WOMEN IN MANAGEMENT

This book presents a realistic perspective on the paradoxes employees face when navigating work and personal responsibilities for career success. The author answers the critical question of how to achieve sustainable and rewarding work–life integration from a perspective of "both/and" rather than "either/or."

While most books focus on a fragmented, hyper-effective view of women and leadership, this book advances the need for an integrated approach. Its Competing Values Framework acts as an organizing model that aligns personal competency with organizational capability, helping readers to identify important leadership roles and competencies, break societal barriers, and choose the right set of behaviors to fit their personal and professional goals. In-chapter text boxes provide personal insight from real employees both entering and established in leadership positions, offering a varied perspective on the challenges and resolutions available to women in management. As men become more engaged with their families, they too will find this book a useful tool.

Students in diversity management, women and management, career development, leadership, and organizational behavior classes will benefit from this realistic and sustainable alternative to the "have it all" model.

Alan T. Belasen is Professor and former Chair of the Graduate Business, Management and Leadership programs at SUNY Empire State College, USA. He is the co-editor of *Confronting Corruption in Business*, published by Routledge in 2015.

"In today's world, women find themselves under tremendous pressure to perform with excellence in all life domains. For many, achieving work–life integration that is both enriching and rewarding is a highly challenging task. This excellent and important book tells the story of women worldwide, and provides valuable information and research-based knowledge, with the potential to improve the lives of millions of women who struggle with work–life conflict."

Sigalit Ronen, *California State University, Northridge, USA*

"Belasen approaches work-life interrelationships for women from an integration rather than a balance perspective, using the competing values framework. In this 'both–and' approach, paradoxes are observed as potential sources of productive tensions rather than liabilities. Strategies for facilitating leadership development for women, as well as the business case for doing so, are compellingly presented."

Annis Golden, *University at Albany, SUNY, USA*

WOMEN IN MANAGEMENT

A Framework for Sustainable Work–Life Integration

Alan T. Belasen

NEW YORK AND LONDON

First published 2017
by Routledge
711 Third Avenue, New York, NY 10017

and by Routledge
2 Park Square, Milton Park, Abingdon, Oxon OX14 4RN

Routledge is an imprint of the Taylor & Francis Group, an informa business

Library of Congress Cataloging-in-Publication Data
A catalog record for this book has been requested

ISBN: 978-1-138-20216-0 (hbk)
ISBN: 978-1-138-20218-4 (pbk)
ISBN: 978-1-315-47457-1 (ebk)

Typeset in Bembo by
Keystroke, Neville Lodge, Tettenhall, Wolverhampton

To my daughters Amy, Anat, Amanda, and Abigail for remaining authentic to the values of "both/and" and work–life integration.

CONTENTS

ILLUSTRATIONS

Figures

Tables

ABBREVIATIONS

CAWP	Center for American Women and Politics
CEO	chief executive officer
COO	chief operating officer
CPS	Current Population Survey
CVF	Competing Values Framework
EEO	equal employment opportunity
EEOC	Equal Employment Opportunity Commission
EU	European Union
FLSA	Fair Labor Standards Act
FMLA	Family Medical Leave Act
GDI	Gender Diversity Index
GDP	gross domestic product
ILM	Institute of Leadership and Management
IPO	initial public offering
IWPR	Institute for Women's Policy Research
J&J	Johnson & Johnson
MBA	Master of Business Administration
MPFC	medial prefrontal cortex
OECD	Organization for Economic Cooperation and Development
P&L	profit and loss
PLC	public limited company
QWL	Quality of Work Life
R&D	research and development
ROE	return on equity
ROI	return on investment
ROIC	return on invested capital

ROS	return on sales
SME	small to medium enterprise
SOX	Sarbanes-Oxley Act
STEM	Science, Technology, Engineering, and Mathematics
TMT	top management team
WBD	women board directors

ACKNOWLEDGMENTS

Many individuals helped to bring this book to fruition through discussions, exchange of ideas, feedback on earlier drafts, as well as comments and suggestions during conference presentations. I would like to acknowledge the insights and feedback of Dr. Sue Faerman and Dr. Sue Epstein whose ideas about work–life integration helped shape the direction of this book. Many thanks to Amy Belasen-Draheim who provided useful suggestions on earlier drafts. I benefited from the advice and insights of many colleagues from numerous networks and associations including the Management Education and Development, Gender and Diversity in Organizations and Organizational Behavior Divisions of the Academy of Management. Special thanks go to my students Courtney Heinbach, Hannah Fairbanks, Kristen Brayden, Bryanna Hebenstreit, Amanda Belasen, Cora Smith, Jordan Carleo-Evangelist, Peter Hooley, Eirinn Norrie, Alissa Petsche, Jamie Zieno, and Morgan Smith from the Department of Communication, University at Albany. Special thanks go to Jennette Tario, Christian Babcock, Alan Finder, Rosario Gallo, Lydia Grant, and Vincenza Macherone from the School of Business, Clarkson University whose ideas inspired me to focus sections of this book on millennials' distinct values and work–life goals.

Special thanks go to Sharon Golan, Acquisitions Editor, Business, Management and Accounting, Routledge, who encouraged and motivated me to go forward with this book project. Erin Arata, Editorial Assistant, US Business and Management, Routledge/Taylor & Francis Group, was instrumental in helping move this book project through the various production phases. Kathryn Fitzgerald's help in making sure that the manuscript follows the publisher's guidelines and formatting requirements was immensurable. Her meticulous attention to detail and the organization of the material is much appreciated as it facilitated the submission of the manuscript on time. Olivia Marine reviewed the figures and tables throughout the book for consistency with the guidelines. I am grateful to my colleagues at SUNY Empire State College for their encouragement and support during the research leading to this book.

My wife Susan provided the social and emotional support as well as the sounding board for many of the ideas in this book. Being surrounded by my five A's was especially rewarding as all provided insights and suggestions from the perspectives of millennials: Ari, an accomplished scholar and professor of economics at SIUE; Amy, an author and marketing director; Anat who is pursuing her PhD in Ecology and Evolutionary Biology, University of Michigan, Ann Arbor; Amanda who is completing her MA in communication, University at Albany; and Abigail, MD Candidate, Class of 2018, Albany Medical College. One more "A" is my granddaughter Adina. I am inspired by their promising future.

FOREWORD

In 2014, over 40 business-school deans, along with leaders from some of America's top corporations, gathered in Washington, DC to discuss and articulate a set of best practices that business schools around the country could adopt to expend opportunities for women in business and provide "know how" for adapting to a twenty-first-century workforce. Convened by members of the Obama administration, this group of leaders engaged with senior White House officials to dialogue on the nature of a changing labor force, the needs of women and companies, and the roles of both business schools and employers in meeting tomorrow's challenges for building a competitive and inclusive workforce.

The convening of the expertise in the room, coupled with the significant research done by the Obama administration and scholars in Gender Studies, led to a draft of "best practices" to be adopted by business-school leaders. I attended this convening and was proud to represent Clarkson University as one of the first 40 schools to be signatories on a commitment to expand opportunities for women and work toward ensuring our "own house" was in order, in addition to working with our stakeholders (faculty, staff, students, and employers) to continuously enhance and improve the curriculum to ensure that we practiced what we preached. This included preparing all of our students to value the contributions of a diverse workforce and understand what access and measuring success actually meant, beginning with a commitment to invite the disenfranchised to be part of the conversation and ultimately innovate on policy and practice for admissions, curriculum, governance, career options, and pathways toward successful lives. Doing so would require a new way of thinking and consideration of alternative perspectives. Thinking entrepreneurially and looking for innovative solutions to old paradigms and challenges that create gender gaps, however unintentional, would be a major priority for all of us as business-school deans (or leaders in other organizations).

As employers focused on how to attract, recruit, and retain the best of a diverse workforce, were we, as business-school deans, doing our part in creating an environment where women felt enabled, and empowered to bring the best of who they are to the business school? We had to look inward and ask the difficult questions related to how we treated our own faculty, staff, and underrepresented students (women, in particular). Were we, as an institution and business school, enabling our female students to pursue the kinds of careers that their white male counterparts often eased into or were we unknowingly creating gender gaps, no matter how pure our motives? Were we eliminating the unintentional and often subtle biases that reinforced a more traditional and outdated classroom? Were we creating the same glass ceilings that we purported to be breaking well into this twenty-first century? Perhaps, even more importantly, were our business schools educating men and women to adapt to changing workforce conditions or were we reinforcing gender stereotypes, cultural biases, and institutional barriers? As deans, we were challenged to explore how we ensured access to business-school education and business careers. As faculty, we were encouraged to look at our curriculum and make the changes that prepare students for the diverse workforce of the future—a workforce of millennials with different attitudes and expectations, challenges around work and family, career paths that may mirror "lattices" rather than "ladders," and a host of other new ways of thinking about career access, success, and how culture and strategy are inextricably linked.

Addressing the gender gap in business education would require deans, faculty, graduate program directors, and others to ensure inclusive and unbiased cultures to support educational and career growth. I was particularly struck by the adage, "Everything Speaks." Case protagonists, textbook examples, guest speakers, tenure review processes, classroom management style, promotion processes, human resources policies and practices around flexibility and child or elder care, mentorship and sponsorships for students and junior faculty, career services that go beyond the needs of traditional students—all of these examples reflect our views on inclusiveness and diversity. Fixing the "gender gap" begins at home. As a signatory to the White House convening, Clarkson University was implicitly agreeing to review how we ensure access and inclusiveness to a diverse set of students and, explicitly, agreeing to an increased awareness on how we set policy and practice, role model behavior, and reflect the workforce of the future.

As a STEM (Science, Technology, Engineering, and Mathematics) institution, we agreed to point out the obvious and not so obvious, whether it was looking at how we role model behavior and create awareness of gender differences in dialogue, negotiation, and communication strategy, or understanding how the wall of pictures of past presidents of the institution in a conference room might suggest, however subtle, that women and people of color need not apply. In all fairness, Clarkson was one of the earlier institutions to matriculate and graduate women engineers and scientists and the precursor to business—industrial distribution specialists. We have worked hard to break down the stereotypes and create a more inclusive culture. As the first female senior administrator on the academic side of the house, I felt welcomed and supported upon arrival. My impressions were reinforced when I challenged President Tony Collins to both sign and commit to the guidelines and best practices coming out of the "recommendations" posed by the White House convening. His enthusiastic support led our business school to integrate many of these best practices into our School of Business Strategic Plan. This served to legitimize conversation around inclusiveness and diversity as strategic imperatives for our business school and the university as a whole.

When Dr. Alan Belasen asked me to write the Foreword for this book, I was truly honored and proud to know that among our faculty Professor Belasen is an outspoken leader on inclusion and creating level playing fields for breaking down barriers and stereotypes. He is committed to ensuring that the talent pool for tomorrow's organizations is truly representative of the demographic realities—women are half the population, are in the pipeline, and are prepared to take on leadership roles. Actively promoting equal pay and opportunity, Belasen goes beyond the obvious to explore the needs of a new generation and non-traditional career paths. While others have written about the gender gap, breaking the glass ceiling and "leaning in," Professor Belasen presses further—exploring the research and reality in preparing for tomorrow's workforce. He ventures into new territory, anticipating attitudinal changes of a millennial generation and understanding the often complex psychology of workplace dynamics and how these dynamics directly impact career choices and opportunities in organizations.

Women in management: A framework for sustainable work–life integration is a comprehensive treatise, providing readers with an in-depth understanding of factors impacting career options. The book helps all of us understand the nuances of work–life integration, exploring more sophisticated strategies for meeting organizational goals while increasing the participation of women in the workforce and leveraging the skills and abilities that women bring to the workplace. The book captures a wide variety of options for making the "business" case for different pathways for women. Whether discussing how to develop succession plans through active identification of qualified women or capturing mentoring and sponsorship strategies required to shepherd top talent to senior management roles, this book focuses on what works, what wins, and what best meets the needs of diverse stakeholders.

Professor Belasen explores a wide range of issues relevant to workforce planning, creating cultures of inclusion, and understanding the demands of leadership in competitive organizations. His perspective is unique—developed from a sophisticated understanding that integration of work–life requires a shift from "either/or" decision making processes around *choice* to a "both/and" way of thinking. Leaders understanding the ground rules of effective "improvisation" may appreciate the outputs from "both/and" thinking—a proven strategy that provides organizations and their members with avenues toward more creative decision making and innovative solutions that satisfy and maximize diverse stakeholder interest.

Discovering a new way of thinking about the interplay between career path and organizational goal attainment is a significant next step in building organizations that benefit from the very strategies and best practices we discussed in Washington, DC several years ago. Belasen's work in this book documents the challenges and opportunities for thinking differently with practical outcomes. From women entrepreneurs to women in the Fortune 500, Belasen's arguments are backed by thoughtful and compelling analysis. A review of labor force data, a glimpse into the extensive interviews with woman managers, and an understanding of the metrics and analytics of corporate board composition all point to considering the myriad paths career pipelines take in different types of organizations. Taken together, one appreciates Belasen's strong thesis that change is necessary if we are to build strong networks, cultures, organizations, or even countries. Avoiding the often "simplistic" recipe of what women need to do, Belasen takes a broader perspective, and demonstrates a sophisticated approach in how we might break down institutional barriers and create true enabling mechanisms that serve all of our society. The implications of his research, findings, and framework can, if acted upon, strengthen the futures of our daughters and sons, as well.

I hope that a read of this book will enable managers and leaders (men and women) to appreciate how much they benefit their organizations when they stop looking at career "requests" as "accommodation" strategy, and, instead, consider "both/and" thinking that leads to a winning strategy for moving organizations ahead with "win–win" outcomes.

Ultimately, Belasen's book is about creating and executing the strategy necessary for the next generation of leaders to function in an increasingly globally competitive world—a landscape that can't afford to leave half the population behind.

Dayle M. Smith, PhD
Professor and Dean
School of Business
Clarkson University

INTRODUCTION

Work–Life Integration

At times when organizations, industries, and markets become increasingly complex and dynamic, successful leaders must have the skills and abilities to look beyond competing tensions and communicate credibly and with high confidence. This book will assist employers in developing organizational strategies that promote work–life integration and in facilitating leadership career paths for high-potential women. While most books focus on a limited or fragmented view of women and leadership, this book advances the need for a broader, integrated approach to women's participation and advancement.

The critical question that this book sets out to answer is how to achieve work–life integration that is sustainable and rewarding. The reality for most women is that they must find ways to combine multiple responsibilities—and they may do so in ways that bring multiple benefits (e.g., less stress, empowerment, financial security). Why not tell that message? The second factor is the notion of perfection and the ways by which the message of perfection in a variety of aspects has been (inappropriately) communicated and accountable for unattainable goals. This includes the very premise of what "all" means. Even Sheryl Sandberg, who does encourage women to "lean in" (Sandberg & Scovell, 2013), is operating from a privileged position (which she acknowledges) that does not mirror the reality of most women. The problem with "lean-in" is that it leads to hyper-effectiveness, which is unsustainable. Does it have to be the very top position in the organization? Everything at one time versus over time? Debora Spar talks about this in her book *Wonder Women: Sex, Power, and the Quest for Perfection* (2013). So why not focus on women who have managed to combine multiple responsibilities in ways that were right for them but do not conform to a notion of perfection (e.g., they are not the chief executive officer—CEO—but have fulfilling, challenging jobs and satisfying personal lives as well)? Combining multiple responsibilities is both beneficial for women and feasible as part of a sustainable work–life plan. The variety of challenges faced by women in different managerial positions coupled with their own sense of priority can make for an interesting set of life choices—not the least of which would center on work–life integration.

Williams and Dempsey, in their recent book *What works for women at work: Four patterns working women need to know* (2014), categorized the set of obstacles women face at work into four overarching patterns or metaphors of gender bias that can limit women's participation and promotion: "Prove it Again" in which women have to provide more evidence of competence to be considered as competent as their male colleagues; "The Tight Rope" where women walk a fine line between being liked but not respected—or respected but not liked; "The Maternal Wall," which pushes working mothers out of the workplace toward full-time caregiving; and "The Tug of War," which compels women to defend their own coping strategies and criticize those of others. They then go on to suggest strategies and lessons to aid women when faced with these patterns. This book is differentiated by combining competing values leadership theory and research with evidence and findings from empirical studies to demonstrate the economic benefits of increasing diversity in management while, at the same time, creating opportunities for inclusive leadership in organizations.

Competing Values Leadership

The Competing Values Framework (CVF) is used as an organizing schema for demonstrating the efficacy of the integrated approach for achieving successful outcomes for both career women and organizations. The *integrative* nature of the CVF allows us to chart internal and external stakeholders, identify important leadership roles and competencies, and help women choose the right set of behaviors that are aligned with their personal and professional goals and priorities.

While the CVF has been used primarily to study organizational and leadership performance, it generally encourages individuals to view work and life responsibilities from a "both/and" rather than an "either/or" perspective. In doing so, it provides a lens for both researchers and managers within organizations to identify processes, practices, and behaviors that allow for the support of integration of work and life responsibilities.

Most importantly, by using the CVF as a lens that allows scholars and practitioners alike to view workplaces through a "both/and" perspective, we can avoid the question that is regularly posed to women regarding whether they can realistically expect to "have it all" in their work and personal life domains. Rather than seeking maximum levels on each dimension (all of family, all of work), the CVF allows us to integrate domains and to raise questions about what it means to maximize outcomes in different circumstances. Additionally, some applications of the CVF caution that the display of extreme behaviors can result in negative consequences. This cautionary note is relevant as career women seeking advancement into higher positions should also consider intended and unintended outcomes of choices.

Profile Awareness

Leaders who are able to master the behaviors and skills associated with the four domains outlined in Figure I.1 also have the cognitive complexity and behavioral flexibility to confront deception and avert corrupt behaviors (Belasen, 2016). Methods or instruments of self-assessment that also consider responses from others (e.g., internal and external stakeholders) are particularly useful for monitoring progress toward desired goals and behaviors (Belasen, 2012). They also provide stakeholders with a dashboard to review potential gaps between actual and desired behaviors, adjust or change criteria as needed, or develop new benchmarks. Social context is important because individuals in leadership positions look to others for validation of their moral judgment and motivation. Senior executives and managers can use these instruments developmentally to examine how well their ratings are balanced across various criteria, check whether important milestones have been accomplished, and revise their development plans accordingly.

The process of integrating differentiated concepts can be illustrated by examining the idea of cognitive complexity. Cognitive complexity refers to the degree of sophisticated understanding of a phenomenon that resides in a person's mind. Individuals who are deeply experienced in a particularly activity have greater cognitive complexity about that activity than those who are novices. Cognitively complex managers are effective leaders who can see the uniqueness embedded in a situation as well as the similarities, which consequently allow them to pursue advanced management strategies. In other words, people with a greater capacity to differentiate and integrate thinking, decisions, and actions can add greater value than less effective managers.

As a *diagnostic tool*, the CVF helps women to see the competing tensions that exist in complex organizational environments and expand the repertoire of their behavioral responses accordingly. Assessment instruments are often used to not only highlight deficiencies in leadership style that cause major breakdowns, but also to improve organizational communication. Managers at all hierarchical levels who used multi-rater tools reportedly developed a clear understanding across hierarchical levels and functional lines and worked effectively as a management team (Belasen, 2008). An individual in a position of authority should create an atmosphere that encourages organizational members to monitor, challenge, and discuss each other's ideas in order to stay open to better and more ethical ways of doing things. Self-assessment tools are designed to help increase self-awareness or understanding of one's strengths and weaknesses, thinking patterns, and motivations. Stakeholders (e.g., board members) can use these instruments to evaluate whether gaps in the behavior of individuals have been addressed and make important decisions about their suitability to lead the organization.

Profile awareness is a powerful medium that allows leaders to understand their strengths and weaknesses, what motivates them, and how they make decisions. Thus, as a *development tool*, the CVF helps women identify personal traits, strengths and weaknesses, and develop self-improvement goals with career choices and outcomes. In other words, the CVF helps women increase their self-efficacy and at the same time link their personal and family goals with their professional needs and goals. Profile awareness and self-regulation are the starting points in a diagnostic process aimed at identifying gaps between actual and desired behaviors and a tracking plan aimed at remedying deficiencies based on input from others.

Paradoxes and Value Creation

Cameron, Quinn, DeGraff, and Thakor (2006) describe "value creation" as a primary motivation that drives both people and businesses. At a personal level, having a positive impact and making a contribution in an area of personal importance is one of the most basic human needs. Creating value is the way people achieve self-fulfillment, realize their unique potential, and reach self-actualization. According to Cameron et al., the most successful organizations and leaders are those that create superior levels of value. These successful leaders and organizations are more differentiated as well as more integrated than their peer systems. They transform themselves by combining stability and flexibility along with internal and external perspectives and by managing paradoxes.

As such, the CVF *creates value* at both the personal competency level and the organizational capability level, matching talents and skills with needs and goals. A version of this framework, developed specifically for this book, appears in Figure I.1. Note how the framework provides a roadmap for identifying the main issues (personal, organizational, institutional, and social) career women face, while at the same time it charts the critical domains of women's work–life aspirations. In this way, the book enables an understanding of the paradoxes faced when navigating work and personal responsibilities and how individuals can realistically manage these sets of responsibilities.

To more fully examine these paradoxes and provide tools for navigating the work–life landscape, I use the CVF because inherent in its theoretical basis is the notion that organizational and managerial performance are ultimately defined (and judged) by a set of competing criteria and that managerial leaders must consistently confront paradoxical choices that emerge from beliefs that are deeply embedded in organizational and life values (Cameron et al., 2006; Quinn, Faerman, Thompson, & McGrath, 2007). For example, managers are expected to ensure stability within the organization yet also face a need to encourage change and innovation in response to external market forces; managers need to look for ways to structure work to enhance employee satisfaction yet must also strive to maximize profitability and meet the demands of external stakeholders.

As another example, the patterns identified by Williams and Dempsey (2014) can be categorized using our framework and therefore portrayed holistically and

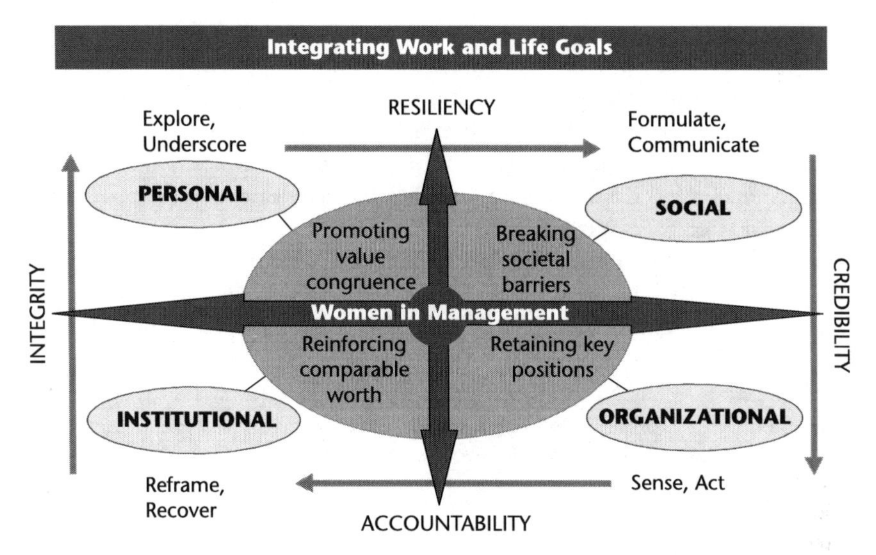

FIGURE I.1 A Framework for Sustainable Work–Life Integration

meaningfully with polar opposites and inherent tensions that otherwise might remain elusive: "Prove it Again" in the lower right quadrant; "The Tight Rope" in the upper left quadrant; "The Maternal Wall" in the lower left quadrant; and "The Tug of War" in the upper right quadrant. The power of using the framework is that it encourages organizational members to see these paradoxes not as "either/or" pressures but, instead, as "both/and" opportunities. In encouraging a "both/and" perspective, our framework calls for executives and organizational leaders to display a range of behaviors to meet these multiple pressures. For example, they can work with their employees to develop new and innovative processes and practices that maintain internal stability and also provide appropriate levels of flexibility.

Role Conflict

Individuals belonging simultaneously to multiple groups (e.g., member of organization, family, community, social club, interest group) often try to meet different responsibilities that relate to these groups (e.g., manager, parent, organizer, player, activist), and these simultaneous role demands can result in interrole conflict (Kahn, Wolfe, Quinn, Snoek, & Rosenthal, 1964). A specific type of interrole conflict is work–family conflict, also called work–family interference. Greenhaus and Beutell (1985) discuss three forms of work–family conflict (i.e., time-based, strain-based, and behavior-based). Alternatively, some have viewed the interaction between work and family roles from a positive perspective. For example, using role accumulation theory some researchers have argued that interactions between multiple roles can have positive consequences (Greenhaus & Powell, 2006). In line with these theories, the notion of work–family enrichment explores the ways in which the presence of and interactions between these two domains can have positive outcomes. A third approach acknowledges that perceptions of conflict and enrichment are influenced by subjective perceptions of gains versus losses of resources (Hobfoll, 1989). For example, a job promotion may be viewed as a gain in resources (e.g., enrichment through increases in money, status, self-esteem) and/or a loss of resources (e.g., conflict due to time no longer available for personal interests, family).

Fittingly, the types of conflicts between work and family interests are not mutually exclusive. That is, an individual can have simultaneous experiences of work–life conflict and work–life enrichment. For example, individuals seeking to engage in their careers and families can, on the one hand, experience conflict when the time they need to be at work conflicts with their ability to attend a family event, while, on the other hand, experiencing enrichment when time spent at work builds their sense of self-identity that then can lead to positive interaction in their family life. Individuals are likely to feel that they need to choose between two positive options, while choosing either one over the other can have extremely negative consequences. In psychology this is also known as cognitive dissonance, often leading to intrapersonal conflict due to the need to choose between two or more equally important goals. In a sense, the paradoxical choice may emerge as a question of whether a promotion will result in conflict (e.g., performance maximizing value with pressures to meet deadlines and milestones) or enrichment (e.g., greater sense of satisfaction in professional life that has positive consequences in personal life). These examples illustrate a few of the paradoxical choices within the work–life landscape that this book sets out to examine.

The four parts of this book parallel the domains of action displayed by the model, each with two chapters. Together with the introduction and conclusion, this book contains 10 chapters.

Part I: Promoting Value Congruence

Promoting value congruence
Women in Management

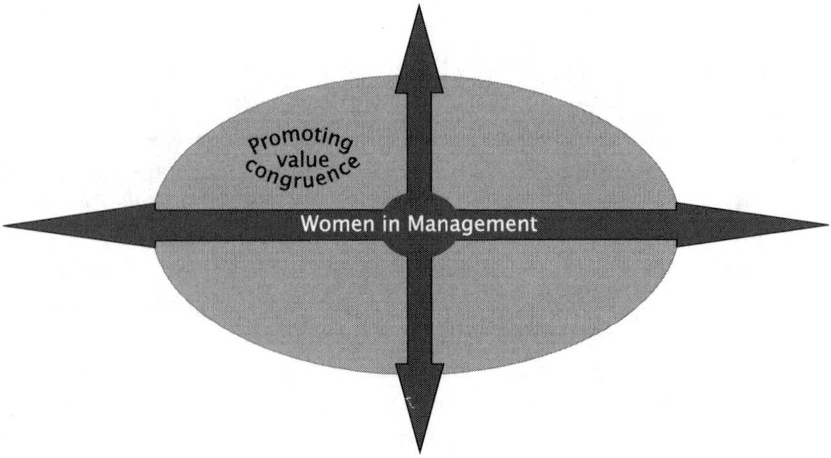

Chapter 1: Challenging the Binary

Some women have simply grown accustomed to making imperfect trade-offs between the demands of professional work and personal responsibilities, yielding unnecessary dissonance, stress, and anxiety while considering their choices. On the one hand, upward obligations toward parents would drive women to succeed even more and attain the top-level position that will allow them to repay the debt to their parents that they feel they owe because of the parents' sacrifice. On the other hand, downward obligations to children would probably deter women from succeeding because they feel torn between spending time with the family and becoming successful. Survey after survey demonstrates that women stay away from seeking managerial or senior executive positions due to lack of workplace flexibility (15%) and family as a bigger priority (26%) but also because of institutional barriers (42%), less willingness to take risks (10%), and lack of mentoring and social support (7%). Nowadays the US Bureau of Labor Statistics reports that nearly 27% of American women work flexible schedules, up from 11% in 1984 (US Bureau of Labor Statistics, 2013). Technologies such as remote server access and videoconferencing as well as telecommuting have made it easier for women to work from home.

Moreover, profound change is forcing organizations to undergo transitions as the so-called millennial generation is entering the workplace and begins to test the more traditional values of command-based structures. Millennials seem to be less motivated by career advancement and more by personal values and aspirations. Women in particular are opting out of the workforce due to absence of flexible work schedules rather than fighting their way through the "labyrinth." To avoid brain-drain and sustain competitive advantage, many organizations will need to know more about this generational shift and its implications.

It is true that women face another catch-22 regarding the path they take with their lives, as criticism seems to come from both directions. Women who attempt to combine work responsibilities with family are either criticized for compromising their familial obligations or for hindering their full professional potential by spending time and effort around their personal life. Conveying a message that highlights the possibility and benefits of integration is definitely advantageous in promoting women's leadership and a healthy outlook on one's personal life. The practicality of this focus makes it both encouraging and relatable for women, and will help reinforce the idea that women do not need to ignore one aspect or attain perfection in both to have what they yearn for. This chapter covers the broader aspects of trends and triggers of work–life interdependence and the shift away from the binary in which the boundaries between family and career are beginning to blur.

Chapter 2: Empowering Women Entrepreneurs

The path to leadership for women in corporate American has not been easy. Despite increasing levels of participation in the workforce and the attainment of high levels of education, women have encountered resistance, prejudice, and hostility—the concrete wall. Even when the overt objections have somewhat diminished, the lingering effects of gender stereotypes have created an obscure barrier to achieving leadership roles—the glass ceiling. The rejection of women from executive suites and corporate boardrooms due to "lack" of vision or innovative thinking, paradoxically, creates opportunities for women to demonstrate their innovation and visionary skills outside corporate America. Over time, pioneering women (some would say superwomen) have succeeded in breaking through the glass ceiling, but their success has not been widely replicated. The pipeline of female middle managers did not result in the expected flood of female executives. Instead, many high-achieving women opted for entrepreneurial activities leading their startup companies from the early stages of development to the growth stage with positive high returns.

This chapter not only covers many success stories but also focuses on unjustified institutional and stereotypical barriers, particularly the second glass ceiling—the stereotype that women are perceived as incapable of leading growing businesses, which is particularly and unnecessarily pervasive among business and government leaders. Our research and analysis show a profound and consistent gender gap in entrepreneur persuasiveness. Investors prefer pitches presented by male entrepreneurs compared with pitches made by female entrepreneurs, even when the content of the pitch is the same.

Women entrepreneurs also face tighter credit availability from financial institutions to start new firms or to fuel the growth of existing small firms. Furthermore, analysis of a longitudinal survey of almost 5,000 entrepreneurial firms shows that not only do women get significantly less external debt and equity than men at firm startup, they also get significantly less capital in the subsequent two years. As a result, many women turn to bootstrap financing and personal sources of funding. However, while there are financial barriers hindering women from reaching their entrepreneurial goals, there are also many programs out there with the sole intent of funding women's business ideas (Goldman Sachs), government (Small Business Administration) nongovernmental (World Bank), or nonprofit organizations (Gates Foundation). Some of these programs, such as Goldman Sachs' 10,000 Women Initiative and Coca-Cola's *5by20* Campaign, are also designed to help women and their communities in developing countries.

Still, progress is being made and the report from the Institute for Women's Policy Research (IWPR, 2015) shows that women are steadily increasing their presence with 29% of America's business owners, up from 26% in 1997. The number of women-owned firms has grown 68% since 2007, compared with 47%

growth for all businesses. As of 2014, there were nearly 9.1 million women-owned businesses in the United States, accounting for 37.8% generating over $1.4 trillion in revenues and employing nearly 7.9 million people. While women-owned firms remain smaller than male-owned firms in terms of average employment and revenues, they are not only showing higher percent growth in numbers but also higher absolute growth in terms of job creation adding an estimated 274,000 jobs since 2007. Leadership talents, attributes, and skills that promote social entrepreneurship are also examined in this chapter.

Part II: Reinforcing Comparable Worth

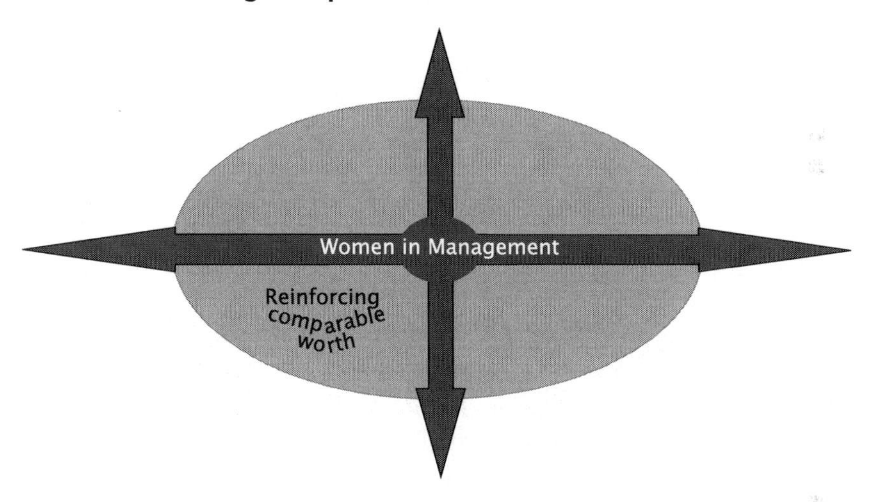

Chapter 3: Promoting Equality in Management

The four barriers to women's promotion—structural obstacles, lifestyle choices, institutional barriers, and individual mindsets—that have traditionally been intensified by the lack of sponsorship, limited flexibility, and unconscious biases are discussed throughout the chapter. Comparable worth pertaining to work-place environments in which men are concentrated in specific job categories and women in other job categories (e.g., staff roles) is discussed. I am using the broader definition that recognizes that many jobs are segregated by gender in which men often receive higher pay in "their categories." The focus is therefore on *equal pay for comparable work*. Comparable worth policies seek to remedy or reduce the effects of wage-based inequities by neutralizing gender as an invisible element.

Many companies today just seem to focus on meeting diversity requirements in the entry-level positions through equal employment opportunity employer laws; however, that is where it ends. US Bureau of Labor Statistics data show that women land 53% of entry-level jobs and make it to mid-level management in large numbers. But then female presence falls to 35% at the director level, 24% at senior vice-president level, and 19% at the C-level (Barsh & Yee, 2012). In a report to the Equal Employment Opportunity Commission (EEOC), Google indicated that of its 36 executives and top-ranking managers, just three were women (Google, 2013). Anecdotally, managers at Google invest time and effort to persuade women engineers to nominate themselves for promotion. In fact, McKinsey's study (Women in the Economy, 2011) shows that women, in general, opt at far higher rates than men for staff jobs, not executive positions. Some 50% to 65% of women at the vice-president level and higher are in staff jobs, compared with only 41% to 48% of men (Shellenbarger, 2012). The other issue involves succession planning and the significance of the limited pool of potentially qualified successors that are being left behind.

To date, women hold only 23 (4.6%) CEO positions at S&P 500 companies and 25 (2.5%) Fortune 1000 companies have women CEOs or presidents. Because CEOs are mostly men and the selection of board members is typically influenced by CEOs, many CEOs will choose board members who possess the qualities that they have. High-ranking female role models are scarce, and they are tough acts to follow. Also, access to middle management and executive positions remains elusive for most women. The most interesting and paradoxical fact is that companies that have more women on their boards and in their senior management teams aren't just opening doors to gender equality but are also reaping greater financial rewards.

This chapter uses data and reports across industries and organizations to evaluate the imbalance of women and men at senior management levels and to suggest diversity as a source of competitive advantage.

Chapter 4: Cracking the Glass Ceiling

The effects of gender on leadership roles and leadership effectiveness have gained renewed attention with Eagly, Johannesen-Schmidt, and Van Engen's (2003) seminal meta-analysis of 45 studies that compared male and female managers on measures of transformational, transactional, and laissez-faire leadership styles. In general, the meta-analysis revealed that, compared with male leaders, female leaders were more transformational as well as engaged in the contingent reward that characterizes transactional behavior. Male leaders were more likely than female leaders to manifest the two other aspects of transactional leadership: active management by exception and passive management by exception. Men were also higher on laissez-faire leadership.

Many of the difficulties and challenges that women face are the result of the incongruity of the traditional women's role and leadership roles. This incongruity creates vulnerability whereby women encounter prejudicial reactions that restrict their access to leadership roles and negatively bias judgments of their performance as leaders. Women encounter resistance when their behaviors go against prevailing gender expectations. For example, their vision might not be recognized if it manifests itself differently from how it is manifested in men.

Easing this dilemma of role incongruity requires that women leaders behave extremely competently while reassuring others that they conform to expectations concerning appropriate behavior for women. This double-standard requirement, observed or expected, to display extra competence in leadership roles, makes it especially difficult for women to gain recognition for high performance and outstanding achievement. Therefore, successful women leaders generally work hard and seek leadership styles that reduce the chance for criticism or that elicit resistance to their authority, challenging them to be egalitarian (Eagly et al., 2003). On the one hand, women are expected to be friendly, supportive, and skilled in socialization processes, yet agreeableness is a handicap in some career advancement (Mueller & Plug, 2006); on the other hand, men who are not friendly (agonistic) are more likely to receive promotions.

This chapter suggests remedies and best practices at the individual (e.g., using self-promotion strategies, increasing self-confidence), interpersonal (active mentoring, sponsorship), and organizational (e.g., cultural transformation, policies, and procedures) levels.

Part III: Retaining Key Positions

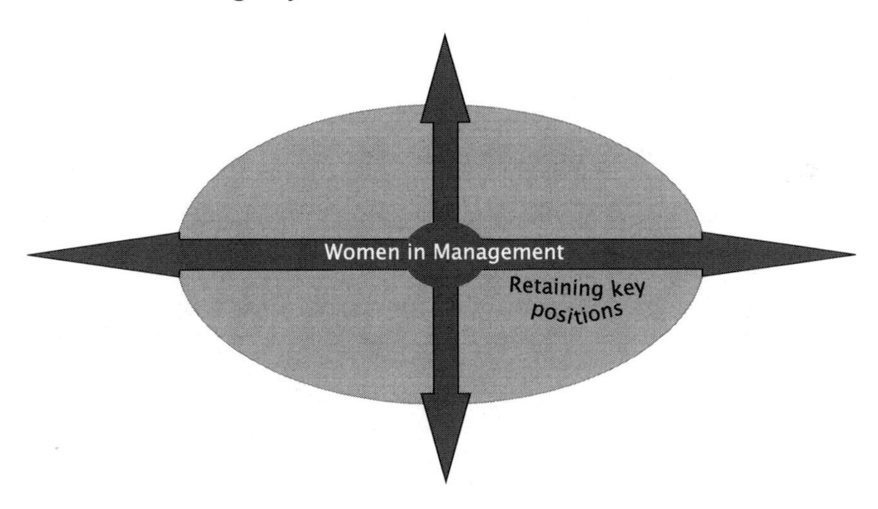

Chapter 5: Creating Effective Boards

Although women and men have reached numerical parity in management, fewer women than men lead from the top. Statistics show that by the end of 2013, women held just 16.9% of Fortune 500 board seats and only 4.6% of Fortune 500 CEOs were women (Warner, 2014). Women also only make 80% of what men make. However, evidence shows that companies with at least one female board member had a return on equity (ROE) of 14.1% over the past nine years, greater than the 11.2% for those without any women. Companies that have focused on increasing gender diversity also saw better results than those who let women's representation slip or fall, a trend that is statistically significant and consistent year after year (Women in Technology, 2015). Fortune 500 firms with a high number of women executives consistently outperformed their industry's median firms on all measures of profitability.

According to Broderick and Keefe (2015), unprecedented economic value will be unleashed, and an unprecedented economic boom will occur, if women are afforded the same educational and economic opportunities as men. Reports have shown that as a result of women entering the workforce over the past four decades, gross domestic product (GDP) in the US is about 25% higher than it would have been. Goldman Sachs economist, Kevin Day, has calculated that eliminating the remaining gap between male and female employment would boost GDP in the US by 9%, by 13% in the Eurozone, and by 13% in Japan. In a stark contrast to this evidence and projections, women's underrepresentation on boards has continued to persist due to unjustified reasons such as lack of qualified candidates; presumed prerequisites of CEO experience; and the belief that women's representation is actually already on the rise (Catalyst, 2012). This chapter traces these reasons and the financial impact of the absence of women on boards on the economic performance of organizations. Mechanisms for greater representation of women on boards, including the benefits of using quotas, and ways to sustain diversity are also discussed.

Chapter 6: Rethinking Women and Leadership

Women are eminently qualified for leadership and management positions in business, government, and the nonprofit sectors. Research has indicated that women's strengths in interpersonal and social skills, e.g., nurturing, compassion, and sharing information, contributes to their effectiveness as leaders and managers. However, I argue that organizational cultures are "gendered" and that gender bias is an invisible barrier—the glass ceiling—preventing women from breaking into the higher levels of management. As a result, women slide out or lay low while others resort to hyper-effective behaviors with considerable loss of discretionary time and feelings of powerlessness.

The stereotypical bias that effective leadership requires masculine behaviors naturally puts women at a disadvantage and men at an advantage as men's inherent demeanor is consistent with what is considered "good leadership." For many women, the balancing act of maintaining masculine roles, while describing themselves as "male-like" when they receive the opportunity to fill traditionally established male leadership roles without "gender-bending," can be quite challenging. In turn, this has led many women to downplay the relevance of upward mobility or avoid targeting promotion to senior management positions. Organizations need to consider tailoring their corporate leadership lifestyles to allow mothers to continue a healthy work–life balance while they are raising children. This is important due to the effects of "brain-drain," especially as many studies have shown that women in corporate leadership positions add value to their companies.

This chapter provides examples of successful leadership practices in business and nonprofit organizations and how women can navigate their careers in gendered-type organizations. Lessons drawn from their experiences to sustain family goals while at the same time succeed in their professional careers are also offered for individuals and organizations. The discussion also draws on Sheryl Sandberg's key messages including becoming engaged in the workplace and promoting yourself; supporting stay-home dads for equal sharing of responsibilities at home; and acting more aggressively in professional endeavors.

PART IV: Breaking Societal Barriers

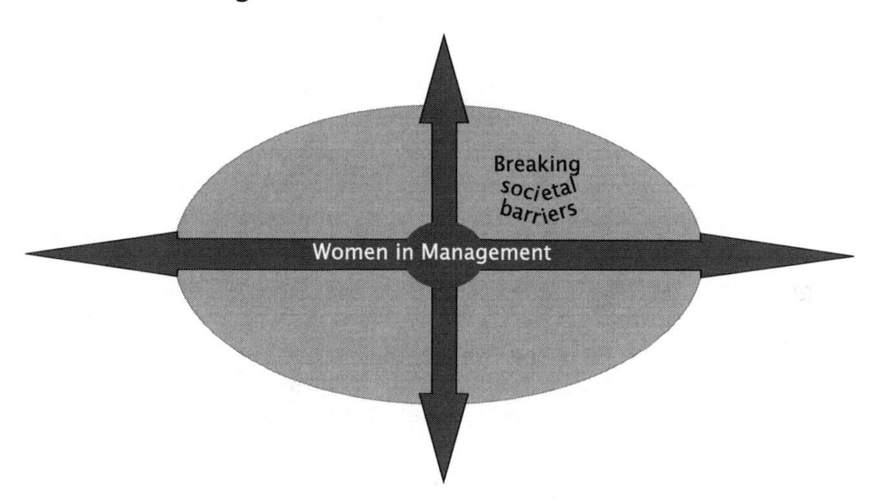

Chapter 7: Changing the Corporate Mindset

Despite being the majority in the population, obtaining 60% of undergraduate and Master's level degrees, and holding almost 52% of all professional-level jobs, American women lag substantially behind men when it comes to their representation in leadership positions (Warner, 2014). A common view is that gender leadership styles reflect the power differentials seen in society as a whole (Fine, 2007) and that masculine qualities such as task focus, assertiveness, authoritativeness, and lack of emotionality, more so than communal qualities, appear synonymous with leadership in US and European cultures (Izraeli & Adler, 1994; Fine & Buzzanell, 2000).

This view will need to change as women have proven to be exceptional leaders in business, government, and nonprofit organizations, as well as political settings. Women have taken on both transformational and transactional roles that have changed the course of major corporations and political institutions. Look at Elizabeth Warren who has challenged the global financial establishment to provide a fair playing field for middle-class individuals. This has led to oversight capabilities that have brought transparency to areas that did not exist before. Similarly, it is important that women are offered the flexibility to develop their careers and family so that a broader base of thought leaders who can benefit employers and stakeholders is cultivated.

This chapter examines societal and legal norms and practices and provides frameworks for cultural transformations and change leadership. The "black box" of the boardroom and dynamics associated with board composition and women participation are also discussed.

Chapter 8: Sustaining Diversity and Inclusion

Women and men in organizations must act in ways that are genuine and honest to their own values and also find the right balance of agentic and communal behaviors through feedback, mentoring, and developmental plans. In most cases women are the primary caregivers and caretakers in the household in addition to being the physical carriers of children, all of which can slow down upward movement at work. This is where the proverbial "glass ceiling" situation appears—as long as standards in business are made and enforced by men, women will continue to be absent from top positions. It is also noted that companies need to systemically break down the cultural barriers and stereotypical biases that prevent women from reaching the top. This chapter offers strategies for reducing bias at work and for empowering women. These strategies include change leadership, cultural transformation, learning, and education. Other tools include teamwork, communication, training, and development.

Conclusion: Quality of Work–Life

The most recent trends in leadership models have sought to shift the paradigm from celebrating overachieving workaholics, to valuing balance, purpose, and mindfulness. There is growing recognition that persons, female or male, who are self-aware, collaborative, and sensitive to the needs of an array of stakeholders make the best leaders. This chapter reviews the key findings and ideas discussed throughout the book and offers a self-assessment instrument, which is based on the framework developed in this book, to help guide career women (and men, too!) achieve work–life integration.

Readership

With an emphasis on balancing theory and practice and with relevant examples that illustrate key points and ideas, this book is suitable as a primary text or important supplement for undergraduate core courses as well as graduate courses in leadership. This book is also relevant to the larger audience of women and men, leaders and managers, company executives, management development consultants, business educators, human resources directors, and trainers.

Many variants of leadership are taught in schools of business (business management, Master of Business Administration—MBA), management programs and different disciplines such as communication, public administration, women's studies, and industrial organization in which this book will be an appealing text. Examples of courses include: Group Communication and Leadership; Organizational Behavior; Management and Leadership; Foundations of Leadership; High-performance Leadership; Leadership Communication; Leading and Managing People; Leadership Development; Women's Leadership; Women and Management; and Managing Human Resources.

References

All weblinks in this book were last accessed on 14 November 2016.

Barsh, J., & Yee, L. (2012). Unlocking the full potential of women at work. *McKinsey & Company*. Retrieved from www.mckinsey.com/business-functions/organization/our-insights/unlocking-the-full-potential-of-women-at-work.

Belasen, A. T. (2008). *The theory and practice of corporate communication: A competing values perspective*. Thousand Oaks, CA: Sage Publications.

Belasen, A. T. (2012). *Developing women leaders in corporate America: Balancing competing demands, transcending traditional boundaries*. Santa Barbara, CA: Praeger.

Belasen, A. T. (2016). Deception and failure: Mitigating leader-centric behaviors. In A. T. Belasen & R. Toma (Eds.), *Confronting corruption in business: Trusted leadership, civic engagement* (pp. 183–216). New York, NY: Routledge.

Broderick, E., & Keefe, J. (2015, May 25). Male business leaders need to support women's empowerment. *The Huffington Post*. Retrieved from www.huffingtonpost.com/elizabeth-broderick/male-business-leaders-nee_b_6939208.html.

Cameron, K. S., Quinn, R. E., DeGraff, J., & Thakor, A. V. (2006). *Competing values leadership: Creating value in organizations*. Cheltenham, UK: Edward Elgar.

Catalyst. (2012). *Catalyst 2012 census of Fortune 500: No change for women in top leadership*. New York, NY: Catalyst.

Eagly, A. H., Johannesen-Schmidt, M. C., & Van Engen, M. L. (2003). Transformational, transactional, and laissez-faire leadership styles: A meta-analysis comparing women and men. *Psychological Bulletin, 129*(4), 569–591.

Fine, M. G. (2007). Women, collaboration, and social change: An ethics-based model of leadership. In J. L. Chin, B. L. Lott, J. K. Rice, & J. Sanchez-Hucles (Eds.), *Women and leadership: Visions and diverse voices* (pp. 177–191). Boston, MA: Blackwell.

Fine, M. G., & Buzzanell, P. M. (2000). Walking the high wire: Leadership theorizing, daily acts, and tensions. In P. M. Buzzanell (Ed.), *Rethinking organizational and managerial communication from feminist perspectives* (pp. 128–156). Thousand Oaks, CA: Sage.

Google. (2013). EEO-1 Report to the Equal Employment Opportunity Commission. Retrieved from http://static.googleusercontent.com/media/www.google.com/en//diversity/2013-EEO-1-consolidated-report.pdf.

Greenhaus, J. H., & Beutell, N. J. (1985). Sources of conflict between work and family roles. *Academy of Management Review, 10*(1), 76–88.

Greenhaus, J. H., & Powell, G. N. (2006). When work and family are allies: A theory of work-family enrichment. *Academy of Management Review, 31*(1), 72–92.

Hobfoll, S. E. (1989). Conservation of resources: A new attempt at conceptualizing stress. *American Psychologist, 44*, 513–524.

IWPR. (2015). *Status of women in the United States*. Retrieved from http://statusofwomendata.org/explore-the-data/data-by-topic/.

Izraeli, D. N., & Adler, N. (1994). Competitive frontiers: Women managers in a global economy. In N. Adler & D. N. Izraeli (Eds.), *Competitive frontiers: Women managers in a global economy* (pp. 3–21). Cambridge, MA: Blackwell.

Kahn, R. L., Wolfe, D. M., Quinn, R. P., Snoek, J. D., & Rosenthal, R. A. (1964). *Organizational stress: Studies in role conflict and ambiguity*. New York, NY: Wiley.

Mueller, G., & Plug, E. (2006). Estimating the effects of personality on men and female earnings. *Industrial & Labor Relations Review, 60*(1), 3–22.

Quinn, R. E., Faerman, S. R., Thompson, M. P., & McGrath, M. R. (2007). *Becoming a master manager – A competency framework*. New York, NY: John Wiley & Sons, Inc.

Sandberg, S., & Scovell, N. (2013). *Lean in: Women, work, and the will to lead*. New York, NY: Alfred A. Knopf.

Shellenbarger, Sue (2012, May 7). The XX factor: What's holding women back? *The Wall Street Journal* [Women in the economy: The journal report]. Retrieved from www.womeninecon.wsj.com/special-report-2012.pdf.

Spar, D. L. (2013). *Wonder women: Sex, power, and the quest for perfection*. New York, NY: Farrar, Straus and Giroux.

US Bureau of Labor Statistics. (February, 2013). *BLS reports: Women in the labor force: A data book* (Report No. 1040). Retrieved from www.bls.gov/cps/wlf-databook-2012.pdf.

Warner, J. (2014, March 7). *Fact sheet—The women's leadership gap: Women's leadership by the numbers*. Center for American Progress. Retrieved from www.americanprogress.org/issues/women/report/2014/03/07/85457/fact-sheet-the-womens-leadership-gap/.

Williams, J. C., & Dempsey, R. (2014). *What works for women at work: Four patterns working women need to know*. New York, NY: New York University Press.

Women in the Economy. (2011, April 11). The journal report: A blueprint for change. *The Wall Street Journal* [Special report]. Retrieved from www.womeninecon.wsj.com/special-report.pdf.

Women in Technology. (2015). *Advancing women to the corporate boardroom*. Retrieved from www.womenintechnology.org/assets/docs/wit_research_report2015_v7_print_web.pdf.

PART I

Promoting Value Congruence

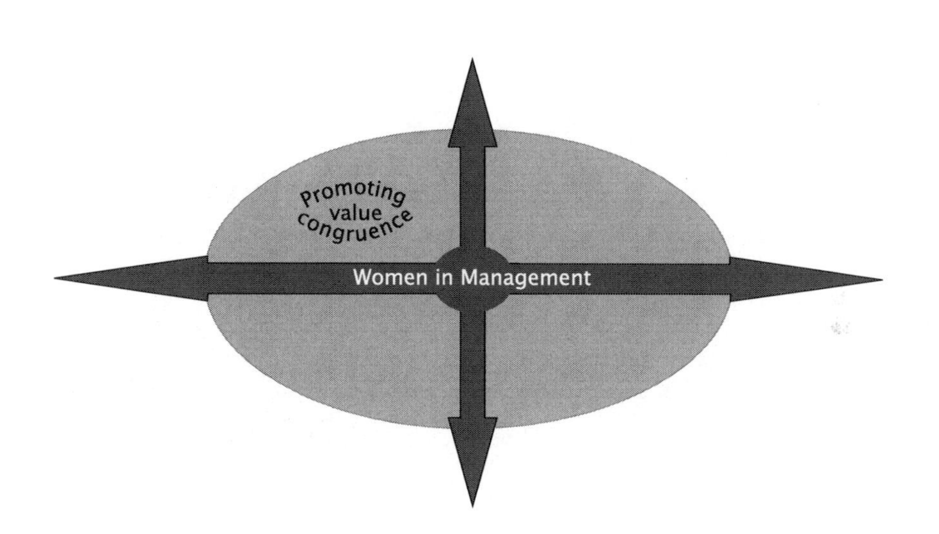

1

CHALLENGING THE BINARY

Brad Harrington, the executive director of the *Boston College Center for Work & Family*, cautions that some women have simply grown accustomed to making imperfect trade-offs between work and their personal lives adding to the dissonance, stress, and anxiety involving the need to face a constant dilemma or make tough choices (Robbins, n.d.). On the one hand, upward obligations toward parents will pull women (especially in the 41–55 age bracket, the "sandwich" generation, positioned between growing children and aging parents) to care for their elderly parents.[1] On the other hand, downward obligations to children would probably deter highly-educated women from pushing their career to the maximum because they feel torn between spending time with the family and work responsibilities. Termed "the rug rat race," economists Garey and Valerie Ramey (2010) of the University of California, San Diego, showed that the increased scarcity of college acceptance and selection rates appears to have heightened rivalry among parents, which takes the form of extra time spent on college preparatory and extracurricular activities. It is for this reason that the most educated parents spend *the most hours parenting, even though they are giving up the most in wages by doing so*. When considering this broader workforce issue, the constructs are often referred to as work–life conflict and work–life enrichment. This will be elaborated on in subsequent sections.

Importantly, the types of interactions between work and life represented by these constructs are not conceptualized as mutually exclusive. That is, an individual can have both work–life conflict and work–life enrichment. For example, employees seeking to engage in their careers and families can, on the one hand, experience conflict when the time they need to be at work conflicts with their ability to attend a family event, while also experiencing enrichment when time spent at work builds their sense of self, which then can lead to positive interaction in their family life. Similarly, employees seeking to attain advanced degrees in order to enhance their marketability can experience conflict when they need to work evenings or weekends and also have course assignments to complete, while also experiencing enrichment when they can see how their work experience enhances their understanding of course concepts.

These situations can potentially present a confusing dilemma that makes it difficult for individuals to assess and articulate smart (but hard) choices for their personal and professional lives. That is, individuals are likely to feel that they need to decide between two positive options, while choosing either one over the other can have extremely negative consequences. Particularly in the case of women, the paradoxical choices are often presented as two extreme ends of a continuum: Should a woman focus on her career or on her family? In a broader employee context, the paradoxical choice may emerge as a question of whether a promotion will result in conflict (e.g., less flexibility in work schedule that has a negative consequence for time for personal interests) or enrichment (e.g., greater sense of satisfaction in professional life that has positive consequences in personal life). In addition to work–family conflict bias, women are also faced with role traps, stereotypes, tokenism, and subconscious biases (Belasen, 2012) that present high-potential women with enormous challenges including:

- *Unequal expectations (double bind)*—Women trying to advance in their careers often find themselves in a double bind. They have learned that they need to act and think like men to succeed, but they are criticized when they do so. The band of acceptable behavior is much more narrow for women than for men. When women managers are assertive and competitive like their male colleagues, they are often judged in performance reviews as being too tough, abrasive, or not supportive of their employees.
- *Glass ceiling*—An invisible barrier that separates women and minorities from top leadership positions. They can look up through the ceiling, but prevailing attitudes are invisible obstacles to their own advancement.
- *Opportunity gap*—The lack of opportunities. In some cases, people fail to advance to higher levels in organizations because they haven't been able to acquire the necessary education and skills.
- *Pipeline condition*—The untested explanation that women leaders with the appropriate skills sets and abilities are very scarce in addition to the fact that mission-critical jobs go to men.

Hewlett (2007) pointed out that nearly four in 10 highly qualified women (37%) reported that they have left work voluntarily at some point in their careers. Women not only stay away from seeking management positions due to lack of workplace flexibility (15%) and family as a bigger priority (26%) but also because of institutional barriers (42%), less willingness to take risks (10%), and lack of mentoring and social support (7%).[2]

"Have it All"

It is true that women face a catch-22 regarding the path they take with their lives, as criticisms seem to amount from both directions: professional and social networks. Women who attempt to combine work responsibilities with family are either chastised for compromising their familial obligations, or for hindering their full professional potential by spending time and effort around their personal life. Lisa Belkin (2003) of the *New York Times* pointed out an alarming trend—large numbers of highly qualified women dropping out of mainstream careers. Labeled as the "opt-out revolution," she traced the reasons and provided evidence why women steer off-ramp or downshift (by moving to less fast-paced jobs to accommodate family needs) at some point on their career highway. The phenomenon of "opt-out" mothers has been a subject of much media fascination—the idea that such ambitious, professionally successful women would put their careers aside, for the opportunity to focus on their families seemed to really strike a chord.

> The truth is the exact opposite. Women faced limited options at work. They failed to realize their aspirations for combining career and family. They suffered a profound loss of identity, not to mention earnings and economic independence. They resumed their careers, but often with considerable redirection to fields less prestigious and less lucrative than their former ones. Theirs were not stories of flow, but of dislocation and personal cost. Employers bore costs too: the loss of highly skilled professional talent, the loss of diverse voices and experiences, and, because women left mid-career just as they were poised for ascent, the loss of women's leadership.
>
> *(Stone, 2013)*

Can the conflicting messages represented recently by Anne-Marie Slaughter and Sheryl Sandberg—"women can't"/"women can" be reconciled (Williams, 2012)? Conveying a message that highlights the possibility and benefits of work–life integration is definitely advantageous in focusing on women's leadership and a healthy outlook on one's personal life. The practicality of this focus makes it both encouraging and relatable for women in addition to reinforcing the idea that women do not need to ignore one aspect or attain perfection in both to feel like they "have it all."

> Women face two life-long developmental tasks: the internal work of forming a vocational identity, and the external work of navigating a career. For women, accomplishing those tasks is complicated by a dilemma imposed by conflicting prescriptions about gender roles – between ambition (choosing a goal and going all-out for it) and drift (taking whatever comes along).
>
> *(Gersick, 2013)*

Are those women who have succeeded in "having it all" any more satisfied with their life than the women who have not met this double goal? Do they experience greater emotional well-being? While there are life satisfaction premiums for career and family individually, there is no additional premium associated with "having it all." A study by Bertrand (2013) found that for the subset of women over 40 years of age who have nearly completed their fertile cycle, the career–life satisfaction premium becomes smaller and is no longer statistically significant. Intuitively, women that "have it all," who are able to meet both professional and personal goals, should report higher levels of well-being. Yet, there are multiple arguments as to why these intuitive answers may not be correct such as changes in life circumstances. It is also possible that highly-educated women might attach different utility values to "having it all" due to their higher social status and greater sense of purpose, even though their well-being scores may not be higher than that of other women who steered toward not maximizing personal values. Bertrand (2013) concluded that there is no evidence of greater life satisfaction or greater emotional well-being among those that have achieved the double goal of combining a successful career with a family life (see Figure 1.1 and Table 1.1).

Less Important Roles

The glass ceiling is a metaphor that explains the subtle, invisible obstacles women face when they try to move up to senior management but are unable to pass

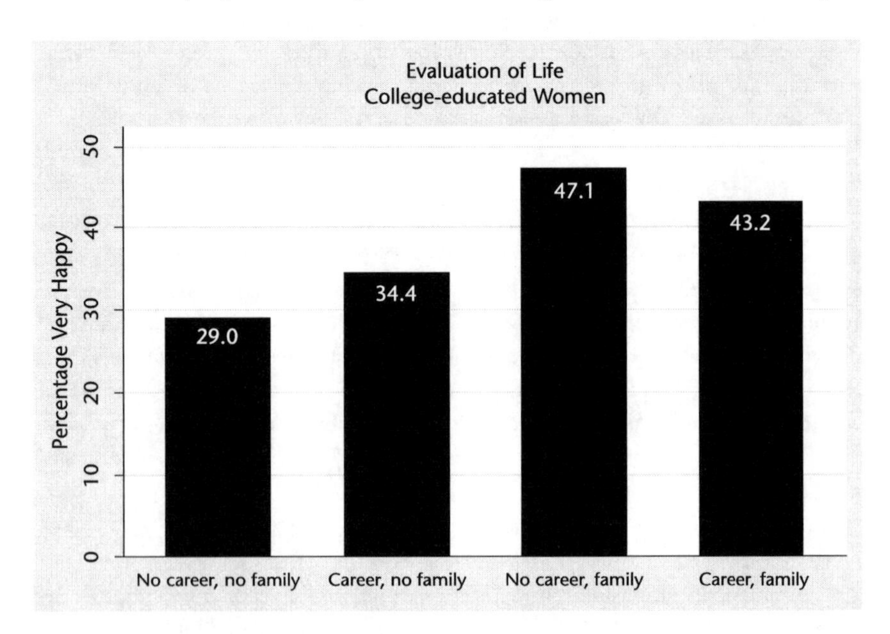

FIGURE 1.1 Life Satisfaction Among College-educated Women

Source: Bertrand (2013).

TABLE 1.1 Emotional Well-being Among College-educated Women. Panel A: Career and Husband

	(1)	*(2)*	*(3)*	*(4)*
Dependent variable:	*Over the Course of the Day, Average:*			
	Happiness	*Sadness*	*Stress*	*Tiredness*
Career	0.088	−0.357	−0.052	−0.21
	[0.121]	[0.098]**	[0.141]	[0.151]
Married	0.259	−0.406	−0.332	−0.019
	[0.109]*	[0.088]**	[0.127]**	[0.136]
Career and married	−0.317	0.567	0.349	0.379
	[0.146]*	[0.118]**	[0.170]*	[0.181]*
Observations	1482	1483	1483	1483
R-squared	0.03	0.04	0.05	0.04

Source: Bertrand (2013).

through middle management. Oakley (2000) described the glass ceiling as not just one wall that women strive to shatter, but many varied pervasive forms of gender bias that occur frequently in both overt and covert ways. Ultimately, women who seek top management positions must sort through culturally formed stereotypes and at the same time avoid crossing culturally generated barriers.

Eagly and Carli (2007) termed the *labyrinth* to describe the complicated, exhausting challenges that women must navigate in pursuit of senior positions. Although gains have been made in many employment areas, women remain significantly underrepresented in positions of power. Women are more likely to be siloed into staff positions such as corporate communication, human resources, and diversity and inclusion and they often play key roles in marketing and customer relations primarily due to their superior people and communication skills in these areas (Belasen, 2012). In addition, women are encouraged to work in departments that have fewer developmental or growth opportunities or do not translate to executive advancement (Guerrero, 2011). Contrast the siloing of women into staff positions with profit and loss responsibilities that are often reserved for men, supporting their upward mobility aspirations.

The fact remains that women are sparsely represented at the upper echelons of business and by 2015 held only 20 (4.0%) of CEO positions at S&P 500 companies, corroborating the substantial evidence of implicit bias against women leaders. Women tend to be viewed as lacking the requisite skills to lead a large organization.

Opportunity Lost

The "glass cliff" describes situations where women are assigned to positions associated with crisis with high risk of failure and criticism (Ryan, Haslam, & Postmes, 2007). Women executives are set up to work under conditions that lead to job dissatisfaction, feelings of disempowerment, and higher risk. Ryan and Haslam (2005) described how women in law firms were given problematic cases and hard-to-win seats compared to men. Other research indicates how women are only considered for leadership positions in companies that are facing financial difficulty and more studies showed how business leaders were more unlikely to pick females to head their companies (Long, 2014). A study by Keziah (2012), for example, showed that male recruiters favored male candidates for low-risk positions. Female recruiters consistently favored a female candidate, with this preference being more marked for a high-risk role. Unless companies develop policies and follow practices to tap into the female talent pool and take proactive steps to reverse this brain-drain, the loss of human capital and underutilization of talent can put companies at disadvantage (Hoobler, Lemmon, & Wayne, 2011). This underscores the fact that companies that achieve diversity and manage it well attain better financial results, on average, than other companies. For example, Catalyst (2011) used three measures in 2010 to examine financial performance: return on sales (ROS); return on invested capital (ROIC); and return on equity (ROE). Previous studies in the series found that there is a connection between gender diversity on corporate boards and financial performance. Findings in this study included:

- Companies with the most women board directors (WBD) outperform those with the least on ROS by 16%.
- Companies with the most WBD outperform those with the least on ROIC by 26%.
- Companies with sustained high representation of WBD, defined as those with three or more WBD in at least four of five years, significantly outperformed those with sustained low representation by 84% on ROS, by 60% on ROIC, and by 46% on ROE.

In *The power of parity: How advancing women's equality can add $12 trillion to global growth*, McKinsey Global Institute (2015) reported that gender parity in economic outcomes is not only a pressing moral and social issue but also a critical global economic challenge. Achieving parity would imply not only the reduction of formidable barriers and change in social attitudes but also personal choices about how to allocate time between domestic and market-based work. The research finds that, in a full-potential scenario in which women play an identical role in labor markets to men's, as much as $28 trillion, or 26%, could be added to the global annual GDP in 2025.

Comparable Skills, Different Preferences

However, for the most part, studies have shown that men and women in comparable positions are actually more alike than different. For example, no differences were found in task-leadership (Won, 2006; Toren, Konrad, Yoshioka, & Kashlak, 1997), no significant differences in the way males and females manage (Vilkinas, 2000), women were stronger in the producer role (Parker, 2004), women were higher in conscientiousness (Gelissen & De Graaf, 2006), women were more analytical (Hays, Allinson, & Armstrong, 2004), women were more detailed (Irby, Brown, Duffy, & Trautman, 2002), and only small differences in women's tendencies toward transformational leadership styles were found in the Eagly and Johannesen-Schmidt (2001) meta-analysis. Some differences, however, were found in motivation and development goals. Most women have multiple goals in life, and don't just set out to snag the biggest monetary prize when they plan their career (Pinker, 2009). Women seem to also prefer intrinsic rewards such as self-development and quality of work–life whereas men value more extrinsic rewards and opportunities to advance up the corporate ladder (Sturges, 1999).

In fact, a new study by Gino, Wilmuth, and Brooks (2015) identified a profound and consistent gender gap in men and women's core life goals: men and women view professional advancement differently, and their views affect their decisions to climb the corporate ladder (or not). Across nine studies using diverse sample populations (executives in high-power positions, recent graduates of a top MBA program, undergraduate students, and online panels of working adults) and over 4,000 participants, they found that, compared to men, women have a higher number of life goals, place less importance on power-related goals, associate more negative outcomes (e.g., time constraints and trade-offs) with high-power positions, perceive power as less desirable, and are less likely to take advantage of opportunities for professional advancement. These findings add another nuance to the already complex set of explanations about gender inequity in business (in addition to institutional barriers and innate differences in men's and women's perceptions and behaviors)—personal preference. Women view high-level positions as equally attainable as men do, but less desirable. Unfortunately, the differences between men and women are not fully understood or valued.

Socialization and Linguistic Differences

Our language and how it is conveyed point to a great number of things about ourselves, including our gender and why masculine stereotypes are still highly valued in workplaces while feminine stereotypes are undervalued (Clason & Turner, 2011). Stereotypes associated with women leaders, on the one hand, include: "communal," which suggests that women are more "cooperative, sensitive, empathetic, nurturing, and more likely to connect with others" than men; "emotional and often cry," which implies the idea that women are generally "unable to control emotion, and are less credible" compared to men; "backstabbing, manipulative," which represents the stereotypical view that women are evil, prone to manipulate others, or conniving. Male leaders, on the other hand, are mostly associated with stereotypes that sound much more positive, including descriptions such as "agentic, autonomous, self-promoting, and tough"; "hard headed and able to control emotion"; and "assertive". By looking at these male stereotypes, we can see how leadership characteristics are being portrayed positively, whereas female stereotypes are connoted with negative or incompetent characteristics.

Stereotypes are learned through the socialization process and result from "nurture" rather than "nature." Because of stereotypes, individuals, in their younger age, are unconsciously led to ignore their natural personal traits, to abandon the unique characteristics that make them who they are, and to passively adopt these stereotypical traits in order to conform to the social notions of masculinity and femininity. Moreover, the language that we use and how we represent femininity and masculinity in language is of great importance because "language is the symbolic embodiment of social values" (Ervin-Tripp, 1987, p. 19). So, the question becomes more like: How are women taught to use language and how are they represented in language?

The traits and behaviors a woman learns as "correct" prevent her from being taken seriously as an individual. Lakoff (1973) argued that the ways in which women are taught to be women, use language, and are represented in language were effectively oppressing women. Socialization teaches women to give way for the superior males and to actively make themselves inferior to men. Lakoff demonstrates how women's "lady-like" language limits their effectiveness. For example, women often use hedges and tag questions, which convey some doubt in statements, lessening their strength. This makes women's language sound more like a question and when paired with a rising intonation at the end of sentences it is not exactly clear whether women are stating something or asking for confirmation of their statement from others.

The representation of women in language, or how we talk about women, is altogether different from how we speak about or refer to men. The underlying theme, the superiority of maleness as the default and female passive expressions or even silence is described in Deborah Tannen's seminal work: *You just don't understand: Women and men in conversation* (1990a). This was produced as more of a layperson's guide to what her research has come to describe as ingrained communicative differences in how women and men speak. In her first chapter she recounts an experience with her ex-husband who screamed: "I do not give you the right to raise your voice at me, because you are a woman and I am a man" (p. 24). This shows how women are overtly expected to behave in relation to men, namely inferior. One of the main communicative differences that her research has shown is that women favor rapport talk, and men prefer report talk (Tannen, 1990b). Each type of talk approaches conversations with others differently and the activity of talking together achieves different ends with women than it does with men.

Communication styles are anchored in or affected by the social context and, as such, gender differences tend to be most pronounced in single-gender groups. When women enter positions of leadership, they experience a deep-rooted complexity of expectations where they are expected to exhibit communal traits as a member of the female gender but at the same time to exhibit agentic traits as a member of leadership (Belasen, 2012). This is a difficult balancing act where women are criticized both for being too masculine and being too feminine (Eagly & Sczesny, 2009).

In her study, Tannen (1990b) had different aged groups of same-sex friends talk together for 15 minutes about "something serious." Girls and women did not have problems choosing a topic, speaking in depth about that topic and on a very personal level. Boys and men had problems choosing a topic and spoke broadly and impersonally. The females spoke about fewer topics with greater inquiry into specific individuals' statements whereas males changed the subjects and only spoke about their side, not using follow-up questions or affiliative comments like the women. If we think further about this, it is not surprising that such a trend can be seen. Growing up at home, children adapt particular gender-based attributes and styles of talking while often participating in separated peer groups or distinct social affiliations. They learn to develop different habits for signaling their intentions and understandings (Tannen, 1990b). Elinor Ochs (1993), speaking more broadly about language acquisition and socialization, states that linguistic constructions of grammar and discourse are crucial indicators of social identity.

Gender is salient to young children's own *identities* and perceptions of others, and parents have an impact on their children's *gender*-role *identity* through day-to-day interactions, by acting as role models, and by *reinforcing* values and attributes of members of the sex that they identify as their own. Gender typing is the process by which a child becomes aware of their gender and thus behaves accordingly by adopting similar values, attitudes, and behaviors. Boys and girls spend large amounts of time playing with *same-sex peers* and go through socialization and identification processes among same-*gender peers*. This socialization of *gender* roles is *reinforced* through the family and observational learning (Shaffer, 2009). As they grow and expand their social circles, children apply their gender-typed attributes from various same-sex models they encounter earlier in society. Of course, this is problematic as the pressure toward the goal of becoming a gender-integrated society and non-gendered organizations requires collaboration, teamwork, and synergy. If gender is a performed identity then growing up in a same-sex peer group reinforces ways of being a woman or man, and those who do not conform are treated as distinct from the peer group.

IN THE MOVIES

One of the most common and noticeable stereotypes at work is based on physical appearance. Women in the workforce have expectations based on their appearance as they are usually seen as unqualified or regarded below men. Hollywood movies such as *The Devil Wears Prada* (2011) depict both the importance of appearance in the workplace as well as reinforcing the stereotypical attitudes toward women:

> The story tells the professional adventure of Andrea; whose greatest dream is to become a journalist. Andrea gets a job in the fashion industry through Runway magazine, the most famous of its type, to make ends meet. But Andrea won't develop her writing skills in the magazine, but her talents as the editor in chief's assistant, Miranda. The problem is that Miranda is a merciless, posh and cruel woman, making the experience a living hell for the girl. The environment in the place will be cold and extremely critical with the physical appearance. The girl will have to change her simple and plain style, for a trendier and elegant one, in order to gain the acceptance of her ruthless boss and colleagues, especially Emily, her unpleasant workmate. Despite everything against Andrea in the office, she will consider the experience as a challenge, drastically changing her clothes and self-image, with the help of Nigel, the magazine's art director. Nevertheless, the job becomes extremely demanding, because of Miranda's tough work rhythm and nearly impossible tasks, leaving Andrea without a private life with her boyfriend, family and friends. Maybe the old Andrea has gone, now more preoccupied about her image and her future in the magazine.
>
> *(Frias, n.d.)*

In *The Intern* (2015), Jules Ostin (Anne Hathaway) plays a woman who "has it all," but who apparently is unsure if she wants any of it in the first place. Robert De Niro plays Ben Whittaker, who shares his wisdom and experience with her. Jules struggles with balancing her work obligations and her responsibilities as a mother and wife. She works long hours in a frustrating corporate environment and without much work–life balance and she is finally convinced by the intern's arguments to hire a CEO. She searches long and hard for the CEO and holds him to high standards. Unfortunately, women and men are viewed differently for the same actions. Jules' skills and talents earn her a leadership position not only because she was able to juggle her responsibilities, but also because she was unwilling to choose between professional success and personal fulfillment. In the end, she made a point to her husband how she wouldn't be happy if she didn't have both her career and family because both made her who she was.

Double-voiced Discourse Strategy

For many female leaders, being in a male-normative work environment is at best stressful and at worst frustrating. The ways in which women are taught to talk seem to be incompatible with a professional identity in a company where maleness is the standard, and those without the ability to communicate within the existing norms are doomed to becoming the silent group. In *The silent sex* (2014), Christopher F. Karpowitz and Tali Mendelberg find particularly troubling evidence with regard to gender equality in deliberative situations in which women speak significantly less than men do and what they do say carries less weight. *A confluence of two factors*—the number of women in a discussion group combined with the group's decision rule—helps to explain when women are more or less involved in group deliberations. Women are at the biggest disadvantage, in terms of speaking, in deliberative bodies that employ unanimous rule (when women are great in number) and in situations that employ majority rule (when women are few in number). Unfortunately, majority rule is the most common configuration for decision making bodies, with the US Congress being the most prominent example. This leads one to question how well women are being represented politically and how different the tenor and outcomes of political discussion might be if institutional configurations were different (Felts, 2015).

WHY WOMEN ARE BETTER LEADERS YET CAN'T BREAK GLASS CEILING

Senator Dianne Feinstein (D-CA) has chaired the Senate's Intelligence Committee for five years. So when she suggested last month that investigators should make public a report on the U.S.'s interrogation techniques because it would "ensure that an un-American, brutal program of detention and interrogation will never again be considered or permitted," one might have seen it as the strong words and fair assessment of a person who has deep experience on the issue. But on Fox News, Bush-era National Security Agency and Central Intelligence Agency Director Michael Hayden suggested that Feinstein actually encouraged the public release of the interrogation techniques report because of her emotions, implying that because Feinstein was a woman she was too emotional to make rational statements.

(Williams, 2014)

Accommodating language to fit particular situations was found to be practiced more often by female leaders in their normal work days than by male leaders in similar situations (Baxter, 2011; Giles, Coupland, & Coupland, 1991). Part of this might well be due to the fact that men already default to "correct" ways of speaking by using the language that they have been accustomed to from a young age, which is congruent with their male identity. For women, however, there is a learning curve where they perceive the need to mirror speaking styles and behaviors, although unnatural to them, with the normative expectations. There are sometimes problems with the implementation of accommodating speech and behavior, such as coming off too masculine, but overall women do more accommodating in the way they speak and present themselves than men.

Baxter (2011) found that female leaders were more critical of their leadership communication than were men and tailored their messages to the individuals who would be receiving them. She uses a Bakhtinian understanding of double-voiced discourse to describe the leadership communication phenomenon that she was observing:

> [S]enior women talked about and demonstrated a heightened awareness of and responsiveness to the concerns and interests of their colleagues, which were then reflected in the different ways they adjusted their language use to serve both their own purposes and those of their team.
>
> *(Baxter, 2011, p. 236)*

An example from her work makes this clearer: "so I've been (.) I've been reading how I've written it and the before I've sent it (.) I've scrolled back through and thought (1) how would (.) how would Dave write this email?" (p. 238). It appears that the person speaking is telling the interviewer that she is cognizant of how she sounds. Moreover, to fit the culture and work environment as a leader she takes into account how the unmarked leader would phrase messages to guide her own messages.

Baxter (2011) concluded that perhaps double-voiced discourse is not simply a survival strategy but a way of practicing different types of leadership at different moments, which lends to the argument that while leaders use different communication styles they do so contingent on the context (Belasen & Frank, 2010, 2012). Women are more likely than men to engage in conversations, elicit opinions, and seek to better understand how their superiors, peers, and subordinates would feel about their attempts at influence (Belasen, 2012). Women have a softer more communal way of making hard decisions. Women in leadership tend to be less abrupt or harsh when trying to obtain "buy-in" from their employees. They have eloquent ways of getting their points across and getting employees to take on difficult tasks without seeming demanding or overbearing.

Role Traps

Kanter (1993) identified four overarching role traps for women in male-normative organizations. These traps, whether they seem to be more positive or negative, are the ways in which a woman could behave and project her professional identity in sanctioned ways while still projecting her feminine leadership traits. These are folk-linguistic stereotypes that exist and factor into how someone's actions are seen as a female leader:

- *Mother:* Traditional authority but expected to be of service to peers on a socio-emotional level and not respected for her independent and professional abilities.
- *Seductress*: Objectified view of women as serving sexual needs of one very senior male. Uses her sexual allure to get promoted rather than professional attributes.
- *Pet:* Adopted by male group as an amusing and cute thing; the mascot for the group.
- *Iron Maiden:* Encapsulates the most explicit power but most masculinized: forceful and aggressive.

Here we can see that women are either hyper-sexualized, as in the seductress, or their sexual identity is taken away from them. When compared to men whose leadership is not characterized by their bodies or their sexuality but by what they do and how they perform as leaders, female leaders are still "trapped" to the extent that there are proverbs, quotations, and folk-linguistic beliefs that offer approved subject positions for women in power. At worst, these may constrain the range of subject positions available to senior women, and thus limit the ways in which they are expected to speak and act. At best, these "stereotypes" can be utilized as discursive resources to offer women in management positions a range of voices and a means of resistance at moments when they are in danger of being undermined. This gendered constraint upon the availability and range of linguistic resources may indeed be one barrier to women's progress to the top (Baxter, 2012).

Baxter extended the notion of Kanter's (1993) argument to suggest that role traps, while constraining, offer a readily available categorization of behavior and identity to actually benefit women's leadership. Even if someone thinks of a leader as an iron maiden, it is connoted with a normative folk-linguistic stereotype and can then rely on that to predict behavior and expect certain kinds of actions from that leader. While it is not ideal to do this, it is a strategy that capitalizes on the already held perceptions of women as leaders and gains them some legitimacy.

Gendered Paths

Gendered career paths and gendered workplaces make it difficult for working women to find their paths and ways to success (Ely, Ibarra, & Kolb, 2011). Historically, the categorization of jobs, the operating model of businesses, and the communication patterns within the workplace were initially reflective of men's lives and situations rather than women's (Acker, 1990; Bailyn, 2006; Hewlett, 2007). According to Clason and Turner (2011), organizations are constructed as places where "men's presence is normative," and women's presence is seen as "an intrusion." With this negative ethos existing in organizations, women generally need to deal with greater challenges and barriers than men before getting to the top of an organization. CEOs and executives are gendered leadership positions; if a woman wants to get to the top of an organization, she has to follow this gendered path, and even though she follows the path, her chances to climb up the hierarchy are quite slim.

Ely et al. (2011) suggest that women in organizations are lacking access to informal networks and sponsors. Informal networks are essential enablers of change in organizations. They can help shape career trajectories by regulating access to jobs, channeling the flow of information and referrals, creating influence and reputation, providing emotional support, feedback, political advice, and protection, and increasing the likelihood and speed of promotion (Burt, 1992; Granovetter, 1985; Higgins & Kram, 2001; Ibarra, 1993; Podolny & Baron, 1997; Westphal & Milton, 2000). Since career paths are gendered in ways that benefit men, it becomes tougher for women to gain access to certain networks that potentially can yield leadership opportunities for individuals. Men's ability to access more networks and resources give them unfair advantage in promotion considerations.

Women are being held back by work–life conflict. Even nowadays, work–family issues are still seen as women's "turf" rather than men's problems, as men executives don't feel guilty for highlighting work as priority. Women, however, are constantly being judged negatively for prioritizing work over family. Indeed, balance is no longer achievable in today's fast-paced world (O'Neil, Hopkins, & Bilimoria, 2008). Instead, integration of work and life is more important and achievable (Kiisel, 2013). Women face the challenge of finding support from female mentors and female role models due to relative scarcity of women in the pipeline or career pathways to executive positions. When aspiring career women or leader-wannabes face problems in the workplace and seek out guidance or inspiration from their female predecessors, they just cannot find many. When male peers are building the foundations of a new identity and are ready to move on, equally high-achieving women may still be searching for role models (Ely & Rhode, 2010). Scarcity of female colleagues in senior management isolates the few women leaders who are often subconsciously viewed by others as symbolic gestures of the company's goodwill efforts to promote equality.

Uphill Battle

The way executives relate to female middle managers is subtly influenced by what they expect of them. If their perceptions of mediocrity lead to setting up low expectations, the productivity of the affected women is likely to be poor, which in turn reinforces that initial perception of uncommitted middle managers. They are perceived as mediocre or weak performers who tend to live down to the low expectations that senior executives have set out for them, in effect perpetuating a vicious cycle of perceived incompetence (Manzoni & Barsoux, 2002). This self-reinforcing process, prime for conditions of failure, is also known as the "Pygmalion Effect" (described in J. Sterling Livingston's 1969 seminal work). Pygmalion refers to a person who consciously or unconsciously is aware of an expectation and acts in a way that is consistent with that expectation. The perception of low value creates another dynamic known as exclusive "clubs" or "golden circles" of winners (in-group) and the less fortunate losers (out-group) with members in the out-group being treated with rules, policy guidelines, and authority, while the members of the in-group enjoy greater feedback, interactions, and close proximity to decision makers.

For example, executives often allocate attractive positions—including line positions—for in-group members (Powell & Butterfield, 2002), a propensity Kanter (1993) termed "homosocial reproduction" whereby male decision makers tend to appoint leaders like themselves in terms of gender, race, age, and background. They may do so out of in-group loyalty, because they are simply more comfortable among members of the in-group or because they view in-group members as more essential to the organization (Cook & Glass, 2014). Not surprisingly, men's overrepresentation in important leadership positions tends to reproduce gender biases and in-group preferences that hinder women's climb to top positions (Chambliss & Uggen, 2000). Indeed, when executives reduce their dependence on men and women middle managers, bypass them, or do not trust their abilities to think and act strategically, a self-reinforcing cycle of failure occurs in which the credibility of middle managers continues to erode. Consequently, unlucky middle managers, particularly women, do not make the short list for upward mobility or are excluded from the succession-planning process altogether (Belasen, 2012). When the emotional impact of the work middle managers perform is not acknowledged, they further feel lonely, *unhappy*, and abandoned (Kuyvenhoven & Buss, 2011).

Zenger and Folkman (2014) examined the demographic characteristics of unhappy employees among more than 320,000 individuals in a variety of organizations and found that 16,000 (5%) were middle managers. The main sources of unhappiness included *poor leadership* as the number one reason followed by "no career or promotion opportunities," "work lacks meaning and purpose," "being treated unfairly compared with others," "feeling under-appreciated," "overworked," and "viewing the organization as inefficient and ineffective."

Tokenism

The advancement of a limited number of women into upper echelons of management can be viewed as "tokenism," the perception of the few women in senior positions as demonstrations of equality, when, in reality, this is far from the truth (Schmitt, Spoor, Danaher, & Branscombe, 2009). The token stands out, becoming more "visible" than other members and feels pressure to demonstrate successful outcomes more so than male counterparts. As tokens, they try to fit within the existing corporate and social structure while the dominant group may keep them on the periphery in subtle rather than overt ways, such as excluding the tokens from social interactions (Brannon, 2010). Token status also leads to weaker social and professional networks and reduced organizational support, information, and assistance from peers and subordinates (Cook & Glass, 2014; Taylor, 2010). Tokens do not become the "good ol‘ boys" or part of the network that offers support to women and allows connections that may be important for their career advancement. Subsequently, token women leaders often experience reduced performance and job satisfaction (Sekaquaptewa & Thompson, 2003). Women from ethnic groups are also trapped in a double-loop disadvantage because they represent tokens in two ways (Murrell & James, 2001).

Queen Bee Syndrome

Since women in senior positions are more likely than men counterparts to suffer from token status, their leadership style is often subject to intense scrutiny and negative evaluation bias. Token women are more likely to experience gender discrimination, receive lower evaluations from male subordinates, and generally experience less career success (Schwanke, 2013). What's more, women's visibility in the workplace is heightened when they make mistakes and is reduced when they make exceptional contributions. Moreover, Hopfl (2010) noted how the two extremes create a dilemma for women at work. Women are not only expected to be invisible or at least unobtrusive but also they are expected to be physically present as a demonstration of their commitment (Clason & Turner, 2011).

A contested behavioral response is the "Queen Bee Syndrome" through which successful women are less likely to share information, let alone guide or even encourage other women to pursue upward mobility. The purpose of this strategy is to maintain a woman's place with the men at her level by aligning herself with the men's perceptions and interests (Hamel, 2009).

> Her behavior might be driven by her insecurity. She doesn't believe that her own innate abilities will help her reach her career goals. Consequently, she is always looking for potential threats to her success. Perhaps the messages she heard growing up confirmed the lessons of Cinderella and Snow White; that other women are out to get you and you better watch out, especially if you are ambitious, certainly if you are beautiful and talented. You always have to guard your back.
>
> *(Marcus, 2016)*

Role Conflict and Work–Life Paradoxes

Individuals typically belong to multiple groups (e.g., member of organization, family, community) in an attempt to fulfill multiple expectations that emerge from different, often overlapping roles (e.g., employee, community organizer, family member, student), and these simultaneous role expectations can result in interrole conflict. A specific type of interrole conflict commonly explored in the extant literature is the conflict between work and family roles. Greenhaus and Beutell (1985) discuss three forms of work–family conflict (i.e., time-based, strain-based, behavior-based). Others viewed the interaction between work and family roles from a positive perspective. For example, using role accumulation theory (Greenhaus & Powell, 2006), researchers have argued that interactions between multiple roles can have positive consequences.

In line with these theories, the notion of work–family enrichment explores the ways in which the presence of and interactions between these two domains can have positive outcomes. A third approach, presented in the conservation of resources theory (Hobfoll, 1989) acknowledges that perceptions of conflict and enrichment are influenced by subjective perceptions of gains versus losses of resources. Arguably, a job promotion may be viewed as a gain in resources (e.g., enrichment through increases in money, status, self-esteem) and/or a loss of resources (e.g., conflict due to time no longer available for personal interests, family).

While much of the literature tends to focus on the interactions between work and family domains, there have been recent calls to expand research efforts to explore non-work areas beyond family (Keeney, Boyd, Sinha, Westring, & Ryan, 2013). This call mirrors the expansion within the workplace of the employee population for whom the coexistence and navigation of work and life responsibilities is relevant. That is, while a work–family focus often leads to discussions centered on women with caregiving responsibilities in a traditional family structure (i.e., woman with children who is married to a male breadwinner), a work–life focus allows for broadening the discourse to include a more diverse workforce. Examples are millennials who seek workplaces that recognize employees' personal responsibilities, baby boomers who are exploring work practices that allow for a phased retirement, men looking for alternative career models that allow for greater involvement in caregiving activities, single parents trying to identify more effective means of integrating work and personal responsibilities, and employees seeking time to pursue educational degrees to advance in their careers. In fact, studies show the millennial generation would take less pay for more flexibility with their work schedule (Asghar, 2014).

RETHINK WHAT YOU 'KNOW' ABOUT HIGH-ACHIEVING WOMEN: THE HBS STUDENT PERSPECTIVE

HBS faculty Robin Ely and Colleen Ammerman along with Pamela Stone (of City University of New York) focused their research on baby boomers (ages 49–67), Generation X (ages 32–48), and millennials (ages 26–31) of both genders, seeking to find out both graduate expectations for their lives after grad school and their experiences in the years since (Ely, Stone, & Ammerman, 2014).

Children do not hold back women's careers but rather the expectations of career prioritization in their relationships hold women back. They found that while the vast majority of female HBS alumnae (75–83%) expected egalitarian relationships, they ended up in traditional relationships (i.e., man's career taking precedence over the woman's) about 40% of the time, leading to dissatisfaction in their careers. Conversely, the minority of men who were in egalitarian relationships but had expected a traditional relationship were also dissatisfied.

Ultimately the authors found that on the whole men expect their careers to be the priority in their partnership and that their expectations are overwhelmingly realized. About half of the women who had egalitarian career expectations also assumed they would perform most of the child care in their families, suggesting women (whether implicitly or explicitly) expect a higher burden from the outset. A number of themes emerged.

First, there was a sense of gratitude and relief that "finally someone has built the data to debunk the myths." There was a general consensus among the students interviewed that the power of the article was to debunk myths with data. The number that stood out most was that 11% of women are opting out for full-time child care—some thought this was high, some thought it was low, but all were struck that the vast majority of women are remaining in the workforce and therefore the fact that women's careers continue to stall must be driven by other factors.

Second, there was pessimism, despair, and discomfort, primarily from female students but also from some male students. One student said she hears the platitudes but doubts action will ensue:

> What I find frustrating about this is that I don't think many of our peers have internalized what it means for them personally. Men and women talk about equality, and I'm sure they believe the words, but they have not truly considered that that means both partners in a relationship making career sacrifices for children.

Third, there was skepticism. Most of the men interviewed suggested women and men wanted different things and therefore the research is not that useful. While this may be true with a broader population, the authors of the research deliberately focused on MBAs, where men and women do not differ much in terms of what they value and hope for in their lives and careers.

The noticeable difference occurs in how men and women's career paths diverge and how likely men are to achieve their ambitions, versus women.

Fourth, a male student recounted his previous discussions with women in which they say they will be less attracted to men who are not the main breadwinner, which, as the student said, "makes it hard to know what we are meant to be—supporters or providers?"

Finally, many students highlighted the need for better government and organizational policies. As long as flexible work arrangements are considered as for mothers only, a stigma will remain.

(Harbus, 2014)

Millennials: Why Companies Should "Lean In"

Moving from work–life balance to work–life integration is not only becoming the new mantra but also a necessity as technologies such as Skype, social networking, and Google Docs and workplace environments continue to change. In fact, millennials have already started to adapt to this reality. They are on Facebook talking to their friends at work and they answer business emails when they leave the office. By 2020, *millennials* will form 50% of the global *workforce* (PricewaterhouseCoopers, 2012). Therefore, it is in every organization's interest to learn how to attract millennials, how to redesign the workplace to meet their expectations, and how to integrate them in a manner that is compelling and consistent with millennials' distinct values. Jamie Gutfreund of the CAA's Intelligence Group (Asghar, 2014) found that:

- 64% of the millennials say it's a priority for them to make the world a better place;
- 72% would like to be their own boss, but if they do have to work for a boss, 79% of them would want that boss to serve more as a coach or mentor;
- 88% prefer a collaborative work culture rather than a competitive one;
- 74% want flexible work schedules; and,
- 88% want "work–life integration," which isn't the same as work–life balance, since work and life now blend together inextricably.

Millennials (both men and women) are rearticulating career goals; the world is currently experiencing a quiet revolution in the re-balancing of the genders' social, educational, and economic power. It may be time for companies to "lean in," in part by considering how they can institutionalize a level playing field for all employees, regardless of gender or caregiver status. Smart leaders have understood for a while that gender balance delivers better and more sustainable performance as companies with more gender-balanced leadership teams outperform those with less (Ely et al., 2014). Could it be that executives need to rearticulate their talent management or diversify leadership competencies to include attributes, behaviors, and expected outcomes that appeal to more women (such as balance, which can contribute to better performance, innovation, and customer satisfaction, for example)?

Social Media and Identity

With the proliferation of social media and web publishing tools, organizations learn to change the way they handle external as well as internal communication since employees are now blogging, tweeting, or responding in open public spaces to queries about their organizations, both positively and negatively. Employees' blogs create an almost unlimited potential for sharing knowledge, fostering dialogue, promoting goods and services, and using multiple and interactive communication channels to enhance the image of the organization. Social media provides meaning and connection between brands and consumers and offers a personal channel and currency for user-centered networking and building relationships (Dong-hun, 2010; Papasolomou & Melanthiou, 2012). In addition, digital media creates options for corporations to tell their story. It serves as a catalyst for creating and influencing external and internal stakeholders (Prasad, 2011). The rising phenomenon of employees' engagement in shaping corporate identity further supports the assumption that reputation and branding are built inside-out as well as shaped by outside-in pressures (Chi, 2011). Corporate branding and brand management are elements of corporate identity.

Indeed, when you respond to work-related email messages or texts over the weekend, you are, in effect, extending the psychological contract with your employer—the unwritten expectations and informal obligations of the employment relationship (which is distinct from the formal, explicit employment contract). Taken together, the psychological contract and the employment contract define the employer–employee relationship in terms of mutual expectations and balanced contributions and inducements. In fact, a study by TeamViewer and Harris Interactive, found that 61% of employees are willing to work during vacation in 2013, up from 52% in 2012 (Harris Interactive, 2013). In another study by Gyro and Forbes Insights (Schawbel, 2014), 98% of executives reported that they check email during their off time and 63% check every one or two hours during their off time. Some employees are doing this because they have no choice, especially managers and executives who have direct reports, and others do it because they feel like they have to. Of course, employees who are really passionate about their work become addicted and are actually excited about new emails coming in.[3]

Work-related email from home blurs work–family boundaries and decreases personal autonomy (Mazmanian, Orlikowski, & Yates, 2013), adds more stress and work overload (Jerejian, Reid, & Rees, 2013), and increases work–family conflict (Boswell & Olson-Buchanan, 2007). Not only that email extends work beyond the regular (obligatory) hours of work, but also it creates the short- and long-term dangers of "on demand" work culture and expectations.

Challenging the Binary

Drawing data from 4,225 publishing scientists and researchers worldwide, the Association for Women in Science (2012) finds that lack of flexibility in the workplace, dissatisfaction with career development opportunities, and low salaries are driving both men and women to re-consider their profession:

- More than half (54%) of all scientists and researchers said that work demands tend to conflict with their personal lives at least two to three times per week.
- Only a third of researchers agreed they work for family-friendly institutions. A number said that their employers do not have spousal hire policies or that such policies are not available because of funding cuts.
- Only half of the women (52%) reported that they are happy with their work–life integration, compared with 61% of men working in research across all fields.
- One-third of researchers say that ensuring good work–life integration has negatively impacted their careers, and women (37%) were more likely than men (30%) to say this was the case. For those researchers with dependent children, 36% reported career problems.
- Nearly 40% of women respondents have delayed having children because of their careers, while 27% of males indicated the same situation. A number of women mentioned waiting until they had a permanent position to get pregnant or noted that they could not afford to start a family on their wages.
- One in 10 researchers indicated that they expect to leave their current job within the next year. Of those intending to leave, females were twice as likely (12%) as males (6%) to cite a spouse's job offer or relocation as the reason. Of researchers intending to leave, 9% indicated it was because they were unable to balance work–life integration overload.

We use the term *Work/Life Integration* instead of *Work/Life Balance* because the latter evokes a binary opposition between work and life. In fact, the traditional image of a scale associated with work/life balance creates a sense of competition between the two elements. Work/life integration instead is an approach that creates more synergies between all areas that define "life": work, home/family, community, personal well-being, and health.

Technological tools have created new ways for us to collaborate and work virtually, bringing with them tailored alternatives for work schedule flexibility. Wellness programs and volunteer opportunities promoted by Berkeley-Haas as well as support for child and elder care at UC Berkeley are just a few examples of programs that facilitate in the workplace the integration between work and personal life.

("Work/Life Integration," 2016)

Flexible Schedules

As work environments become more complex and interdependent, the boundaries between family and career begin to blur and women and men have to blend what they do personally and professionally in order to make both work. Research by Fuwa and Cohen (2007) indicates that the average American woman works 13.2 hours per week on housework, compared to her spouse who works approximately 6.6 hours. This disparity creates an undesirable scenario for women, who are forced to choose an unhealthy work–life balance in order to pursue their careers.

In total, 30 million Americans work from home at least once each week, which is expected to increase by 63% by 2018 (Rapoza, 2013). About 3 million Americans never go to an office and 54% are happier working from home than in an office. Furthermore, 70% of employees work from alternative locations (not just home) on a regular basis (Brooks, 2012). A total of 47% of individuals who have the option to telework are "very satisfied" with their jobs, compared to 27% of those who are office-bound (Rapoza, 2013).

HOW DOES THE US RANK IN WORK POLICIES FOR INDIVIDUALS AND FAMILIES?

Out of 173 countries studied, 168 countries offer guaranteed paid leave to women in connection with childbirth; 98 of these countries offer 14 or more weeks paid leave. Although in a number of countries, many women work in the informal sector where these government guarantees do not always apply, the fact remains that the U.S. guarantees no paid leave for mothers in any segment of the work force, leaving it in the company of only 4 other nations: Lesotho, Liberia, Papua New Guinea, and Swaziland.

(Heymann, Earle, & Hayes, 2007)

Over two-thirds of employers reported increased productivity among their teleworkers. Contributing factors included fewer interruptions from colleagues, more effective time management, feelings of empowerment, flexible hours and, of course, even longer hours. The home office never closes. The result is increased productivity, reduced facility costs, lowered absenteeism, and reduced turnover. Employees save somewhere between $1,600 to $6,800 and 15 days of time once used driving to work or taking public transportation (Rapoza, 2013). What these numbers illustrate is that millions of people are working in a personal setting, primarily from home. When this happens, it's hard to separate work and life. They are fully integrated (Schawbel, 2014).

Interestingly, women are not alone in favoring a change in work schedules to help reconcile the competing commitments of family and work (Vanderkam, 2015). Men do too, as the cover of *Fortune*'s November 2005 issue has shown (see box "What Do Men Really Want?"). In fact, as the share of dual-income households has risen, the roles of mothers and fathers have begun to converge. Men today are now reporting high levels of work–family conflict (Harrington, Van Deusen, & Mazar, 2012)· They feel not just pressure, but also the desire to be more involved in family life, childcare, housework, and cooking.

At the same time, polls have been showing that women are now just as likely as men to say that they want to have challenging careers (Ludden, 2013). Male executives seem to agree that restructuring senior management jobs in ways that would both increase productivity and make more time for a life outside the office would also have a competitive advantage in attracting talent.

WHAT DO MEN REALLY WANT?

Our new survey of senior FORTUNE 500 male executives offers surprising answers. Fully 84% say they'd like job options that let them realize their professional aspirations while having more time for things outside work; 55% say they're willing to sacrifice income. Half say they wonder if the sacrifices they've made for their careers are worth it. In addition, 73% believe it's possible to restructure senior management jobs in ways that would both increase productivity and make more time available for life outside the office. And 87% believe that companies that enable such changes will have a competitive advantage in attracting talent. Other interviews suggest that the younger a male executive is, the more likely he is to say he cares about all of this.

Of course there's a roadblock to reform: fear. FORTUNE's survey found that even though most senior-level men want better options, nearly half believe that for an executive to take up the matter with his boss will hurt his career.

Still, two things seem clear. First, men and women are far more alike in their desires than the debate over these issues has assumed. Second, as talented men raise their voices with women who have been irate about this for decades, the 24/7 ethic is pretty clearly on borrowed time.

(Miller, 2005)

Changes in corporate practices and policies begin to take shape. The US Bureau of Labor Statistics reports show that by 1997 nearly 27% of American women experienced flexible schedules as an alternative to the traditional 9 to 5, 40-hour workweek, up from 11% in 1984 (Beers, 2000). The US Bureau of Labor Statistics also reports that in May 2004, over 27 million full-time wage and salary workers had flexible work schedules that allowed them to vary the time they began or ended work (US Department of Labor, 2005). These workers comprised 27.5% of all full-time wage and salary workers, down from 28.6% in May 2001, when these data were last collected. The proportion who usually worked a shift other than a daytime schedule (14.8%) remained close to the 2001 level. These findings were obtained from a supplement to the May 2004 Current Population Survey (CPS).[4] The survey also collected information about flexible schedules, shift work, and other related topics.[5]

Results showed that men are more likely to have flexible schedules than women (28.1% and 26.7%, respectively). Overall reasons for requesting flexible work hours included: "nature of the job," e.g., employer-arranged irregular schedules (54.6%), "personal preference" (11.5%), "better arrangements for family or childcare" (8.2%), "could not get any other job" (8.1%), and "better pay" (6.8%). Many of those who worked night and evening shifts chose such schedules due to personal preference (21% and 15.9%, respectively) or because these shifts facilitated better arrangements for family or childcare (15.9% and 11%, respectively). For these women, well-paying professional jobs that allow *flexibility to handle their family needs* are "very appealing" (Goudreau, 2011).

Pew Research surveys (Parker & Livingston, 2016) have found that, just like mothers, 50% of working fathers find it enormously challenging to balance the competing demands of family obligations and work responsibilities as well as earning the additional income to support their families. In fact, 48% of working fathers with children under age 18 say they'd prefer to be home. About the same share of working fathers (34%) and mothers (40%) say they "always feel rushed" in their day-to-day lives. These facts are also consistent with the change from "housewife" to "independent/working mother." With the rising cost of daycare, some women are forced to leave their jobs because it has become more cost effective to stay at home and take care of the baby if they are not the breadwinner of the family.

It is important to note that The Fair Labor Standards Act (FLSA) does not address flexible work schedules (US Department of Labor, n.d.). Alternative work arrangements such as flexible work schedules are a matter of agreement between the employer and the employee (or the employee's representative). Technologies such as remote server access and videoconferencing as well as telecommuting have facilitated the trend toward flexible work arrangements.

Paid Parental Leave

Companies must hunt for unconscious biases that may affect women's careers as well as grow beyond the premise that offering flextime or "family friendly" options are enough to retain and develop high-potential women (Ely et al., 2014). Moreover, they need to support men who take on flexible arrangements, thereby mainstreaming flexibility and removing the stigma of childcare responsibilities. The benefits will be twofold: women who use flexible arrangements will not be penalized, and men will be able to be more involved in their families as many desire to be (Harbus, 2014). Likewise, companies can benefit from providing paid leave to women. Paid leave provides much needed flexibility to women caregivers as well as helping companies retain talent and avoid additional costs of replacing employees or retraining. Jobs that are very complex and that require higher levels of education and specialized training tend to have even higher turnover costs.[6]

Some companies offer in-house daycare, extended maternity and paternity leaves, and flexible schedules, making it easier to maintain work and family responsibilities without fear of being penalized. The government has important responsibilities, too. When Australia passed a parental leave law in 2010, it left the US among very few countries as the top industrialized nation that does not have a mandated paid leave for mothers of newborns. Many countries give new fathers paid time off as well or allow parents to share paid leave. It is astounding that the US does not require paid maternity leave. Consider for a moment what other countries offer to new mothers in comparison to the United States' zero paid weeks and 12 unpaid: Denmark—42 paid weeks and 54 unpaid; Sweden—40 paid weeks and 85 unpaid; France—73 paid weeks and 162 unpaid; Germany—38 paid weeks and 162 unpaid; Italy—30 paid weeks and 65 unpaid (Wittenburg-Cox & Maitland, 2009). New parents in the US are guaranteed their jobs for 12 weeks after the arrival of a new baby, thanks to the Family Medical Leave Act (FMLA) of 1993, but they do not have to be paid during that time and exemptions apply for small companies.

If an organization is not covered by FMLA or state laws, what steps can be taken to ensure that employees get the appropriate level of maternity leave? Providing maternity leave is a smart option for small businesses with fewer than 50 employees. According to the US Department of Labor (2013), which surveyed employers and employees nationwide on leave taking under the FMLA, providing both maternity and medical leave is proven to make a positive impact on the lives of employees without placing an undue burden on employers.

THE FAMILY AND MEDICAL LEAVE ACT

The ... FMLA, has been helping families overcome work-family challenges since its passage 22 years ago by enabling employees to take unpaid job-protected leave to recover from personal illnesses, care for a new child, or care for another family member. While the FMLA was an important first step toward creating more equitable work environments, it leaves out around 40% of the workforce and only guarantees unpaid leave, which many workers cannot afford to take. On its own, the FMLA fails to provide the resources that many families, especially Millennial families, need to be able to take time off without risking their economic stability.

Families deserve to know they will not be thrown into hardship if breadwinners have to take time off from work to care for a family member or themselves. Paid family and medical leave is critical to the stability and success of Millennials who are working hard to make ends meet as they launch their careers, start families, and pay off student loan debts.

(Frothingham, 2015)

Abuse of these policies is also much lower than expected, and 90% of employees return to their jobs after taking FMLA leave (Beesley, 2013). Other economic benefits to both employees and employers include (Gault, Hartmann, Hegewisch, Milli, & Reichlin 2014):

- increased likelihood of workers returning to work after childbirth;
- improved employee morale;
- neutral and/or positive effect on workplace productivity;
- reduced costs to employers through lower employee attrition rates;
- improved family income; and
- fostering gender equity in the office and at home.

NEWBURGH HEIGHTS PASSES RECORD-SETTING PARENTAL-LEAVE LAW

NEWBURGH HEIGHTS, OH – A big day for parents in Northeast Ohio as a record-setting parental-leave law was passed in Newburgh Heights.

City council unanimously approved Ordinance 201628, which gives full-time employees six months paid maternity and paternity leave.

According to Mayor Trevor Elkins, Newburgh Heights becomes the first city in the state of Ohio to give paid maternity leave and the first in the nation to offer six months.

"I'm very excited because it sends a clear message that we value our employees' families," said Mayor Elkins.

Both female and male employees are eligible for the leave.

The law does not apply to the Mayor and other elected officials.

The leave will run concurrently with FMLA leave, if the employee wishes.

"The rest of the world is far more generous and values that first couple years. Some European nations give more than two years. I think we are behind the times. I think this is just a step to catch us up," said Mayor Elkins.

(Reid, 2016)

This means that more women will continue to be in the workforce and will not be faced with a binary choice between career and family, or rather, one at the expense of the other. Furthermore, more women in management positions, as argued throughout the book, leads to increased profits for the employer.

NEW YORK JUST CREATED A REVOLUTIONARY NEW FAMILY-LEAVE POLICY

New York has just become the fifth state — after California, which passed its family-leave insurance program in 2002 and implemented it in 2004, New Jersey (2009), Rhode Island (2014), and Washington (which passed its measure in 2007 but has not yet put it into effect) — to mandate paid leave. And compared to its progressive predecessors, New York's bill is startlingly robust.

The program will mandate up to 12 weeks of paid time off from a job to bond with a new child (including adopted or foster children), or to care for a gravely ill parent, child, spouse, domestic partner, or other family member. The duration of the leave, while still far from the 40 weeks guaranteed in the U.K. or even the 16 weeks provided in Bangladesh, doubles the 6 weeks allotted in California and New Jersey, and triples the 4 weeks of paid leave offered by Rhode Island.

New York's new bill does away with many of these exceptions. The paid leave program will cover full-time and part-time employees. There will be no exemptions for small businesses. And to take advantage of the program, you only have to have been employed by the company for six months. The program will be funded on an insurance model, in which roughly a dollar a week will be deducted from employee paychecks; there is no employer contribution.

(Traister, 2016)

Changes, indeed, are taking shape. Among women in the United States, post-graduate education and motherhood are increasingly going hand-in-hand according to the Pew Research Center (Livingston, 2015). The share of highly-educated women who are remaining childless into their mid-40s has fallen significantly over the past two decades. Today, 22% ages 40 to 44 with a Master's degree or higher have no children—down from 30% in 1994. The decline is particularly dramatic among women with an MD or PhD—fully 35% were childless in 1994, while today the share stands at 20%.

Not only are highly-educated women more likely to have children these days, but also they are having bigger families than in the past. Among women with at least a Master's degree, 60% had two or more children, up from 51% in 1994. These findings could also signal the shift away from traditional ideas of gender roles and, instead, embrace the "millennial women," who may prefer to integrate a post-graduate education and a career as well as raise a family (Clark, 2015).

Notes

1 According to Amanda Hess (2013), women were much more likely to provide care for elderly parents than men were; 7% of the women in the sample "assisted with parents' personal needs," compared to 3.6% of men; 20% of women "helped parents with chores, errands, and transportation," compared to 16% of men. And female caregivers were much more likely to exit the workforce to execute these duties. When men took on caregiving roles, their employment status was unaffected.

The cost impact of caregiving on the individual female caregiver in terms of lost wages and Social Security benefits equals $324,044. See The MetLife Study of Caregiving Costs to Working Caregivers: Double Jeopardy for Baby Boomers Caring for Their Parents, www.metlife.com/mmi/research/caregiving-cost-working-caregivers.html#key findings.

2 See, for example, www.transformleaders.tv/why-arent-there-more-women-ceos/.

3 "[T]echnology means that we're all available 24/7. And, because everyone demands instant gratification and instant connectivity, there are no boundaries, no breaks." David Solomon, Global Co-head of investment banking at Goldman Sachs. See www.newyorker.com/magazine/2014/01/27/the-cult-of-overwork.

4 The CPS is the monthly household survey that provides information on national employment and unemployment.

5 The sample included wage and salary workers who usually work full time (35 or over hour/week) on their main job.

6 There are significant business costs to replacing employees, Center for American Progress. See www.americanprogress.org/issues/labor/report/2012/11/16/44464/there-are-significant-business-costs-to-replacing-employees/.

References

Acker, J. (1990). Hierarchies, jobs, bodies: A theory of gendered organizations. *Gender and Society*, *4*, 139–158.

Asghar, R. (2014, January 13). What millennials want in the workplace (and why you should start giving it to them). *Forbes*. Retrieved from www.forbes.com/sites/robasghar/2014/01/13/what-millennials-want-in-the-workplace-and-why-you-should-start-giving-it-to-them/#74db5c3f2fdf.

Association for Women in Science. (2012, March 9). The work–life integration overload: Thousands of researchers weigh in on outmoded work environments, unfriendly family policies. *PR Newswire*. Retrieved from www.prnewswire.com/news-releases/the-work-life-integration-overload-thousands-of-researchers-weigh-in-on-outmoded-work-environments-unfriendly-family-policies-142044843.html.

Bailyn, L. (2006). *Breaking the mold: Redesigning work for productive and satisfying lives*. Ithaca, NY: Cornell University Press.

Baxter, J. (2011). Survival or success? A critical exploration of the use of "double-voiced discourse" by women business leaders in the UK. *Discourse & Communication, 5*(3), 231–245.

Baxter, J. (2012). Women of the corporation: A sociolinguistic perspective of senior women's leadership language in the U.K. *Journal of Sociolinguistics, 16*(1), 81–107.

Beers, T. M. (2000). Flexible schedules and shift work: replacing the 9-to-5 workday. *Monthly Labor Review, 123*, 33.

Beesley, C. (2013, July 31). Maternity leave benefits – What are your small business obligations and options? Small Business Administration. Retrieved from www.sba.gov/blogs/maternity-leave-benefits-what-are-your-small-business-obligations-and-options.

Belasen, A. T. (2012). *Developing women leaders in corporate America: balancing competing demands, transcending traditional boundaries*. Santa Barbara, CA: Praeger.

Belasen, A. T., & Frank, N. M. (2010). A peek through the lens of the Competing Values Framework: What managers communicate and how. *The Atlantic Journal of Communication, 18*(3), 5–30.

Belasen, A. T., & Frank, N. M. (2012). Using the Competing Values Framework to evaluate the interactive effects of gender and personality traits on leadership roles. *The International Journal of Leadership Studies*, 7(2), 192–215.

Belkin, L. (2003, October 26). The opt-out revolution. *The New York Times Magazine*. Retrieved from www.nytimes.com/2003/10/26/magazine/26WOMEN.html?pagewanted=all.

Bertrand, M. (2013). Career, family, and the well-being of college-educated women. *American Economic Review*, 103(3), 244–250. DOI:10.1257/aer.103.3.244

Boswell, W. R., & Olson-Buchanan, J. (2007). The use of communication technologies after hours: The role of work attitudes and work-life conflict. *Journal of Management, 33*(4), 592–610.

Brannon, L. (2010). *Gender: Psychological perspectives*. New York, NY: Psychology Press.

Brooks, C. (2012, October 22). Most employees take the office on the road. *Business News Daily*. Retrieved from www.businessnewsdaily.com/3300-employees-work-home-office.html§hash.HwdE2TV7.dpuf%20at.

Burt, R. (1992). *Structural holes*. Cambridge, MA: Harvard University Press.

Catalyst. (2011). The bottom line: Corporate performance and women's representation on boards (2004–2008). *Catalyst Knowledge Center*. Retrieved from www.catalyst.org/knowledge/bottom-line-corporate-performance-and-womens-representation-boards-20042008.

Chambliss, E., & Uggen, C. (2000). Men and women of elite law firms: Reevaluating Kanter's legacy. *Law and Social Inquiry, 25*, 41–68.

Chi, H. (2011). Interactive digital advertising vs. virtual brand community: Exploratory study of user motivation and social media marketing responses in Taiwan. *Journal of Interactive Advertising, 12*(1), 44–61.

Clark, K. (2015, May 15). Study: Highly educated women are choosing both career and motherhood. *USA Today/College*. Retrieved from http://college.usatoday.com/2015/05/15/study-highly-educated-women-are-choosing-both-career-and-motherhood/.

Clason, M. A., & Turner, L. H. (2011). Communicating manufacturing as masculine domain: How women get noticed at work. *Women & Language*, *34*(2), 41–59.

Cook, A., & Glass, C. (2014). Women and top leadership positions: Towards an institutional analysis. *Gender, Work and Organization*, *21*(1), 91–103. DOI:10.1111/gwao.12018

Dong-Hun, L. (2010). Korean consumer & society: Growing popularity of social media and business strategy. *SERI Quarterly*, *3*(4), 112–117.

Eagly, A. H., & Carli, L. L. (2007). *Through the labyrinth: The truth about how women become leaders*. Cambridge, MA: Harvard Press.

Eagly, A. H., & Johannesen-Schmidt, M. C. (2001). The leadership styles of women and men. *Journal of Social Issues*, 57, 781–797.

Eagly, A., & Sczesny, S. (2009). Stereotypes about women, men and leaders: Have times changed? In M. Barreto, M. Ryan, & M. Schmitt (Eds.), *The glass ceiling in the 21st century: Understanding barriers to gender equality* (pp. 21–48). Washington, DC: American Psychological Association.

Ely, R., Stone, P., & Ammerman, C. (2014). Rethink what you "know" about high-achieving women, R1412G. *Harvard Business Review*, *92*(12), 101–109.

Ely, R. J., Ibarra, H., & Kolb, D. M. (2011). Taking gender into account: Theory and design for women's leadership development programs. *Academy of Management Learning & Education*, *10*(3), 474–493.

Ely, R. J., & Rhode, D. L. (2010). Women and leadership: Defining the challenges. In N. Nohria, & R. Khurana (Eds.), *Handbook of leadership theory and practice* (pp. 377–410). Boston: Harvard Business Publishing.

Ervin-Tripp, S. M. (1987). About, by, and to women. In D. Brouwer & D. de Haan (Eds.), *Women's language, socialization, and self-image* (pp. 17–26). Dordrecht and Providence: Foris.

Felts, N. A. (2015). Review of *The Silent Sex: Gender, Deliberation, and Institutions* by Christopher F. Karpowitz and Tali Mendelberg (Princeton, NJ: Princeton University Press, 2014). *Journal of Public Deliberation*, *11*(1), Article 10. Available at: www.publicdeliberation.net/jpd/vol11/iss1/art10.

Frias, A. (n.d.). Re: *The Devil Wears Prada* (2006), plot summary [Online forum comment]. Retrieved from www.imdb.com/title/tt0458352/plotsummary.

Frothingham, S. (2015, December 10). Broader paid leave would provide opportunity and security for millennial caregivers. *Center for American Progress*. Retrieved from https://cdn.americanprogress.org/wp-content/uploads/2015/12/09143828/PaidLeaveMillennials.pdf.

Fuwa, M., & Cohen, P. (2007). Housework and social policy. *Social Science Research*, *36*, 512–530.

Gault, B., Hartmann, H., Hegewisch, A., Milli, J., & Reichlin, L. (2014). Paid parental leave in the United States: What the data tell us about access, usage, and economic and health benefits. *Institute for Women's Policy Research*. Retrieved from www.iwpr.org/publications/pubs/paid-parental-leave-in-the-united-states-what-the-data-tell-us-about-access-usage-and-economic-and-health-benefits/.

Gelissen, J., & De Graaf, P. (2006). Personality, social background, and occupational career success. *Social Science Research*, *35*, 702–726.

Gersick, C. (2013, August 23). Getting from "keep out" to "lean in": A new roadmap for women's careers. Yale SOM Working Paper. Retrieved from http://ssrn.com/abstract=2315013.

Giles, H., Coupland, J., & Coupland, N. (1991). *Contexts of accommodation: Developments in applied sociolinguistics*. Cambridge, UK: Cambridge University Press.

Gino, F., Wilmuth, C. A., & Brooks, A. W. (2015). Compared to men, women view professional advancement as equally attainable, but less desirable. *Proceedings of the National Academy of Sciences*, *112*(40), 12354–12359.

Goudreau, J. (2011, March 7). 20 Surprising jobs women are taking over. *Forbes*. Retrieved from www.forbes.com/sites/jennagoudreau/2011/03/07/20-surprising-jobs-women-are-taking-over/#365e16766f0b.

Granovetter, M. (1985). Economic action and social structure: The problem of embeddedness. *American Journal of Sociology*, *91*, 481–510.

Greenhaus, G., & Powell. G. (2006). When work and family are allies: A theory of work–family enrichment. *Academy of Management Review*, *31*(1), 72–92.

Greenhaus, J. H., & Beutell, N. J. (1985). Sources and conflict between work and family roles. *Academy of Management Review*, *10*(1), 76–88.

Guerrero, L. (2011). Women and leadership. In W. Rowe & L. Guerrero (Eds.), *Cases in leadership* (pp. 380–412). Thousand Oaks, CA: SAFE Publications.

Hamel, S. (2009). Exit, voice, and sense-making following psychological contract violations. *Journal of Business Communication*, *46*(2), 234–261.

Harbus, The. (2014, December 25). Rethink what you "know" about high-achieving women: The HBS student perspective. Harvard Business School, The Harbus News Corporation. Retrieved from www.beatthegmat.com/mba/2014/12/25/rethink-what-you-know-about-high-achieving-women-the-hbs-student-perspective.

Harrington, B., Van Deusen, F., & Mazar, I. (2012). The new dad: Right at home. Boston College Center for Work and Family. Boston: Carroll School of Management. Retrieved from www.bc.edu/content/dam/files/centers/cwf/pdf/The%20New%20Dad%20Right%20at%20Home%20BCCWF%202012.pdf.

Harris Interactive on behalf of TeamViewer. (2013). 2013 Work/life balance index. *Visually*. Retrieved from http://visual.ly/2013-worklife-balance-americans.

Hays, J., Allinson, C. W., & Armstrong, S. (2004). Intuition, women managers, and gendered stereotypes. *Personnel Psychology*, *33*(4), 403–417.

Hess, A. (2013, November 21). Women are more likely to care for aging parents—and drop out of the workforce to do it. *Slate*. Retrieved from www.slate.com/blogs/xx_factor/2013/11/21/elder_caregiving_women_are_more_likely_to_drop_out_of_work_to_care_for_aging.html.

Hewlett, S. A. (2007). *Off ramps and on ramps: Keeping talented women on the road to success*. Boston: Harvard Business School Press.

Heymann, J., Earle, A., & Hayes, J. (2007, February 1). *How does the U.S. rank in work policies for individuals and families? A briefing paper prepared for the Council on Contemporary Families*. Retrieved from https://contemporaryfamilies.org/wp-content/uploads/2013/10/2007_Briefing_Heymann_Work-policies-US-rank.pdf.

Higgins, M. C., & Kram, K. E. (2001). Reconceptualizing mentoring at work: A developmental network perspective. *Academy of Management Review*, *26*, 264–288.

Hobfoll, S. E. (1989). Conservation of resources: A new attempt at conceptualizing stress. *American Psychologist*, *44*, 513–524.

Hopfl, H. (2010). A question of membership. In P. Lewis & R. Simpson (Eds.), *Revealing and concealing gender: Issues of visibility in organizations* (pp. 39–53). Basingstoke, UK: Palgrave Macmillian.

Hoobler, J. M., Lemmon, G., & Wayne, S. J. (2011). Women's underrepresentation in upper management: New insights on a persistent problem. *Organization Dynamics, 40,* 151–156.

Ibarra, H. (1993). Personal networks of women and minorities in management: A conceptual framework. *Academy of Management Review, 18,* 56–87.

Irby, B. J., Brown, G., Duffy, J. A., & Trautman, D. (2002). The synergistic leadership theory. *Journal of Educational Administration, 40*(4/5), 304–322.

Jerejian, A. C. M., Reid, C., & Rees, C. S. (2013). The contribution of email volume, email management strategies and propensity to worry in predicting email stress among academics. *Computers in Human Behavior, 29*(3), 991–996.

Kanter, R. (1993). *Men and women of the corporation.* New York, NY: Basics Press.

Karpowitz, C., & Mendelberg, T. (2014). *The silent sex: Gender, deliberation, and institutions.* Princeton, NJ: Princeton University Press.

Keeney, J., Boyd, E., Sinha, R., Westring, A., & Ryan, M. (2013). From "work-family" to "work–life": Broadening our conceptualization and measurement. *Journal of Vocational Behavior, 82*(3), 221–237.

Keziah, H. E. (2012). Falling over a glass cliff: A study of the recruitment of women to leadership roles in troubled enterprises global business and organizational excellence. *Global Business and Organizational Excellence, 31*(5), 44–53.

Kiisel, T. (2013, July 16). "Work–life balance" should be "work–life integration." *Forbes.* Retrieved from www.forbes.com/sites/tykiisel/2013/07/16/work-life-balance-maybe-we-should-recognize-its-really-work-life-integration/#7daac1982f1f.

Kuyvenhoven, R., & Buss, C. (2011). A normative view of the role of middle management in the implementation of strategic change. *Journal of Management and Marketing Research, 8*(1), 1–14.

Lakoff, R. (1973). The logic of politeness; or, minding your Ps and Qs. In C. Corum, T. C. Smith-Stark, & A. Weiser (Eds.), *Papers from the ninth regional meeting of the Chicago Linguistics Society* (pp 292–305). Chicago: Department of Linguistics, University of Chicago.

Livingston, G. (2015). Childlessness falls, family size grows among highly educated women. *Pew Research Center.* Retrieved from www.pewsocialtrends.org/2015/05/07/childlessness-falls-family-size-grows-among-highly-educated-women/.

Livingston, J. S. (1969). Pygmalion in management. *Harvard Business Review,* July/August, 81–89.

Long, C. (2014, July 17). Women, leadership and the "glass cliff": Research roundup. *Journalist's Resource.* Retrieved from http://journalistsresource.org/studies/society/gender-society/women-leadership-glass-cliff-research-roundup.

Ludden, J. (2013, May 15). Stay-at-home dads, breadwinner moms and making it all work. *NPR [Morning edition].* Retrieved from www.npr.org/2013/05/15/180300236/stay-at-home-dads-breadwinner-moms-and-making-it-all-work.

McKinsey Global Institute. (2015). *The power of parity: How advancing women's equality can add $12 trillion to global growth.* Retrieved from www.wocan.org/resources/power-parity-how-advancing-womens-equality-can-add-12-trillion-global-growth.

Manzoni, J. F., & Barsoux, J. L. (2002). *The set-up-to-fail syndrome: How good managers cause great people to fail.* Boston: Harvard Business School Press.

Marcus, B. (2016, January 13). The dark side of female rivalry in the workplace and what to do about it. *Forbes*. Retrieved from www.forbes.com/sites/bonniemarcus/2016/01/13/the-dark-side-of-female-rivalry-in-the-workplace-and-what-to-do-about-it/#13f432bc3854.

Mazmanian, M., Orlikowski, W. J., & Yates, J. (2013). The autonomy paradox: The implications of mobile email devices for knowledge professionals. *Organization Science*. Printed in *Articles in Advance, Organization Science*, *24*(5), 1337–1357.

Miller, J. (2005, November 28). Get a life! Working 24/7 may seem good for companies, but it's often bad for the talent—and men finally agree. So businesses are hatching alternatives to the punishing, productivity-sapping norm. *Fortune*. Retrieved from http://archive.fortune.com/magazines/fortune/fortune_archive/2005/11/28/8361955/index.htm.

Murrell, A. J., & James, E. H. (2001). Gender and diversity in organizations: Past, present, and future directions. *Sex Roles*, *45*(5–6), 243–257.

O'Neil, D. A., Hopkins, M. M., & Bilimoria, D. (2008). Women's careers at the start of the 21st century: Patterns and paradoxes. *Journal of Business Ethics*, *80*, 727–743.

Oakley, J. G. (2000). Gender-based barriers to senior management positions: Understanding the scarcity of female CEOs. *Journal of Business Ethics*, *27*(4), 321–334.

Ochs, E. (1993). Constructing social identity: A language socialization perspective. *Research on language and Social Interaction*, *26*(3), 287–306.

Papasolomou, J., & Melanthiou, Y. (2012). Social media: Marketing public relations' new best friend. *Journal of Promotion Management*, *18*, 319–328.

Parker, K., & Livingston, G. (2016, June 16). 6 facts about American fathers. *Pew Research Center, Fact Tank*. Retrieved from www.pewresearch.org/fact-tank/2016/06/16/fathers-day-facts/.

Parker, K. L. (2004). Leadership styles of agricultural communications and information technology managers: What does the Competing Values Framework tell us about them? *Journal of Extension*, *42*(1). Retrieved from www.joe.org/joe/2004february/a1.php.

Pinker, S. (2009). Why women earn less, men are fragile and more. *Today-MSNBC.com*. Retrieved from www.msnbc.msn.com/id/23558979/.

Podolny, J., & Baron, J. (1997). Resources and relationships: Social networks and mobility in the workplace. *American Sociological Review*, *62*, 673–693.

Powell, G. N., & Butterfield, D. A. (2002). Exploring the influence of decision makers' race and gender on actual promotions to top management. *Personnel Psychology*, *55*, 397–428.

Prasad, K. (2011). New media and public relations in Oman: Embracing innovation in the digital era. *Global Media Journal: Mediterranean Edition*, *6*(1), 53–57.

PricewaterhouseCoopers. (2012). *Millennials at work: Reshaping the workplace*. Retrieved from www.pwc.com/m1/en/services/consulting/documents/millennials-at-work.pdf.

Ramey, G., & Ramey, V. (2010). The rug rat race. Economic Studies Program, The Brookings Institution, *Brookings Papers on Economic Activity*, *41*(1), 129–199.

Rapoza, K. (2013, February 18). One in five Americans work from home, numbers seen rising over 60%. *Forbes*. Retrieved from www.forbes.com/sites/kenrapoza/2013/02/18/one-in-five-americans-work-from-home-numbers-seen-rising-over-60/#7e4f08e14768.

Reid, M. (2016, May 17). Newburgh Heights passes record-setting parental-leave law. *Fox 8 Cleveland*. Retrieved from http://fox8.com/2016/05/17/newburgh-heights-passes-record-setting-parental-leave-law/.

Robbins, S. (n.d.). Have women found work/life balance? *Real Simple*. Retrieved from www.realsimple.com/work-life/life-strategies/time-management/work-life-balance.

Ryan, M. K., & Haslam, S. A. (2005). The glass cliff: Evidence that women are over-represented in precarious leadership positions. *British Journal of Management, 16*(2), 81–90.

Ryan, M. K., Haslam, S. A., & Postmes, T. (2007). Reactions to the glass cliff; Gender differences in the explanations for the precariousness of women's leadership positions. *Journal of Organizational Change Management, 20*(2), 182–197.

Schmitt, M., Spoor, J., Danaher, K., & Branscombe, N. (2009). Rose-colored glasses: How tokenism and comparisons with the past reduce the visibility of gender inequality. In M. Barreto, M. K. Ryan, & M. Schmitt (Eds.), *The glass ceiling in the 21st century: Understanding barriers to gender equality* (pp. 49–71). Washington, DC: American Psychological Association.

Schwanke, D. (2013). Barriers for women to positions of power: How societal and corporate structures, perceptions of leadership and discrimination restrict women's advancement to authority. *Earth Common Journal, 3*(2). Retrieved from www.studentpulse.com/a?id=864.

Schawbel, D. (2014, January 21). Work life integration: The new norm. *Forbes*. Retrieved from www.forbes.com/sites/danschawbel/2014/01/21/work-life-integration-the-new-norm/#6a730aaa2184.

Sekaquaptewa, D., & Thompson, M. (2003). Solo status, stereotype threat and performance expectancies: Their effects on women's performance. *Journal of Experimental Social Psychology, 39*(1), 68–74.

Shaffer, D. R. (2009). *Social and personality development* (6th ed.). Belmont, CA: Wadsworth.

Stone, P. (2013). "Opting out": Challenging stereotypes and creating real options for women in the professions. Gender and work research symposium: Challenging conventional wisdom. *Harvard Business School*. Retrieved from www.hbs.edu/faculty/conferences/2013-w50-research-symposium/Documents/stone.pdf.

Sturges, J. (1999). What it means to succeed: Personal conceptions of career success held by male and female managers at different ages. *British Journal of Management, 10*, 239–252.

Tannen, D. (1990a). *You just don't understand: Women and men in conversation*. New York, NY: Morrow.

Tannen, D. (1990b). Gender differences in topical coherence: Creating involvement in best friends' talk. *Discourse Processes, 13*, 73–90.

Taylor, C. (2010). Occupational sex composition and the gendered availability of workplace support. *Gender & Society, 24*(2), 189–212.

Toren, N., Konrad, A. M., Yoshioka, I., & Kashlak, R. (1997). A cross-national cross-gender study of managerial task preferences and evaluation of work characteristics. *Women in Management Review, 12*(6), 234–243.

Traister, R. (2016, April 1). New York just created a revolutionary new family-leave policy. *New York Magazine*. Retrieved from http://nymag.com/thecut/2016/03/new-york-revolutionary-family-leave-paid-time-off.html.

US Department of Labor, Bureau of Labor Statistics. (2005, July 1). *Workers on flexible and shift schedules in 2004 summary* [Press release]. Retrieved from www.bls.gov/news.release/flex.nr0.htm.

US Department of Labor, Wage and Hour Division. (n.d.). *Compliance assistance—Wages and the Fair Labor Standards Act (FLSA)*. Retrieved from www.dol.gov/whd/flsa/.

US Department of Labor, Wage and Hour Division. (2013). *FMLA Surveys*. Retrieved from www.dol.gov/whd/fmla/survey/.

Vanderkam, L. (2015, June 6). Women with big jobs and big families: Balancing really isn't that hard. *Fortune*. Retrieved from http://fortune.com/2015/06/06/women-with-big-jobs-and-big-families-balancing-really-isnt-that-hard/.

Vilkinas, T. (2000). The gender factor in management: How significant others perceive effectiveness. *Women in Management Review*, *15*(5/6), 261–271.

Westphal, J. D., & Milton, L. P. (2000). How experience and network ties affect the influence of demographic minorities on corporate boards. *Administrative Science Quarterly*, *45*, 366–398.

Williams, J. (2012). Slaughter vs. Sandberg: Both right. *The Huffington Post*. Retrieved from www.huffingtonpost.com/joan-williams/ann-marie-slaughter_b_1619324.html.

Williams, R. (2014, April 8). Why women are better leaders yet can't break glass ceiling. *Psychology Today*. Retrieved from www.psychologytoday.com/blog/wired-success/201404/why-women-are-better-leaders-yet-cant-break-glass-ceiling.

Wittenburg-Cox, A., & Maitland, A. (2009). *Why women mean business*. Chichester, UK: John Wiley & Sons Ltd.

Won, H. (2006). Links between personalities and leadership perceptions in problem-solving groups. *The Social Science Journal*, *43*(4), 659–672.

Work/Life Integration. (2016). Human Resources. Hass School of Business, University of California, Berkeley. Retrieved from www.haas.berkeley.edu/human-resources/life-integration/.

Zenger, J., & Folkman, J. (2014, November 24). Why middle managers are so unhappy. *Harvard Business Review*. Retrieved from https://hbr.org/2014/11/why-middle-managers-are-so-unhappy.

2

EMPOWERING WOMEN ENTREPRENEURS

The leaking pipeline, limited flexibility on the part of employers, and lack of upward mobility leave many women who are stuck in lower or mid-level positions with staff roles, not line roles, to contemplate the possibilities outside the organization. Even as women are exhorted to "lean in" (Sandberg, 2013), many are hoping for work–life integration, independence, purpose, and fulfillment, more so than prestige, titles, and monetary rewards. Belasen (2012) reported a higher turnover rate of women with at least 10 years of executive experience than males at the same level. Between the stress of balancing work and home and other workplace barriers, one can understand why many women feel frustrated when bias-based objections become a reality or when peripheral considerations become the center for vicious office politics and power struggles. A study by John Becker-Blease from Oregon State University that was conducted in 2010 found that about 7.2% of women executives in the survey left their jobs, compared to 3.8% of men. Both the voluntary rates (4.3% versus 2.8%) and the involuntary rates (2.9% versus 0.9%) were higher for women executives. Research has shown that women are more likely than men to leave a job due to domestic or social responsibilities, which could explain the higher voluntary departure rate (Klampe, 2010).

Compared to men, women are less motivated to manifest agentic behaviors that enhance personal status and influence and that could promote their chances to gain access to favorable funding sources. As a result, only 6% of women founders get funding from investors (Greenberg & Mollick, 2016). Possible reasons include:

1. Lower propensity of women to negotiate for themselves.
2. Gender stereotypes for women asking for "things" in society.
3. Reputation issues.

4. Societal norms: "women are generally seen as inferior to men on qualities believed to be necessary to succeed in the business world."
5. Risk aversion: lower level of risk tolerance or confidence: men often equate negotiation as "fun" whereas women equate negotiation as "scary."
6. Less or inadequate support.
7. Different demand patterns (smaller businesses, service sectors) but women have a greater need for credit than men when starting new businesses (Marlow & Patton, 2005).
8. Women lack information about key influential networks.
9. Women do not identify themselves with or are not welcomed in established traditional business social associations. Social identification facilitates assimilation processes, feelings of belongings, and recognition by the group (Ashforth & Mael, 1989).
10. Women are perceived to be less ambitious or have lower levels of self-efficacy when approaching venture capitalists who are looking for "entrepreneurial passion," positive signals, and high confidence as important criteria for funding decisions (Cardon, Wincent, Singh, & Drnovsek, 2009; Hmieleski & Baron, 2008).

Most startups are initiated with support from others (Reynolds & Curtin, 2009) as entrepreneurship is the result of sustained networking activity. Nascent ventures benefit from helpers or non-owner founders (or not employed by the startup) who provide material investment, guidance, key tacit information, advice, access to important networks, and training to the founding teams in various stages of startups' development (Ruef, 2010; Burton, Anderson, & Aldrich, 2009). Evidence suggests that entrepreneurial helpers have significant impact on startups' performance and sustainability. Venture capitalists tend to back those startups when they are familiar with the founding (Zhang, Souitaris, Soh, & Wong, 2008). It is therefore fair to assume that the increase number of helpers is associated with boosting the probability of female entrepreneurs asking for financing (Kwapisz & Hechavarria, 2016).

Conscious Choices and Hybrid Entrepreneurship

Raffiee and Feng (2014) noted that entrepreneurs who gave up their day jobs in stages through "hybrid entrepreneurship" were 33% less likely to fail in their startups than those who leave their jobs precipitously to run their new business on a full-time basis. The reason is that hybrid entrepreneurship facilitates learning of two key dimensions that impact the viability of the startup: (1) the quality and attractiveness of the venture idea; and (2) the individual's capabilities in the entrepreneurial context. It allows entrepreneurs to gain important knowledge about their new business while phasing out their paying jobs. This has also become much easier with the rise of digital technologies that reduce the cost and time commitment of starting new ventures. The reduced sunk cost and risk exposure associated with hybrid entrepreneurship (i.e., phasing gradually into the new venture) appear to make an attractive exploitation strategy. Women entrepreneurs may intentionally use hybrid entrepreneurship as a means to reduce demand uncertainty prior to committing to their business.

Creativity and Innovation

The article by Ray Williams, "Why women may be better leaders than men" (2012) brings to light many examples of how women are making significant strides as entrepreneurs and intrapreneurs but still suffer from the constraints of the glass ceiling. Intrapreneurship is the act of behaving like an entrepreneur while working within a large organization. New research by Proudfoot, Kay, and Koval (2015) confirms that people tend to associate creativity with stereotypically masculine traits such as risk-taking, self-reliance, and adventurousness. If men are perceived to be better when it comes to creativity and innovative thinking—two traits that are valued in top management positions—then gender inequality in the workforce is continually perpetuated. The rejection of women from executive suites and corporate boardrooms due to "lack" of vision, creativity, or innovative thinking, paradoxically has created opportunities for women to apply their innovation and creativity skills elsewhere, primarily through the formation of startups.

A GENDER BIAS IN THE ATTRIBUTION OF CREATIVITY: ARCHIVAL AND EXPERIMENTAL EVIDENCE FOR THE PERCEIVED ASSOCIATION BETWEEN MASCULINITY AND CREATIVE THINKING

We propose that the propensity to think creatively tends to be associated with independence and self-direction—qualities generally ascribed to men—so that men are often perceived to be more creative than women. In two experiments, we found that "outside the box" creativity is more strongly associated with stereotypically masculine characteristics (e.g., daring and self-reliance) than with stereotypically feminine characteristics (e.g., cooperativeness and supportiveness; Study 1) and that a man is ascribed more creativity than a woman when they produce identical output (Study 2). Analyzing archival data, we found that men's ideas are evaluated as more ingenious than women's ideas (Study 3) and that female executives are stereotyped as less innovative than their male counterparts when evaluated by their supervisors (Study 4). Finally, we observed that stereotypically masculine behavior enhances a man's perceived creativity, whereas identical behavior does not enhance a woman's perceived creativity (Study 5). This boost in men's perceived creativity is mediated by attributions of agency, not competence, and predicts perceptions of reward deservingness.

(Proudfoot, Kay, & Koval, 2015)

Work–Family Conflict Motivates Women Entrepreneurs

The US Small Business Administration, Office of Advocacy (2014) defines a small business as an independent business having fewer than 500 employees. In 2011, there were 28.2 million small businesses, and 17,700 firms with 500 employees or more. Small businesses make up 99.7% of the US employer firms, 63% of net new private-sector jobs, 48.5% of private-sector employment, 42% of private-sector payroll, 46% of private-sector output, 37% of high-tech employment, 98% of firms exporting goods, and 33% of exporting value.

Entrepreneurship is an essential part of today's business organizations and until about 20 years ago it has been a mainly male-dominated industry (Wilson, Kickul, & Marlino, 2007). Like entrepreneurship, politics is dominated by men's characteristics such as assertiveness and self-promotion, tactics used to control impressions and exercise influence. Political skills can potentially reveal important findings concerning gender and entrepreneurship. Phipps and Prieto (2015) found that males have greater propensity than females to be entrepreneurs in the future. The lack of female presence also contributed to the unavailability of female mentors indirectly affecting women's entrepreneurial self-efficacy, and consequently their entrepreneurial endeavors (Phipps & Prieto, 2015). Since creativity is positively correlated with entrepreneurial intentions (Hamidi, Wennberg, & Berglund, 2008; Olawale, 2010; Phipps, 2012), it may be a determinant of entrepreneurial self-efficacy.

These results are consistent with other studies in which women reported lower entrepreneurial career intentions (Wilson et al., 2007; Zhao, Seibert & Hills, 2005), and since intentions are the precursors to actual behavior, the results suggest compatibility with the ongoing tendency of fewer women than men seeking entrepreneurial endeavors or engagement in entrepreneurial behavior. Is there any relationship between workplace inequalities or accommodations, for that matter (e.g., flexible work schedule, part-time opportunities, paid leave) and the incentive women have to pursue an entrepreneurial activity?

Thébaud (2015) evaluated empirically the question of gender inequalities in business startup, ownership, and growth arguing that in organizations with paid leave, subsidized childcare, and part-time employment opportunities that mitigate work–family conflict, women are less likely to opt for business ownership as a fall-back income-driven employment strategy. Figure 2.1 shows predicted probabilities for men and women at different levels of childcare spending and part-time employment. Women's predicted probability of having been motivated by limited employment options is lower by about nine percentage points in countries spending the most versus the least on childcare (0.24 versus 0.33, respectively), and that probability is lower by about four percentage points in countries with the highest rate of women's part-time employment versus the lowest rate of women's part-time employment (0.27 versus 0.31, respectively). This finding is consistent with the claim that work–family policies yield gender-differentiated incentives to become a business owner. The larger gender gaps in the odds of

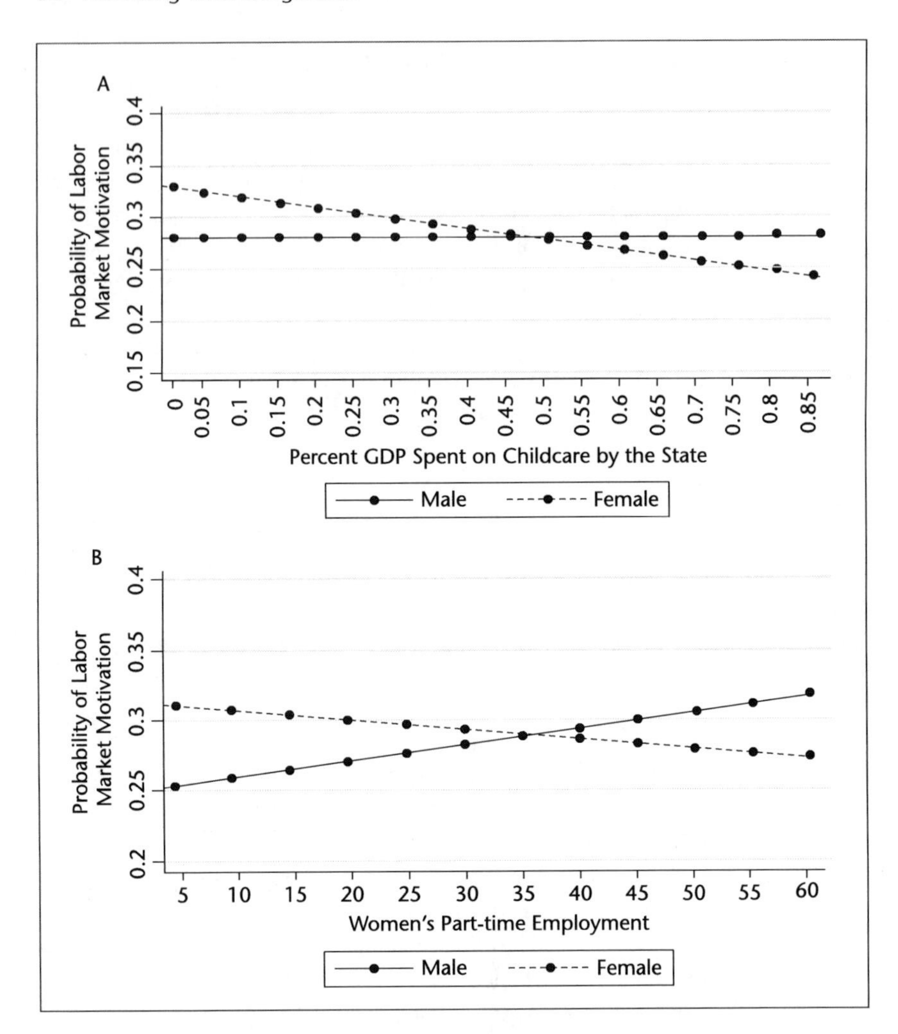

FIGURE 2.1 Predicted Probabilities of Being Motivated by Limited Employment Options for Men and Women Business Owners

Source: Thébaud (2015).

being an entrepreneur in countries that reconcile work and family through paid childcare may arise, in part, because fewer women in these contexts are attracted to entrepreneurship out of a need to resolve work–family conflicts.

Startups and Venture-backed Companies

However, the motivation of women in initiation of new businesses and fulfilling leadership roles in new ventures or startups has recently begun to shift. As of 2014, there were nearly 9.1 million women-owned businesses in the United States, accounting for 37.8% and generating over $1.4 trillion in revenues and employing nearly 7.9 million people. While women-owned firms remain smaller than male-owned firms in terms of average employment and revenues, they are not only showing higher percent growth in numbers but also higher absolute growth in terms of job creation adding an estimated 274,000 jobs since 2007. For comparison, in men-owned and equally owned firms, employment has declined over the past seven years. Between 1997 and 2014, when the number of businesses in the United States increased by 47%, the number of women-owned firms increased by 68%—a rate 145% greater than the national average. Indeed, the growth in the number (up 68%), employment (up 11%), and revenues (up 72%) of women-owned firms from 1997 to 2014 exceeded the growth rates of all but the largest publicly traded firms (Womenable, 2014).

According to Astia, a network that includes investors, entrepreneurs, and executives and that supports women-led small companies, women make up less than 10% of venture-backed startups (Stengel, 2013): a gloomy condition that represents a missed opportunity for the American economy. Women-led companies generate great business ideas and strong returns but have been systematically underinvested. Compare this with evidence that shows that companies with more gender diversity delivered better results from initial public offerings (IPOs), by as much as 30% on average (Markowitz, 2011).

Further evidence comes from the results of a study conducted by Dow Jones in 2011, which focused on US-based venture-backed companies and how the inclusion of women on management teams affected the success of startups. The study concluded with a remarkable notation: "Participation from female executives makes a significant difference in pushing a company to its success" (Canning, Haque, & Wang, 2012). In 2011 the privately held companies made up 44% of this sample. Nearly half of these 9,978 companies had at least one female executive. Of the 94,000 employees who have worked in a director-level position or higher at these companies, 10% (9,300) were female. In addition, 1.3% of the privately held companies had a female founder, 6.5% had a female CEO, and 20% had one or more female C-level executives.

The Dow Jones study examined over 20,000 venture capital-backed companies and 167,556 executives, of whom 11,193 were female. Results show that venture-backed startups with women in senior executive roles are more likely to succeed than companies where only men are in senior executive roles. The study also found that the overall median proportion of female executives was 7.1% at successful companies and 3.1% at unsuccessful companies, demonstrating the value that having more females can potentially bring to a management team.

Success of startups was measured by an exit through IPO, IPO registration, privately held and consistently profitable, or acquisition for an amount greater than its total venture capital amount raised. Failure was measured by the count of companies that ceased operations, went bankrupt, or exited at a valuation below their total venture-capital funding. The same study found that companies with an executive team composed of 5% to 25% female executives have been successful. It concluded that having female executives, particularly at vice-president and director levels positively helps venture capital-backed companies. Another study concluded with the same finding: women-led tech companies are less capital intensive and have fewer failures (Padnos, 2010).

The results of the Dow Jones study (Canning et al., 2012) were consistent with the comprehensive overview of women's entrepreneurship conducted by the Global Entrepreneurship Monitor research consortium, which reported on the results of a 2012–2014 study covering 83 countries. Key findings were the total early-stage entrepreneurship activity rates, which have increased by 7% since 2012, and the decrease of the gender gap (ratio of women to men participating in entrepreneurship) by 6% (Kelley, Brush, Greene, Herrington, Ali, & Kew 2014). Furthermore, female entrepreneurs in 75% of the European countries reported higher levels of innovation than male entrepreneurs. Like in North America, this can also be attributed to the fact that there are proportionately more educated women (than men) entrepreneurs in Europe. In Chile and India, more than half of women entrepreneurs believe they offer innovative products or services.

Another study by the Goldman Sachs 10,000 Women initiative in 2013–2014 shows that women entrepreneurs participating in the program from 43 developing countries dramatically expanded their businesses. The businesses grew employment an average of 50% within six months after program completion, and revenues increased by 480% within 18 months post-program (Brush, Balachandra, Davis, & Greene, 2014).

Social Enterprise

More than 75% of female-owned businesses operate in service and retail industries in which women's attributes and inner capabilities prove advantageous. Social feminist theory views gender as socially constructed and embedded in complex processes that also give meaning and distinctiveness to men and women who are socialized differently. Men are expected to have agentic (e.g., assertive) traits, while women are socialized to have communal (e.g., nurturing) traits. Women's inner capabilities are translated into strategic maturity, good practices, and superior performance especially during the early stages of startup development when relationship, participation, and collaboration are vital for the success of the business.

Not only do women managers play a significant role in corporate intrapreneurship but also they align company messages so that the market credits the company with receiving and delivering the social innovation. In fact, big companies that embrace intrapreneurship will thrive in the future (Debb, 2015). Women intrapreneurs help make innovation happen for the customer and enable the company to communicate its success through open innovation initiatives.

Women can model the way for infusing companies with the triple bottom line—social, environmental, financial—that goes beyond the traditional measures of profits, return on investment, and shareholder value to include environmental and social dimensions as open innovation and social entrepreneurship are becoming crucial for addressing social and environmental issues (Konda, Starc, & Rodica, 2015). Not only does innovation create a market advantage, but also it can entice countless solutions to social problems.

MEET THE WORLD'S YOUNGEST FEMALE BILLIONAIRE: A COLLEGE DROPOUT AND MEDICAL GENIUS

When Elizabeth Holmes was a 19-year-old sophomore at Stanford University in 2003, she decided to drop out and start her own company, Theranos. She felt strongly that her tuition money could be used for a greater and more benevolent purpose: revolutionizing healthcare.

When she first told Channing Robertson, her chemical engineering professor, what she planned to do, he was concerned about the implications of Holmes leaving her degree unfinished. He asked her why she wanted to risk everything in order to pursue this plan. Holmes replied: "I want to create a whole new technology, and one that is aimed at helping humanity at all levels regardless of geography or ethnicity or age or gender."

The fire in Holmes' eyes convinced her professor that she would succeed, and she received his blessing.

Making Medical History

Holmes wanted to create a technology that would make blood tests easier. She hates needles, and wanted to make blood tests simpler, cheaper and more accessible for all people. For a decade, she quietly worked on a technology that would make blood tests nothing more than a painless finger prick. Holmes has created hardware and software that allow for blood tests to be done by pricking someone's finger and storing the blood in a tiny vial called a nanotainer.

Some people are so afraid of needles and blood, they would rather avoid getting blood tests than obtaining potentially life-saving medical information. Surprisingly, about half of all Americans do not comply when their doctors ask them to get blood work done. Holmes' technology eliminates that fear, and makes it easier and more likely that people will get necessary blood tests. Not to mention, traditional blood tests typically involve sending multiple vials of blood to separate labs for evaluation. This takes weeks for the results to come through, and also leaves a lot of room for error.

With the single prick of a finger, the technology Holmes has created can provide a wealth of information with exceptional efficiency. The new tests can be done at a pharmacy without going to a doctor or lab, and the results only take about four hours. Furthermore, the same drop of blood can be used for multiple tests with this technology. Blood work can also be very expensive, depending on your insurance coverage. This new test, however, is much cheaper, which was always one of Holmes' goals when she started Theranos. It's painless, more accurate, cheaper and quicker. Simply put, this technology is revolutionary, and it will save lives.

Blood Money

Holmes' company, Theranos, is now worth $9 billion. She owns 50 percent of it and is worth $4.5 billion, making her the youngest female and third-youngest billionaire on the recently released list of the 400 richest Americans from Forbes. She is the youngest woman to become a self-made billionaire. Her company has also partnered with Walgreens, and it seems that it will only continue to grow. Yet, Holmes did not create her company to get rich, she sincerely wanted to make a change in the world. As she puts it:

> We're successful if person by person we help make a difference in their lives. Our purpose is to give people access to the basic right of being (blood) tested when they need to or want to. If we can do that, then we will have made a difference.
>
> She believes that affordable and efficient healthcare is a human and civil right. Elizabeth Holmes is proof that greatness is achieved by combining passion, innovation and the desire to better the lives of those around you.

(Haltiwanger, 2014)

Work–Life Integration: Mompreneurship

Caregiver discrimination or the Family Responsibilities Discrimination Act (EEOC, 2007) is designed to protect workers against unfair practices based on their family caregiving responsibilities. Pregnant women, mothers and fathers of young children, and employees with aging parents or sick spouses or partners may encounter family responsibilities discrimination. They may be rejected for hire, eliminated from considerations for promotion, demoted, transferred, harassed, or terminated—despite good or even superb performance—simply because their employers make personnel decisions based on biased judgment or preconceived assumptions how they will or should act given their family responsibilities.

MORE WOMEN ARE IN THE WORKFORCE—SO WHY ARE THEY STILL DOING SO MANY CHORES?

In 2011, 83% of women and 65% of men "spent some time doing household activities such as housework, cooking, lawn care or financial and other household management," according to the U.S. Department of Labor, Bureau of Labor Statistics (2016b). The year earlier, the spread was 84% to 67%, respectively. Flash back to 2003 and the numbers were at 84% and 63%. So, sure, we're seeing some change but none that I'd classify as particularly profound—especially when you look at how the workforce is divided today.

(Tennery, 2012)

The strongest motivations for women starting their own businesses involve setting their own work schedule and the opportunity to integrate family and work. Flexibility is needed to handle childcare obligations, participate in community affairs, respond to personal health concerns, provide caregiving for aging parents, and perform other family obligations. Flexibility does not necessarily mean working fewer hours, but having more control over when those hours are worked. This gives women at work the ability to manage their family responsibilities and at the same time have successful careers. The idea of women seeking entrepreneurial opportunities to achieve greater flexibility to better balance work and family life has been manifested through the concept of "mompreneur." First coined by and Ellen Parlapiano and Patricia Cobe in 1996, the term reflects the creation of a new business venture by a woman who is both a mother and a business woman and who is motivated by the need to integrate work and family (Parlapiano & Cobe, 2002). It is estimated that there are more than 5 million mompreneurs in the United States alone. These women, for the most part, broke out of traditional thinking and used what may have been perceived as a barrier as the motivation to build their own business (Richomme-Huet, Vial, & d'Andria, 2013).

While it might seem that motherhood gives women a great opportunity to experience alternative career and market opportunities, there are still institutional barriers that inhibit their full success as a mompreneurs. One of these barriers is external sources of funding. The "Cupcake Challenge" is a title given to a certain kind of financial discrimination mompreneurs experience when trying to get loans to start a business (Casserly, 2011). It involves the challenge or the stigma of selling a "cute" consumer business idea to funders, whether it's a cupcake bakery, a line of wooden toys, or a sign-language school for parents of infants. When these entrepreneurs go to the bank to get financing for their ideas, they are often met with skepticism about the viability and commercialization of their business ventures. Mompreneurs are not treated as seriously, their ideas are undervalued, and their market analysis (e.g., time to market, inventory cost, customer acquisition, and so on) and valuation are undermined. As Birchbox CEO and co-founder Katia Beauchamp stated, after she was turned down by many male investors she pitched: it is easier for men to get funding (Beauchamp, 2016). However, it is important to note that most ventures do not qualify for venture capital and never will. According to the Small Business Administration, about 600,000 new businesses are started in the US each year, and the number of startups funded by venture capital is about 300 (Rao, 2013).

Second Glass Ceiling

Bosse and Porcher (2012) suggested that the second glass ceiling appears like an entrepreneurship corollary to the first glass ceiling except that it centers on the capital markets that serve small firms. They pointed out that mompreneurs face tighter credit availability from financial institutions to start new firms or to fuel the growth of existing small firms. The use of *gender as a grouping criterion* is widely observed in sociological research. People feel most comfortable working with others of their own gender based on deeply held gender stereotypes (Blau, Ferber, & Winkler, 2006). Thus, as long as there are many more males than females at banks and investment firms in positions to allocate financial capital, it follows that males who seek capital may receive a disproportionate share, *ceteris paribus*. In a recent study of 3,000 managers, women report lower self-belief and confidence than men, implying that women take a comparatively cautious approach to business decisions (Institute of Leadership and Management, 2011). We know that women are not likely to put themselves forward for new roles unless they feel 95% capable, whereas men will happily do so at 65%, so what happens is that when women are promoted, they are very familiar with the tasks their people are doing (Dickson, 2011).

Bellucci, Borisov, and Zazzaro (2010) also found that women business managers tend to be perceived as more risk-averse than men, particularly in the areas of financial and investment decisions. In a study that tracked high-growth companies, men appeared to understand how leverage can support growth better than women, with 52% of the male-owned firms incurring debt funding for growth compared to only 29% of women-owned firms (Klein, 2010). Hadary (2010) suggested that the stereotype that women are perceived as incapable of leading growing businesses is pervasive among business and government leaders. She also points to some women's own perceptions of incompetence as a key reason why others do not believe their firms will grow. Self-confidence and self-trust are often the biggest hurdles to women's advancement and the reason women hold back from putting themselves forward for promotions (Hall, 2011).

Underfunded

The research by Wood Brooks, Huang, Wood Kearney, and Murray (2014) documents critical criteria that investors use to make allocation decisions: the gender and physical attractiveness of the entrepreneurs themselves. Across a field setting (three entrepreneurial pitch competitions in the United States) and two experiments, they identified a profound and consistent gender gap in entrepreneur persuasiveness. Investors prefer pitches presented by male entrepreneurs compared with pitches made by female entrepreneurs, even when the content of the pitch is the same. This effect is moderated by male physical attractiveness: attractive males were perceived as particularly persuasive, whereas physical attractiveness did not matter among female entrepreneurs (see Figures 2.2 and 2.3).

Bosse and Porcher (2012) cite strong evidence from a multi-country database of 14,000 firms that shows that women-managed firms are 5% less likely to get a bank loan approved compared to men and when they do get a bank loan, on average, they pay half a percentage point more in interest (Muravyev, Talavera, & Schafer, 2009). Furthermore, analysis of a longitudinal survey of almost 5,000 entrepreneurial firms shows that not only do women get significantly less external debt and equity than men at firm startup, but they also get significantly less capital in the subsequent two years (Coleman & Robb, 2009).

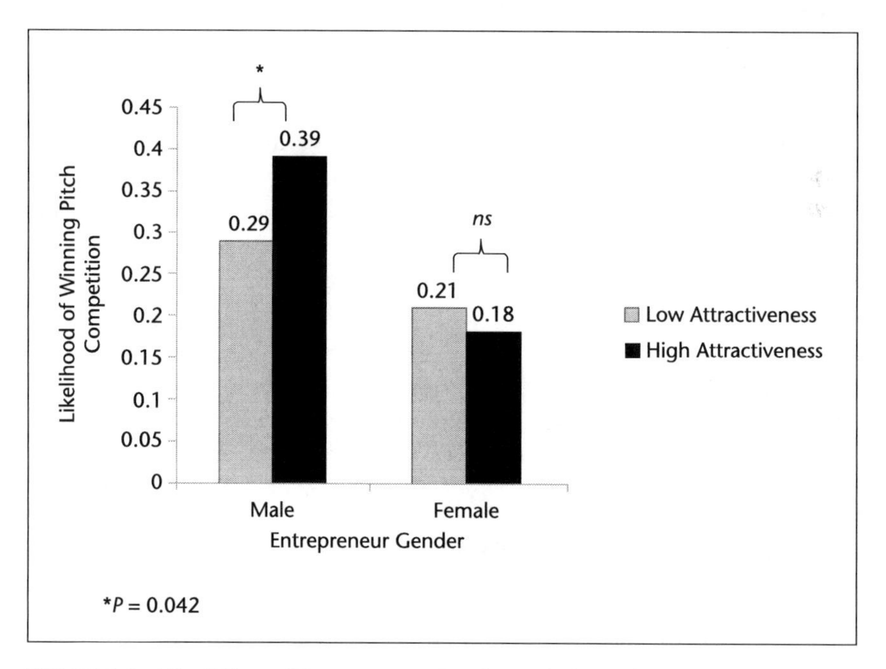

FIGURE 2.2 The Effect of Entrepreneur Gender and Physical Attractiveness on Pitch Success Rate in a Field Setting

Source: Wood Brooks et al. (2014).

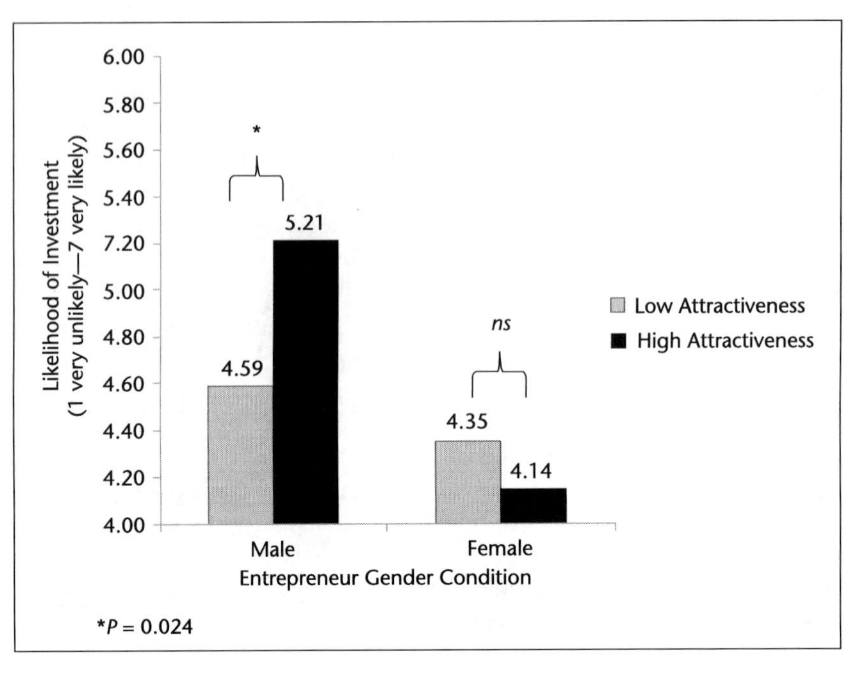

FIGURE 2.3 The Effect of Entrepreneur Gender and Physical Attractiveness on Ratings of Investment Likelihood in an Experimental Setting

Source: Wood Brooks et al. (2014).

The Center for Women's Business Research's (2010) Key4Women Confidence Index reported that women business owners continue to cite problems getting loans. Bosse and Porcher (2012) agree that more women business owners are seeking credit, but fewer report that they are getting all of the credit they want (9.5% versus 6.3%) and more report that they are getting none of the credit they want (20% in 2009 versus 25% in 2010). Even for firms with higher annual revenues (greater than $500,000) only 10.3% received all the credit they wanted, while 65.5% stated that they were able to obtain at least some, most, or all credit sought. In contrast, only a third (33.3%) of those with smaller annual revenues (less than $500,000) were able to obtain at least some, most, or all credit sought.

WHY DON'T WOMEN GET MORE SMALL BUSINESS LOANS?

Although 40% of small businesses in the United States are owned by women and women account for the fastest-growing segment of entrepreneurs, they still lag behind male-owned businesses in their ability to access borrowed money to fuel growth and fund working capital. "In 2014 the Subcommittee on Small Businesses and Entrepreneurism published a report that said only 4% of the total dollar amount of business loans go to women-owned businesses," said Peter Bolin, Experian Director of Consulting and Analytics.

> After hearing of this report, ... Experian recently conducted a study of male-owned businesses and female-owned businesses to compare how they manage their personal and business credit to see if there were significant differences. ... It's less about gender bias and more about the type of businesses women start and how they access credit in the beginning. Women tend to leave the workforce to stay at home and start a business that can be run out of a spare room or the garage—like a salon, an eBay distribution business, or some other personal services business. Men, on the other hand, are more likely to start businesses in construction, real estate, restaurants, or retail businesses that take them out of the home.
>
> *(Kiisel, 2015)*

Contrary to existing perceptions, many fundable women entrepreneurs have the requisite skills and experience to lead high-growth ventures. Nonetheless, women were consistently left out of the networks of growth capital and appeared to lack the contacts needed to break through. The research by a Babson College team aimed at comparing the statistics presented in 1999 to what is actually happening in the marketplace today:

> Our data show that during 2011–2013 more than 15% of the companies receiving venture capital investment had a woman on the executive team. Compared with our finding in 1999, when businesses with women on the executive team received fewer than 5% of all venture capital investments, this sure represents important progress.
>
> *(Brush, Greene, Balachandra, & Davis, 2014)*

A few other staggering statistics: A study by the Kaufman Institute and reported by *The Atlantic* found that women are recipients of just 19% of angel investor funding. For male entrepreneurs, 60% of startup funding was raised from outside sources, such as bank loans or angel investors, compared to 48% for women entrepreneurs (Khazan, 2015). The total dollar investment in companies with a woman on the executive team during 2011–2013 was 21% or $10.9 billion out of $50.8 billion. This figure also rose annually: in 2011 companies with women on the executive team received 9% ($816 million) of the total $8.9 billion invested, while in 2013 they received 27% ($7.1 billion) of the total $26.4 billion invested.

However, companies with a woman CEO only received 3% of the total venture capital dollars, or $1.5 billion out of the total of $50.8 billion invested during 2011–2013.

The evidence appears to be very clear. Women-led startup ventures receive significantly less funding from venture capital than do their male counterparts. Is it simple sexism? I don't think it's simple, but sexism may play a role.

With all things said, women are facing serious challenges with all the misperceptions established by a majority of male venture capitalists. Progress is being made and the report from the IWPR shows that women are steadily increasing their presence with 29% of America's business owners, up from 26% in 1997. The number of women-owned firms has grown 68% since 2007, compared with 47% for all businesses (White, 2015).

Even as women-owned businesses continue to grow at rates exceeding the national average in the US, these firms "are not moving along the growth continuum" (American Express, 2011, p. 3). Men-owned businesses are also, on average, larger than women-owned businesses—about twice as many have 10 or more employees and three times as many have reached the $1 million revenue mark (American Express, 2011).

Women disproportionately face financial access barriers to affordable bank loans (e.g., long-term loans) that prevent them from pursuing their entrepreneurial goals. However, there are many programs out there with the sole intent of funding women's business ventures. Examples include Goldman Sachs, US Small Business Administration, nongovernmental agencies such as the World Bank, and nonprofit organizations such as the Gates Foundation. Some of these programs, such as the Goldman Sachs 10,000 Women Initiative and Coca-Cola's *5by20* campaign, have greater scope as they are also designed to help women and their communities in developing countries.

Bootstrap Financing and Access to Capital

While women may have broader goals for their social enterprise, men may focus on a narrower set of goals, primarily securing access to capital outside bootstrap financing. Bootstrap financing can help mitigate liquidity issues, especially during periods of declining sales when capital acquisition is unavailable, hindering the performance and growth goals of the small startup. Issues of self-funding, high debt conversion, and lack of or limited access to financial markets and commercial banks (Carpenter & Petersen, 2002; Watson, 2002; Watson & Robinson, 2003) may limit the ability of small to medium enterprises (SMEs) to acquire more capital. Berger and Udell (2002) also suggested that challenges of information transparency often constrain external funders' willingness to providing financing. Small firms most commonly access capital from personal sources (e.g., savings and friends/family) and debt from financial institutions. Berger and Udell (2002) indicated that small firms' capital structure is comprised of about 49.6% equity and 50.3% debt. About one-third of total equity is provided by the owner, and almost 35% of debt comes from commercial banks and trade credit accounts. Coleman (2007) and Harrison and Mason (2007) reported that younger firms might rely on bootstrap financing because they generally have less access to capital markets.

Challenges associated with information asymmetry, high transaction costs, and credit rationing (Levenson & Willard, 2000) contributed to slow growth or decline of SMEs. Differences in access to capital have been a reason attributed as an obstacle to women launching and growing small firms and the lower growth rate and smaller size of female-owned firms than that of male-owned firms. Neeley and Van Auken (2010) found that female owners' use of bootstrap capital was inversely associated with access to overdraft privileges at their financial institution. Bootstrap sources of capital are relatively less restricted (Ebben & Johnson, 2006; Winborg & Landstrom, 2001) and provide SME owners with the flexibility to allocate their funds and lower the costs of capital effectively (Collins-Dodd, Gordon, & Smart, 2004).

Poorly developed capital acquisition plans often lead to financial distress and even failure commonly experienced by SME owners (Carter & Van Auken, 2005; Van Praag, 2003). According to a new study by Neeley and Van Auken (2012), the five most frequently used financial methods of funding were invoicing customers promptly (96%), buying used equipment (77%), minimizing inventory (76.2%), stop selling to late-paying customers (73.4%) and giving preference to early-paying customers (71.8%). The least used funding methods were delaying employee pay (6.0%), factoring accounts receivable (5.7%), applying for government grants (5.2%), obtaining foundation grants (1.2%), and receiving corporate grants (0.4%).

Limited access to financial institutions and capital markets suggest that female entrepreneurs and female-owned SMEs should be aware of the options associated with bootstrap financing to supplement capital needs, as well as effectively develop capital acquisition strategies for accessing short- and long-term debt capital for creating and sustaining value.

Empowering Women

The Goldman Sachs 10,000 Women Initiative was created with the goal of educating women entrepreneurs in emerging economies. The program helps women to reach their entrepreneurial goals. By funding women entrepreneurs, the Goldman Sachs 10,000 Women Initiative hopes to help stimulate the overall economy in the communities that these women serve. By the close of 2013, the initiative had enrolled its 10,000th woman (Blair, 2014). Similarly, the Coca-Cola *5by20* campaign was launched in 2010 to help women reach their entrepreneurial goals and create sustainable economic climates in their communities by providing them access to business skills, financial services, assets, and support networks.

The name "*5by20*" comes from Coca-Cola's goal of positively affecting 5 million women by 2020. The campaign currently has programs in 12 countries (Coca-Cola Company, 2013). Recently, Dell launched the "Pay it Forward" initiative to use the power of women's networks to expand opportunities for women entrepreneurs (Dell, 2013). The campaign works on the premise that if women reciprocate in helping other women achieve their business goals, they can create a global community of women supporting women and these efforts will create a ripple effect. Through this process, Dell has set a goal to track support for 1 million aspiring women entrepreneurs by the end of 2015. According to Ingrid Vanderveldt, a well-respected American businesswoman, media personality, and investor: "Empowering women worldwide and investing in their futures can help drive growth in the global economy and promote economic vitality and security" (Vanderveldt, 2014).

Another female education and funding foundation is Tory Burch.[1] Burch founded her fashion company, Tory Burch, in 2004 while in her kitchen and opened her first store in New York City. The high-end fashion brand is most popularly known for its classic ballet flat embossed with the gold Tory Burch crest. According to *Forbes* magazine, Tory Burch is worth about $1 billion (Kanani, 2014). Because early on Burch endured the challenges of balancing work–life goals along with the systemic barriers securing funding, she decided to also launch the "Tory Burch Foundation" in 2009, in order to support female entrepreneurs in overcoming their own obstacles. The foundation offers access to capital for loans, specifically through Bank of America through community lenders (Kanani, 2014). The foundation also offers business education, mentoring, and networking opportunities. Funding is selective. In order to be eligible, entrepreneurs must have $500,000 in annual revenues.[2]

Entrepreneurship and Leadership Roles

The process of entrepreneurship is typically broken down into the stages of: idea generation; opportunity evaluation; planning; the company formation and launch; and growth (The Duke Entrepreneurship Manual, n.d.). During each one of these stages, there are different processes that take place. The "idea generation" stage is the starting point of initiating the innovation. This is the first step toward being able to convince others, whether they are prospective customers, employees, partners, or investors, in the viability of the concept idea. The opportunity evaluation stage is a value proposition or feasibility test with a particular emphasis on answering the following questions:

1. Is there a sufficiently attractive market opportunity?
2. Is your proposed solution feasible, both from a market perspective and a technology perspective?

3. Can you compete (over a sufficiently interesting time horizon)? Is there sustainable competitive advantage?
4. Do you have a team that can effectively capitalize of this opportunity?
5. What is the risk-tolerance profile of this opportunity, and does it justify the investment of time and money?

Planning includes articulation of the value proposition, how the organization is differentiated from the competition, supply-chain management strategies, target market and potential buyers, and a robust business model for serving customers' needs. An essential part of positioning the organization in the marketplace is the company's *vision*: how it wants to be known or thought of. A compelling vision is necessary to inspire investors, recruit and motivate employees, and to motivate customers and equity holders. Planning also includes operational plans and forecasts about revenue streams, objectives, priorities, and milestones in important functional areas for the new venture: marketing; selling; operations; finance; and human resources.

There are four main areas of strategy: determination of the target customer set; business model; position; and objectives. The formation stage includes the incorporation of the organization as a legal entity and the investments in capabilities and delivery systems. The growth stage reflects revenues and expansion through product innovation and market-penetration strategies. Studies by Babson College (Brush, Greene, Balachandra, & Davis, 2014) found that women-led companies during the early stages of development enjoyed a much higher success rate as opposed to male-led companies. The Dow Jones also conducted a similar study with the finding that business startups were more likely to succeed if they had women on their executive teams (Canning et al., 2012).

Evidently, women have the behavioral flexibility needed to play multiple roles: a transactional manager with well-defined expectations and responsibilities who is not necessarily a risk-taker; a transformational leader who focuses on the future, facilitates change, and has a vision of success; and an entrepreneur who can champion innovation and create new opportunities (Dover & Dierk, 2009). Notably, feminist researchers have strongly reasoned that transformational leadership might be particularly advantageous to women because of its genderless qualities. Transformational leadership draws on the confluence of vision and interpersonal communication to mobilize support and commitment of followers. If women have the ability to influence followers to embrace and then implement the vision, then they certainly possess qualities of successful visionary leaders. For aspirational managers seeking career advancement to higher levels of the organization, vision and innovation are strong markers for promotion potential. A primary reason is the perceived causal path that exists between vision and forward thinking, business performance, financial performance, and overall stakeholder satisfaction (Cameron, Quinn, DeGraff & Thakor, 2006). The distinction between transformational leadership and transactional roles is also captured by the CVF.

Competing Values and Leadership Roles

Inherent in the CVF is the notion that organizational and managerial performance are ultimately defined (and judged) by a set of competing criteria and that managerial leaders must consistently confront paradoxical choices that emerge from beliefs that are deeply embedded in organizational and life values (Cameron et al., 2006). Managers are expected to ensure stability within the organization and yet are also faced with a need to encourage change and innovation in response to external market forces. Thus, managerial responses include a variety of transactional and transformational roles differentiated by job requirements or tasks. The CVF displays the repertoire of leadership roles by aligning pairs of roles with specific organizational environments (Figure 2.4).

For example, the *innovator* and *broker* roles rely on creativity and communication skills to bring about change and acquire the resources necessary for change management. The *monitor* and *coordinator* roles are more relevant for system maintenance and integration and require project management and supervision skills. While the *director* and *producer* roles are geared toward goal achievement, the *facilitator* and *mentor* roles focus on employee motivation, facilitation, and development.

The upper part of the framework reflects transformational roles while the lower part includes transactional roles. Transformational leadership, on the one

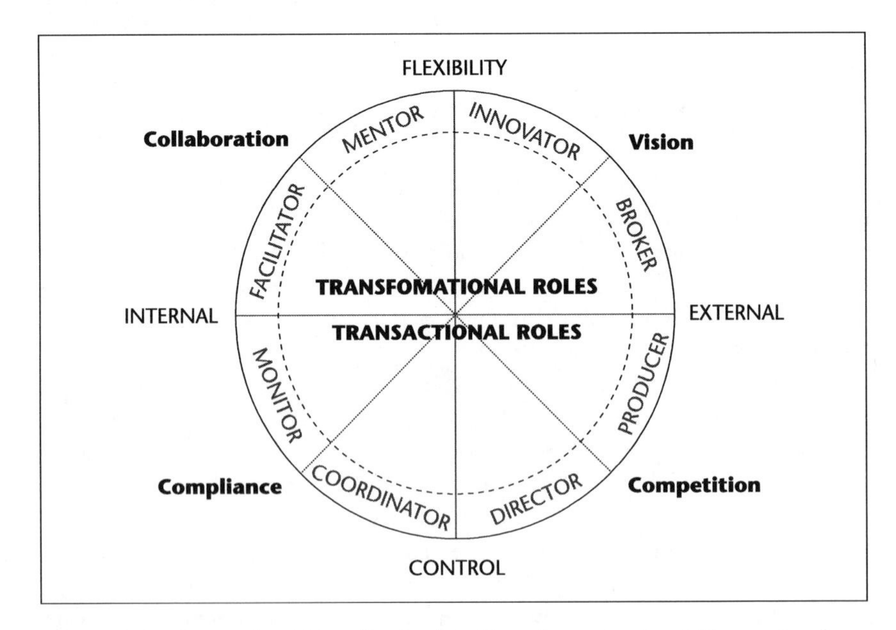

FIGURE 2.4 Competing Values Leadership: Transformational and Transactional Roles

Source: Cameron, Quinn, DeGraff, & Thakor (2006).

hand, inspires followers to do more than they originally intended to do by presenting them with a compelling vision and by encouraging them to transcend their own interests for those of the group or work unit. Transactional leaders, on the other hand, rely upon the economic value of transaction (i.e., exchange of performance for reward) to motivate employees to achieve desired outcomes. Unlike transformational leaders who rely on intangible sources of motivation to energize employees, transactional leaders focus on structuring the incentive system using rules and policies to achieve conformance. The two types of leadership, transformational and transactional, therefore seek to accomplish organizational goals by motivating employees on a continuum that ranges from extrinsic to intrinsic values.

Role Conflict

One example of self-assessment and feedback provided by peers (men and women performing lower middle management duties and responsibilities) in one organization with highly interdependent units appears in Figure 2.5. While the peers expected to see greater involvement of the female manager in performing the CVF roles (5.8 on a scale of 1–7), her self-ratings were quite lower (average score of 4.89), indicating a possible mismatch between expectations and the need to evaluate the reasons leading to the gap in perceptions. In addition, women managers may face a problem of incongruity between expectations about the actual and desired behavior of women and men on the one hand and the attributes typically associated with masculine aspects of competence in performing leadership roles on the other (Ely & Meyerson, 2000). Based on the descriptive aspects of communal characteristics and differences in managerial behavioral tendencies,

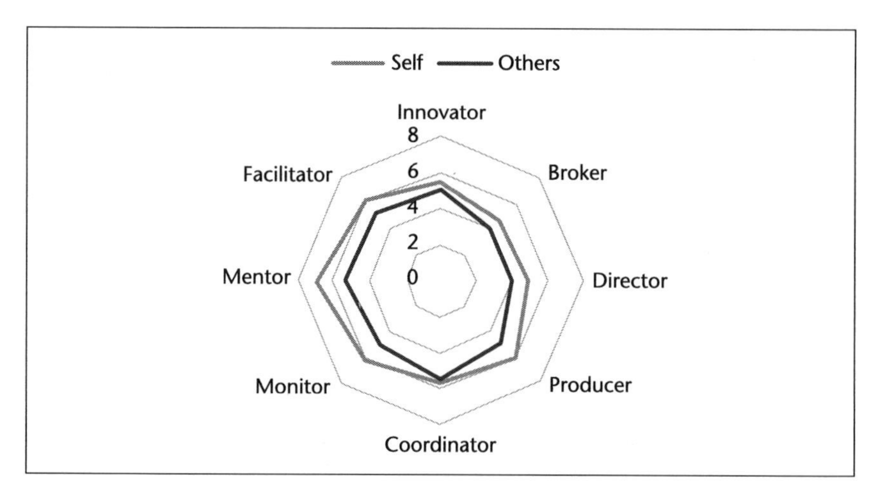

FIGURE 2.5 Self-assessment Ratings and Ratings from Others

women are perceived to possess suboptimal leadership abilities. When women fail to meet expectations (i.e., perform well on masculine aspects of competence), their failures are interpreted as confirming these stereotypes. However, in organizations with supportive culture and well-integrated roles (as opposed to gendered organizations), women and men in managerial positions use behavioral flexibility and apply situational leadership according to the demands of the task, rather than in conformity with stereotypical gender characteristics (i.e., agentic versus communal) or historical gender norms.

Some applications of the CVF caution that the display of extreme behaviors can result in negative consequences, especially when certain roles are used extensively without considering the other roles (Quinn, 1988). Belasen and Frank (2004) found that, on the one hand, when managers perform all the roles indiscriminately or with limited or selective delegation, managers might become hyper-effective, a dysfunctional and unsustainable behavior with negative health and performance consequences. Effective managers, on the other hand, display behavioral flexibility that allows them to master contradictory behaviors while also keep some measure of behavioral integrity and credibility.

Of the quadrants in Table 2.1, the *compliance* quadrant might arguably be considered as the safest for women if they must have very strong skills in at least one other area. High collaboration competencies would be playing right into gender stereotypes, just as high scores in the *vision* quadrant wouldn't be taken seriously. For competition competencies, very high strengths could be seen as going head-to-head with men as behaving in a non-traditional way, which might also be perceived as tipping toward the negative zone for women. *Compliance* roles, however, as long as they are well balanced, are the only ones left where

TABLE 2.1 Transformational and Transactional Roles

Transformational	*Feminist Theme*	*CVF Focus*
Collaboration	Caring	Mentor
	Empowering	Facilitator
Vision	Forward Thinking	Broker
	Innovative	Innovator
Transactional		
Competition	Consultative	Director
	Inclusive	Producer
Compliance	Fair	Coordinator
	Equitable	Monitor

Source: Adapted from Belasen & Frank (2012).

strong skills are highly valued and are not inconsistent with traditional gender role perceptions (Belasen & Frank, 2012).

Life Cycle

Structurally, organizations evolve through predictable stages of development, each with particular characteristics of structure, control systems, goals, and innovation. Each stage has also a new set of rules that emerge for how the organization functions internally and how it relates to important stakeholders: investors, customers, regulators, employees, and so on. These stages are consistent with the dimensions of the CVF (Quinn, 1988) and include: entrepreneurial; collectivity; formalization; and elaboration (see Figure 2.6).

Indeed, a study found that the business mantra to "think leader, think male" may begin to fade as employees and other stakeholders gradually begin to value those leadership skills that focus on relationships and not just traditional leader traits that are more in line with masculinity. This is consistent with a trend toward more communal management styles and demonstrates that women who lead from the top can succeed and provide both people oriented skills and performance-based management advocated by many organization behaviorists (Nauert, 2015). The dynamics associated with each stage of development are described below.

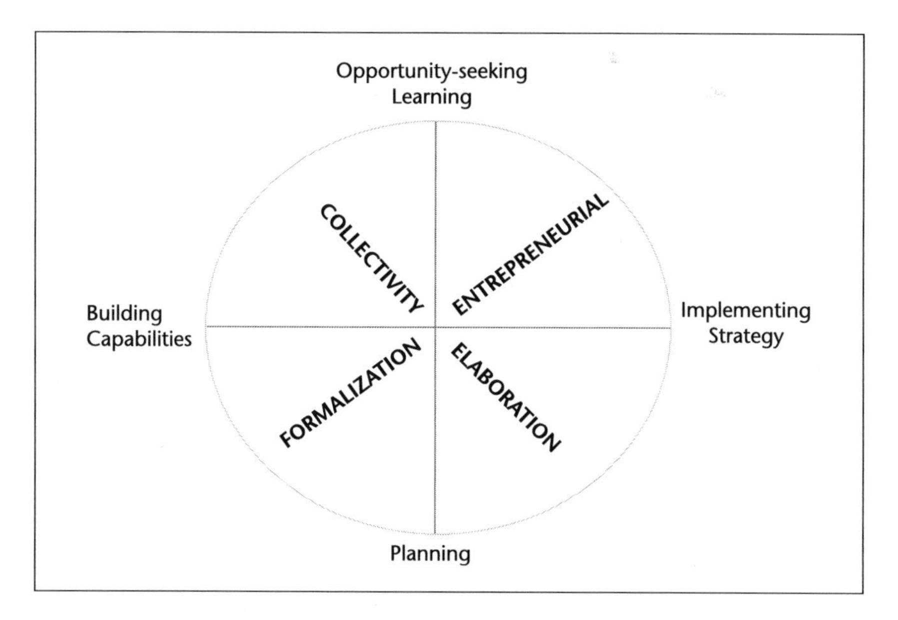

FIGURE 2.6 Organizational Life Cycle

Entrepreneurial stage: Emphasis is outward—creating a product or service and surviving in the marketplace. The founders devote their energies to production and marketing and long hours of work. Creativity and innovation are high. Creative and technically oriented owners are confronted with management issues. The organization is small and most engagements are through informal lines of communication with the top manager/owner providing the structure and concertive control via mutual adjustment and personal supervision. Rewards are personal.

Collectivity stage: Growth is rapid and employees are excited and committed. The structure is still informal, although some departments are established along with job responsibilities and high specialization. Direction is provided through strong charismatic leadership. Commitment, loyalty, and cohesiveness are vital although some conflict begins to emerge over goals and responsibilities as managers seek greater freedom.

Formalization stage: Focus is inward—on internal capabilities, systems, and processes. The organization adds staff support groups, formalizes procedures, and the hierarchy begins to form through centralized authority, established rules and formal procedures, and standardization of work processes. Product groups may be formed to improve coordination and stabilize the organization. Top management becomes concerned with strategy planning and implementation issues and leaves operations to middle managers. Delegation is selective and limited. Conflict and tension emerge around control and autonomy, access, and influence.

Elaboration stage: The organization is stabilized around rules, plans, and objectives that various work units follow. Teamwork and interfunctional collaboration are encouraged. Tough competition may lead to temporary decline and a push toward revitalization. The organization is larger but with social control and self-discipline, which reduce the need for formal controls. Managers are skilled in interpersonal relations and the use of rewards to motivate and achieve high performance.

Table 2.2 illustrates the relationship between the internal and external aspects of initiating a new organization with the female leadership roles listed in Table 2.1.

Innovation and Social Entrepreneurship

The concept of innovation is central to the process of entrepreneurship. In a changing environment and tough competition, innovation is a key process of strategic value for achieving competitive advantage (O'Regan, 2012). Innovation is market driven and customer focused. By disrupting existing processes or practices and by doing things more effectively and efficiently, innovative firms enable economic growth, trigger rise in wages, bring greater quality of work life,

TABLE 2.2 Stages of Organizational Development

Stages	*Women's Leadership*	*Roles*	*Orientations*	*Milestones*
Entrepreneurial	*Vision*: Forward thinking, innovative	*Broker*: Selling ideas, effective speaking and persuasion skills *Innovator*: Creative, imaginative, resilient	*Purpose*: challenge receivers to accept mind-stretching vision *Medium and tone*: visionary, charismatic, vivid, colorful metaphors, symbols, oral delivery, enthusiastic, emphatic, unorthodox written communication *Focus*: idea-centered, futuristic, and rhetorical *Audience*: customers, investors *Example*: CEO speech, written strategic plan, smart talk, communicating vision	Idea generation, opportunity evaluation
Collectivity	*Collaboration*: Caring, empowering	*Facilitator*: Interaction and problem solving skills, interpersonal communication *Mentor*: Strong emotional intelligence skills; inspiring coaching and guiding followers	*Purpose*: establish integrity, rapport, trust, confidence, and commitment *Medium and tone*: conversational, familiar words, inclusive pronouns, personal examples, honesty, committed *Focus*: receiver-centered *Audience*: employees *Example*: informal chats, cafeteria talks, reflective listening, personal, supportive, communicative, reinforcing feedback, evocative	Goal setting, planning

(continued)

TABLE 2.2 Stages of Organizational Development *(continued)*

Stages	*Women's Leadership*	*Roles*	*Orientations*	*Milestones*
Formalization	*Compliance*: Fair, equitable	*Coordinator*: Integrating functional units, maximizing operating efficiency *Monitor*: Using analytics to drive performance, developing standards and compliance systems	*Purpose*: providing clear directions to receivers *Medium and tone*: neutral, precise words, controlled, sequential, standard constructions, factual accuracy, structural rigor, logical progression, realistic presentation, conventional documents, concrete examples, lists, tables, audit reports *Focus*: channel-centered *Audience:* regulators *Example*: policy statements, procedural specifications, rules, standards, written documents, computer printouts, unaddressed letters, memos, directives	Formation, infrastructure and control systems
Elaboration	*Competition*: Consultative, inclusive	*Producer*: Motivating others, rewarding good performance *Director:* Inspiring action, modeling the way, setting goals, allocating resources	*Purpose*: promoting an idea, selling product or service, persuading receivers, establish credibility *Medium and tone*: decisive, engaging, original, supported by credible evidence, prepositional, assertive, declarative, vivid examples, sense of urgency *Focus*: argument-centered *Audience*: owners, analysts *Example*: sales presentations, recommendations to senior managers, press releases, directives, quarterly results, financial reports	Launch and growth

and create higher standards of living (Ascher, 2012). With knowledge so widely distributed and easily accessible, companies increasingly are pursuing the strategy of crowdsourcing and open innovation (De Wit, Dankbaar, and Vissers, 2007). Open innovation helps companies reduce the cost of product development and process improvement, accelerate time to market for new products, improve product quality, and access customer and supplier expertise outside the organization (Wallin & Krogh, 2010).

For open innovation to be successful, it has to be distributed both internally and externally through collaborative networks or ecosystems (Chesbrough & Appleyard, 2007; Giannopoulou, Ystrom, Ollila, Tobias, & Elmquist, 2010). These networks operate by openly sharing early-stage research and allowing all the parties to use the collective knowledge to solve particular problems. Since the main premise of open innovation is to extend the pursuit for and commercialization of new products, open innovation organizations use multiple forms of communication including social media outlets to reach out to customers and innovators.

Implementing innovation requires an effective balance of strategic awareness with operating experience and an optimal mix of leadership and management roles. This is important as crowdsourcing often creates different identities for the organization that also require effective communication strategies (Belasen & Rufer, 2013). A broader identity gives employees the permission to engage in various strategies—to exploit existing products and services while simultaneously explore new offerings and business models. Female managers, especially in middle management positions, more so than senior managers or operating-level managers, have the communication competencies to handle the complexity of information and high number of interactions (Belasen & Luber, 2017).

Another mix of leadership and management roles involves interpersonal communication and strategy implementation. Women managers have the talents, skills, and experience to lead the collaboration process with external networks. According to Wallin and Krogh (2010), when firms invite users to contribute their knowledge to innovation, they cannot apply traditional rules or centralized authority to directing, incentivizing, and monitoring their efforts. Instead, positive and supportive communication as well as a climate that embraces interactive relationships should be used. This is where women excel by adding value to organizations and customers alike. They facilitate adaptation using the *innovator* and *broker* roles and manage innovation implementation using the *director* and *producer* roles (see Table 2.2). This is where women's leadership strengths and their fine communication skills come in quite handy as they master the "both/and" persuasion strategies (Belasen, 2008).

Facilitating adaptability requires that managers relax control to get new projects started, secure time for experimental programs, locate and provide resources for trial projects, and encourage informal discussion and information sharing.

They can implement intended strategy by monitoring activities to support organizational goals, translate strategies into action plans and work unit objectives, and make effective presentations to boards of directors. Women managers, in *mentor and facilitator* roles, have the knowledge and skills to shift from the role of a manager to the roles of *team builder and team leader* as well as to implement innovation.

Team leadership evolves through two different phases: the transition phase and the action phase (Morgeson, DeRue & Karam, 2010). Throughout each of these phases, the team responds to different needs. For example, during the transition phase the team needs a team charter outlined with goals and objectives, developing positive team norms, clarifying task performance strategy, sense making, and providing feedback. In the action phase, *monitoring* output inside and outside the teams, *coordinating* team actions, engaging in effective communication, and maintaining boundaries are important aspects of positive relationships and effective interfunctional collaboration. Eventually these roles, combined, can elevate the team to a higher level of performance with rotating leadership roles, which, on average, evolve with greater maturity, competence, and confidence. These differences (before and after the transition) are also illustrated in the CVF chart in Figure 2.7.

In order to fulfill all these needs, a driving force must be present—a high-impact manager who is both task and relationship oriented with situational skills (Belasen & Luber, 2017). High-achieving women have the right combination of functional knowledge, leadership competencies, and adaptability skills to lead innovative organizations. Wei, Khoury and Grobmeier (2010) found, for example, that most leaders at the research and development (R&D) collaborative group have a "steering" rather than "directing" approach, motivating innovators, communicating, and clarifying goals and expectations. Within the R&D collaboration, cross-functional teams are often the most prominent and a leader of such collaboration requires technical skills, personal skills, cognitive ability, and

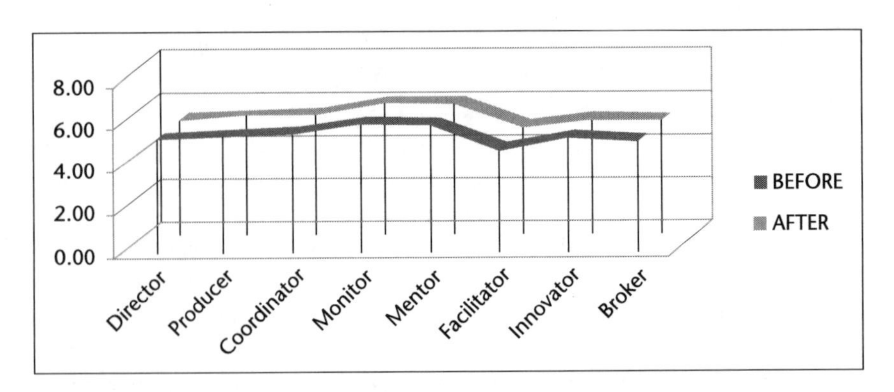

FIGURE 2.7 Before and After the Transition

political and project management skills, which are shared by many high-achieving women.

WOMEN IN INDUSTRIAL RESEARCH: A WAKE UP CALL FOR EUROPEAN INDUSTRY

The European Commission's Directorate-General for Research launched the Women in Industrial Research (WIR) expert group in January 2002 at a time when the problems of recruiting sufficient numbers of highly qualified researchers and engineers had already been identified as a policy concern. It is one of a series of initiatives from the DG Research to foster better use of the talent pool of women in science and in science policy.

The European Council agreed at the Barcelona summit that the proportion of Gross Domestic Product (GDP) spent on R&D in the European Union (EU) should increase from 1.9% in 2000 to 3% by 2010. This will mean substantially increasing the numbers of researchers: indeed, investment in industrial R&D is expected to double by 2010. Given that it plays the leading role in R&D, this is a major challenge for industry.

The report to the European Commission from the High Level Expert Group on Women in Industrial Research for strategic analysis of specific science and technology policy issues (STRATA), the position of women in industrial research was analyzed and recommendations as to how this talent pool could better be used were presented.

By 2002, women constitute only around 15% of industrial researchers in the EU. As significantly more women are graduating in science and engineering, they are an obvious source of new recruits. In addition, the disproportionate loss of women from scientific careers needs to be overcome. Old-fashioned ideas and practices still impede women's careers in industrial research. Their input into innovation, and creativity of science does not reflect their buying power or their growing role as decision-makers.

(Rübsamen-Waigmann, Sohlberg, Rees, Berry, Bismuth, D'Antona et al., 2003)

As shown in Figure 2.8, innovation implementation is exercised through behavioral (e.g., broker, facilitator) and task (e.g., coordinator, monitor) behaviors (Madlock, 2008). In addition to the persuasion aspect of managerial communication and the ability to control language, gestures, and tone of voice, for managers to be perceived as competent communicators by their subordinates, Shaw (2005) suggested that they must also share and respond to information in a timely manner. Moreover, they should integrate the activities of interfunctional project teams, monitor progress toward implementation, and evaluate and control the process. Women share the personality traits and behavioral flexibility to deal effectively

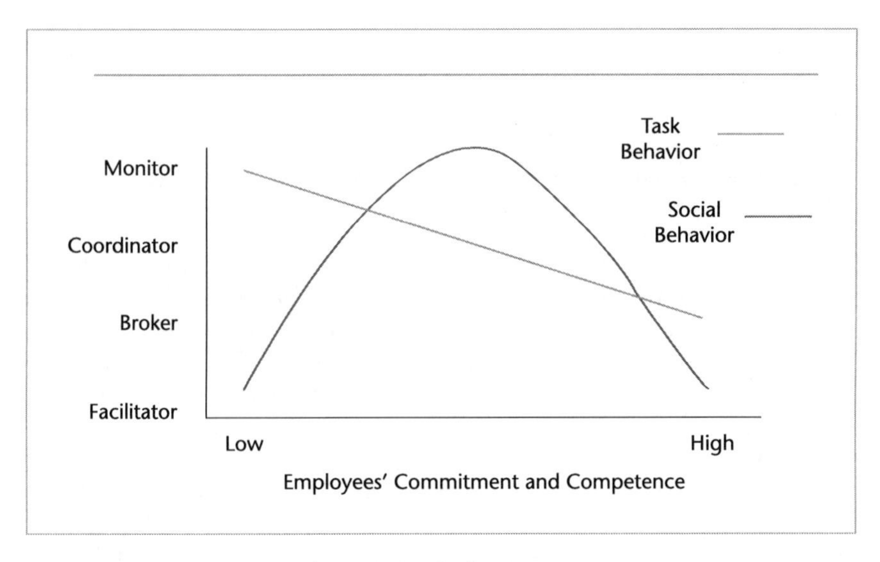

FIGURE 2.8 Innovation Implementation Roles

with various stakeholders (Belasen & Frank, 2010) and equally mitigate resistance to innovation implementation both internally, employees with difficulty to steer away from routine processes, and externally, consumers who might resist product innovation (Heidenreich & Spieth, 2013).

While upper management does most market communication, message alignment falls to middle managers. The same way that women intrapreneurs know how to balance corporate interests with broad social and environmental needs in developing sustainable solutions, they also know how to balance the corporate identity against the brand promises and the company's sense of responsibility against its earnings consistency (Belasen, Eisenberg, & Huppertz, 2015).

Success Rates

Geibel, Askari, and Heinzel (2014) used the *Global entrepreneurship monitor report* (Bosma & Levie, 2009) to measure the "fear of failure rate" in 26 countries. This rate is defined as the percentage of the age "18–64 population with positive perceived opportunities who indicate that fear of failure would prevent them from setting up a business." Those individuals are currently not involved in entrepreneurship activity. The rate was about 27% in 2012 in America, which means that 27% of the individuals with entrepreneurial aspirations recognized opportunities but did not materialize on their plans, even if the expected utility was projected to be higher than the next best alternative. Factors included the availability of startup capital (liquidity constraints), economic growth (level of industrialization, employment), entrepreneurship education (building skills and knowledge of entrepreneurship), reputation (image), and startup activity (level of involvement). One of the findings was that even if the economy of a country is well developed, a recession might raise the fear of failure due to the negative development and therefore prevent people from starting a business. Furthermore, a low startup activity increases the fear of failure rate. Possibly, individuals who are currently not involved in a startup have less confidence concerning the potential of their idea if they don't observe other people being successful or trying to be successful. Observing a higher degree of entrepreneurial activity could raise their trust in the market conditions required for successfully setting up their own business.

Given the number of startups that are established daily in America, it seems that the "fear factor" among women compared to men is relatively the same, and therefore it is quite mindboggling that one of the stereotypical biases in executive suites and boardrooms is that women lack confidence. Let's look at the numbers.

While there has been a net average of 506 new women-owned firms started per day since 2007, the daily average was 602 per day from 2011–2012, 744 per day from 2012–2013, and fully 1,288 per day in 2014—showing that the number of new women-owned firms launched each day has doubled over the past three years. During the most recent period, from 2007–2014, the number of women-owned firms increased by 17% compared to an overall increase of 13%—a ratio of 1.3:1. As mentioned earlier, over the entire 1997–2014 period, the number of women-owned firms has increased at a rate 1.5 times the national average (Womenable, 2014). About 50% of all new establishments survive five years or more and about one-third survive 10 years or more.

Government reports (Figure 2.9) show that the period from 1993 to 2006 was marked by an increase in the number of startups births and deaths, indicating a

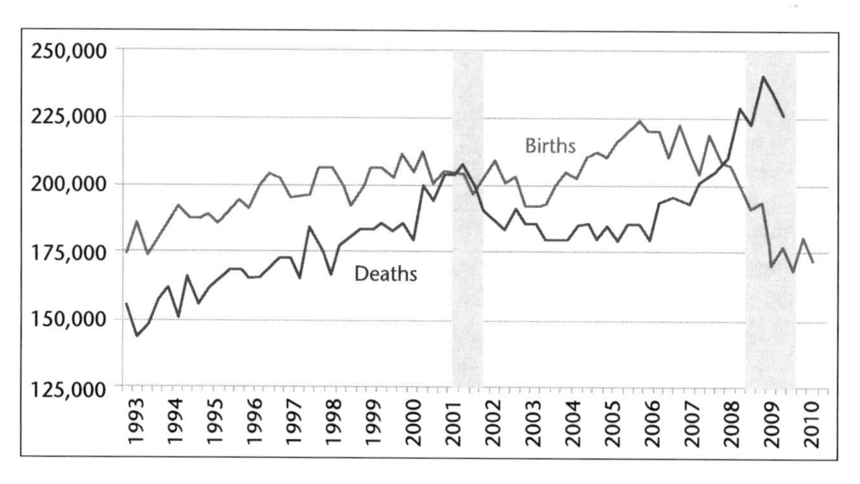

FIGURE 2.9 Quarterly Establishment—Births and Deaths, 1993–2010

Source: US Department of Labor, Bureau of Labor Statistics (2016b).

higher amount of business "churn"—that is, new business establishments entered and old establishments exited the economy in greater numbers. Since the most recent recession began in December 2007, births have experienced the steepest decline in the history of the series. New establishments have not been formed at the same levels seen before the economic downturn began, and the number has been much lower than it was during the 2001 recession. Still, women-owned firms have increased as a share of total businesses over the years, but they remain smaller, on average, than male-owned firms.

In 2012 alone, 36% of business owners were women. The most recently available data on the number of women-owned businesses are from 2007. These data indicate that there were 7.8 million women-owned firms (US Department of Labor, Bureau of Labor Statistics, 2016a). The death rates were lower for female-owned than male-owned establishments within enterprises of 50 or more employees (US Department of Commerce, 2010).

Training and Education

The Global Women Entrepreneur Leaders Scorecard (Aidis, Weeks, & Anacker, 2015), which ranks countries based on business environment, access to resources, leadership and rights, existing pipelines for entrepreneurship, potential women leaders in entrepreneurship, and government practices, recently named the US as the most favorable environment for women entrepreneurs among 31 countries. The publication also identified significant gender impediments and weaknesses in fostering female entrepreneur leaders and networks that persist even in top-performing nations, including the US. Effective entrepreneurship education and training can assist women entrepreneurs in their business and leadership goals (Bullough, Sully De Luque, Abdelzaher, & Heim, 2015). These women become leaders in their communities and inspire other women as well as members of their own families to take risks and achieve their dreams.

From a gender perspective, the leadership field is strongly focused on, and influenced by, men. While the US is ranked as number one, it also exhibited weakness in fostering female entrepreneur leaders and networks (Narea, 2015). Some scholars have even argued that the term leadership is "conventionally constructed in masculine terms" (Kyriakidou, 2012, p. 4; Vinkenburg, van Engen, Eagly, & Johannesen-Schmidt, 2011). In order to overcome this limitation, leadership should be examined through a gender lens (Eagly & Heilman, 2015; Peus, Braun, & Knipfer, 2015), adopt an equity and fairness perspective to evaluate gender gaps in leadership (Hausmann, Tyson, & Zahidi, 2011; Peus et al., 2015; Schuh, Hernandez Bark, Van Quaquebeke, Hossiep, Frieg, & Van Dick, 2014), and reviewed within the context of gender roles, identity, social location, and relationships (Glynn & Raffaelli, 2010). While some aspects of entrepreneurial skills are difficult to develop (e.g., creativity, energy, passion), other aspects such as business planning and capital options can be learned (Henry, Hill, & Leitch, 2005).

Leadership capabilities include public speaking and presenting skills, developing confidence, and taking charge. Soft skills might include mentoring others, inspiring followers, and influencing the attitudes and behaviors of others (Belasen, 2012). Education and training on topics related specifically to networking, negotiation, and leading change, critical thinking, decision making, problem solving, and creativity skills as well as managing career transitions and work–life balance issues, may also help women navigate gendered challenges (Eagly & Carli, 2007; Ely, Ibarra, & Kolb, 2011). Most importantly, business-plan development should also be included for both existing entrepreneurs who have not conducted a full business analysis and potential entrepreneurs who need to gain familiarity with the anatomy of a business plan and methods for completing research to improve their chances of success (Russell, Atchison, & Brooks, 2008).

Some studies have shown that women-only training and education programs are useful and derive positive outcomes for female participants (Debebe, 2011). Participants feel more comfortable, less pressured, as well as enjoy an improved sense of safety as tokenism is mitigated. For example, a survey of 1,452 women attending a women-only management training program in the UK, found that women developed greater confidence and trusting relationship in sharing insights and ideas. They took risks, interacted well with each other, and spoke up with confidence (Willis & Daisley, 2008). However, the value of co-educational programs cannot be underestimated as men and women need to learn to "coexist" and work together in the most complementary way to offset cultural barriers and widen access to entrepreneurship education.

Continuous Improvement

This chapter traced issues and dynamics of mobility of career women into executive suites and conscious choices made by successful women. It examined career opportunities outside the realm of corporations through intrapreneurial leadership roles in venture capital-backed companies or entrepreneurial roles in women-owned firms. The CVF was used as the organizing schema to describe these roles since the model captures both transformational and transactional roles that are also important for managing organizational transitions.

As discussed earlier in this chapter, the CVF highlights the contradictory nature inherent in organizational environments and the complexity of choices faced by managers when responding to competing tensions. These choices include a variety of managerial roles differentiated by specific managerial situations. The *innovator and broker* roles rely on creativity and persuasion to bring about change and acquire resources necessary for change management. The *monitor and coordinator* roles are more relevant for system maintenance and integration and require project management and supervision. While the *director and producer* roles are geared toward goal achievement, planning, and initiating structures and actions, the *facilitator and mentor* roles are aimed at motivating, guiding, and engaging employees

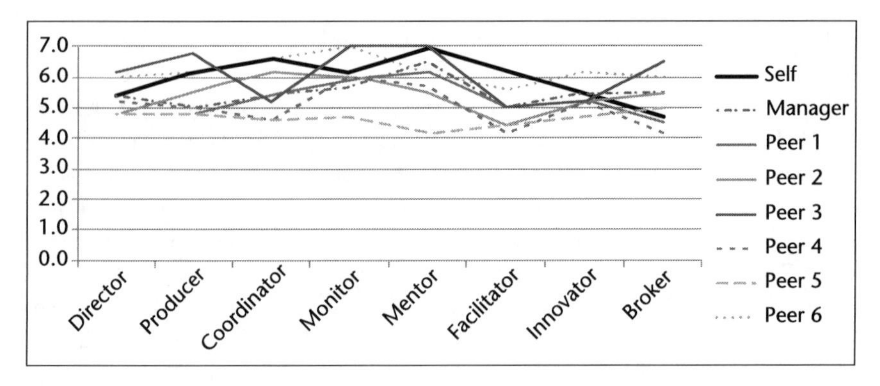

FIGURE 2.10 Assessment Based on Inputs from Others

through commitment and involvement. The upper part of the framework reflects transformational roles while the lower part mirrors transactional roles.

Charting these roles on the CVF diagram (as shown earlier in Figures 2.5 and 2.7) gives participants in a training program a chance to see how well they "cover" these eight roles while at the same time review their strongest role(s) and those in need of further development. Figure 2.10, however, shows the range of responses by others (how well they perceive the effectiveness of the focal person) in comparison to the self-assessment of the focal person.

In my executive development programs, I often tell managers to chart (self-assess) themselves twice—first, as they actually perform these roles and, second, as they wish to perform these roles. The gap between the two charts can represent an opportunity for personal development and personal improvement. As mentioned earlier, another way of doing this assessment is to compare how well a manager or an entrepreneur performs these roles versus how well others (e.g., manager, peers) perceive them in these roles. This should provide some sense of validation. Figure 2.7, for example, shows the "before" and "after" charts in which the individual involved took steps to remedy their weaknesses based on the feedback from others. Still another exercise that I initiate in my executive development programs is to have executives chart their roles versus where their organizations expect them to be. This gives them the opportunity to examine their "profiles" against the goals of their organizations and develop improvement plans that more strategically address their professional goals in light of organizational goals and expectations.

Notes

1 www.toryburchfoundation.org/programs/.
2 www.toryburchfoundation.org/fellows/eligibility/.

References

Aidis, R., Weeks, J., & Anacker, K. (2015). The global women entrepreneur leaders' scorecard 2015: From awareness to action report. *ACG Inc.* Retrieved from http://i.dell.com/sites/doccontent/corporate/secure/en/Documents/2015-GWEL-Scorecard-Executive-Summary.pdf.

American Express. (2011). The American Express OPEN State of women-owned business report: A summary of important trends, 1997–2011. *American Express: New York City.* Retrieved from https://c401345.ssl.cf1.rackcdn.com/pdf/WomanReport_FINAL.pdf.

Ascher, J. (2012). Female entrepreneurship: An appropriate response to gender discrimination. *Journal of Entrepreneurship, Management & Innovation, 8*(4), 97–114.

Ashforth, B. E., & Mael, F. (1989). Social identity theory and the organization. *The Academy of Management Review, 14*(1), 20–39.

Belasen, A. T. (2008). *The theory and practice of corporate communication: A competing values perspective.* Thousand Oaks, CA: Sage Publications.

Belasen, A. T. (2012). *Developing women leaders in corporate America: Balancing competing demands, transcending traditional boundaries.* Santa Barbara, CA: Praeger.

Belasen, A. T., & Frank, N. M. (2004). The perceptions of human resource managers of the shifting importance of managerial roles in downsizing organizations. *International Journal of Human Resources Development and Management, 4*(2), 144–163.

Belasen, A. T., & Frank, N. M. (2010). A peek through the lens of the competing values framework: What managers communicate and how. *The Atlantic Journal of Communication, 18*, 280–296.

Belasen, A. T., & Frank, N. M. (2012). Using the Competing Values Framework to evaluate the interactive effects of gender and personality traits on leadership roles. *The International Journal of Leadership Studies,* 7(2), 192–215.

Belasen, A. T., & Luber, E. (2017). Innovation implementation: Leading from the middle out. In N. Pfeffermann & J. Gould (Eds.), *Strategy and communication for innovation: Integrative perspectives on innovation in the digital economy* (3rd ed.) (pp. 229–243). Berlin, Germany: Springer.

Belasen, A. T., & Rufer, R. (2013) Innovation communication for effective inter-professional collaboration: A stakeholder perspective. In N. Pfeffermann, T. Minshall, & L. Mortara (Eds.), *Strategy and communication for innovation* (2nd ed.) (pp. 227–240). Berlin, Germany: Springer.

Belasen, A. T., Eisenberg, B., & Huppertz, J. (2015). *Mastering leadership: A vital resource for healthcare organizations.* Boston: Jones Bartlett Learning.

Bellucci, A., Borisov, A., & Zazzaro, A. (2010). Does gender matter in bank-firm relationships? Evidence from small business lending. *Journal of Banking & Finance, 34*, 2968–2984.

Berger, U., & Udell, G. (2002). Small business credit availability and relationship lending: The importance of bank organizational structure. *The Economic Journal, 112* (477): F32–F53.

Beauchamp, K. (2016, April 8). Birchbox CEO: "Easier for men to get funding." *CNN/Money.* [Video file]. Retrieved from http://money.cnn.com/video/news/2016/04/08/birchbox-ceo-beauty-products-investors.cnnmoney/.

Blair, B. (2014, September 11). Investing in the power of women: A report on the 10,000 women program. *Babson College Announcements.* Retrieved from www.babson.edu/news-events/babson-news/Pages/140911-babson-goldman-sachs-report-on-women-entrepreneurs.aspx.

Blau, F. D., Ferber, M. A., & Winkler, A. E. (2006). *The economics of women, men, and work* (5th ed.). Upper Saddle River, NJ: Pearson Prentice Hall.

Bosma, N., & Levie, J. (2009). *Global entrepreneurship monitor (GEM) 2009 executive report.* Global Entrepreneurship Research Association (GERA). Retrieved from http://entreprenorskapsforum.se/wp-content/uploads/2010/02/GEM-Global-2009-Report.pdf.

Bosse, D., & Porcher, P. (2012). The second glass ceiling impedes women entrepreneurs. *The Journal of Applied Management and Entrepreneurship, 17*(1), 51–68.

Brush, C., Balachandra, L., Davis, A., & Greene, P. (2014). Investing in the power of women: Progress report on the Goldman Sachs *10,000 women* initiative. Babson Park, MA: Babson College. Retrieved from www.goldmansachs.com/citizenship/10000women/news-and-events/10kw-progress-report/progress-report-full.pdf.

Brush, C., Greene, P. G., Balachandra, L., & Davis, A. E. (2014). Diana report: Women entrepreneurs 2014—bridging the gender gap in venture capital. *Arthur M. Blank Center for Entrepreneurship Babson College.* Retrieved from www.babson.edu/Academics/centers/blank-center/global-research/diana/Documents/diana-project-executive-summary-2014.pdf.

Bullough, A., Sully De Luque, M., Abdelzaher, D., & Heim, W. (2015). Developing women leaders through entrepreneurship education and training. *Academy of Management Perspectives, 29*(2), 250–270. DOI:10.5465/amp.2012.0169

Burton, D., Anderson, P., & Aldrich, H. (2009). Owner founders, non-owner founders, and helpers. In P. D. Reynolds & R. T. Curtin (Eds.), *New firm creation in the United States: Initial explorations with the PSED II data set* (pp. 115–136). New York, NY: Springer.

Cameron, K. S., Quinn, R. E., DeGraff, J., & Thakor, A. V. (2006). *Competing values leadership: Creating value in organizations.* Cheltenham, UK: Edward Elgar.

Canning, J., Haque, M., & Wang, Y. (2012). *Women at the wheel: Do female executives drive start-up success?* New York, NY: Dow Jones & Company, Inc. Retrieved from https://issuu.com/ladywyspr/docs/womenpe_report_final.

Cardon, M., Wincent, J., Singh, J., & Drnovsek, M. (2009). The nature and experience of entrepreneurial passion. *The Academy of Management Review, 34*(3), 511–532.

Carpenter, R., & Petersen, B. (2002). Is the growth of small firms constrained by internal finance? *The Review of Economics and Statistics, 84*(2): 298–309.

Carter, R., & Van Auken, H. (2005). Bootstrap financing and owner's perceptions of their business constraints and opportunities. *Entrepreneurship & Regional Development, 17*(2), 129–144.

Casserly, M. (2011). Female founders: Overcoming the cupcake challenge and "mompreneur" stigma. *Forbes.Com*, p. 11. Retrieved from www.forbes.com/sites/meghancasserly/2011/03/22/female-founders-cupcake-challenge-gilt-groupe-learnvest-zipcar/#3cee17cf3b80.

Center for Women's Business Research. (2010, June). Key4Women confidence index. Retrieved from www.key.com/pdf/women-confidence-index-summer10.pdf.

Chesbrough, H. W., & Appleyard, M. M. (2007). Open innovation and strategy. *California Management Review, 50*(1), 57–76.

Coca-Cola Company. (2013, March 11). The Coca-Cola Company and IFC announce initiative to support women entrepreneurs across emerging markets [Press release]. Retrieved from www.coca-colacompany.com/press-center/press-releases/the-coca-cola-company-and-ifc-announce-initiative-to-support-women-entrepreneurs-across-emerging-markets.

Coleman, S. (2007). The role of human and financial capital in the profitability and growth of women-owned small firms. *Journal of Small Business Management, 45*(3), 303–319.

Coleman, S., & Robb, A. (2009). A comparison of new firm financing by gender: Evidence from the Kauffman firm survey data. *Small Business Economics, 33*, 397–411.

Collins-Dodd, C., Gordon, I., & Smart, C. (2004). Further evidence on the role of gender in financial performance. *Journal of Small Business Management, 42*(4), 395–417.

Debb, G. (2015, March 19). Big companies that embrace intrapreneurship will thrive. *Entrepreneur*. Retrieved from www.entrepreneur.com/article/243884.

Debebe, G. (2011). Creating a safe environment for women's leadership transformation. *Journal of Management Education, 35*(5), 679–712.

Dell. (2013, June 3). Dell launches Pay It Forward initiative to support one million female entrepreneurs by 2015 [Press release]. Retrieved from www.mybusiness.com.au/news/952-dell-launches-initiative-to-support-one-million-female-entrepreneurs.

De Wit, J., Dankbaar, B., & Vissers G. (2007). Open innovation: The new way of knowledge transfer? *Journal of Business Chemistry, 4*(1), 11–19.

Dickson, L. (2011, May 4). Women managers balance the yin and yang of good communication skills. *Voicepro*. Retrieved from www.voiceproinc.com/women-managers-balance-the-yin-and-yang-of-good-communication-skills/.

Dover, P., & Dierk, U. (2009). Sustaining innovation in the global corporation: The role of managers, entrepreneurs and leaders. *Proceedings of The European Conference on Management, Leadership & Governance*, 19–29.

The Duke Entrepreneurship Manual: A Resource for Entrepreneurs. (n.d.). "Entrepreneurial process—a framework." Duke the Fuqua School of Business Center for Entrepreneurship and Innovation. Retrieved from www.dukeven.com/Home/old-material/entrepreneurship-overview—a-framework.

Eagly, A. H., & Carli, L. (2007). *Through the labyrinth: The truth about how women become leaders*. Boston: Harvard Business School Press.

Eagly, A., & Heilman, M. (2015). Call for papers: Special issue of *Leadership Quarterly* on gender and leadership. Retrieved from www.eawop.org/news/special-issue-of-leadership-quarterly-on-gender-and-leadership.

Ebben, J., & Johnson, A. (2006). Bootstrapping in small firms: An empirical analysis of change over time. *Journal of Business Venturing, 21*(6), 851–865.

Ely, R. J., Ibarra, H., & Kolb, D. M. (2011). Taking gender into account: Theory and design for women's leadership development programs. *Academy of Management Learning & Education, 10*(3), 474–493.

Ely, R., & Meyerson, D. (2000). Theories of gender in organizations: A new approach to organizational analysis and change. In B. M. Staw & R. Sutton (Eds.), *Research in Organizational Behavior* (pp. 103–151). New York, NY: Elsevier/JAI.

EEOC. (2007). Enforcement guidance: Unlawful disparate treatment of workers with caregiving responsibilities. (Notice number 915.002). Retrieved from www.eeoc.gov/policy/docs/caregiving.html@regive.

Geibel, R., Askari, H., & Heinzel, J. (2014). Identification of factors that prevent potential entrepreneurs from founding. *GSTF Business Review (GBR), 3*(4), 27–33.

Giannopoulou, E., Ystrom, A., Ollila, S., Tobias, F., & Elmquist. (2010). Implications of openness: A study into (all) the growing literature on open innovation. *Journal of Technology Management and Innovation, 5*(3), 162–180.

Glynn, M. A., & Raffaelli, R. (2010). Uncovering mechanisms of theory development in an academic field: Lessons from leadership research. *Academy of Management Annals, 4*(1), 359–401.

Greenberg, J., & Mollick, E. R. (2016). Leaning in or leaning on? Gender, homophily, and activism in crowdfunding. *Administrative Science Quarterly*. Retrieved from http://ssrn.com/abstract=2462254.

Hadary, S. G. (2010). What's holding back women entrepreneurs? *The Wall Street Journal*, May 17, R1, R3.

Hall, V. (2011, March 11). Why women are more trusted than men, and how to use trust to our advantage. *The Glass Hammer*. Retrieved from http://theglasshammer.com/2011/03/11/why-women-are-more-trusted-than-men-and-how-to-use-trust-to-our-advantage/.

Haltiwanger, J. (2014, October 7). Meet the world's youngest female billionaire: A college dropout and medical genius. *Elite Daily*/Entrepreneurship. Retrieved from http://elitedaily.com/money/entrepreneurship/meet-elizabeth-holmes/788918/.

Hamidi, D. Y., Wennberg, K., & Berglund, H. (2008). Creativity in entrepreneurship education. *Journal of Small Business and Enterprise Development, 15*(2), 304–320.

Harrison, R., & Mason, C. (2007). Does gender matter? Women business angels and the supply of entrepreneurial finance. *Entrepreneurship Theory and Practice, 31*(3), 445–472.

Hausmann, R., Tyson, L. D., & Zahidi, S. (2011). The global gender gap report 2011. Retrieved from www3.weforum.org/docs/WEF_GenderGap_Report_2011.pdf.

Heidenreich, S., & Spieth, P. (2013). Why innovations fail – The case of passive and active innovation resistance. *International Journal of Innovation Management, 17*(5), 1. DOI:10.1142/S1363919613500217

Henry, C., Hill, F., & Leitch, C. (2005). Entrepreneurship education and training: Can entrepreneurship be taught? Part II. *Education + Training, 47*(3), 158–169.

Hmieleski, K. M., & Baron, R. A. (2008). When does entrepreneurial self-efficacy enhance versus reduce firm performance? *Strategic Entrepreneurship Journal, 2*(1), 57–72.

Institute of Leadership and Management. (2011). *Ambition and gender at work*. London: Institute of Leadership and Management.

Kanani, R. (2014, February 20). Why Tory Burch wants to empower women entrepreneurs. *Forbes*. Retrieved from www.forbes.com/sites/rahimkanani/2014/02/20/why-tory-burch-wants-to-empower-women-entrepreneurs/.

Kelley, D., Brush, C., Greene, P., Herrington, M., Ali, A., & Kew, P. (2014). GEM Special report: Women's entrepreneurship. *The Global Entrepreneurship Monitor*. Babson Park, MA: Babson College.

Khazan, O. (2015, March 12). The sexism of startup land. *The Atlantic*. Retrieved from www.theatlantic.com/business/archive/2015/03/the-sexism-of-startup-land/387184/.

Kiisel, T. (2015, April 30). Why don't women get more small business loans? – An interview with Experian director Peter Bolin. *BusinessLoans.com*. Retrieved from www.businessloans.com/article/why-dont-women-get-more-small-business-loans-an-interview-with-experian-director-peter-bolin/.

Klampe, M. (2010, October 4). Women executives twice as likely to leave their jobs as men. *Oregon State University News and Research Communications*. Retrieved from http://oregonstate.edu/ua/ncs/archives/2010/oct/women-executives-twice-likely-leave-their-jobs-men.

Klein, K. E. (2010, November 2). How women business owners are held back. *Bloomberg Businessweek*, 14.

Konda, I., Starc, J., & Rodica, B. (2015). Social challenges are opportunities for sustainable development: Tracing impacts of social entrepreneurship through innovations and value creation. *Economic Themes*, *53*(2), 215–233.

Kwapisz, A., & Hechavarria, D. M. (2016). Women don't ask: An investigation of start-up financing and gender. Paper presented at the Academy of Management, Anaheim, CA.

Kyriakidou, O. (2012). Gender, management and leadership. *Equality, Diversity and Inclusion: An International Journal*, *31*(1), 4–9.

Levenson, A., & Willard, K. (2000). Do firms get the financing they want? Measuring credit rationing experiences by small businesses in the U.S. *Small Business Economics*, *14*(2), 83–94.

Madlock, P. (2008). The link between leadership style, communicator competence, and employee satisfaction. *Journal of Business Communication*, *45*(1), 61–78.

Markowitz, E. (2011, September 30). Truth: Women-led startups have fewer failures. *Business Insider*. Retrieved from www.businessinsider.com/truth-women-led-startups-generate-higher-revenues-and-have-fewer-failures-2011-9.

Marlow, S., & Patton, D. (2005). All credit to men? Entrepreneurship, finance, and gender. *Entrepreneurships Theory and Practice*, 717–735.

Morgeson, F. P., DeRue, S., & Karam, E. (2010). Leadership in teams: A functional approach to understanding leadership structures and processes. *Journal of Management*, *36*(1), 5–39.

Muravyev, A., Talavera, O., & Schafer, D. (2009). Entrepreneurs' gender and financial constraints: Evidence from international data. *Journal of Comparative Economics*, *37*(2), 270–286.

Narea, N. (2015). U.S. is women's entrepreneurship frontrunner, but lags in fostering leaders. *Forbes.Com*, 38. Retrieved from www.forbes.com/sites/nicolenarea/2015/07/01/u-s-is-womens-entrepreneurship-frontrunner-but-lags-in-fostering-leaders/#43c421765ad5.

Nauert, R. (2015). Women well-suited to be leaders. *Psych Central*. Retrieved from http://psychcentral.com/news/2010/05/14/women-well-suited-to-be-leaders/13829.html.

Neeley, L., & Van Auken, H. (2010). Differences between female and male entrepreneurs' use of bootstrap financing. *Journal of Developmental Entrepreneurship*, *15*(1), 19–34.

Neeley, L., & Van Auken, H. (2012). An examination of small firm bootstrap financing and use of debt. *Journal of Developmental Entrepreneurship*, *17*(1), 1–12.

Olawale, F. (2010). Graduate entrepreneurial intention in South Africa: Motivations and obstacles. *International Journal of Business and Management*, *5*(9), 87–98.

O'Regan, N. (2012). Entrepreneurship and innovation: Overview. *Strategic Change*, *21*(5/6), 193–198. DOI:10.1002/jsc.1903

Padnos, C. (2010, February). High performance entrepreneurs: Women in high tech. *Illuminate Ventures*. Retrieved from www.txwsw.com/pdf/IlluminateWPSummary6-10.pdf.

Parlapiano, P., & Cobe, E. (2002). *Mompreneurs: A mother's practical step-by-step guide to work-at-home success* (Revised and updated). New York, NY: Perigee Books.

Peus, C., Braun, S., & Knipfer, K. (2015). On becoming a leader in Asia and America: Empirical evidence from women managers. *The Leadership Quarterly*, *26*, 55–67.

Phipps, S. (2012). Contributors to an enterprising gender: Examining the influence of creativity on entrepreneurial intentions and the moderating role of political skill controlling for gender. *Academy of Entrepreneurship Journal, 18*(1), 77–90.

Phipps, S., & Prieto, L. (2015). Women versus men in entrepreneurship: A comparison of the sexes on creativity, political skill, and entrepreneurial intentions. *Academy of Entrepreneurship Journal, 21*(1), 32–43.

Proudfoot, D., Kay, A., & Koval, C. (2015). A gender bias in the attribution of creativity: archival and experimental evidence for the perceived association between masculinity and creative thinking. *Psychological Science, 26*(11), 1751–1761.

Quinn, R. E. (1988). *Beyond Rational Management.* San Francisco: Jossey-Bass.

Raffiee, J., & Feng, J. (2014). Should I quit my day job? A hybrid path to entrepreneurship. *Academy of Management Journal, 57*(4), 936–963.

Rao, D. (2013, July 22). Why 99.95% of entrepreneurs should stop wasting time seeking venture capital. *Forbes.* Retrieved from www.forbes.com/sites/dileeprao/2013/07/22/why-99-95-of-entrepreneurs-should-stop-wasting-time-seeking-venture-capital/#5d13ff85296d.

Reynolds, P. D., & Curtin, R. T. (Eds.) (2009). *New firm creation in the United States: Initial explorations with the PSED II data set.* New York, NY: Springer.

Richomme-Huet, K., Vial, V., & d'Andria, A. (2013). Mumpreneurship: A new concept for an old phenomenon? *International Journal of Entrepreneurship and Small Business, 19*(2), 251–275.

Rübsamen-Waigmann, H., Sohlberg, R., Rees, T., Berry, O., Bismuth, P., D'Antona, R. et al. (2003). Women in industrial research: A wake up call for European industry (Luxembourg: Office for Official Publications of the European Communities). Retrieved from https://ec.europa.eu/research/swafs/pdf/pub_gender_equality/wir_final.pdf.

Ruef, M. (2010). *The entrepreneurial group: Social identities, relations, and collective action.* Princeton, NJ: Princeton University Press.

Russell, R., Atchison, M., & Brooks, R. (2008). Business plan competitions in tertiary institutions: Encouraging entrepreneurship education. *Journal of Higher Education Policy and Management, 30*(2), 123–138.

Sandberg, S. (2013). *Lean in: Women, work, and the will to lead.* New York, NY: Knopf.

Schuh, S. C., Hernandez Bark, A. S., Van Quaquebeke, N., Hossiep, R., Frieg, P., & Van Dick, R. (2014). Gender differences in leadership role occupancy: The mediating role of power motivation. *Journal of Business Ethics, 120*(3), 363–379.

Shaw, K. (2005). Getting leaders involved in communication strategy: Breaking down the barriers to effective leadership communication. *Strategic Communication Management, 9*, 14–17.

Stengel, G. (2013, February 6). Funding: There's a new source for women entrepreneurs. *Forbes.* Retrieved from www.forbes.com/sites/geristengel/2013/02/06/funding-theres-a-new-source-for-women-entrepreneurs/#48992f8012b3.

Tennery, A. (2012, June 28). More women are in the workforce—so why are they still doing so many chores? *Business Money, Time Magazine.* Retrieved from http://business.time.com/2012/06/28/more-women-are-in-the-workforce-so-why-are-we-still-doing-so-many-chores/.

Thébaud, S. (2015). Business as plan B: Institutional foundations of gender inequality in entrepreneurship across 24 industrialized countries. *Administrative Science Quarterly, 60*(4), 671. DOI:10.1177/0001839215591627

US Department of Commerce, Economics and Statistics Administration. (2010, October). *Women-owned businesses in the 21st century*. Retrieved from www.esa.doc.gov/sites/default/files/women-owned-businesses.pdf.

US Department of Labor, Bureau of Labor Statistics. (2016a, April 28). *Business employment dynamics: Entrepreneurship and the US economy*. Retrieved from www.bls.gov/bdm/entrepreneurship/entrepreneurship.htm.

US Department of Labor, Bureau of Labor Statistics. (2016b, June 24). American time use survey. *News Release USDL-16-1250*. Retrieved from www.dol.gov/whd/fmla/survey/.

US Small Business Administration, Office of Advocacy. (2014, March). *Frequently asked questions. Advocacy: the voice of small business in government*. Washington, DC: US Small Business Administration. Retrieved from www.sba.gov/sites/default/files/FAQ_March_2014_0.pdf.

Vanderveldt, I. (2014, January 6). Resolutions: Female entrepreneurs are key to sustainable global development. *United Nations Foundation*. Retrieved from www.unfoundation.org/blog/female-entrepreneurs.html.

Van Praag, C. (2003). Business survival and success of young small business owners. *Small Business Economics*, *21*, 1–17.

Vinkenburg, C. J., van Engen, M. L., Eagly, A. H., & Johannesen-Schmidt, M. C. (2011). An exploration of stereotypical beliefs about leadership styles: Is transformational leadership a route to women's promotion? *The Leadership Quarterly*, *22*, 10–21.

Wallin, M., & Krogh, G. (2010). Focus on the integration of knowledge. *Organizational Dynamics*, *39*(2), 145–154.

Watson, J. (2002). Comparing the performance of male- and female-controlled businesses: Relating outputs to inputs. *Entrepreneurship Theory and Practice*, 26(3), 91–100.

Watson, J., & Robinson, S. (2003). Adjusting for risk in comparing the performances of male- and female-controlled SMEs. *Journal of Business Venturing*, *18*(6), 773–788.

Wei, Z., Khoury, A. E., & Grobmeier, C. (2010). How do leadership and context matter in R&D team innovation? A multiple case study. *Human Resource Development International*, *13*(3), 265–283.

White, G. (2015, April 17). Women are owning more and more small businesses. *The Atlantic*. Retrieved from www.theatlantic.com/business/archive/2015/04/women-are-owning-more-and-more-small-businesses/390642/.

Williams, R. (2012, December 15). Why women may be better leaders than men: Women's leadership style more suited to modern organizations? *Psychology Today*. Retrieved from www.psychologytoday.com/blog/wired-success/201212/why-women-may-be-better-leaders-men.

Willis, L., & Daisley, J. (2008). Women's reactions to women-only training. *Women in Management Review*, *12*(2), 56–60.

Wilson, F., Kickul, J., & Marlino, D. (2007). Gender, entrepreneurial self-efficacy, and entrepreneurial career intentions: Implications for entrepreneurship education. *Entrepreneurship: Theory & Practice*, *31*(3), 387–406.

Winborg, J., & Landstrom, H. (2001). Financial bootstrapping in small businesses: Examining small business managers' resource acquisition behaviors. *Journal of Business Venturing*, *16*(3), 235–254.

Womenable. (2014, March). *The 2014 State of Women-Owned Businesses Report: A Summary of Important Trends 1997–2014*. Commissioned by American Express OPEN.

Los Angeles, CA: LaLa Press. Retrieved from www.womenable.com/content/userfiles/2014_State_of_Women-owned_Businesses_public.pdf.

Wood Brooks, A., Huang, L., Wood Kearney, S., & Murray, F. E. (2014). Investors prefer entrepreneurial ventures pitched by attractive men. *Proceedings of the National Academy of Sciences (PNAS)*, *111*(12), 4427–4431. DOI:10.1073/pnas.1321202111

Zhang, J., Souitaris, V., Soh, P., & Wong, P. (2008). A contingent model of network utilization in early financing of technology ventures. *Entrepreneurship Theory and Practice*, *32*(4), 593–613.

Zhao, H., Seibert, S. E., & Hills, G. E. (2005). The mediating role of self-efficacy in the development of entrepreneurial intentions. *Journal of Applied Psychology*, *90*(6), 1265–1272.

PART II

Reinforcing Comparable Worth

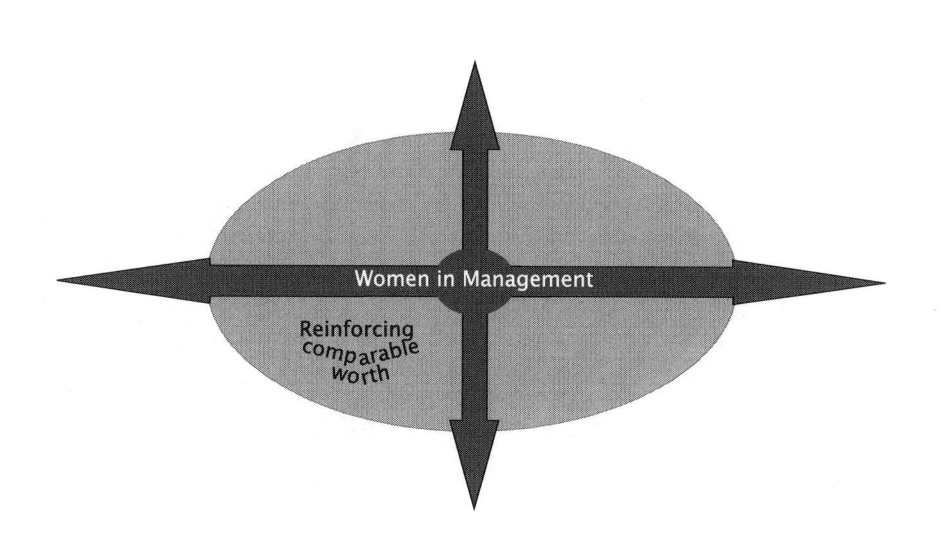

3

PROMOTING EQUALITY IN MANAGEMENT

Many companies today just seem to focus on meeting diversity in entry-level positions through equal employment opportunity (EEO) regulations, however that is where it ends. According to the 2011 Catalyst census women have made no significant inroads into management positions and are no further along the corporate ladder than they were six years ago. From the report:

- Women held 16.1% of board seats in 2011, compared to 15.7% in 2010.
- Less than one-fifth of companies had 25% or more women board directors.
- About 10% companies had no women serving on their boards.
- Women of color still held only 3% of corporate board seats.
- Women held 14.1% of executive officer positions in 2011, compared to 14.4% in 2010.
- Women held only 7.5% of executive officer top-earner positions in 2011, while men accounted for 92.5% of top earners.
- Less than 20% companies had 25% or more women executive officers and more than 25% had no women executives.
- White men held 74.5% of board seats on the 500 largest publicly traded companies, versus 5.7% for African American men and 1.9% for African American women.

By 2012, the percentage of African American male directors declined to 5.5%, while the percentage of African American female directors remained flat. White men continued to hold roughly 95% of board chair positions and 86% of lead director slots. McKinsey & Company, an international management consulting firm, found that in 2012 women accounted for 53% of entry-level jobs and made it to "the belly of the pipeline" in large numbers. But then female presence fell off a cliff, to 35% at the director level, 24% among senior vice-presidents and 19% in the executive suite (Barsh & Yee, 2012). These percentages are intriguing as they punctuate the problem with the leaking pipeline with a downward trend from 37% in 2012 to 28% women-to-men ratios at the director and vice-president levels respectively the prior year (2011). The gender gap was even wider for women of color. Among African American employees, both men and women expressed an above-average desire to advance to the next level. McKinsey's study (Women in the Economy, 2011), for example, found that 81% of African American men and 86% of African American women aspire to advance, compared with 74% of all men and 69% of all women, but only 35% of the African American women believed they will have a chance to move up, compared with 41% of all women. Black men felt even more empowered than whites as 49% believed they will move up, compared with 43% of men on average.

As members of two devalued identities, African American women face a very unique experience of dual discrimination. In the early 1970s, discrimination based on sexism and racism was termed "double jeopardy" to denote that the minority woman's experience in society is manifested simultaneously on the two fronts of gender and ethnic prejudices (Beale, 1970). This term is still applicable as no significant change to the presence of African American women in executive suites or boardrooms has recently been recorded. In 2013, 30% of the 250 largest corporations did not have a single African American director indicating that corporate boards have become less diverse over the past several years (Black Enterprise, 2013).

Barriers to Promotion and Participation

One of the most serious issues regarding the scarcity of women in top management teams (TMTs) and corporate boards is the perseverance of gendered leadership. Symptomatic to gender leadership is the use of negative stereotyping, discrimination, and prejudice, which traverse from traits (women are friendly, cooperative, relational, inclusive) to consequences (women are dominated and opportunities for upward mobility are blocked), creating a *chilling effect* discouraging and deterring women from reaching the top (Carnes & Radojevich-Kelley, 2011; McEldowney, Bobrowski, & Gramberg, 2009). High-potential women advance more slowly in both pay and career progression than men even though they are on par in employing career management strategies. Due to the expanded female stereotypes in the workplace, women may forgo applying for higher positions in a company.

Barsh and Yee (2012), who conducted a study of 60 leading Fortune 500 companies, found that diverse leadership programs in these organizations triggered stronger business results. They went on to suggest that other companies should get "closer to unlocking the full potential of women at work" (p. 2). However, these 60 companies had nearly 140,000 mid-level women managers but only about 7,000 (5%) became vice-presidents, senior vice-presidents, or members of the C-suite. The fact remains the same—regardless of their enormous value to the management of organizations, women are underrepresented in TMT positions and still have a long way to go before achieving parity with their male counterparts in the workplace.

Alice Eagly and Linda Carli (2007) describe the problem of gendered leadership and accessibility as *labyrinth leadership*. Ultimately, women who seek top management positions must weed through culturally formed stereotypes and at the same time avoid crossing culturally generated barriers. They work against a centripetal force, invariably unicursal, moving in a curvilinear path that is directed inward, keeping women from reaching upper-level positions. The prevailing gap between women's education and workforce participation has continued to persist, too: "In an era when women have made sweeping strides in educational attainment and workforce participation, relatively few have made the journey all the way to the highest levels of political or corporate leadership" (Pew Research Center, 2008, p. 3).

Organizational and cultural barriers converge with stereotypical biases, preconceptions of roles and abilities, and misrepresentation of the commitment to personal and family responsibilities as an inability to meet tough schedules (primarily for women) to block women's access to top positions. Furthermore, the systematic exclusion from informal networks of communication, lack of opportunities to assume line roles, and limited access to visible and/or challenging assignments prevent women from advancing to higher-level positions at the same rate as men. High-potential women are less likely to promote themselves as well as men, have less mobility within the organization, and are more dependent on formal advancement procedures than are men (Lyness & Thompson, 2000). This is especially true in highly male-dominated or masculine settings where women are challenged to act tough and exercise competitive styles to gain acceptance into influential networks (Timberlake, 2005). Unfortunately, it was found to be true also in academic settings.

Sarsons (2015) set out to explore whether bias arising from collaborative work helps explain the gender promotion gap in academic institutions by testing whether coauthored publications matter differently for tenure by gender. While solo-authored papers send a clear signal about one's ability, coauthored papers do not provide specific information about each contributor's skills. She found that female authors often suffered a "coauthor penalty" when they coauthored with men. The penalty was lower when coauthorship involves no men. The results provide suggestive evidence that gender bias exists in academic promotion decisions. The bias occurs when reviewers make a judgment on the part of the employer as to which author has made the greatest contribution to the paper. Figure 3.1 shows that when women solo-author, they also signal their abilities explicitly and therefore have roughly the same chance of receiving tenure as a man, but women who coauthor most of their work have a significantly lower probability of receiving tenure.

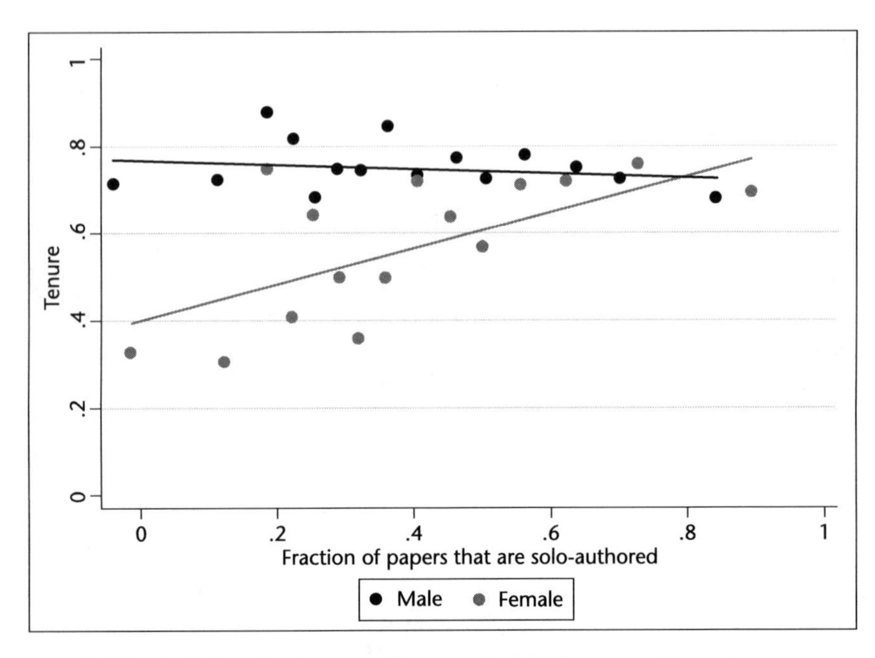

FIGURE 3.1 Relationship Between Composition of Papers and Tenure

Source: Sarsons (2015).

Employers update their beliefs upward as more solo signals are generated until both men and women are believed to be high types. The gap in tenure rates, therefore, should be smaller or eliminated as more solo-authored papers are produced by women. However, bias, whether conscious or subconscious, can have significant implications for the gender gap in promotion decisions. Table 3.1 shows that while 77% of the men in the sample study received tenure, only 52% of the women received tenure. There is no statistically significant difference in

TABLE 3.1 Summary Statistics

	Full	*Male*	*Female*	p-*value*
Tenure	0.71	0.77	0.52	0.001
	(0.45)	(0.42)	(0.50)	
Total Papers	8.6	8.7	8.2	0.164
	(4.0)	(4.1)	(3.4)	
Solo-authored	3.1	3.1	3.1	0.997
	(2.4)	(2.4)	(2.3)	
Coauthored	5.5	5.7	5.1	0.135
	(3.7)	(3.8)	(3.3)	
Years to Tenure	6.7	6.6	7.1	0.021
	(1.9)	(1.9)	(1.9)	

	Full	*Male*	*Female*	p-*value*
Avg. Journal Rank:				
All Publications	45.5	46.3	42.6	0.048
	(18.8)	(19.1)	(17.3)	
Solo Publications	46.4	47.0	44.4	0.300
	(24.2)	(24.5)	(22.9)	
Coauthored Publications	45.6	46.6	42.2	0.054
	(22.3)	(22.8)	(20.1)	
Observations	552	422	130	

Source: Sarsons (2015).

the number of papers that men and women produced although men have slightly more papers in high-ranked journals. Sarsons (2015) concluded that if women are tenured at lower rates because of such productivity differences, controlling for the number and rank of publications should explain the tenure gap.

Self-promotion and the Ability to Network

Women are still perceived as "risky" appointments for line roles that are often staffed by decisions of male-dominated committees (Herminia, Carter, & Silva, 2010). Successful completion of high-risk assignments typically comes with public recognition that is often translated into top positions. High-potential women have less access to challenging projects (e.g., international assignments) and high-risk assignments that also lead to visibility, so important for advancement to senior executive positions (Belasen, 2012). However, while men tend to place a high priority on visibility and recognition, women with a track record of success depend on peer support to advance their career. Paradoxically, just when women are most likely to need active mentoring or even sponsorship—as they aim for positions of power—they may be least likely to find it. Women executives are concentrated into certain types of jobs—mostly staff and support jobs—that offer little opportunity for getting to the top (Feminist Majority Foundation, 2014).

Women have limited access to or are excluded from informal networks in the workplace. These networks are vital during socialization processes, decision making communications, and conflict resolutions. Limited access can also make it more difficult for women to create willing or supporting alliances, negotiate their "cards" more aggressively, or become "go to" leaders. Exacerbating the problem is the fact that often human-resources officers may emphasize the positive skills that women possess, but may not actually follow through on supporting women's advancement. Existing training and development programs tend to focus on current competencies and short-term performance expectations rather than long-term strategic goals putting women at an obvious disadvantage.

> When you ask women, 77% of them will tell you they believe promotions are driven by a combination of hard work, long hours, and education credentials. However, 83% of men will readily acknowledge that "who you know" counts for a lot, or at least as much as "how well you do your job" . . . Hard work alone is not enough to get you promoted if nobody knows and acknowledges it. Many women work hard and expect their boss to realize it and it's just not enough. If you aren't standing up for yourself, who will?
>
> *(Halter, 2015)*

Frustrated by the uphill battle and the injustice and without opportunities for self-promotion, women increasingly assume staff roles (as opposed to line roles) where there is little opportunity for advancing to the top. Reportedly (Belasen, 2012), by 2010, the largest proportion of women managers was in healthcare and social assistance (70%), educational services (57%), financial activities (50%), and leisure and hospitality (45%). A 2012 report by McKinsey (Women in the Economy, 2011) indicates that women, in general, opt at far higher rates than men for staff roles, not executive line positions. Some 50% to 65% of women at the vice-president level and higher are in staff roles, compared with only 41% to 48% of men. Contrast the siloing of women into strategic or line roles with significant profit and loss responsibilities, which are often reserved for men, with staff roles that limit women's upward mobility aspirations

RECOUNT BY A STUDENT IN PROFESSOR BELASEN'S LEADERSHIP DEVELOPMENT PROGRAM, APRIL 2016

I was in the field operations organization that consisted almost entirely of men. There were a few female supervisors and technicians and only one female mid-level manager. Female employees were generally placed in sales and human resources. For years, the company placed new hires in what they perceived to be appropriate for their gender. Women were not expected to be able to perform field jobs as well as a man could because it was more physical and "rough." Women were given office positions where it was believed they were better suited. Advancement in the company, however, depended on field operations experience. There was a common belief that to move up in the company you had to be able to manage a field team. Since women were rarely placed in field positions, their opportunities for advancement were very limited or confined to just their business department.

By denying women field experience, the male-dominated culture continued to thrive in upper management. Some managers would communicate in a hostile and hyper-aggressive manner. These managers viewed feedback or opposing opinions as push back or as obstruction to their goals. Employees would not voice their opinions or ideas in fear of being berated or viewed as incompetent. Upper management was mostly male dominated and this type of management style was accepted and even encouraged through targeted promotion.

The culture took a swing when the company made a concerted effort to diversify its management and non-management teams across all departments. More females were placed in field supervisor and tech positions. Lower level managers were now included in decision making processes. Diversity and harassment training were mandatory and frequent. How employees communicated started to change. Terms like manpower were changed to workforce to reflect the reality. More importantly, female employees were now gaining needed experience to advance. In fact, at one point I reported to a female director who reported to a female regional vice president who herself reported to a female senior vice president. This was not only empowering and rewarding for employees, but it also created a sense of cohesion and trust.

Family Pulls and Work Pushes

High-ranking female role models are relatively scarce in middle management and executive positions remain elusive for most women. Known as the "leaky pipeline," this has significant implications for succession planning and the perpetuation of unreachability due to the limited pool of potentially qualified women successors who are being left behind. Take Google as an example, in a report to the EEOC, Google indicated that of its 36 executives and top-ranking managers, just three are women (Google, 2013). Anecdotally, managers at Google invest time and effort to persuade women engineers to nominate themselves for promotion (Shellenbarger, 2012).

Barsh and Yee (2012) reported that women in their sample of Fortune 500 companies opted to take staff roles, got stuck in middle management, or simply left their organization. For example, about 50% of the mid-level women managers indicated that they are both the primary breadwinners and primary caregivers. And yet, only 3% of the male and female managers worked part time and less than 1% of the senior executives worked part time, making the balance of work and family quite challenging for women. Consequently, women appeared to slow their careers or downshift to less important roles to reduce uncertainty or lessen travel constraints.

> Indeed, even among the successful women we interviewed, more than half felt they held themselves back from accelerated growth. Most said they should have cultivated sponsors earlier because a sponsor would have

> pushed them to take opportunities. These women said they did not raise their hands or even consider stretch roles. And when surveyed, more women than men reported that they would likely move next into support roles.
>
> *(Barsh & Yee, 2012, p. 7)*

The pipeline, in effect, continues to suffer from leaks and blockages. Indeed, Kurtulus and Tomaskovic-Devey (2012) confirmed that an increase in the share of female top managers is associated with subsequent increases in the share of women in mid-level management positions. The four barriers to women's promotion—structural obstacles, lifestyle choices, institutional barriers and individual mindsets—have traditionally been intensified by the lack of sponsorship, limited flexibility and unconscious biases. They also restrict the movement of women into influential executive positions (see Figure 3.2).

> Early in the pipeline, women and men are distributed across line and staff roles at similar levels, but women begin a steady shift into staff roles by the time they reach the director level. Structurally, women do not have the same opportunities to benefit from sponsor discussions, and so they lack support to stay in the line. Line jobs are less flexible than staff jobs, so as women form families, staff jobs look more appealing. Well intentioned leaders often do not even ask mothers to consider a tough assignment. And women know that line jobs carry greater pressure. The more issues like this we explored, the more we found the four barriers working in combination to make the problem impenetrable.
>
> *(Barsh & Yee, 2012, p. 6)*

Hard Choices

Many women report that to be successful, they need to demonstrate consistent levels of commitment, higher levels of technical proficiency, show adherence to bottom-line results, have demonstrated competency in strategic thinking and decision making, be creative, have effective conflict resolution skills, and cope effectively with change and uncertainty—all coupled with long hours at work. What's more, women have to deal with the inconsistency of their own sense of success and the way organizations measure it. Women also experience cross-pressures for their time and the constant need to balance competing priorities across life and career goals that are different for men (Mainiero & Sullivan, 2006; O'Neil & Bilimoria, 2005). Consequently, many women choose to work part-time or not at all so they can attend to their families at home. Others telework from home, most commonly on a part-time basis. Indeed, Ruderman and Ohlott (2004) reported a higher turnover rate for women than male counterparts in executive positions with at least 10 years of experience.

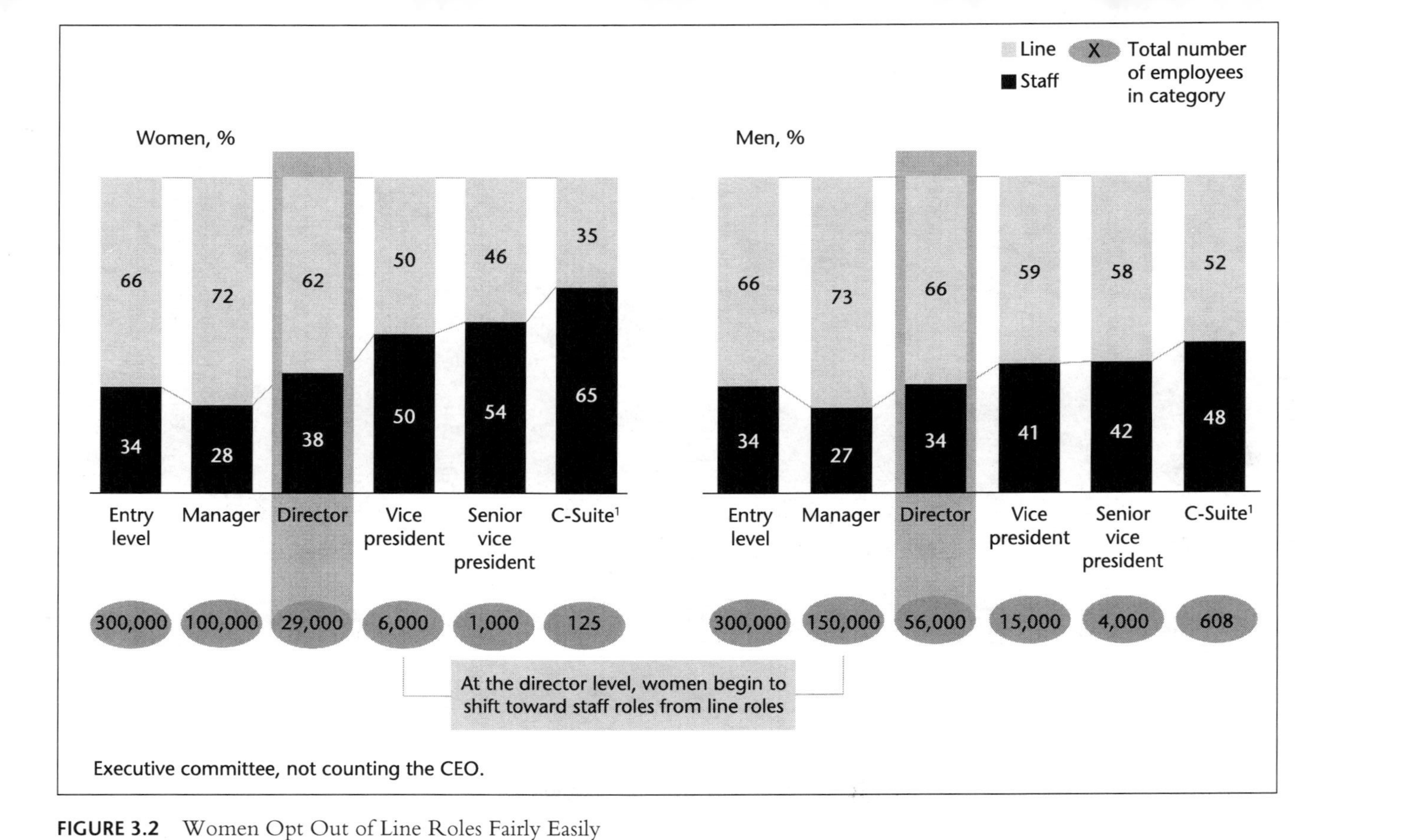

FIGURE 3.2 Women Opt Out of Line Roles Fairly Easily

Source: Barsh and Yee (2012, p. 6).

EXTREME WORK DEMANDS CAN DRUM WOMEN OUT

The extreme demands of many 24/7 work corporate environments today represent an impasse to many women who wish to prioritize life outside of work more highly. I've written before and believe this wholeheartedly – women are not less ambitious than men. It is the COST of ambition – and the struggle women face in pursuing their professional ambitions – that is at the heart of why we have so few women leaders today, and why women are achieving less and not reaching as high as men in corporate America. As Betsy Myers, President Clinton's senior adviser on women's issues shared with me recently, women tend to view their work as only one piece of the pie that represents their total life experience. If they're forced to focus 24/7 on work for a majority of their professional lives, most women will choose not to pay that price.

(Caprino, 2013)

The majority of women, nonetheless, plan to return to work after a certain period of "leave of absence" but even if the break is only for a few months it becomes difficult to continue the intended career path or climb the senior leadership ladder. So the continuity of career advancement becomes a crucial factor for reaching the top of the pyramid. Any interruptions in working life reduce the likelihood to reach the highest positions in a company. And companies, aiming at frictionless flow, facility, and optimization rather than accommodating talented women seem to stay on course. For example, one study found that only 4% of companies surveyed even attempted to put women on a growth path towards becoming CEO (Oakley, 2000). And much of the buzz about the appropriate ways for "opted out" women to re-enter the workforce is met with a tough reality. JP Morgan and its "Workforce Re-entry Program", which was launched in 2013, focused on recruiting out-of-work talent who once worked in financial services, but left the challenge of raising children or caring for the elderly to others. The program started with the asset management division and expanded to the legal and investment bank divisions in 2014 (Schonberger, 2015).

> Today, however, family happiness, relationships, and balancing life and work, along with community service and helping others, are much more on the minds of Generation X and Baby Boomers. When the researchers asked respondents to rate the importance of nine career and life dimensions, nearly 100%, regardless of gender, said that "quality of personal and family relationships" was "very" or "extremely" important . . . . Whereas about 50% to 60% of men across the three generations told the researchers they were "extremely satisfied" or "very satisfied" with their experiences of

> meaningful work, professional accomplishments, opportunities for career growth, and compatibility of work and personal life, only 40% to 50% of women were similarly satisfied on the same dimensions.
>
> *(Ely, Stone, & Ammerman, 2014)*

Some organizations, however, offer on-site daycare as well as flex-time where an employee can choose to work four days a week for 10 hours rather than five days a week for eight hours. The Johnson & Johnson (J&J) Finance Vice-President Kendall O'Brien stated:

> If J&J hadn't had on-site daycare, if I hadn't had a supervisor supportive of my working flexible hours, if I weren't part of an organization that's cognizant of the talent pipeline and that recognized I didn't want to leave, I wouldn't be here today.
>
> *(Spence, 2010, p. 5)*

Organizations must not only recognize the barriers that exist which prevent women from fully committing to work, but also offer support to help women balance their contradictory roles. Work–life integration and the willingness to relocate provide flexibility that can make women's talents and contributions both competitive and attractive for employers.

Diversity as a Source of Competitive Advantage

Inclusive leadership and participation of women on TMTs help boost companies' public image and reputation through support of social responsibility and philanthropic programs. They add value to the company with unique adaptability skills and are masters in creating positive work climates based on inclusion and diversity. Not only does greater diversity help the business—and possibly creates a competitive advantage—it also creates an actively engaged workplace culture, which typically indicates satisfied employees, a win–win situation (Baldoni, 2013). Women-friendly organizations typically have a stronger moral orientation and project more social sensitivity than other organizations, a necessary attribute for a socially accountable company's board. It is not that women and men compete in a zero-sum game—it is that women bring something new and different to the table for an organization. Understanding consumers' shopping habits and buying decisions is a good example. Women notoriously spend more time shopping and therefore purchase a greater amount of goods, whereas men tend to be more focused and just grab what they need and intended to purchase. Marketers need to focus on both genders but place more emphasis on women as

> women make more than 85% of the consumer purchases in the United States, and reputedly influence over 95% of total goods and services

purchased. Women as a whole are considered more sophisticated shoppers than men, taking longer to make a buying decision.

(Lewis, 2013)

Roy D. Adler, Professor of Marketing at Pepperdine University, conducted a comparative analysis involving the effects of women's presence on TMTs on firm performance. Data from Fortune 500 companies for the 1980 to 1998 period were collected to measure firm profits as a percentage of revenues, assets, and stockholders' equity (Adler, 2001). A fourth measure of profitability was used to determine whether each firm was higher or lower than its relevant industry median. These results showed a clear pattern. Fortune 500 firms with a high number of women executives outperformed their industry median firms on all three:

- On the measure of profits as a percentage of revenues, the subject firms outperformed the corresponding industry medians by 34%. The women-friendly firms averaged 6.4% while the average of their industry medians was 4.8%. When taken individually, almost two-thirds of the subject firms (66%) outperformed their median counterparts.
- On the measure of profits as a percentage of assets, the subject firms outperformed the industry medians by 18%. The women-friendly firms averaged 6.5% while the average of their industry medians was 5.5%. When taken individually, 62% of the subject firms outperformed their median counterparts.
- On the measure of profits as a percentage of stockholders' equity, the 25 firms outperformed the industry medians by 69%. The women-friendly firms averaged 26.5% while the average of their industry medians was 15.7%. When taken individually, 68% of the subject firms outperformed their median counterparts.

DIVERSITY A SOURCE OF COMPETITIVE ADVANTAGE

Vanessa Torres, Head of Group Investments and Value Management, BHP Billiton—Women in Energy and Resources Leadership Summit

At BHP Billiton, we are working very seriously in order to reduce the time we need to achieve an inclusive environment and an optimal diversity balance which will make our organization not only better in terms of our workforce satisfaction, but also more and more productive through time. And, at BHP Billiton, it starts with our CEO, Andrew Mackenzie, who named diversity and inclusion as one of the strategic priorities in his message that informs business planning for the whole organization. As one of our business priorities, this focus translates in initiatives such as:

1. Assessment of our own data to support the business case, as our 2013 Employee Perception Survey showed that increased inclusion correlates with increased performance;
2. Establishment of Inclusion and Diversity councils throughout our organization;
3. Deployment of unconscious bias training in large scale, which has already started with our Group Management Committee and will be ultimately delivered to all our leaders and employees;
4. Indigenous representation targets throughout our businesses;
5. Identifying qualified women in succession plans for key leadership roles as well as piloting senior executive female sponsorship program;
6. Company-wide female retention and recruitment targets for each financial year, including a focus on recruiting female Graduates;
7. And, finally, by establishing inclusion and diversity as KPIs in the scorecards of all leaders across the company.

Importantly, inclusion is one of the themes of our Leadership Development Program which will ultimately reach 10,000 leaders in BHP Billiton. By investing in our leadership, we will be creating more inclusive environments where our employees feel valued and heard.

(Torres, 2015)

Successful female executives who have gone through accelerated career choices also enjoyed the benefit of a sponsor, have the know-how to build relationships, and step outside their comfort zone to fuel their personal and professional growth. High-achiever women adapt better to the male environments in their executive circles and have the ability to overcome the extraordinary challenges of meeting a variety of expectations through endurance, sponsor relationships, and high stamina. They are perceived by their male counterparts as having high work ethics, relentless focus on performance and results, are resilient to change, and are persistent in getting constructive feedback for self-improvement. These women managers are inspirational, collaborative, and inclusive, highly competent, and very effective team leaders.

The "Asking Advantage"

Babcock and Laschever (2007), co-authors of *Women don't ask*, found that male graduate students starting out in their first job earn 7.6% or almost $4,000 more than female grads. It turned out that only 7% of the female students had negotiated their starting salaries as compared to 57% of men who had asked for more money than they were offered. The most striking finding, however, was that the students who had negotiated (most of them men) were able to increase their starting salaries by 7.4% on average—a figure nearly matching the gender gap between men and women's starting salaries. This has implications as to why and how the gender pay gap is created and sustained due to socio-psychological forces that reinforce gender differences. White female physicians, for example, earn 40% less than white men. Women also tend to assume they will be offered compensation that is fair for the job—an assumption that sabotages future attempts at negotiation (Ly, Seabury, & Jena, 2016). Changes, however, have begun to take shape as millennials are now asking for (and getting) more pay than men. Women in technology, sales, or marketing with two years' or less experience actually got salary offers that were 7% higher than those received by equally inexperienced men (Sahadi, 2016).

Girls are taught from early childhood to build relationship capital by focusing on what they need rather than what they're worth. Women are satisfied with relatively less pay. Both sexes subscribe to powerful stereotypes that keep women from asserting themselves—even if they repudiate the stereotype or feel immune to it. Women are more likely to experience barriers due to the masculinity of the negotiation process, which is not congruent with their authentic or prototypical behaviors. If they don't force their desired outcome, they'll be completely overlooked, and if they do, they'll be resented or even thwarted because they will be perceived as self-serving.

Women have traditionally adapted to such environments in a few different ways. One is "going along to get along," in which females play along with locker-room talk in particular and do not report it. Another is to become "more male" by shedding traditionally "female" attributes such as empathy. The problem is that once women adopt the going along to get along style, they lose their authenticity and prototyped behavior. As Caprino (2013) suggested: "Whole-self authenticity is a must-have for many women, yet still impossible in many corporate environments." The idea that authenticity and transparency, and being who women *really* are—and being recognized and appreciated for that—is a vitally important criterion for women's career success.

Consequently, women don't ask for what they want or feel they deserve because they're fearful they will not be liked, whereas men perceive asking as a useful means to achieve greater gains. This is what sociologists call "accumulation of disadvantage." The bottom line is that even if women were asking for comparable things and were equally successful at getting what they ask for, this simple difference in the "asking propensity" of men and women inevitably leads to men having more opportunities in accumulating more resources. The net result is a sustained gender pay gap. Behaviorally and cognitively, women must understand, at a very deep level, the forces that shape their beliefs, attitudes, and impulses. Simply telling women what they should do differently without helping them understand the root causes of their behavior will not help them achieve meaningful change.

Gender Gap in Executive Pay

Shin (2012) analyzed a sample of 7,711 executives (of which 6% were women and 94% men) employed by 831 publicly traded US firms from 1998 to 2005 examining the relationship between female representation in compensation committees, the presence of female CEOs, and the reduction of wage disparities. Findings included:

- In real dollar terms, men in the sample study were paid $1,443,607 (in 2000 dollars) on average, while women received $1,018,107 (in 2000 dollars) on average, or 42% less than men.
- Having a greater proportion of women on compensation committees was found to reduce inequality in salaries paid to women compared to their male counterparts. The increase in the representation of women was not correlated with any adverse impact on salaries paid to male executives.
- An overwhelming 81% of the firms in the sample had no female representation in their compensation committees, while only 10% of the firms had equal gender representation in compensation committees.
- Firms with one woman on the compensation committee experienced an average total compensation (including annual salary, bonuses, stock options, and other long-term incentive pay) increase for women by $302,000, up 34%. Adding another woman to the compensation committee was correlated with yet another 38% jump in salaries for women, to an overall average of $1,635,000. Firms with at least two women on compensation committees (which is usually comprised of four members) eliminated salary disparities altogether.
- Among top positions, females were more likely to hold lower-ranking positions of executive vice-president, senior vice-president, counsel, and secretary. Male executives typically landed the positions of CEO, chief operating officer (COO), president, and chairman.
- Overall, the presence of female CEOs was not associated with a reduction in wage discrimination faced by other women executives in the same company.

Why is there no strong linkage between the presence of female CEOs and executive compensation for women (Shin, 2012)? One explanation is associated with the limited active mentoring relationships. For top managers who need to juggle demanding job requirements and performance pressures, developing effective mentoring relationships may be a challenge. Some female executives might succumb to the *Queen Bee Syndrome* (see Chapter 1), relegating the need to act as a supportive mentor to other women. This syndrome places a woman executive in the strained position of wanting to integrate herself with her network of associates but at the same time feeling pressured to separate herself from her female colleagues at lower ranks (Knight, 2011). In some cases, isolation, marginalization, and vulnerability to judgment of others create complex chain of mutually reinforcing events that cause women to gradually and subconsciously become risk-averse, overly focused on details, and prone to micromanagement (Kanter, 1993; Kram & McCollom-Hampton, 1998). Eventually they lose sight of the larger purpose as leaders and are framed into existing or known stereotypes (Ely, Ibarra, & Kolb, 2011). Unfortunately, if women have to hide their own values and submit to organizational pressure to mold into current norms and practices, their motivation to remain with the organization for a long period of time is lessened (Ruderman & Ohlott, 2004).

The US EEOC[1]

The US EEOC is responsible for enforcing federal laws that make it illegal to discriminate against a job applicant or an employee because of the person's race, color, religion, sex (including pregnancy), national origin, age (40 or older), disability, or genetic information. It is also illegal to discriminate against a person because the person complained about discrimination, filed a charge of discrimination, or participated in an employment discrimination investigation or lawsuit. Most employers with at least 15 employees are covered by EEOC laws (20 employees in age-discrimination cases). Most labor unions and employment agencies are also covered.

The laws and regulations apply to all types of work situations, including hiring, firing, promotions, harassment, training, wages, and benefits. The EEOC has the authority to investigate charges of discrimination against employers who are covered by the law. The Commission's role in an investigation is to fairly and accurately assess the allegations in the charge and then make a finding. If it finds that discrimination has occurred, the Commission will try to settle the charge.[2] If unsuccessful, EEOC has the legal authority to use its judgment and in some cases file a lawsuit to protect the rights of individuals and the interests of the public. The EEOC, however, works to prevent discrimination before it occurs through outreach, education, and technical assistance programs.

The EEOC provides leadership and guidance to federal agencies on all aspects of the federal government's EEO program.[3] EEOC assures federal agency and department compliance with EEOC regulations, provides technical assistance to federal agencies concerning EEO complaint adjudication, monitors and evaluates federal agencies' affirmative employment programs, develops and distributes federal sector educational materials and conducts training for stakeholders, provides guidance and assistance to Administrative Judges who conduct hearings on EEO complaints, and adjudicates appeals from administrative decisions made by federal agencies on EEO complaints.

COMMENT SUBMITTED IN PROFESSOR BELASEN'S CLASS, FALL 2015

In my previous employment, there was one department that notoriously poached/hired friends they had worked with in other organizations—they all looked alike, thought alike, behaved alike, etc. As HR [human resources], my role was not to make the actual selection; rather, it was to ensure the applicants forwarded to the hiring manager met the minimum requirements for the job. However, once I noticed the pattern (during the third hiring process), I started forwarding blind resumes (i.e., redacting all names/addresses/phone numbers—anything that would directly identify a candidate—I would even redact and categorize current and/or previous employer names—i.e., multinational Fortune 500 company, local non-profit organization, state-level government agency, etc.) so that the hiring manager could only compare applicants based on the qualifications listed on the resume. Certainly, this was not fool-proof, and categorizing the current/previous employer names was a bit drastic, but given the circumstances, it helped level the playing field for all applicants and minimized the risk of wrongful hire or other discrimination-based lawsuits. For standard external hires (or even first round internal promotions), organizations could use blind resumes to help initially level the playing field for all applicants. Once it goes to the interview round(s), it may or may not change the end result, but at least the qualified applicants have a fighting chance.

Inconsequential Enforcement of Equality Laws

Some concerns about the inability of the EEOC to fulfill its mission of handling employment discrimination complaints due to limited resources and inadequate budget were raised in 2001 and again a decade later. While EEOC developed a priority system in 1995 to facilitate the processing of cases, the huge backlog of unresolved complaints were piling up with extraordinary variation across offices in categorization practices and outcomes in resolving cases (Moss, Burris, Ullman, Johnsen & Swanson, 2001). A decade later, in 2011, the problem of unfunded mandate has continued to limit the EEOC ability to provide adequate resolutions to claims. In fact, the Evaluation of the Management of the EEOC's State and Local Programs (EEOC, 2011) showed clearly that from 2000–2008, as a result of declining appropriation levels and hiring freezes, EEOC lost approximately 25% of its full-time employees and its case backlog increased.

The evaluator concluded that

> EEOC has not established any performance goals or objectives related to the Fair Employment Practices Agencies (FEPA) performance. Without any performance goals and objectives, the EEOC is not holding itself accountable for achieving program results. We recommend that management develop and implement strategic performance goals and objectives that are reflective of the program; are measurable and in accordance with the requirements of Government Performance and Results Act; and that the goals and objectives are included in the annual performance and accountability report.[4]

CENSUS BUREAU

Mom Is Designated "Parent," Dad Is "Childcare Arrangement"

In a move that should frustrate advocates, mothers and fathers alike, the Census Bureau's recently compiled "Who's Minding the Kids?" report counts fathers staying home with their children as a "child care arrangement." This puts fathers looking after their children—or what most people call *parenting*—in the same category as a working mother hiring a babysitter or sending her kids to day-care.

(Women's Law Project, 2012)

Employers' Common Mistakes

During the Annual Meeting of the American Corporate Counsel Association in fall 2002, in her speech, EEOC Chair Cari Dominguez placed some of the burden of nonconformance issues on "judgment lapses" or common mistakes made by employers when dealing with EEOC regulations. She also offered ways to minimize conflict with EEOC (Dawson, n.d.; Shea, 2003):

- *Employers underestimate EEOC.* Many employers and their counsel underestimate the competence and professionalism of the EEOC staff primarily to preconceived notions of a pro-employee bias by the Commission. Dominguez suggested that employers become prepared and stay out of EEOC's line of vision by playing fair and having a respectful work environment.
- *Employers do not communicate.* Many employers and their attorneys fail to stay in touch with the EEOC while an investigation is taking place. Once the complaint has been initiated, the employer has the burden to show actions were nondiscriminatory. Proactive communication with the EEOC

investigator builds credibility for the company and for the attorney who represents it.

- *Employers are dismissive.* Apparently, too many on the employer's side assume that the EEOC will not litigate due to shortage of resources. Although litigation (rather than a dismissal and notice of rights) is definitely the exception, the EEOC has been known to go to court—especially when class relief is possible. The EEOC is generally a hard-working and effective adversary for any employer when they believe discrimination exists.
- *Employers retaliate.* Retaliation charges count for about 28% of all of EEOC's charges. Even if the original charge is unfounded, the employer could still be found guilty of retaliation discrimination.
- *Employers avoid mediation.* Employers tend to believe that EEOC mediators would not give them a fair shake. In many cases, the mediators are generally quite fair and savvy and have facilitated very economical resolutions for companies. Not every case is suitable for mediation, but more cases are mediation worthy. Passing up mediation, when offered, can suggest that you have no intention of resolution or to even listen to the employee(s).
- *Employers wait.* Employers employ delay tactics in an attempt to weaken the EEOC. Employers should realize that once an employee files a charge, the statute of limitations on the federal antidiscrimination claims stops running until the EEOC disposes of the case. If found guilty, the liability, e.g., back pay, continues to accrue until the case is closed.
- *Employers act inappropriately.* Employers do not always take corrective action when problems arise, and without an effective EEO policy and procedures to process EEO complaints of discrimination they fail to take proactive or preventive approaches to tackle discrimination issues. When EEO procedures are implemented and followed consequentially, they also help develop a good culture and expected norms of behaviors.
- *Employers prevaricate.* To the extent that employers provide non-coercive advance preparation for their employees before EEOC interviews, or obtain legal representation before responding to charges, this is all perfectly legitimate and more than fair. However, employers who try to improperly conceal witnesses or evidence, falsify documents, threaten potentially adverse witnesses with discipline or discharge (or blacklisting), lie to the EEOC, or engage in other improper activity should watch it—they are hurting no one but themselves. Things will only get worse when employers are not open and honest with the EEOC.
- *Employers do not calibrate.* Employers often fail to monitor the demographics of employment activity or enforcement of EEO procedures. This is the EEOC's top complaint. Many employers are not proactive with EEO laws, waiting until the risk becomes the problem. If you are a medium to large employer (over 50 employees), keep EEO and harassment policies up to date; have good processes in place for employees to complain if they believe that

they have been treated unfairly; and provide effective management training on employee relations, discipline and discharge, discrimination, reasonable accommodation, retaliation, and harassment. It is also advisable to monitor legal actions filed against the company (including lawsuits and administrative charges), even if frivolous, because heavy activity may indicate serious morale or perception issues if not bona fide discrimination issues.

TOP FEMALE PLAYERS ACCUSE US SOCCER OF WAGE DISCRIMINATION

US Soccer, the governing body for the sport in America, pays the members of the men's and women's national teams who represent the United States in international competitions. The men's team has historically been mediocre. The women's team has been a quadrennial phenomenon, winning world and Olympic championships and bringing much of the country to a standstill in the process.

Citing this disparity, as well as rising revenue numbers, five players on the women's team filed a federal complaint . . . accusing US Soccer of wage discrimination because, they said, they earned as little as 40% of what players on the United States men's national team earned even as they marched to the team's third World Cup championship last year. The five players, some of the world's most prominent women's athletes, said they were being shortchanged on everything from bonuses to appearance fees to per diems.

The case, submitted to the *Equal Employment Opportunity Commission*, the federal agency that enforces civil rights laws against workplace discrimination, is the latest front in the spreading debate over equal treatment of female athletes. A tennis tournament director was forced to resign recently after saying that female players "ride on the coattails of the men," and the N.C.A.A. has drawn scrutiny for the financial disparities between the men's and women's basketball tournaments.

(Das, 2016)

Best Practices for Employers and Human Resources/EEO Professionals

The following propositions and means to avert inequality, encourage diversity, and reinforce equity and civility in organizations are offered on the EEOC site.[5]

General

- Train human resources managers and all employees on EEO laws. Implement a strong EEO policy that is embraced at the top levels of the organization.

Train managers, supervisors, and employees on its contents, enforce it, and hold them accountable.

- Promote an inclusive culture in the workplace by fostering an environment of professionalism and respect for personal differences.
- Foster open communication and early dispute resolution. This may minimize the chance of misunderstandings escalating into legally actionable EEO problems. An alternative dispute-resolution program can help resolve EEO problems without the acrimony associated with an adversarial process.
- Establish neutral and objective criteria to avoid subjective employment decisions based on personal stereotypes or hidden biases.

Recruitment, Hiring, and Promotion

- Recruit, hire, and promote with EEO principles in mind, by implementing practices designed to widen and diversify the pool of candidates considered for employment openings, including openings in upper-level management.
- Monitor for EEO compliance by conducting self-analyses to determine whether current employment practices disadvantage people of color, treat them differently, or leave uncorrected the effects of historical discrimination in the company.
- Analyze the duties, functions, and competencies relevant to jobs. Then create objective, job-related qualification standards related to those duties, functions, and competencies. Make sure they are consistently applied when choosing among candidates.
- Ensure selection criteria do not disproportionately exclude certain racial groups unless the criteria are valid predictors of successful job performance and meet the employer's business needs. For example, if educational requirements disproportionately exclude certain minority or racial groups, they may be illegal if not important for job performance or business needs.
- Make sure promotion criteria are made known, and that job openings are communicated to all eligible employees.
- When using an outside agency for recruitment, make sure the agency does not search for candidates of a particular race or color. Both the employer that made the request and the employment agency that honored it would be liable.

Terms, Conditions, and Privileges of Employment

- Monitor compensation practices and performance appraisal systems for patterns of potential discrimination. Make sure performance appraisals are based on employees' actual job performance. Ensure consistency, i.e., that comparable job performances receive comparable ratings regardless of the evaluator, and that appraisals are neither artificially low nor artificially high.

- Develop the potential of employees, supervisors, and managers with EEO in mind, by providing training and mentoring that provides workers of all backgrounds the opportunity, skill, experience, and information necessary to perform well, and to ascend to upper-level jobs. In addition, employees of all backgrounds should have equal access to workplace networks.
- Protect against retaliation. Provide clear and credible assurances that if employees make complaints or provide information related to complaints, the employer will protect employees from retaliation, and consistently follow through on this guarantee.

Harassment

- Adopt a strong anti-harassment policy, periodically train each employee on its contents, and vigorously follow and enforce it.
- Develop a clear explanation of prohibited conduct, including examples.
- Have a clear assurance that employees who make complaints or provide information related to complaints will be protected against retaliation.
- Articulate clearly the complaint process that provides multiple, accessible avenues of complaint.
- Provide assurances that the employer will protect the confidentiality of harassment complaints to the extent possible.
- Have a complaint process that provides a prompt, thorough, and impartial investigation.
- Ensure that the employer will take immediate and appropriate corrective action when it determines that harassment has occurred.

MAVIS DISCOUNT TIRE TO PAY $2.1 MILLION TO SETTLE EEOC CLASS SEX DISCRIMINATION LAWSUIT

Tire Retailer Violated Federal Law by Systemically Refusing to Hire Women in Its Field Locations, Federal Agency Charged

Mavis Discount Tire, Inc./Mavis Tire Supply Corp./Mavis Tire NY, Inc./Cole Muffler, Inc., a large tire retailer based in the New York metropolitan area, will pay $2.1 million and provide other relief to settle a class sex discrimination lawsuit by the U.S. Equal Employment Opportunity Commission (EEOC), the agency announced today.

According to EEOC's lawsuit, Mavis engaged in a pattern or practice of sex discrimination by refusing to hire women for its field positions—managers, assistant managers, mechanics, and tire technicians—in the company's over 140 stores throughout Connecticut, Massachusetts, New York, and Pennsylvania. EEOC also charged that Mavis failed to make, keep, and preserve employment records.

Such alleged conduct violates Title VII of the Civil Rights Act of 1964. EEOC filed its lawsuit in U.S. District Court for the Southern District of New York (Case No. 12-CV-00741) after first attempting to reach a pre-litigation settlement through its conciliation process.

The consent decree settling the suit, entered by Judge Katherine P. Failla on March 24, 2016, provides that Mavis will pay $2.1 million, to be divided among 46 aggrieved women. Also, the decree provides for extensive safeguards to prevent future discrimination by implementing hiring goals for women, a comprehensive recruitment and hiring protocol, and anti-discrimination policies and training. "We are pleased that as a result of this settlement, Mavis will be making concerted, verifiable efforts to hire more women at all of its field locations," EEOC Acting Regional Attorney Raechel Adams said.

EEOC New York District Director Kevin Berry added,

> This case exemplifies EEOC's commitment to remedying systemic bias. EEOC found that Mavis for years had maintained a pattern of not hiring women at its field locations. This settlement ensures that qualified women will continue to be hired in the future – and advances EEOC's first priority in its Strategic Enforcement Plan, eliminating barriers in recruitment and hiring.

EEOC General Counsel David Lopez said:

> We are pleased that during Women's History Month, we were able to announce this settlement, which is one in a series of EEOC cases nationally to address discriminatory barriers for women. Moving forward, qualified female applicants will be judged by their talents and skill and not simply passed over because of their gender – and women who were denied positions will be compensated.

The elimination of recruiting and hiring practices that discriminate against women, racial, ethnic and religious groups, older workers, and people with disabilities is one of six national priorities identified by EEOC's Strategic Enforcement Plan (SEP).

EEOC's New York District Office oversees New York, Connecticut, Maine, Vermont, New Hampshire, Massachusetts, Rhode Island, and parts of New Jersey. EEOC enforces federal laws prohibiting employment discrimination.

(EEOC, 2016)

Fair Pay Act

In a 2010 World Economic Forum report on corporate practices for gender diversity in 20 countries, 15% of the total set of responding companies track salary gaps between women and men, 13% track salary gaps between women and men and implement corrective measures, 54% do not track salary gaps and affirm that generally there are no gaps between male and female employees' salaries in their companies, and, finally, 18% of the companies responded that they do not formally track salary gaps. Hence, 72% of the companies surveyed do not monitor gender pay gaps at all. The complete results are displayed in Figure 3.3.

In January 2016, President Obama renewed his call to Congress to pass the Paycheck Fairness Act, which would potentially close loopholes in the Equal Pay Act of 1963 and require employers to prove that pay gaps are due to legitimate business reasons, not discrimination. The proposal would cover more than 63 million employees—potentially providing a new wealth of data for understanding the pay gap issue and determining whether certain workers are getting short-changed (Ortiz, 2016).

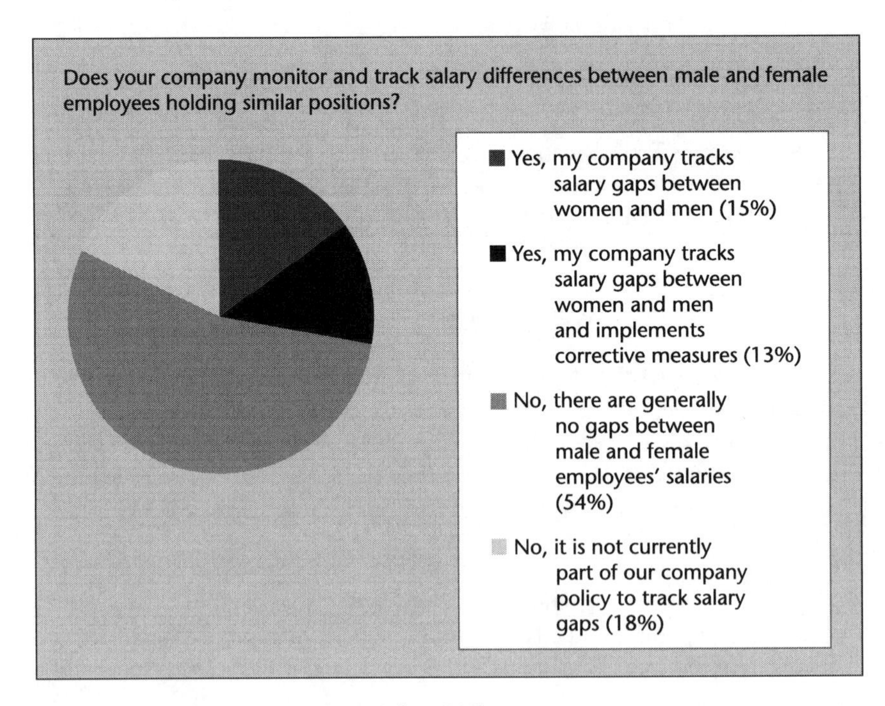

FIGURE 3.3 Policies on Tracking Salary Differences

Source: Zahidi & Ibarra (2010).

OBAMA MOVES TO EXPAND RULES AIMED AT CLOSING GENDER PAY GAP

President Obama on Friday moved to require companies to report to the federal government what they pay employees by race, gender and ethnicity, part of his push to crack down on firms that pay women less for doing the same work as men.

"Women are not getting the fair shot that we believe every single American deserves," Mr. Obama said in announcing the proposal, timed to coincide with the seventh anniversary of his signing of the Lilly Ledbetter Fair Pay Act, which makes it easier for people to challenge discriminatory pay. "What kind of example does paying women less set for our sons and daughters?"

The new rules, Mr. Obama's latest bid to use his executive power to address a priority of his that Congress has resisted acting on, would mandate *that companies with 100 employees or more include salary information on a form they already submit annually* that reports employees' sex, age and job groups.

"Too often, pay discrimination goes undetected because of a lack of accurate information about what people are paid," said Jenny Yang, the chairwoman of the Equal Employment Opportunity Commission, which will publish the proposed regulation jointly with the Department of Labor. "We will be using the information that we're collecting as one piece of information that can inform our investigations."

The requirement would expand on an executive order Mr. Obama issued[6] nearly two years ago that called for federal contractors to submit salary information for women and men. Ms. Yang said the rules would be completed in September, with the first reports due a year later.

(Hirschfeld, 2016)

Linking Diversity with Performance and Rewards

Organizations must undergo a fundamental change in the hiring, evaluation, selection, and promotion policies and criteria used to fill top leadership positions. They need to reassess their missions and core values and remove barriers that limit or inhibit women's access to upper-level positions. Even a small increase in the percentage of female managers is expected to contribute to the implementation of successful practices, such as participative decision making, equity, and transparent communications. Furthermore, research shows that employee participation in decision making is positively correlated with superior organizational performance (Fernie & Metcalf, 1995) as also evident in the fact that many decisions in organizations are made by groups, teams, or committees (Foote, Matson, Weiss, & Wenger, 2002). If women have preferences for specific leadership styles (i.e., democratic) that contribute to effective decisions (and outcomes), the likelihood that such styles and practices (i.e., involvement, interpersonal orientation) will become prevalent across organizational lines could also increase.

Women leaders have the capacity to be more balanced and seek out win–win solutions in their decision making. They examine causes and consequences of decisions and their potential impact on affected employees, customers, and shareholders. This big-picture thinking may help women deal more successfully with ambiguity in business (Coughlin, Wingard, & Hollihan, 2005). It is unlikely that a woman will consciously go through a logical decision making sequence to select the best option (Belasen & Frank, 2008). Instead, women, on the one hand, tend to look at details to create a bigger, more holistic picture of a situation before making a decision. Men, on the other hand, tend to gather as much information as women, but analyze it in a more linear path. Indeed, women scored higher on traits associated with conscientiousness (Belasen & Frank, 2012). Women were found to be better suited for leadership than their male colleagues when it comes to clarity, innovation, support, and targeted meticulousness (Øyvind & Glasø, 2013).

Melero (2011) found that workplaces with a higher percentage of female managers tend to allocate more time to group decision making processes and to giving and receiving feedback. In fact, Cook and Glass (2014) suggested that the integration of women into decision making roles reduces both the impact of male-to-female evaluation bias and the inclination for men to prefer hiring other men (Carrington & Troske, 1995; Cohen, Broschak, & Haveman, 1998; Ely, 1995). Managers are also more open to improving the collective performance and discussing career development opportunities with employees. When organizations include women in their management teams, they should expect above the average performance. Prejudices against female managers are also expected to become less pervasive, and the perception of tokens by peers and superiors when women participate in decision making will lessen.

Tokenism, on the one hand, is a phenomenon that leads to the informal isolation of minority members who, in turn, respond by keeping low profiles. On the other hand, participative decision making is inclusive and generates more discussions and options for solving problems as well as increases diversity and acceptance of viewpoints. Linking diversity goals with performance goals and financial incentives should be formalized through human-resources policies and reinforced through senior management commitment (Giscombe & Mattis, 2002). For example, Sodexo USA has developed a diversity scorecard (Anand, 2014) that links the human-resources cycle (i.e., recruitment, retention, development, promotion) with diversity and engagement goals, business goals, and strategies (Dolezalek, 2008). Senior executives must communicate the message that gender diversity is a business imperative and actively model the way through decisions and actions. Senior executives should also encourage performance dialogues, invest in women's leadership development, and use evidence-based discussions to spearhead best practices that drive success. Establishing a leadership priority for change has been the most successful of all diversity initiatives (Kalev, Dobbin, & Kelly, 2006). Gender diversity should become the new organizational mantra, the DNA of successful organizations.

Notes

1 Adapted from: www.eeoc.gov/eeoc/index.cfm.
2 www.eeoc.gov/federal/adr/resolvehandbook.cfm.
3 www.eeoc.gov/federal/fed_employees/faq_hearing.cfm.
4 www1.eeoc.gov//eeoc/oig/2010-09-aep.cfm?renderforprint=1.
5 www.eeoc.gov/eeoc/initiatives/e-race/bestpractices-employers.cfm.
6 President Obama signs a new Executive Order to prevent workplace discrimination and empower workers to take control over negotiations regarding their pay, www.whitehouse.gov/blog/2014/04/08/taking-action-honor-national-equal-pay-day.

References

Adler, R. D. (2001). Women in the executive suite correlate to high profits. *Harvard Business Review, 79*(3), 30–32. Retrieved from www.researchgate.net/publication/267822127.

Anand, R. (2014). Diversity and inclusion, a strategic business imperative: The Sodexo story. *Sodexo Quality of Life Services*. Retrieved from www.desmoinesmetro.com/documents/filelibrary/webinars/20141119_DIForum_Sodexo_5CC76947E7958.pdf.

Babcock, L., & Laschever, S. (2007). *Women don't ask: The high cost of avoiding negotiation and positive strategies for change*. New York: Bantam Books.

Baldoni, J. (2013, July 4). Employee engagement does more than boost productivity. *Harvard Business Review*. Retrieved from https://hbr.org/2013/07/employee-engagement-does-more/.

Barsh, J., & Yee, L. (2012). Unlocking the full potential of women at work. *McKinsey & Company*. Retrieved from www.mckinsey.com/business-functions/organization/our-insights/unlocking-the-full-potential-of-women-at-work.

Beale, Frances M. (1970). *Double jeopardy: To be black and female*. New York, NY: Washington Square Press. Retrieved from http://intellhisblackamerica.voices.wooster.edu/files/2012/03/Frances-Beale_Double-Jeopardy-To-Be-Black-and-Female1.pdf.

Belasen, A. T. (2012). *Developing women leaders in corporate America, balancing competing demands, transcending traditional boundaries*. Santa Barbara, CA: Praeger Publishing.

Belasen, A. T., & Frank, N. M. (2008). Competing values leadership: Quadrant roles and personality traits. *Leadership and Organizational Development Journal, 29*(2), 127–143.

Belasen, A. T., & Frank, N. M. (2012). Using the competing values framework to evaluate the interactive effects of gender and personality traits on leadership roles. *The International Journal of Leadership Studies*, 7(2), 192–215.

Black Enterprise. (2013, September 6). *Black enterprise releases exclusive report on African American corporate directors*. Retrieved from www.blackenterprise.com/news/report-black-corporate-directors-study-boardrooms/.

Caprino, K. (2013, February 12). The top 6 reasons women are not leading in corporate America as we need them to. *Forbes/Leadership*. Retrieved from www.forbes.com/sites/kathycaprino/2013/02/12/the-top-6-reasons-women-are-not-leading-in-corporate-america-as-we-need-them-to/#20ba413e6d6d.

Carnes, W. J., & Radojevich-Kelley, N. (2011). The effects of the glass ceiling on women in the workforce: Where are they and where are they going? *Review of Management Innovation & Creativity*, *4*(10), 70–79.

Carrington, W., & Troske, K. (1995). The gender segregation in small firms. *Journal of Human Resources*, *30*, 503–533.

Catalyst. (2011). *No news is bad news: Women's leadership still stalled in corporate America* [News and announcements]. New York, NY: Catalyst. Retrieved from www.catalyst.org/media/no-news-bad-news-womens-leadership-still-stalled-corporate-america.

Cohen, L., Broschak, J., & Haveman, H. (1998). And then there were more? The effect of organizational sex composition on the hiring and promotion of managers. *American Sociological Review*, *63*, 711–727.

Cook, A., & Glass, C. (2014). Women and top leadership positions: Towards an institutional analysis. *Gender, Work and Organization*, *21*(1), 91–103. DOI:10.1111/gwao.12018

Coughlin, L., Wingard, E., & Hollihan, K. (2005). *Enlightened power: How women are transforming the practice of leadership*. San Francisco: Jossey-Bass.

Das, A. (2016, March 31). Top female players accuse US soccer of wage discrimination. *The New York Times*. Retrieved from www.nytimes.com/2016/04/01/sports/soccer/uswnt-us-women-carli-lloyd-alex-morgan-hope-solo-complain.html.

Dawson, C. A. (n.d.). EEOC tales of top mistakes made by employers: Have you felt the power of Uncle Sam's Equal Employment Opportunity Commission (EEOC)? Retrieved from www.multiculturaladvantage.com/recruit/eeo-employment-law/EEOC-Tales-of-Top-Mistakes-Made-by-Employers.asp.

Dolezalek, H. (2008). The path to inclusion. *Training*, *45*(4), 52–54.

Eagly, A. H., & Carli, L. L. (2007). *Through the labyrinth: The truth about how women become leaders*. Cambridge, MA: Harvard Press.

EEOC. (2011, March 10). *Evaluation of the management of the EEOC's state and local programs project number 2010-09-AEP final evaluation report*. Williams, Adley & Company-DC, LLP. Retrieved from www1.eeoc.gov/eeoc/oig/2010-09-aep.cfm?renderforprint=1.

EEOC. (2016, March 25). Mavis Discount Tire to pay $2.1 million to settle EEOC class sex discrimination lawsuit. US EEOC [Press release]. Retrieved from www.eeoc.gov/eeoc/newsroom/release/3-25-16.cfm.

Ely, R. (1995). The power in demography: Women's social constructions of gender identity at work. *Academy of Management Journal*, *38*, 589–634.

Ely, R. J., Ibarra, H., & Kolb, D. M. (2011). Taking gender into account: Theory and design for women's leadership development programs. *Academy of Management Learning & Education*, *10*(3), 474–493.

Ely, R., Stone, P., & Ammerman, C. (2014). Rethink what you "know" about high-achieving women, R1412G. *Harvard Business Review*, *92*(12), 101–109.

Feminist Majority Foundation. (2014). *Empowering women in business: The glass ceiling: How women are blocked from getting to the top*. Retrieved from www.feminist.org/research/business/ewb_glass.html.

Fernie, S., & Metcalf, D. (1995). Participation, contingent pay, representation and workplace performance: Evidence from Great Britain. *Britain Journal of Industrial Relations, 33*(3), 379–415.

Foote, N., Matson, E., Weiss, L., & Wenger, E. (2002). Leveraging group knowledge for high-performance decision making. *Organizational Dynamics, 31*(2), 280–295.

Giscombe, K., & Mattis, M. (2002). Leveling the playing field for women of color in corporate management: Is the business case enough? *Journal of Business Ethics, 37*(1), 103–119.

Google. (2013). EEO-1 report to the Equal Employment Opportunity Commission. Retrieved from http://static.googleusercontent.com/media/www.google.com/en//diversity/2013-EEO-1-consolidated-report.pdf.

Halter, J. T. (2015, June 26). Women in the workplace: If women don't stand-up for themselves, who will? *Huffington Post*. Retrieved from www.huffingtonpost.com/jeffery-tobias-halter/women-in-the-workplace-if-women-dont-stand-up-for-themselves-who-will_b_7656612.html.

Herminia, I., Carter, N., & Silva, C. (2010). Why men still get more promotions than women. *Harvard Business Review*, https://hbr.org/2010/09/why-men-still-get-more-promotions-than-women.

Hirschfeld, J. (2016, January 29). Obama moves to expand rules aimed at closing gender pay gap. *The New York Times*. Retrieved from www.nytimes.com/2016/01/29/us/politics/obama-moves-to-expand-rules-aimed-at-closing-gender-pay-gap.html?_r=0.

Kalev, A., Dobbin, F., & Kelly, E. (2006). Best practices or best guesses? Assessing the efficacy of corporate affirmative action and diversity policies. *American Sociological Review, 71*(4), 589–617.

Kanter, R. (1993). *Men and women of the corporation*. New York: Basics Press.

Knight, R. (2011). Queen bee in the office: Who gets stung? http://blogs.ft.com/women-at-the-top/2011/06/27/queen-bee-in-the-office-who-gets-stung/#axzz1wFoZTOae.

Kram, K., & McCollom-Hampton, M. (1998). When women lead: The visibility-vulnerability spiral. In E. Klein, F. Gabelnick, & P. Herr (Eds.), *The psychodynamics of leadership* (pp. 193–218). Madison, CT: Psychosocial Publishing Group.

Kurtulus, F. A., & Tomaskovic-Devey, D. (2012). Do female top managers help women to advance? A panel study using EEO-1 records. *The ANNALS of the American Academy of Political and Social Science, 639*, 173–197.

Lewis, M. (2013). Men vs. women: Differences in shopping habits and buying decisions. *Money Crashers*. Retrieved from www.moneycrashers.com/men-vs-women-shopping-habits-buying-decisions/.

Ly, D. P., Seabury, S. A., & Jena, A. B. (2016). Differences in incomes of physicians in the United States by race and sex: Observational study. *British Medical Journal, 353*, i2923. Retrieved from www.bmj.com/content/353/bmj.i2923.full.

Lyness, K. S., & Thompson, D. E. (2000). Climbing the corporate ladder: Do female and male executives follow the same route? *Journal of Applied Psychology, 85*, 86–101.

McEldowney, R. P., Bobrowski, P., & Gramberg, A. (2009). Factors affecting the next generation of women leaders: Mapping the challenges, antecedents, and consequences of effective leadership. *Journal of Leadership Studies*, 3(2): 24–30.

Mainiero, L. A., & Sullivan, S. E. (2006). *The opt-out revolt: Why people are leaving companies to create kaleidoscope careers*. Mountain View, CA: Davies-Black Publishing.

Melero, E. (2011). Are workplaces with many women in management run differently? *Journal of Business Research*, *64*, 385–393.

Moss, K., Burris, S., Ullman, M., Johnsen, M., & Swanson, J. (2001). Unfunded mandate: An empirical study of the implementation of the Americans with Disabilities Act by the Equal Employment Opportunity Commission. *University of Kansas Law Review*, *50*, 1–110.

O'Neil, D. A., & Bilimoria, D. (2005). Women's career development phases: Idealism, endurance, and reinvention. *Career Development International*, *10*, 168–189.

Oakley, J. G. (2000). Gender-based barriers to senior management positions: Understanding the scarcity of female CEOs. *Journal of Business Ethics*, *27*(4), 321–334.

Ortiz, E. (2016, January 29). President Obama announces rules for closing gender pay gap. *NBC News*. Retrieved from www.nbcnews.com/news/us-news/obama-announce-new-rules-closing-gender-pay-gap-n506941.

Øyvind, M., & Glasø, L. (2013). Character and leadership. In R. Rønning, W. Brochs-Haukedal, L. Glasø, & S. B. Matthiesen (Eds.), *Life as a leader. Lederundersøkelsen 3.0* (pp. 47–72). Fagbokforlaget: Bergen.

Pew Research Center. (2008). Men or women: Who's the better leader? A paradox in public attitudes. Retrieved from http://pewsocialtrends.org/2008/08/25/men-or-women-whos-the-better-leader/.

Ruderman, M. N., & Ohlott, P. J. (2004). What women leaders want? *Leader to Leader*, 41–47.

Sahadi, J. (2016, April 12). Young women are asking for (and getting) more pay than men. *CNN Money*. Retrieved from http://money.cnn.com/2016/04/12/pf/gender-pay-gap/index.html.

Sarsons, H. (2015, December 3). Gender differences in recognition for group work. (No. 254946). Retrieved from http://scholar.harvard.edu/files/sarsons/files/gender_groupwork.pdf?m=1449178759.

Schonberger, J. (2015, January 12). JPMorgan helps women re-enter the workforce. *FOXBusiness, Career*. Retrieved from www.foxbusiness.com/features/2015/01/12/jpmorgan-helps-women-re-enter-workforce.html.

Shea, R. E. (2003). Agency identifies top mistakes made by employers the EEOC's "notorious nine." *Labor & Employment Insights*, Winter/Spring. Retrieved from www.constangy.com/communications-69.html#agency.

Shellenbarger, S. (2012, May 7). The XX factor: What's holding women back? *The Wall Street Journal* [Women in the Economy: The Journal Report]. Retrieved from: www.womeninecon.wsj.com/special-report-2012.pdf.

Shin, T. (2012). The gender gap in executive compensation: The role of female directors and chief executive officers. *The ANNALS of the American Academy of Political and Social Science*, *639*(1), 258–278.

Spence, B. (2010). 2010 NAFE top 50 companies. *NAFE Magazine*, *33*(1), 4–14.

Timberlake, S. (2005). Social capital and gender in the workplace. *Journal of Management Development*, *24*, 34–44.

Torres, V. (2015, April 22). *Diversity a source of competitive advantage*. Presented at the Women in Energy and Resources Leadership Summit, Perth, Australia.

Women in the Economy, The Journal Report. (2011, April 11). A blueprint for change. *The Wall Street Journal* [Special report]. Retrieved from www.womeninecon.wsj.com/special-report.pdf.

Women's Law Project. (2012, February 17). Census bureau: Mom is designated "parent," dad is "childcare arrangement." Retrieved from https://womenslawproject.wordpress.com/2012/02/17/census-bureau-mom-is-designated-parent-dad-is-childcare-arrangement/.

Zahidi, S., & Ibarra, H. (2010). The corporate gender gap report 2010. World Economic Forum. Geneva, Switzerland. Retrieved from www3.weforum.org/docs/WEF_GenderGap_CorporateReport_2010.pdf.

4

CRACKING THE GLASS CEILING

Gender Differences and Similarities

The literature on women and leadership often seeks to identify unique attributes that distinguish between the styles of men and women performing leadership roles. A common view is that gender leadership styles reflect the power differentials seen in society as a whole (Fine, 2007; Fine & Buzzanell, 2000) and that masculine qualities, such as task focus, assertiveness, authoritativeness, and lack of emotionality, more so than communal qualities, appear synonymous with leadership within North American and European cultures (Izraeli & Adler, 1994; Schein, 2001). Evolutionary psychology postulates that human behavior is flexible due to the large number of contextual and psychological adaptations that shape human behavior. The mind is viewed as an integrated collection of cognitive mechanisms or evolved adaptations that affect and guide human behavior.

> Women and men are expected to differ in domains in which they have faced recurrently different adaptive problems over human evolutionary history. They are expected to be similar in all domains in which they have faced similar adaptive problems over human evolutionary history.
>
> *(Buss & Schmitt, 2011, p. 770)*

Evolutionary psychology research generally supports the claim that males are more dominant and competitive than women and naturally they are more likely to obtain positions of power.

MEN AND WOMEN: NO BIG DIFFERENCE

Hyde observed that across the dozens of studies, consistent with the gender similarities hypothesis, gender differences had either no or a very small effect on most of the psychological variables examined.

Hyde found that gender differences seem to depend on the context in which they were measured. In studies designed to eliminate gender norms, researchers demonstrated that gender roles and social context strongly determined a person's actions. For example, after participants in one experiment were told that they would not be identified as male or female, nor did they wear any identification, none conformed to stereotypes about their sex when given the chance to be aggressive. In fact, they did the opposite of what would be expected—women were more aggressive and men were more passive.

(American Psychological Association, 2005)

This approach stresses the "gender similarities hypothesis," which holds the view "that males and females are similar on most, but not all, psychological variables. That is, men and women, as well as boys and girls, are more alike than they are different" (Hyde, 2005, p. 581).[1] In contrast to the similarity hypothesis, Eagly (1995) argued that gender differences exist, are consistent across studies, and should not be ignored merely because they are perceived to conflict with certain political agendas.[2] Thus, Eagly and Carli (2007, p. 29) reject the notion that men, unlike women, possess a "naturally dominant and competitive psychology that facilitates leadership" and raise questions about the robustness of the claims concerning the predominance of men as leaders. Women are different from men by virtue of their innate sex-based traits, and their communication and leadership styles reflect this difference. Treating or evaluating women like men, or trying to "retrofit them" so they will conform to a male-centric work culture has not been efficacious in stopping the leaky pipeline of women advancement, as demonstrated by the dearth of women presence on boards and TMTs. Therefore, senior executives must reframe the gender debate and fix their biased systems to remedy the problem of underrepresentation and avoid organizational brain-drain due to departure of talented women from the workforce.

Wittenberg-Cox and Maitland (2008) pointed out that although companies are used to analyzing workforce turnover, they are not used to analyzing it by gender. Companies that have done so know that women do not generally quit to stay at home although that is still a commonly held view. Many leave for a more attractive workplace, or greater control over their lives, or for the renewed meaning and motivation offered by alternative careers such as entrepreneurship.

EVALUATING GENDER SIMILARITIES AND DIFFERENCES: RESEARCH EVIDENCE

We utilized this enormous collection of 106 meta-analyses and 386 individual meta-analytic effects to re-evaluate the gender similarities hypothesis. Furthermore, we employed a novel data-analytic approach called meta-synthesis (Zell & Krizan, 2014) to estimate the average difference between males and females and to explore moderators of gender differences. The average, absolute difference between males and females across domains was relatively small ($d = 0.21$, SD = 0.14), with the majority of effects being either small (46%) or very small (39%). Magnitude of differences fluctuated somewhat as a function of the psychological domain (e.g., cognitive variables, social and personality variables, well-being), but remained largely constant across age, culture, and generations. These findings provide compelling support for the gender similarities hypothesis, but also underscore conditions under which gender differences are most pronounced. Further, there was a distinct, albeit small difference between males and females when aggregating effects across domains. Thus, although our results suggest that the overall difference between males and females is relatively small, we caution against the conclusion that gender differences are trivial or non-existent.

Finally, although our results provide suggestive evidence that overall gender differences may not fluctuate substantially across age, culture, and generations, we do not believe that these data should be used to infer that gender differences are static or fixed. Indeed, prior research examining gender differences in specific domains has found important fluctuations in gender effects as a function of age, culture, and time period (see Eagly & Wood, 2013; Hyde, 2014). Scholars should continue to examine whether and when these potentially important theoretical variables moderate psychological gender differences both within and across domains.

(Zell, Krizan, & Teeter, 2015)

In a study of senior managers' stereotypical perceptions of leadership behaviors, Prime, Carter, and Welbourne (2009) found that with the exception of "networking," female respondents perceived that women were more effective than men on "supporting," "rewarding," "mentoring," "consulting," "team-building," and "inspiring." Male respondents attributed female effectiveness to "supporting others" and "rewarding subordinates" behaviors. Male respondents perceived male managers as more effective than women in "inspiring others." In terms of "problem solving," "upward influence," and "delegation," male respondents rated male managers as more effective than women on all three variables while women rated male managers higher on all three except for "problem solving." A follow-up study conducted by the same researchers revealed mixed results with male respondents designating inspiring, consulting, and rewarding behaviors as gender-neutral behaviors.

These findings could not support the congruence gender role theory which postulates that gender is not a reliable indicator of leadership behavior. Instead, Prime et al.'s (2009) divergence theory suggests that gender is a reliable indicator of perceived differences in women's and men's leadership performance. In other words, men and women are expected to behave differently from one another rendering gender a dichotomous variable. Certain mutually exclusive roles are appropriate and socially "acceptable" for men and women and are reflected through organizational norms and expectations. Other than demonstrating the complexity of gender effects on perceptions of leadership effectiveness, these findings have implications for women moving through the corporate ladder and who are evaluated strictly on performance-based criteria such as critical thinking and identifying innovative solutions to problems. This is important since even senior managers may be prone to personal biases when evaluating women's suitability for leadership positions.

> Believing that women lack the expertise to navigate through business problems, the followers of women leaders—especially men—may be more likely to question their recommendations and doubt whether it is worth following their directions. By casting doubt on the problem-solving competence of women leaders, men's stereotypes can potentially make it more difficult for women leaders to gain buy-in from their followers and peers on their problem-solving proposals.
>
> *(Prime et al., 2009, p. 46)*

Hardworking and Purpose-driven

The argument based on biology and evolutionary psychology that men and women are socially different would certainly suggest basic dispositional and personality differences between men and women. Women managers see themselves as being more agreeable while men see themselves as being agreeable at times and assertive at other times (Judge, Higgins, Thoresen, & Barrick, 1999). Fittingly, when researchers studied perceptions of effective leadership skills, women were seen as giving more attention to detail, as being more emotional, and as being more likely to seek input from others. Men were seen as more likely to delegate detail work to others (Irby, Brown, Duffy, & Trautman, 2002).

Women often score significantly higher than men on conscientiousness and national cultures frequently signify this. In Russia, for example, men exhibit internal locus of control, while women were found to have external locus of control (Semykina & Linz, 2007). Even in terms of Prediger's (1982) "people–things" and "ideas–data" dimensions, both men and women related to the people–things dimension with women leaning more toward the people side and men leaning more toward the task side (Lippa, 1998). Yet other approaches made the case that, although relations leadership was associated with agreeableness and task leadership was associated with assertiveness and conscientiousness (Won, 2006), there was no support for gender differences in relationship versus task orientation (Toren, Konrad, Yoshioka, & Kashlak, 1997).

Female leaders were rated as having more idealized influence, providing more inspirational motivation, being more individually considerate and offering more intellectual stimulation (Daft, 2011). For example, no differences were found in task-leadership (Won, 2006; Toren et al., 1997), women were stronger in the producer role (Parker, 2004), women were higher in conscientiousness (Belasen & Frank, 2012), women are more analytical (Hays, Allinson, & Armstrong, 2004), women are more detailed (Irby et al., 2002), and yet no support was found for how significant others perceive effectiveness between genders (Vilkinas, 2000; Vilkinas & Cartan, 2006) and only small differences were found in women's tendencies toward transformational leadership styles in the Eagly, Johannesen-Schmidt, and Van Engen (2003) meta-analysis. Traits such as emotional intelligence, empathy, and compassion have been found to be more prevalent in women. Women also seem to regard ethics and integrity at a higher level than men, with women being less accepting than men of dishonest and deceitful tactics (Belasen, 2012; Eagly & Carli, 2007).

One of the crucial survival skills that successful female leaders have in common is *adaptability*, which is a good thing until it is used unwisely (Belasen, 2012). Instead of exhibiting their strong characteristics, women suppress them while relying on adaptive strategies to be accepted and advance their careers. The adaptation is a process of blending in with the male cohorts in leadership positions. In corporate America, the common misperception exists that leaders need to adopt hard and aggressive demeanors in order to be strong leaders. The issue revolves around the lack of education about the differences between male and female leaders. Research points out that some steps need to be taken by companies to rectify this situation. It's not enough to identify and instill the "right" skills and competencies as if we exist in a *social vacuum*. Others need to recognize and support women's motivation to lead and increase the likelihood that others within the organization will encourage women's efforts.

Even though a woman does not look or behave similarly to current leadership, she will lead the change in her own way as soon as we as society recognize that leaders do not need to fit a specific mold that corporate America has created. Ibarra, Ely, and Kolb (2013) suggest three actions to support women's access to leadership positions: (1) educate women and men about second-generation gender bias; (2) create safe "identity workspaces" to support transitions to bigger roles; and (3) anchor women's development efforts in a sense of leadership purpose rather than in how women are perceived. Hopefully, the actions outlined will give women insight into their true self and their organizations, which will enable them to discover their own path to becoming great leaders utilizing their authentic traits. The evolving platform relies on current leadership's ability to communicate and educate its workforce.

Transformational and Transactional Roles

As the number of women in the workforce and in leadership roles begins to shift, it is also important to understand the intersection of gender and leadership. Debates about the leadership styles of women and men gained momentum in the 1990s because of new research attempting to identify the styles that are especially attuned to contemporary organizational conditions (Eagly & Carli, 2004). The new emphasis was on leadership that is transformational in the sense that it is insightful and inspiring (future oriented), rather than operational or hierarchical, and that provides a vision that strengthens the organization by inspiring followers' commitment and creativity. As its name implies, transformational leadership is a process that changes and transforms individuals.

Transformational leadership offers an emotional bond that raises the level of motivation, commitment, and morality of followers by articulating a compelling vision that transcends leader-centric goals and interests. Leadership is quite different from the wielding power of transactional management because it is inseparable from followers' needs. The transformational leader affects the feelings of the follower, creating positive identification with both the leader and the work unit. Ironically, this interaction is characterized by both dependence and independence, an interpersonal dependence between the leader and constituents and an empowering independence that encourages work group identification (Kark, Shamir, & Chen, 2003).

Transformational roles have been typically categorized into four types: idealized influence; inspirational motivation; intellectual stimulation; and individual consideration. Idealized influence refers to leaders who have high standards of moral and ethical conduct, who are held in high personal regard, and who engender loyalty from followers. Inspirational motivation refers to leaders with a strong vision for the future based on values and ideas that generate enthusiasm, build confidence, and inspire followers using symbolic actions and persuasive language. These two traits, idealized influence and inspirational motivation, are highly correlated and are sometimes combined to form a measure of charisma. The third trait, intellectual stimulation, refers to leaders who challenge existing organizational norms, encourage divergent thinking, and who push followers to develop innovative strategies. Individual consideration, the fourth transformational leadership trait, refers to leader behaviors aimed at recognizing the unique growth and developmental needs of followers as well as coaching followers and consulting with them.

Transactional leadership behaviors are aimed at monitoring and controlling employees through rational or economic means. Using contingent rewards, transactional leaders focus their attention on exchange or trade relationships providing tangible or intangible support and resources to followers in exchange for their efforts and performance and sanctioning undesired behaviors or unattained performance levels. To deal with unexpected surprises or non-routine events, transactional leaders may also rely on management by exception, revising and updating standards, and monitoring deviations from these standards. In the passive version of management by exception, leaders take an inactive approach, intervening only when problems become serious. Active management by exception characterizes enhanced monitoring activities by transactional managers who initiate corrective actions and intensely evaluate progress toward achieving desired performance levels (Bono & Judge, 2004). Bass (1990) included laissez-faire under the transactional leadership label, though it can be viewed as non-leadership or the abdication of leadership responsibilities.

Eagly et al.'s (2003) seminal meta-analysis of 45 studies compared male and female managers on measures of transformational, transactional, and laissez-faire leadership styles. In general, the meta-analysis revealed that, compared with male leaders, female leaders were more transformational as well as engaged in the contingent reward that characterizes transactional behavior. Male leaders were more likely than female leaders to manifest the two other aspects of transactional leadership: active management by exception and passive management by exception. Men were also higher on laissez-faire leadership.

Feminist researchers have strongly reasoned that transformational leadership might be particularly advantageous to women because of its androgynous qualities. Women's self-reports of assertiveness, dominance, and masculinity (Twenge, 1997, 2001), and the value that women place on job attributes such as freedom, challenges, leadership, prestige, and influence (Konrad, Ritchie, Lieb, & Corrigall, 2000), have all become as prevalent as in men. They also work harder and wisely choose the leadership style that they feel comfortable with, and that does not contradict their feminine image. Ibarra and Obodaru (2008), for example, found that, with one exception—*forwardness of thinking*, women managers displayed stronger skills than men in all measurement areas, including process and practicality. Women can be go-getters in management and at the same time inspire others and model the way as trusted leaders.

Trustworthiness

The relationship between expected return and trusting behavior is stronger among men than women, suggesting that men view social interactions more strategically than women. Women feel more obligated to trust and reciprocate, but the impact of obligation on behavior varies (Buchan & Solnick, 2008). These findings support the argument by Walters, Stuhlmacher, and Meyer (1998), who suggested that in negotiations, men are more task oriented and women are more interpersonally oriented. The scenario with the highest level of trust is a male sender (negotiator) who would be more trusting presenting to a female who would be more trustworthy.

According to the 2013 Edelman Trust Barometer, only 15% of Americans trust their leaders to tell the truth. Globally, only 28% of respondents believe that businesses follow ethical practices (Edelman, 2013). Meanwhile, the percentage of companies with "strong" or "strong-leaning" ethics cultures climbed to 66% in 2013, up from 60% in 2011, according to the National Business Ethics Survey of 6,420 employees (Institute of Business Ethics, 2014). When companies value ethical performance, misconduct is substantially lower. In 2013, only 20% of workers reported seeing misconduct in companies where ethical cultures are "strong," compared with 88% who witnessed wrongdoing in companies with the weakest cultures, according to the survey. Trusted leadership and employee engagement accounts for many of the good practices and ethical behaviors in organizations (Belasen, 2016a), and women in leadership positions in organizations help foster positive relationships (Belasen, 2012). Given their strong emotional intelligence skills (Goleman, 2009), women also manifest in their behavior the four "S's" of trusted leadership—selflessness, safety, service, and sacrifices. They are capable of acting selflessly when the time comes, being safe and making others feel safe, performing services, and making personal sacrifices for the benefits of the collective (Dame, 2014).

Forwardness of Thinking and Perceptions of Competence

Unfortunately for women seeking career advancement to higher levels of the organization, vision and innovation are strong markers for promotion potential. A primary reason is the perceived causal path that exists between vision and forward thinking, business performance, financial performance, and overall stakeholder satisfaction (Cameron, Quinn, DeGraff, & Thakor, 2006). Strengths in other areas may not always compensate for perceptions of weakness in innovativeness and vision. Innovativeness is also a stronger predictor of promotability to positions of power than relationship skills (Post, DiTomaso, Lowe, Farris, & Cordero, 2009).

There are three strong reasons why innovation and vision (forward thinking) are essential elements for achieving senior positions and are the obstacles women face in advancement to top levels. First, although, women managers are often thought to have a "female advantage" of greater *relationship capital* than men, giving them an edge when both are equally qualified for promotions, that "advantage" is only materialized when the female is also perceived as being visionary and innovative (Post et al., 2009). Thus, the transformational leadership advantage exists only when the candidate for promotion displays not only strong relationship capital, but also visionary, forward-thinking skills. Unfortunately, women are less likely to promote themselves than men due to systemic and stereotypical barriers (Bowles & McGinn, 2005). Second, vision appears more frequently as an essential quality in senior management than in middle management (Belasen, Eisenberg, & Huppertz, 2015). As a personal and executive characteristic, vision distinguishes top-level managers from other managers. Finally, when asked to rate the relative contribution of managerial attributes to leadership effectiveness, graduates of executive leadership programs selected "ability to inspire others," a reflection of vision, as the top requirement for successful leadership (Prime et al., 2009).

If women are perceived as being less visionary and innovative (Ibarra & Obodaru, 2008) and if they are seen as being less successful in handling novel or exceptional situations, does this lead to the common view that they are less effective managers than men and therefore less qualified to perform top-level leadership roles? If so, then how can we explain the evidence[3] that a higher proportion of women on TMTs is a driver for better business performance and influences the bottom line in both the short and long terms (Woetzel, Madgavkar, Ellingrud, Labaye, & Devillard et al., 2015)?

The claim for vision as an essential requirement for entering TMTs underpins the context of the executive glass ceiling, and gives shape to four obstacles women face in upward mobility: Women are seen as being lower in vision than men by their male peers (Ibarra & Obodaru, 2008); women are perceived as being stronger in relationship oriented skills, which are of low priority in top-level leadership skills (Prime et al., 2009); women are seen as being stronger in transactional, organizational skills (Belasen & Frank, 2012); and, finally, the so-called "female qualities" of relationship and organizational skills are seen as more important at lower levels of the managerial hierarchy (Belasen, 2012).

Role Incongruity and Authentic Leadership

Trustworthiness needs to be established from the top of the pyramid by leaders with a strong conviction to bring about equality and fairness in hiring and promoting women to TMTs. Meanwhile, as organizations reinforce masculine qualities through rewards and incentives (Chin, 2004), images such as "the glass ceiling," which precludes women from positions at the highest levels and "the concrete wall" with its emphasis on inequitable rules and norms have persisted (Weyer, 2007). Further research by Haslam and Ryan (2005) and Ryan, Haslam, and Postmes (2007) has presented evidence of the tenacity of "the glass cliff," which puts women in positions associated with crises that carry a high risk of failure and criticism reflecting more barriers to women's leadership. Eagly and Carli (2007) have gone so far as to argue that since there are actually several barriers that women must overcome to reach senior positions, a more appropriate metaphor to describe the challenges women face in ascending the corporate ladder would be the "labyrinth." The labyrinth is a negotiable yet challenging, non-linear path that is both elusive and complex.

Many of the difficulties and challenges that women face arise from the incongruity of the traditional women's role and leadership roles. This incongruity creates vulnerability whereby women encounter prejudicial reactions and evaluation biases that restrict their access to leadership roles (Weyer, 2007). Women are more likely to experience barriers due to the masculinity of positions that are not congruent with their authentic or prototypical behaviors. Authentic leaders have the ability to acknowledge their thoughts, emotions, needs, wants, preferences, and beliefs and act consistently with those inner feelings and beliefs. They have strong self-awareness and self-regulation, internalized regulation, balanced processing of information, and relational transparency.

Schwartz (2012), writing in the *Harvard Business Review* blog, describes what women know about leadership that men do not, observing that

> an effective modern leader requires a blend of intellectual qualities—the ability to think analytically, strategically and creatively—and emotional ones, including self-awareness, empathy and humility . . . I meet far more women with this blend of qualities than I do men.

In his experience, men tend to overvalue strengths rather than humility:

> [T]he vast majority of CEOs and senior executives I've met over the past decade are men [who] resist introspection, feel more comfortable measuring outcomes than they do managing emotions, and under-appreciate the powerful connection between how people feel and how they perform . . . For the most part, women, more than men, bring to leadership a more complete range of the qualities modern leaders need, including self-awareness, emotional attunement and authenticity.

Authentic leaders display genuine behaviors that create positive leader-follower relationships, increased follower trust, and sustainable employee performance (Gardner, Avolio, Luthans, May, & Walumbwa, 2005). They have a deep sense of purpose, possess ethical and moral values, lead with their hearts, establish close relationships with followers, and demonstrate self-control and self-discipline (George, 2003).

Self-control is a skill that when used correctly can help in life's journeys such as education and employment. The ability to show self-control early is a good precursor for success in life. Studies show that girls have 5–20% more self-control than boys, and women, on average, have a 14% higher grade point average than men (Amin, 2014). According to a study conducted in 2013, the average man doesn't reach full emotional maturity until age 43, and without a higher level of maturity self-control is less achievable (Olson, 2013).

Authentic leaders have the capacity to unleash their subordinates' full potential; they are effective in creating positive work environments and in achieving positive and enduring outcomes in organizations (Gardner & Schermerhorn, 2004). Authentic leaders manifest trust, hope, emotion, and identification in their behaviors to exert influence over followers (Avolio, Gardner, Walumbwa, Luthans, & May, 2004; Avolio & Gardner, 2005). Authenticity is associated with positive employees' outcomes and job satisfaction (Azanzaa, Moriano, & Molero, 2013). Authentic leadership and prototypical traits (i.e., representing the group) promote trustworthiness and respect (Belasen, 2016b). Being prototypical helps women to be perceived as authentic. At critical times it may also help women avoid glass cliffs and typecast jobs.

Role incongruity between female gender role (communal) and perceived leader role (agentic) leads to prejudice against female leaders, diminished leadership potential, biased evaluations, and more barriers to being authentic in leadership roles. Women encounter resistance when their behaviors are measured against prevailing gender expectations. For example, their vision might not be recognized if it manifests itself differently than in men. Women are more conscientious and analytical, are both people and task oriented, and have a more transformational rather than contractual leadership style (Belasen & Frank, 2012). Yet, men are granted power automatically, while women have to earn it. It is unlikely that a woman will consciously go through a logical decision making sequence to select the best behavioral styles. More likely she will exercise her natural strengths, or automated responses (Belasen & Frank, 2008), and only those whose strengths survive the demanding selection process will become managers. If men have an unfair advantage over women because people attribute male qualities to leadership regardless of their qualifications, how do women earn authority in a gendered organization?

Easing this dilemma of role incongruity requires that women leaders behave extremely competently while reassuring others that they conform to expectations concerning appropriate behavior for women. This double-bind requirement, observed or expected, to display extra competence, makes it especially difficult for women to gain recognition for high performance and outstanding achievement. Therefore, successful women leaders generally work harder and seek leadership styles that reduce the chance for criticism or that elicit resistance to their authority challenging them to be egalitarian (Eagly & Carli, 2003, p. 825). Women are assumed to be warm and selfless (typical female gender roles) while at the same time expected to be assertive and competent (attributes of agentic leaders). Communal characteristics do not "produce respect for women as authorities and leaders" (Eagly & Carli, 2007, p. 102). On the one hand, women are expected to be friendly, supportive, and skilled in socialization processes, yet agreeableness is a handicap in career advancement (Mueller & Plug, 2006); on the other hand, men who are not friendly (agonistic) are more likely to receive promotions.

Holes in the Glass Ceiling: The Public Sector

Bowling, Kelleher, Jones, and Wright (2006) found that women face fewer blockages in securing top state public-agency posts, in effect, poking holes in the

TABLE 4.1 Women US Officeholders Serving in 2016

Women Officeholders Serving in 2016	*Number of Women*	*% of Total*
Federal Executive (Cabinet)	7	46.7%
US Supreme Court	3	42.9%
Congress	104	19.4% of 535 seats
US Senate	20	20% of 100 seats
US House	84	19.3% of 435 seats
Statewide Executive	77	24.7% of 312 seats
State Legislature	1,808	24.5% of 7,383 seats
State Senate	445	22.6% of 1,972 seats
State House/Assembly	1,363	25.2% of 5,411 seats
Mayors—Cities over 30,000	257 (2015)	18.4% of 1,393 seats
Mayors—100 Largest Cities	19 (2015)	19% of 100 seats

Source: Adapted from CAWP (2016).

glass ceiling. Women's access to positions of authority in politics and government has been facilitated by their educational levels, career aspirations, and organizational experiences. Moreover, lateral career movements of women have begun to crack the concrete walls around them. Women in politics have an edge over their counterparts in the C-suite. Many adults (34%) think that female politicians are better at working out compromises than their male counterparts. Only 9% say men are better. A larger number of adults (55%) believes there is no difference between men and women in this regard. Women are also perceived to have advantage over men (34% to 3% respectively) when it comes to being honest and ethical (Figure 4.1). Recent women officeholders in federal and state offices from the Center for American Women and Politics (CAWP) are presented in Table 4.1.

In government, in which state executives include six governors and 12 lieutenant governors according to a March 2014 report by the US Office of Personnel Management, 34% of Senior Executive Service positions at federal agencies are held by women as compared to 14.6% in the private sector.

Notably, younger women who are currently entering the federal work-force are more likely to be on a management track than they previously were. In 2014, the gap between men and women was much less pronounced among supervisors aged 25–34 than among older supervisors. Nearly 44% of supervisors and managers aged 25–34 were women, versus about 35% of managers aged 55–64 (US Office of Personnel Management, 2014).

WOMEN IN LAW ENFORCEMENT

Women represented nearly 12% of about 700,000 police officers in the U.S., according to data submitted to the FBI in 2011. That number is up only slightly from 11.2% in 2001.Women still are vastly underrepresented at the top ranks of law enforcement. Law enforcement is a career dominated largely by male officers, and especially male administrators. The *National Association of Women Law Enforcement Executives* reported that in 2011, there were just 219 women holding chiefs' jobs in the U.S., where there are now more than 14,000 police agencies.

(Johnson, 2015)

In the nonprofit sector, results from a 2003 to 2007 survey indicate that the so-called "feminine" industries are concentrated in the nonprofit sector, and this "gendered industry" involves overrepresentation of women to the tune of 68%. The results also suggest that women with more education and experience may choose nonprofit jobs over jobs in the other sectors while nonprofit employment is generally associated with negative wage differentials (Lee, 2014).

In politics and government, unlike in business, women typically do not always face the need to be tested across divisional lines to be promoted. In government, the career paths are more linear and the opportunities for women's inclusion are much greater than in business. To become top executive in business, however, candidates typically have to have prior line experience in critical profit and loss (P&L) jobs. Consequently, many successful women end up in staff roles e.g., human resources and investor relations that, while important, do not carry the weight and visibility needed to land a top position in the executive suite.

In Fortune 200 companies, for example, a woman's chance of advancing from an executive committee to a CEO position is about 3% as compared to 12% for a man, partly because almost twice as many women as men (60% versus 35%) choose staff roles for their mid-career (Barsh & Yee, 2012). "We need to give women more full P&L experience and the task of managing brands—the nuts and bolts of the corporations," Denise Morrison, CEO of Campbell Soup Company, told CNN Money (Egan, 2015). When a critical mass of high-performing men and women middle managers strive to grow and continue at higher levels, the company builds an advantage that's among the hardest for competitors to copy.

Active Mentoring and the Sponsorship Effect

Mentoring and sponsorship are particularly important for women, especially since they lag behind men when it comes to promotion opportunities. In fact, women

*In **politics**, the % saying women/men in top positions are better at ...*

	WOMEN ARE BETTER	MEN ARE BETTER	NO DIFFERENCE
Working out compromises	34%	9%	55%
Being honest and ethical	34	3	62
Working to improve U.S. quality of life	26	5	68
Standing up for beliefs	26	10	63

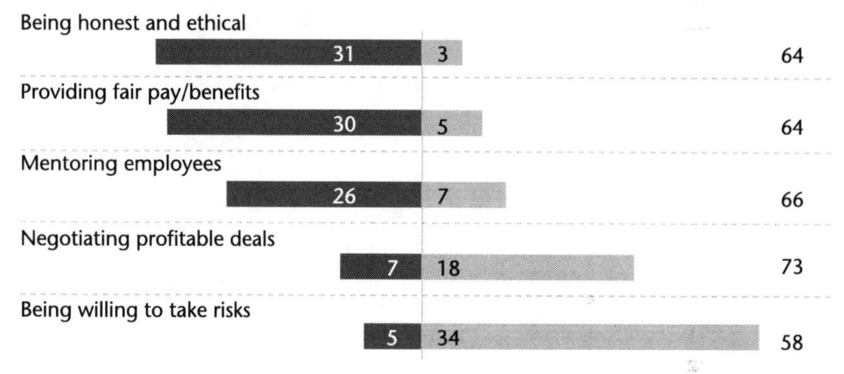

FIGURE 4.1 Women Excel at Compromise, Men at Risk-taking but Overall, Majority of Public Sees Little Difference

Source: Pew Research Center (2015).

Note: "No answer" not shown.

with a mentor increase their chances of being promoted to middle management by 56% over women without a mentor (Roebuck & Smith, 2011). These researchers also noted that mentoring and sponsorship initiated by senior-level executives lead to career advancement for both men and women. Research found that women are less likely to be promoted at the same rate as men; however, with a sponsor, women are just as likely to be promoted as men (Foust-Cummings, Dinolfo, & Kohler, 2011). Hewlett (2013) describes how employees are more likely to obtain promotions, pay raises, and high-profile assignments when they have sponsors. She also found that having a sponsor helps predict satisfaction of promotion rate and that working increases mothers' likelihood of staying in the workforce.

However, most women lag behind men when it comes to having a sponsor. According to Hewlett, Peraino, Sherbin, and Sumberg (2010) a mere 13% of full-time female employees at large companies (over 50,000 employees) have sponsors to help them step up the corporate ladder or shield them from undesired situations. Men are 46% more likely than women to have a sponsor—a gender gap.

Sponsors go beyond the traditional social, emotional, and personal growth development provided by mentors. A mentor listens and provides suggestions and insights based on experience and intuition, but a sponsor typically talks about the protégé. A sponsor is essentially a power broker who endorses a high-potential woman (the protégée) in conversations and decision situations in closed-door meetings and supports her in stormy moments.

> Sponsors not only promote their charges, they also protect, prepare, and push them—all the way to the top. In fact, after surveying more than four thousand U.S. men and women with college educations working in white-collar jobs, listening intently to the discussion in our Virtual Strategy Sessions, a particularly effective online focus group, and interviewing the leaders of the Hidden Brain Drain Task Force, we're convinced that promotion to top jobs depends on sponsorship—which women have a hard time accessing. If today's female executives find themselves outside the inner sanctum, it's not only because they're removed from the crucial conversations that determine who moves up, but because they have no proxy. Sponsorship corrects that. By providing women the authoritative voice they lack, the backroom access they're often denied, and the advocacy they desperately need, sponsorship truly levels the playing field.
>
> *(Hewlett et al., 2010, p. 4)*

Sponsors act like champions or advocates who are influential actors with proximity to decision authority centers. They know the "ins and outs" of organizational dynamics and internal affairs and often act as the "go to" persons with updated information about important outcomes, anticipated or actual. A highly placed, influential mentor, often called a sponsor, goes beyond giving general career feedback and advice. A sponsor can propel a protégé to the top of a list or pile of candidates or even eliminate the list itself (Foust-Cummings et al., 2011). The advice and coaching provided by a sponsor facilitate understanding, mediate between interests and parties, enable stretch assignments, and mitigate the perceived uncertainty that comes with less experience or little familiarity with executive decision processes.

> Indeed, the impact of sponsorship appears to be remarkably consistent for both men and women across all measures. Some 43% of male employees and 36% of females will ask their manager for a stretch assignment; when a sponsor gets behind them, the numbers rise, respectively, to 56% and 44%.

> When it comes to asking for a pay raise, the majority of men (67%) and women (70%) resist confronting their boss. With a sponsor in their corner, however, nearly half of men and 38% of women summon the courage to negotiate.
>
> *(Hewlett et al., 2010, p. 11)*

Effective sponsors that are also located at the top of the organization create upward pressure in pay for their endorsed protégés, help connect them with senior leaders and increase the protégés' visibility. Sponsorship draws its success from a trusting relationship, honesty, mutual respect, positive communication, and strong emotional support and empathy. According to Hewlett et al. (2010) fully 70% of men with sponsors and 68% of women reported feeling satisfied with their rate of advancement, which translated into a 23% sponsorship effect for men and a 19% effect for women.

> Men and women alike say they get valuable career advice from their mentors, but it's mostly men who describe being sponsored. Many women explain how mentoring relationships have helped them understand themselves, their preferred styles of operating, and ways they might need to change as they move up the leadership pipeline. By contrast, men tell stories about how their bosses and informal mentors have helped them plan their moves and take charge in new roles, in addition to endorsing their authority publicly. As one male mentee recounts, in a typical comment: "My boss said, 'You are ready for a general management job. You can do it. Now we need to find you a job: What are the tricks we need to figure out? You have to talk to this person and to that one and that one.' They are all executive committee members. My boss was a network type of a person . . . . Before he left, he put me in touch with the head of supply chain, which is how I managed to get this job."
>
> *(Herminia, Carter, & Silva, 2010)*

According to Hewlett (2013), sponsors do three things that mentors do not: (1) they go out on a limb on behalf of their protégés; (2) they provide support in the form of defense against critics and advocate for promotions; and (3) they provide "air cover" that allows protégés to take risks. Hewlett also shows that sponsors also expand the protégées' perception of their potential; provide opportunities to stretch talents; give advice on how to present themselves as professional leaders; make connections to clients and customers; and give the kind of honest, critical feedback on skill gaps that mentors may not recognize or want to provide. These may lead to positive outcomes such as greater promotion opportunities for protégées, higher retention rates, better pay, greater satisfaction, and quality of work life.

SPONSORING WOMEN TO SUCCESS

What Organizations Can Do

1. Develop company-specific formal sponsorship programs that identify high-performing women that go beyond mentorship.
2. Involve entire senior leadership team in sponsorship efforts and request that they drive the dialogue from the top around such efforts.
3. Tie sponsorship goals to performance evaluation criteria in a visible manner.
4. Implement sponsorship programs as part of succession planning.
5. Implement assessments to help sponsors and protégés identify the specific goals and areas on which they should focus their attention and sponsorship efforts.

What Sponsors Can Do

1. Sponsorship is key to advancing women into senior positions, and sponsors can provide greater opportunities for their protégés to develop the necessary skills to excel and advance.
2. Sponsors can provide sophisticated coaching, advice, and specification steps to enable protégés to move to new roles and positions and take new assignments.
3. Sponsors can help protégés gain visibility within the organization and, at times, outside the organization.
4. Acting as a sponsor can enhance one's own reputation for developing talent and leaders. The success of the protégé thus enhances the sponsor's own reputational capital.
5. Sponsors need to persuade their peers to support the sponsor's protégés.

What Protégés Can Do

1. Identify your goals and accomplishments and identify individuals within the organization who could serve as an appropriate sponsor for you.
2. Identify the benefits to the sponsor of a sponsorship relationship and how sponsorship will help the organization, the sponsor, and you.
3. Be open to honest and constructive advice and criticism from sponsors.
4. Be committed to making the sponsorship relationship work effectively and understand the risk a sponsor may take on your behalf.
5. Once you have been sponsored, remember to "pay it forward" and sponsor another woman.

What Each of Us Can Now Do

1. Familiarize yourself with the studies and research on the importance of sponsorship.
2. Leverage the power of women at the conference by informing your organization and others of the benefits of sponsorship.

(Foust-Cummings et al., 2011)

Trusted Leadership

Two levels of intervention must be considered for minimizing the negative effects of evaluative biases: (1) informal or personal initiatives by women and men in organizations; and (2) change in formal institutional mechanisms such as policies, evaluation criteria, and codes of behavior. Training for senior executives as potential sponsors and for protégées should increase the mutual commitment and joint accountability of both sides. Formally matching of sponsors and protégées based on skills and availability, goals and position within the company is a good starting point. The timeline of the relationship is important, too, as studies report that individuals with extensive mentoring relationships, as opposed to short-term relationships, reported greater gains, had higher pay, and were more satisfied. The majority (76%) of protégées surveyed agreed that their relationships with sponsors and mentors are most important primarily during their early stages of their careers (Dworkin, Maurer, & Schipani, 2012).

Institutionally, organizations need to reassess their mission statements and remove corporate barriers that limit or inhibit women's access to upper-level positions. On the personal side, senior executives need to be attentive to their blind spots, or the behavioral and perceptual areas known to others but unknown to them, to maintain a good balance, and avoid poorly made judgments or dysfunctional forms of behavior. Acknowledging women's contributions to the workplace requires two-way leadership in which care and sensitivity, transparency and accountability are the principles that drive mutual respect and confidence. Ultimately, leadership is about character and doing the right things, moral maturity, self-control, and appreciation of others. Trust-based reciprocal relationships enable leaders to serve the people that rely on them, listen to their needs, give praise and recognition, show kindness, display true honesty, and be authentic. Trusted leadership is characterized by the absence of arrogance, pride, and deception. It is acting unselfishly. The challenge is systemic but the solution involves first and foremost a shift in mindset.

The framework for trusted leadership (Belasen, 2016a) is presented in Figure 4.2. Based on rules of disclosure, transparency, and public accountability, a well-organized exchange system should include sharing of information with the public (INFORM) to achieve greater transparency; using communications to

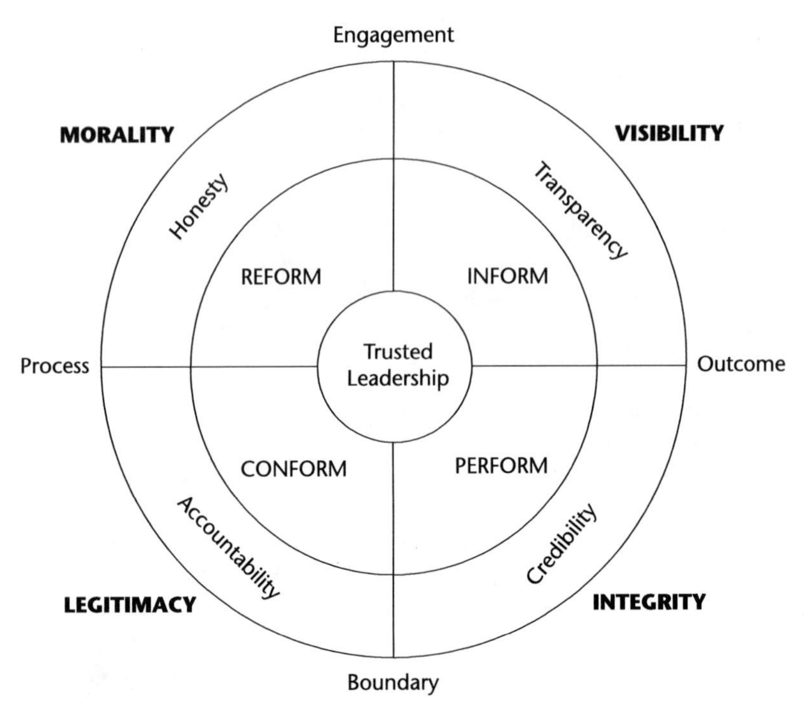

FIGURE 4.2 Trusted Leadership

Source: Belasen (2016a).

mobilize employees and stakeholders to tackle deficiencies such as inequity or unfair practices (REFORM); developing rules of conduct and codes of ethics to guide future actions and to increase equality (CONFORM); and moving forward to meet new performance goals and expectations such as promoting women (PERFORM). Embedded in the model are core assumptions and positive outcomes with parallels around the model—visibility and integrity are associated with external communications, outcomes, public image, and reputation. Integrity and legitimacy reflect strong adherence to codes of ethics, rules of conduct, and governance. Legitimacy and morality preserve high standards of ethical behavior, moral values, equity, and sensitivity to members' needs and goals. Morality and visibility reinforce the social identity and public image of the organization and shape it as responsible and responsive.

Leaders who are able to master the behaviors and skills associated with the four domains outlined in the model also have the cognitive complexity and behavioral flexibility to make smart choices that benefit the organization and its stakeholders. Methods of self-assessment that also consider responses from others (e.g., followers, protégés) are particularly useful for monitoring progress toward desired goals and behaviors. They also provide others with a dashboard to review potential gaps between actual and desired behaviors, adjust or change criteria as needed, or develop new benchmarks. The social context is important because women and men in leadership positions look to others for validation of their moral judgment and motivation. Senior executives and potential sponsors can use these instruments developmentally to examine how well their ratings are balanced across the various criteria (see the Trusted Leadership Questionnaire below), check whether important milestones have been accomplished, and revise their attitudes and behaviors accordingly. Self-assessment tools are designed to help increase self-awareness or understanding of one's strengths and weaknesses, thinking patterns, and motivations.

Self-regulation

Board members can use the instruments provided below to evaluate whether gaps in the behaviors and attitudes of senior executives toward women have been addressed and make important decisions about their suitability to lead the organization. Assessment instruments are often used to not only highlight deficiencies in leadership style that cause major breakdowns, but also to improve organizational communication. Managers at all hierarchical levels who used multi-rater tools reportedly developed a clear understanding across hierarchical levels and functional lines and worked effectively as a management team (Belasen, 2008). An individual in a position of authority should create an atmosphere that encourages organizational members to monitor, challenge, and discuss organizational discourse and biases in order to remain open to better and more ethical ways of doing things.

Porter and Daniel's (2007) definition of transformational women leadership includes the following dimensions: *values, vision, action, learning, understanding, ethical practices, and social constructivism*. These seven dimensions, when combined, form a robust definition of effective leadership (Belasen, 2012), which is also consistent with Goleman's (2009, p. 44) description of emotional intelligence as the "sine qua non of leadership." According to Goleman, emotional intelligence skills are significantly more important than cognitive abilities and technical skills when moving up the corporate ladder. These emotional intelligence skills include self-awareness (e.g., self-confidence and acceptance of constructive criticisms), self-regulation (trustworthiness, integrity), motivation (a passion for new challenges, optimism in the face of failure), empathy (developing and coaching others, cultural sensitivity), and social skills (expertise in building and leading teams, persuasiveness). Goleman (2009, p. 45) noted about women's strengths in TMTs: "When I compared star performers with average ones in senior leadership positions, nearly 90% of the difference in their profiles was attributable to emotional intelligence rather than cognitive abilities."

Moral awareness is a powerful medium that allows leaders to understand their strengths and weaknesses, what motivates them, and how they make decisions. Moral awareness and self-regulation are the initial points in a diagnostic process aimed at identifying gaps between actual and desired behaviors and a tracking plan aimed at remedying deficiencies based on input from others. In many ways, this process is a multi-stage decision making process similar to the one described by Trevino and Brown (2004) that moves from moral awareness to moral judgment (deciding which course of action is justifiable), to moral motivation (or the commitment to pursue actions), and moral character (or the persistence to sustain the behavior).

Diagnosing and Tracking Leadership Behavior

A milestone for ongoing conversations and exchange of ideas is an assessment instrument aimed at measuring the trustworthiness of leaders, articulating self-improvement plans, and monitoring progress aimed at closing the gaps between current and desired behaviors (Belasen, 2016b). The Trusted Leadership Questionnaire is designed to measure the dimensions that comprise the model in Figure 4.2. Examples of current and desired profiles are provided in Figures 4.3 and 4.4 consecutively.

Trusted Leadership Questionnaire

Rate each item on a scale from 1 to 5 where:

1 = I do not demonstrate this behavior
2 = I demonstrate this behavior to a small degree
3 = I demonstrate this behavior to a moderate degree
4 = I demonstrate this behavior frequently
5 = I demonstrate this behavior to a great degree

Next, rate yourself again, this time by considering expectations from others (e.g., women reporting to you; a high-achieving woman who is sponsored by you, and so on) or by reflecting on how you would like to be perceived by others. Take a look at the gaps. Where do you need to change to become a trusted leader?

Transparency

1. I feel my diversity goals are accepted by others
2. I strive to achieve successful outcomes through inclusive leadership
3. I pay close attention to how well I work with men and women
4. I use a plan that is shared publically and that guides the evaluation criteria
5. I make sure that we understand each other's concerns
6. I seek to understand the needs of my followers
7. I revise my vision and goals based on inputs from diverse stakeholders

Credibility

8. I am candid, honest and openly express my thoughts and concerns
9. I articulate shared goals and interests consistently
10. I tell the truth with high conviction
11. When I withhold information, I let people know the reason
12. I consistently share personal commitments in the open
13. I admit to personal mistakes and do not blame others for my failure
14. I listen to my followers and peers attentively
15. I welcome constructive criticism
16. At times of change I remain open to new ideas
17. I value feedback from others even if it negates my thinking
18. I ask stakeholders if I meet their expectations or for ideas to help support their goals

Accountability

19. I clarify my actions to various stakeholders
20. I encourage employees to explain our behavior to stakeholders
21. I emphasize the importance of complying with regulations fairly and objectively
22. I strive to ensure that we openly and honestly share practices and outcomes
23. I emphasize the obligation of carrying out government policies (e.g., EEO) properly
24. I ensure that we follow rules and procedures consistently and equitably
25. I adhere to ethical codes of conduct
26. I communicate and reinforce integrity guidelines
27. I clarify the personal and collective consequences of misconduct and unfair treatment
28. I encourage joint decision making processes
29. I support lateral communication, employee engagement, and inclusive leadership

Honesty

30. I am approachable when others need me
31. I support giving back to the community
32. I encourage women to participate in decision making
33. I act with respect for others
34. I seek to meet others' expectation of me
35. I hold myself and others to high ethical standards
36. I put others' best interests above my own
37. I have a thorough understanding of social values

38. I would not compromise ethical principles in order to gain personal benefits
39. I make a sincere effort to know about others' career goals
40. I value honesty and equal opportunity

Figures 4.3 and 4.4 depict the ratings involving the actual behavior (baseline) and the desired behavior (benchmark). Understandably, the ratings in Figure 4.3, which denote current behaviors, are lower than the ratings in Figure 4.4, which represents future behaviors. The gap between the two sets (see Figure 4.5) signifies opportunities for improvement.

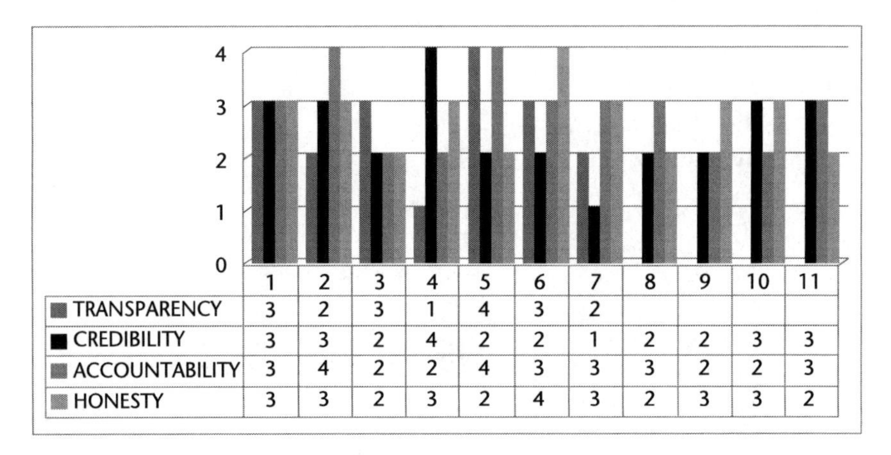

	1	2	3	4	5	6	7	8	9	10	11
TRANSPARENCY	3	2	3	1	4	3	2				
CREDIBILITY	3	3	2	4	2	2	1	2	2	3	3
ACCOUNTABILITY	3	4	2	2	4	3	3	3	2	2	3
HONESTY	3	3	2	3	2	4	3	2	3	3	2

FIGURE 4.3 Current Profile

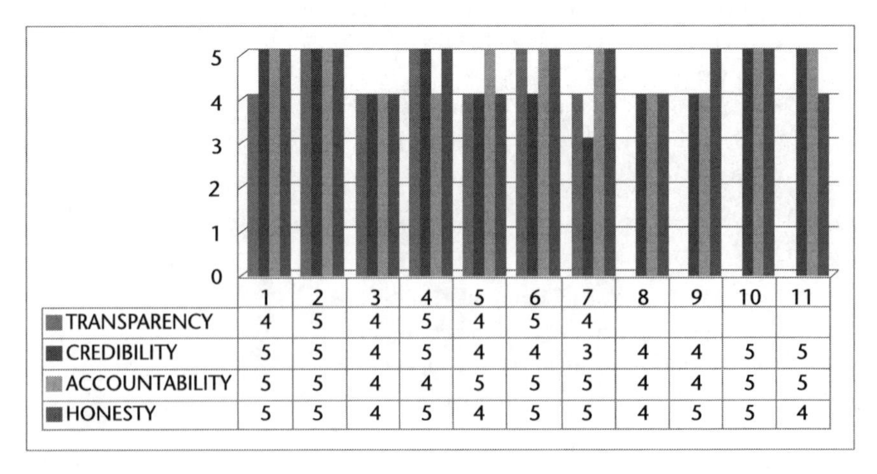

	1	2	3	4	5	6	7	8	9	10	11
TRANSPARENCY	4	5	4	5	4	5	4				
CREDIBILITY	5	5	4	5	4	4	3	4	4	5	5
ACCOUNTABILITY	5	5	4	4	5	5	5	4	4	5	5
HONESTY	5	5	4	5	4	5	5	4	5	5	4

FIGURE 4.4 Desired Profile

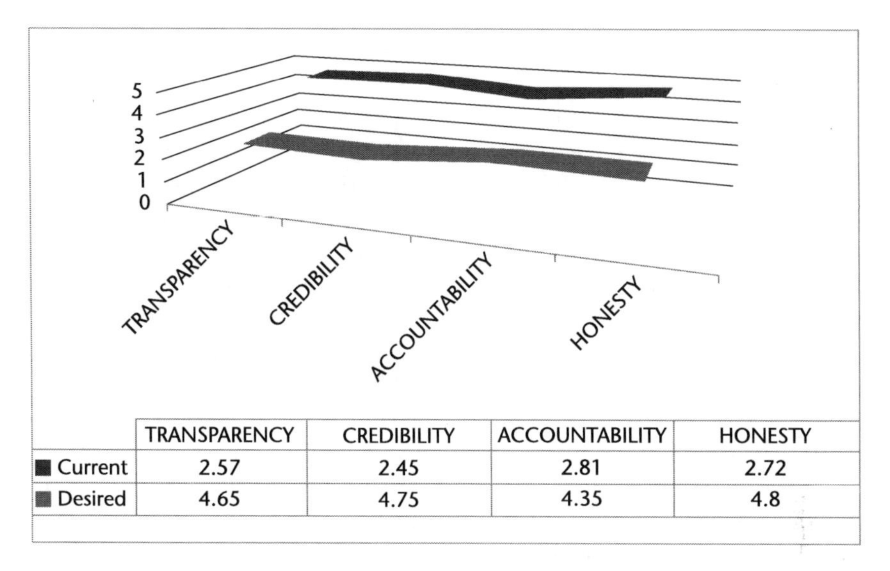

	TRANSPARENCY	CREDIBILITY	ACCOUNTABILITY	HONESTY
Current	2.57	2.45	2.81	2.72
Desired	4.65	4.75	4.35	4.8

FIGURE 4.5 Current and Desired Profiles

Developing improvement strategies should also include several milestones and checkpoints when the survey may be taken again to see whether the gap has been eliminated. Another option is to obtain feedback from others and even allow board members to assess the attributes of the leader using the same survey. The differences between the self-assessment and assessment from others could be very revealing and should lead to a more valid and reliable understanding of the distance between behaviors and expectations. Subsequently, ideas and actions for improvement could be prioritized to reflect inputs from others and eventually lead to a better alignment between the leader's profile on the four dimensions and the ratings by others. Figure 4.5 transposes the two profiles to provide a single view of the gaps across the four domains of trusted leadership.

A leader's failure or incapacity to acknowledge the gap and initiate a shift from the current mindset or behavior to the acceptable level (one that is appreciated or recognized publically) might potentially lead to failure. Trusted leadership is sustained through honesty and trustworthiness. When a top executive employs self-regulation and shows genuine concern for diversity or makes a personal sacrifice for others, a true form of leadership emerges. Acting authentically—ensuring employees' safety, treating them with respect, and making sacrifices that benefit them—generates a high level of commitment to the leader and organizational goals (Belasen, 2016b).

Profile Awareness

The four dimensions that interlink these values and outcomes—transparency, credibility, accountability, and honesty—must be present simultaneously to increase the prospects for greater diversity and inclusiveness. A deficiency in *transparency* (see Figure 4.6) occurs when a leader is too inwardly focused, paying attention to operational and financial objectives, as well as to managing internal dynamics. While these are important matters and they cannot be ignored, the temptation among many leaders is to act with a sense of urgency rather than strategy. Refocusing on purposeful ideas as the basis for strengthening equity and fairness in TMTs and for a good alignment between the image and identity of the organization are at the core of trusted leadership. Yet other leaders experience a deficiency in accountability, as depicted in Figure 4.7. This deficiency is usually marked by a tendency to shoot from the hip, resulting in making authoritative decisions without the benefit of input from affected stakeholders (e.g., high potential women) or all the available information.

Executives who demonstrate lower levels of *accountability* need to resist the temptation to make decisions quickly, even though the urgent pressures of the moment may push them into deciding too quickly. Unless the matter is extremely urgent and a decision absolutely must be made on the spot, leaders should pause and ask a few questions: Is there information or data to support the

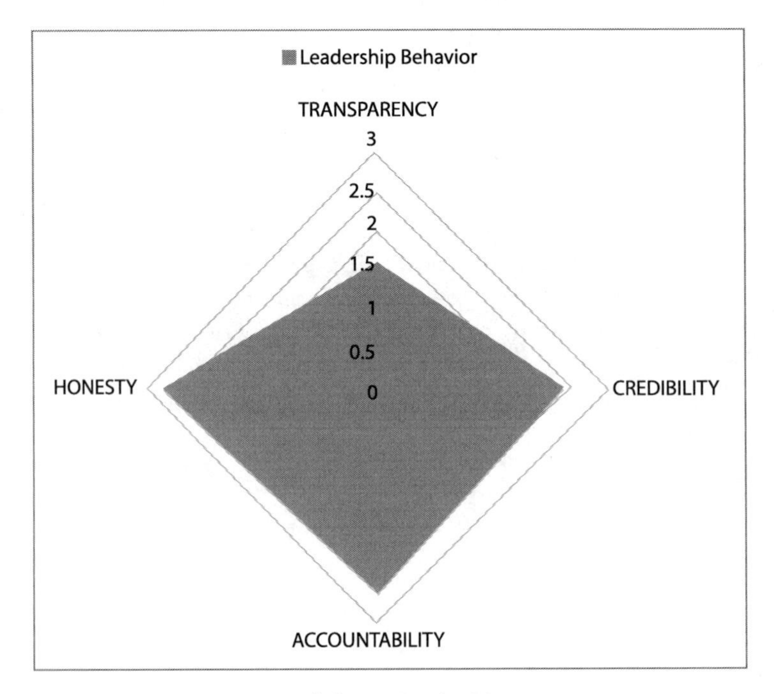

FIGURE 4.6 Transparency-deficient Leadership

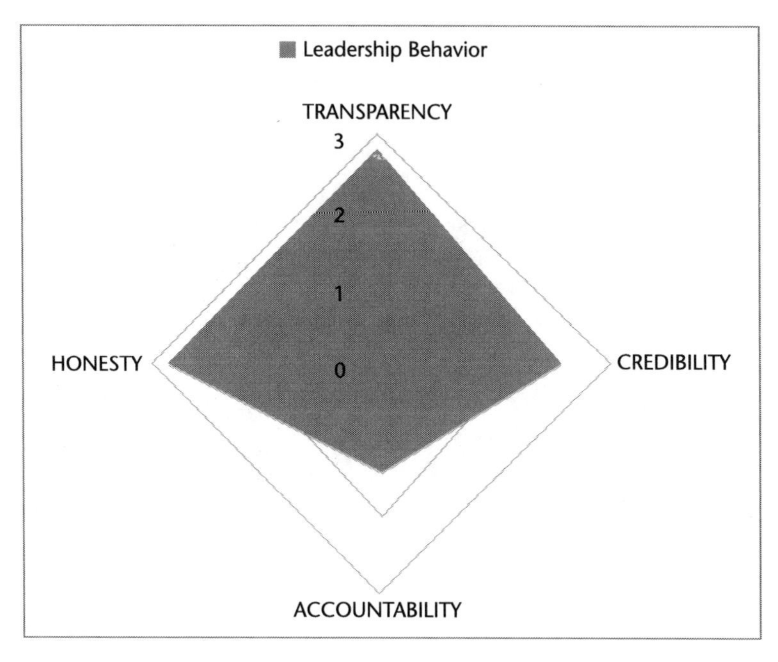

FIGURE 4.7 Accountability-deficient Leadership

decision? What do we know? What don't we know? How long do we have to decide this? How long will it take to get the data? Who has it? Who is working on it? What are the risk and cost of making the wrong decision?

Figure 4.8 illustrates the profile of a leader who is deficient in the *honesty* quadrant. This may prove to be the most difficult deficiency to remedy, since it relies on the individual's emotional intelligence and the socio-psychological ability to empathize with others, especially followers. Bosses have tremendous impact on those who work in an organization. Recent surveys of employees have found extremely high levels of dissatisfaction with the workplace environment and more specifically managers they work for. A random poll by Gallup (Adkins, 2015) of more than 80,000 full- and part-time workers in 2014 found that only 31.5% of employees are engaged and inspired at work. The vast majority—68.5%—is not engaged with their employers with severe consequences to organizational performance. The 2014 Deloitte Global Human Capital Trends report shows that 79% of business and human resources leaders worldwide believe they have significant retention and engagement issues (Deloitte, 2014). Openness, honesty, authenticity, and mutual respect are great mitigations for building relationship capital in organizations.

Finally, leaders deficient in *credibility* (Figure 4.9) often lose their reputation and ability to marshal resources for the common good. They are perceived as political and manipulative. Unable to mobilize support for their vision, they resort

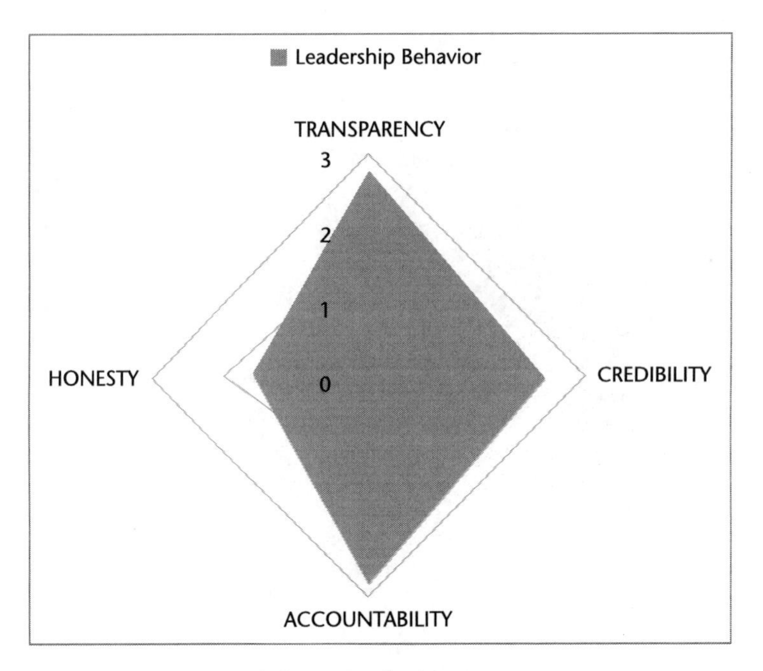

FIGURE 4.8 Honesty-deficient Leadership

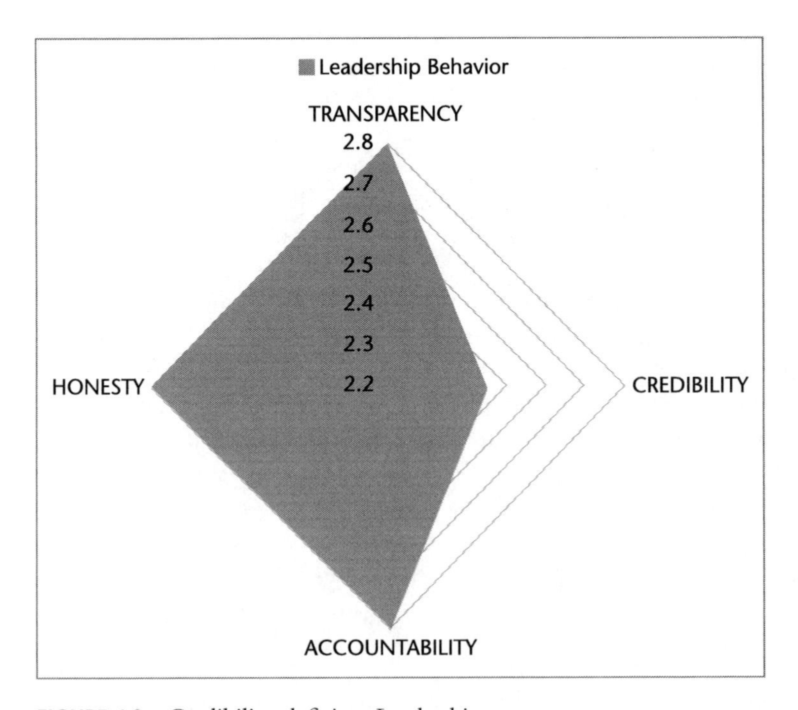

FIGURE 4.9 Credibility-deficient Leadership

to making solo decisions. These leaders tend to withhold information and resort to secrecy and closed-door decisions.

Authentic leaders are those who lead by example in fostering healthy ethical climates characterized by transparency, trust, integrity, and high moral standard. Gardner et al. (2005, p. 344) refer to these individuals as authentic leaders who are not only true to themselves but also help others to sustain their authenticity. To achieve authenticity, trusted leaders must first evaluate their core characteristics, skills, strengths and weaknesses, values and behavioral patterns, and the predominant ways they exercise influence (Miller, 2012). Authenticity is associated with heightened levels of self-awareness, self-clarity, and self-confidence.

Leaders practicing self-regulation must be mindful to remain authentic.

> Self-regulation involves the exertion of self-control through (a) the setting of internal standards, which can be existing standards or newly formulated ones, (b) the evaluation of discrepancies between these standards and actual or potential outcomes, and (c) the identification of intended actions for resolving these discrepancies.
>
> *(Gardner et al., 2005, p. 354)*

In other words, a leader must self-understand that true leadership is a balancing act that requires effective sensitivity and communication skills. When leaders and followers alike are engaged in transparent, honest, accountable, and credible communications they will give more attention to self-reflection, which can result in effective behavioral change.

Leaders who consistently share information about themselves and the organization and who tie ethics and diversity to the long-term success of the organization build a culture of trust with followers and enhance organizational credibility with stakeholders. When people are entrusted with all the necessary information to make wise choices, they are likely to act responsibly and sustain a culture of higher purpose. Authentic corporate leaders who champion diversity and inclusion as part of the new mindset and who sponsor the integration of talent pipeline development in the overall strategy of the organization can also help high-potential women achieve parity with men in corporate officer positions.

Notes

1 Psychologist Diane Halpern, PhD, a professor at Claremont College and past-president (2005) of the American Psychological Association, points out that even where there are patterns of cognitive differences between males and females, "differences are not deficiencies." She continues: "Even when differences are found, we cannot conclude that they are immutable because the continuous interplay of biological and environmental influences can change the size and direction of the effects sometime in the future" (American Psychological Association, 2005).

2 Contrast Eagly's view with Hyde's who stated that "[t]he claims [of gender difference] can hurt women's opportunities in the workplace, dissuade couples from trying to resolve conflict and communication problems and cause unnecessary obstacles that hurt children and adolescents' self-esteem" (American Psychological Association, 2005).
3 In a 2011 study, Catalyst looked at Fortune 500 companies and found that those in the top quartile in terms of female board representation—with women making up 19–44% of board members, had a 16% ROS (i.e., return on sales or net income as a percentage of revenue) higher than companies with no women on their boards (Carter & Wagner, 2011).

References

Adkins, A. (2015, January 28). Majority of US employees not engaged despite gains in 2014. *Gallup*. Retrieved from www.gallup.com/poll/181289/majority-employees-not-engaged-despite-gains-2014.aspx.

American Psychological Association. (2005, October 20). Men and women: No big difference. Retrieved from www.apa.org/research/action/difference.aspx.

Amin, A. (2014). Self-discipline gives girls the edge: Gender in self-discipline, grades, and achievement test scores. *Happier Human*. Retrieved from http://happierhuman.com/self-discipline-gives-girls-the-edge-gender-in-self-discipline-grades-and-achievement-test-scores/.

Avolio, B., & Gardner, W. (2005). Authentic leadership development: Getting to the root of positive forms of leadership. *The Leadership Quarterly*, *16*(3), 315–338.

Avolio, B., Gardner, W., Walumbwa, F., Luthans, F., & May, D. (2004). Unlocking the mask: A look at the process by which authentic leader's impact follower attitudes and behaviors. *The Leadership Quarterly*, *15*(6), 801–823.

Azanzaa, G., Moriano, J. A., & Molero, F. (2013). Authentic leadership and organizational culture as drivers of employees' job satisfaction. *Journal of Work and Organizational Psychology*, *29*, 45–50.

Barsh, J., & Yee, L. (2012). Unlocking the full potential of women at work. *McKinsey & Company*. Retrieved from www.mckinsey.com/business-functions/organization/our-insights/unlocking-the-full-potential-of-women-at-work.

Bass, B. M. (1990). From transactional to transformational leadership: Learning to share the vision. *Organizational Dynamics*, Winter, 19–31.

Belasen, A. T. (2008). *The theory and practice of corporate communication: A competing values perspective*. Thousand Oaks, CA: Sage Publications.

Belasen, A. T. (2012). *Developing women leaders in corporate America, balancing competing demands, transcending traditional boundaries*. Santa Barbara, CA: Praeger Publishing.

Belasen, A. T. (2016a). Introduction: Corruption and destructive leadership. In A. T. Belasen & R. Toma (Eds.), *Confronting corruption in business: Trusted leadership, civic engagement* (pp. 1–29). New York, NY: Routledge.

Belasen, A. T. (2016b). Deception and failure: Mitigating leader-centric behaviors. In A. T. Belasen & R. Toma (Eds.), *Confronting corruption in business: Trusted leadership, civic engagement* (pp. 183–216). New York, NY: Routledge.

Belasen, A. T., & Frank, N. M. (2008). Competing values leadership: Quadrant roles and personality traits. *Leadership and Organizational Development Journal*, *29*(2), 127–143.

Belasen, A. T., & Frank, N. M. (2012). Using the competing values framework to evaluate the interactive effects of gender and personality traits on leadership roles. *The International Journal of Leadership Studies*, 7(2), 192–215.
Belasen, A. T., Eisenberg, B., & Huppertz, J. (2015). *Mastering leadership: A vital resource for healthcare organizations*. Boston: Jones Bartlett Learning.
Bono, J. E., & Judge, T. A. (2004). Personality and transformational and transactional leadership: A meta-analysis. *Journal of Applied Psychology, 89*(5), 901–910.
Bowles, H. R., & McGinn, K. (2005). Claiming authority: Negotiating challenges for women leaders. In D. M. Messick & R. Kramer (Eds.), *The psychology of leadership: some new approaches* (pp. 191–208). Mahway, NJ: Erlbaum.
Bowling, C. J., Kelleher, C. A., Jones, J., & Wright, D. S. (2006). Cracked ceilings, firmer floors and weakening walls: Trends and patterns in gender representation among executives leading American state agencies, 1970–2000. *Public Administration Review, 66*(6), 823–836.
Buchan, N. R., & Solnick, S. J. (2008). Trust and gender: An examination of behavior and beliefs in the investment game. *Journal of Economic Behavior & Organization, 68*(3–4), 466–476.
Buss, D., & Schmitt, D. (2011). Evolutionary psychology and feminism. *Sex Roles, 64*, 768–787.
Cameron, K. S., Quinn, R. E., DeGraff, J., & Thakor, A. V. (2006). *Competing values leadership: Creating value in organizations*. Northampton, MA: Edward Elgar.
Carter, N. M., & Wagner, H. M. (2011). The bottom line: Corporate performance and women's representation on boards (2004–2008). *Catalyst, 1*. Retrieved from www.catalyst.org/knowledge/bottom-line-corporate-performance-and-womens-representation-boards-20042008.
CAWP. (2016). Facts/current numbers. *Eagleton Institute of Politics, Rutgers University*. Retrieved from www.cawp.rutgers.edu/current-numbers.
Chin, J. L. (2004). Feminist leadership: Feminist visions and diverse voices. *Psychology of Women Quarterly, 28*, 1–8.
Daft, R. (2011). *The leadership experience* (5th ed.) Mason, OH: South-Western, Cengage Learning.
Dame, J. (2014). The four keys to being a trusted leader. *Harvard Business Review*. Retrieved from https://hbr.org/2014/03/the-four-keys-to-being-a-trusted-leader/.
Deloitte. (2014). Engaging the 21st-century workforce. A report by Deloitte Consulting LLP and Bersin. Retrieved from http://dupress.com/periodical/trends/global-human-capital-trends-2014.
Dworkin, T. M., Maurer, V., & Schipani, C. A. (2012). Career mentoring for women: New horizons, expanded methods. *Business Horizons, 55*(4), 363–372.
Eagly, A. H. (1995). The science and politics of comparing women and men. *The American Psychologist, 50*, 145–158.
Eagly, A. H., & Carli, L. L. (2003). The female leadership advantage: An evaluation of the evidence. *The Leadership Quarterly, 14*, 807–834.
Eagly, A. H., & Carli, L. L. (2004). Women and men as leaders. In J. Antonakis, R. J. Sternberg, & A. T. Cianciolo (Eds.), *The nature of leadership* (pp. 279–301). Thousand Oaks, CA: Sage.
Eagly, A. H., & Carli, L. L. (2007). *Through the labyrinth: The truth about how women become leaders*, Boston: Harvard Business School Press.

Eagly, A. H., Johannesen-Schmidt, M. C., & Van Engen, M. L. (2003). Transformational, transactional, and laissez-faire leadership styles: A meta-analysis comparing women and men. *Psychological Bulletin, 129*(4), 569–591.

Eagly, A. H., & Wood, W. (2013). The nature-nurture debates: 25 years of challenges in the psychology of gender. *Perspectives on Psychological Science, 8*, 340–357.

Edelman, R. (2013). Edelman Trust Barometer 2013. Retrieved from www.edelman.com/insights/intellectual-property/trust-2013/.

Egan, M. (2015, March 24). Still missing: Female business leaders. *CNNMoney*. Retrieved from http://money.cnn.com/2015/03/24/investing/female-ceo-pipeline-leadership/.

Fine, M. G. (2007). Women, collaboration, and social change: An ethics-based model of leadership. In J. L. Chin, B. L. Lott, J. K. Rice, & J. Sanchez-Hucles (Eds.), *Women and leadership: Visions and diverse voices* (pp. 177–191). Boston: Blackwell.

Fine, M. G., & Buzzanell, P. M. (2000). Walking the high wire: Leadership theorizing, daily acts, and tensions. In P. M. Buzzanell (Ed.), *Rethinking organizational and managerial communication from feminist perspectives* (pp. 128–156). Thousand Oaks, CA: Sage.

Foust-Cummings, H., Dinolfo, S., & Kohler, J. (2011, August). Sponsoring women to success. *Catalyst, 201*(1). Retrieved from www.catalyst.org/publication/485/sponsoring-women-to-success.

Gardner, W., & Schermerhorn, J. (2004). Unleashing individual potential: Performance gains through positive organizational behavior and authentic leadership. *Organizational Dynamics, 33*(3), 270–279.

Gardner, W., Avolio, B., Luthans, F., May, D., & Walumbwa, F. (2005). Can you see the real me? A self-based model of authentic leader and follower development. *The Leadership Quarterly, 16*(3), 343–372.

George, B. (2003). *Authentic leadership*. San Francisco: Jossey-Bass.

Goleman, D. (2009). What makes a leader? *Harvard Business Review*, Winter, 44–53.

Haslam, S., & Ryan, M. K. (2005). The glass cliff: Evidence that women are over-represented in precarious leadership positions. *British Journal of Management, 16*(2), 81–99.

Hays, J., Allinson, C. W., & Armstrong, S. (2004). Intuition, women managers, and gendered stereotypes. *Personnel Psychology, 33*(4), 403–417.

Herminia, I., Carter, N., & Silva, C. (2010). Why men still get more promotions than women. *Harvard Business Review*. Retrieved from https://hbr.org/2010/09/why-men-still-get-more-promotions-than-women.

Hewlett, S. A. (2013). *Forget a mentor, find a sponsor: The new way to fast-track your career*. Boston: Harvard Business Review Press.

Hewlett, S., Peraino, K., Sherbin, L., & Sumberg, K. (2010). The sponsor effect: Breaking through the last glass ceiling. *Center for Work-Life Policy Survey*. Research sponsored by American Express, Deloitte, Intel, and Morgan Stanley. Retrieved fromhttps://30percentclub.org/assets/uploads/UK/Third_Party_Reports/TheSponsorEffect_execsummry.pdf.

Hyde, J. S. (2005). The gender similarities hypothesis. *The American Psychologist, 60*(6), 581–592.

Hyde, J. S. (2014). Gender similarities and differences. *Annual Review of Psychology*, 65, 373–398.

Ibarra, H., & Obodaru, O. (2008). Women and the vision thing. *Harvard Business Review, 85*(1), 40–47.

Ibarra, H., Ely, R. J., & Kolb, D. M. (2013). Women rising: The unseen barriers, *Harvard Business Review*. Retrieved from https://hbr.org/2013/09/women-rising-the-unseen-barriers.

Institute of Business Ethics. (2014). National Business Ethics Survey 2013 Summary—US. Retrieved from www.ibe.org.uk/userassets/survey%20summaries/nbes2013ibe summary.pdf.

Irby, B. J., Brown, G., Duffy, J. A., & Trautman, D. (2002). The synergistic leadership theory. *Journal of Educational Administration*, *40*(4/5), 304–322.

Izraeli, D. N., & Adler, N. (1994). Competitive frontiers: Women managers in a global economy. In N. Adler & D.N. Izraeli (Eds.), *Competitive frontiers: women managers in a global economy* (pp. 3–21). Cambridge, MA: Blackwell.

Johnson, K. (2015, December 2). Women move into law enforcement's highest ranks. *USA Today*. Retrieved from www.usatoday.com/story/news/nation/2013/08/13/women-law-enforcement-police-dea-secret-service/2635407/.

Judge, T. A., Higgins, C. A., Thoresen, C. J., & Barrick, M. R. (1999). The big five personality traits, general mental ability, and career success across the life span. *Personnel Psychology*, *52*(3), 621–652.

Kark, R., Shamir, B., & Chen, G. (2003). The two faces of transformational leadership: Empowerment and dependency. *Journal of Applied Psychology*, *88*(2), 246–255.

Konrad, A. M., Ritchie Jr., J. E., Lieb, P., & Corrigall, E. (2000). Sex differences and similarities in job attribute preferences: A meta-analysis. *Psychological Bulletin*, *126*, 593–641.

Lee, Y. J. (2014). The feminine sector: Explaining the overrepresentation of women in the nonprofit sector in the USA. *International Journal of Social Economics*, *41*(7), 556–572.

Lippa, R. (1998). Gender related individual differences, and the structure of vocational interests: The importance of the people–things dimension. *Journal of Personality and Social Psychology*, *74*(4), 996–1009.

Miller, P. (2012). Self-reflection: The key to effective leadership. *Today's Manager*, December 2011–January 2012.

Mueller, G., & Plug, E. (2006). Estimating the effects of personality on men and female earnings. *Industrial & Labor Relations Review*, *60*(1), 3–22.

Olson, S. (2013, June 11). Men mature after women—11 years after, to be exact—a British study reveals. *Medical Daily*. Retrieved from www.medicaldaily.com/men-mature-after-women-11-years-after-be-exact-british-study-reveals-246716.

Parker, K. L. (2004). Leadership styles of agricultural communications and information technology managers: What does the Competing Values Framework tell us about them? *Journal of Extension*, *42*(1). Retrieved from https://joe.org/joe/2004february/a1.php.

Pew Research Center. (2015). Public says women are equally qualified, but barriers persist. Retrieved from www.pewsocialtrends.org/2015/01/14/women-and-leadership/.

Porter, N., & Daniel, J. H. (2007). Developing transformational leaders: Theory to practice. In J. L. Chin, B. Lott, J. K. Rice, & J. Sanchez-Hucles (Eds.), *Women and leadership: Transforming visions and diverse voices* (pp. 245–263). Malden, MA: Blackwell.

Post, C., DiTomaso, N., Lowe, S. R., Farris, G. F., & Cordero, R. (2009). A few good women: Gender differences in evaluations of promotability in industrial research and development. *Journal of Managerial Psychology*, *24*(4), 348–371.

Prediger, D. J. (1982). Dimensions underlying Holland's hexagon: Missing link between interests and occupations? *Journal of Vocational Behavior, 21*, 259–287.

Prime, J. L., Carter, N. M., & Welbourne, T. M. (2009). Women "take care," men "take charge": Managers' stereotypic perceptions of women and men leaders. *The Psychologist-Manager Journal, 12*, 25–49.

Roebuck, D. B., & Smith, D. N. (2011). Wisdom from executive female leaders: What can organizations, executive education programs, and graduate students learn? *Journal of Executive Education, 10*(1), 43–73.

Ryan, M. K., Haslam, S. A., & Postmes, T. (2007). Reactions to the glass cliff: Gender differences in the explanations for the precariousness of women's leadership positions. *Journal of Organizational Change Management, 20*(2), 182–197.

Schein, V. E. (2001). A global look at psychological barriers to women's progress in management. *Journal of Social Issues, 57*(4), 675–688.

Schwartz, T. (2012). What women know about leadership that men don't. *Harvard Business Review* [blog]. Retrieved from https://hbr.org/2012/10/what-women-know-that-men-dont.html.

Semykina, A., & Linz, S. J. (2007). Gender differences in personality and earnings: Evidence from Russia. *Journal of Economic Psychology, 28*(3), 387–410.

Toren, N., Konrad, A. M., Yoshioka, I., & Kashlak, R. (1997). A cross-national cross-gender study of managerial task preferences and evaluation of work characteristics. *Women in Management Review, 12*(6), 234–243.

Trevino, L. K., & Brown, M. E. (2004). Managing to be ethical: Debunking five business ethics myths. *Academy of Management Executive, 18*(2), 69–81.

Twenge, J. M. (1997). Changes in masculine and feminine traits over time: A meta-analysis. *Sex Roles, 36*, 305–325.

Twenge, J. M. (2001). Changes in women's assertiveness in response to status and roles: A cross-temporal metaanalysis, 1931–1993. *Journal of Personality and Social Psychology, 81*, 133–145.

US Office of Personnel Management. (2014). Women in federal service: A seat at every table. Retrieved from www.fedview.opm.gov/2014files/2014_Womens_Report.pdf.

Vilkinas, T. (2000). The gender factor in management: How significant others perceive effectiveness. *Women in Management Review, 15*(5/6), 261–271.

Vilkinas, T., & Cartan, G. (2006). The integrated competing values framework: Its spatial configuration. *Journal of Management Development, 25*(6), 505–521.

Walters, A. E, Stuhlmacher, A. F., & Meyer, L. L. (1998). Gender and negotiator competitiveness: A meta-analysis. *Organizational Behavior & Human Decision Processes, 76*, 1–29.

Weyer, B. (2007). Twenty years later: Explaining the persistence of the glass ceiling for women leaders. *Women in Management Review, 22*(6), 482–496.

Wittenberg-Cox, A., & Maitland, A. (2008). *Why women mean business: Understanding the emergence of our next economic revolution*. Chichester, UK: Wiley.

Woetzel, J., Madgavkar, A., Ellingrud, K., Labaye, E., Devillard, S., Kutcher, E., Manyika, J., Dobbs, R., & Krishnan, M. (2015). How advancing women's equality can add $12 trillion to global growth. *McKinsey Global Institute Report, September*. Retrieved from www.mckinsey.com/global-themes/employment-and-growth/how-advancing-womens-equality-can-add-12-trillion-to-global-growth.

Won, H. (2006). Links between personalities and leadership perceptions in problem-solving groups. *The Social Science Journal, 43*(4), 659–672.

Zell, E., & Krizan, Z. (2014). Do people have insight into their abilities? A meta-synthesis. *Perspectives on Psychological Science, 9*, 111–125.

Zell, E., Krizan, Z., & Teeter, S. R. (2015). Evaluating gender similarities and differences using metasynthesis. *American Psychologist, 70*(1), 10–20.

PART III

Retaining Key Positions

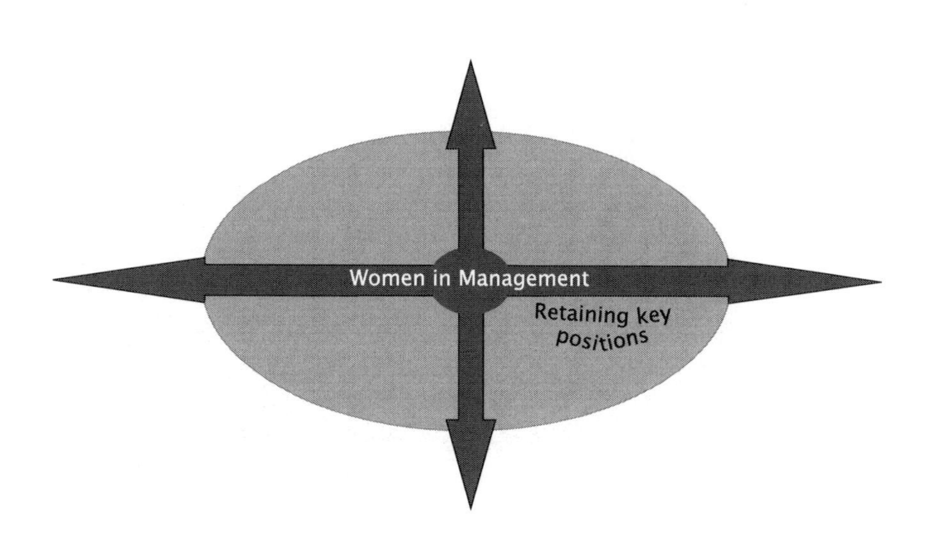

5

CREATING EFFECTIVE BOARDS

Unfair Share, Unwise Choices

Company boards serve numerous roles, some of which include providing continuity for the organization and selecting and appointing a CEO who is charged with the administration of the organization. The board governs using broad objectives and policies and publicly accounts for all organizational expenditures and funds. Because CEOs are mostly men (by mid-2014, about 5% of the Fortune 1000 companies had women CEOs or presidents (Fairchild, 2014) and as of January 2016, women held 20 (4.0%) of CEO positions at S&P 500 companies (Catalyst, 2016)) and the selection of board members is typically influenced by CEOs, many CEOs tend to choose board members who possess the qualities that they themselves have (Arfken, Bellar, & Helms, 2004). They will likely select individuals with whom they feel more comfortable to maintain the "critical competencies" or preserve the "traditional aspects of the board," leaving the opposite gender (women) behind.

A report by Ernst & Young, *Women on US boards: what are we seeing?*, indicates that by February 2015, the number of women occupying board positions on S&P 1500 companies was 2,150 (out of 13,850 seats). It also found that more of those positions—2,200—were held by men named John, James, William, or Robert. The figures for CEO positions were far worse. There are four times as many men named John, James, William, or Robert currently serving as chief executives than there are women (Ernst & Young, 2015). Women don't fare any better in Australia where a recent study cited in Women's Agenda (Dent, 2015) found that there are more men called Peter (6.5%) leading ASX 200 companies than there are women (5.75%).

The "opposites attract" theory when it comes to forming effective teams with complementary skills and co-leadership abilities has been disproven as evident in the underrepresentation of women on boards. Humans tend to lean toward the old adage of "birds of a feather flock together." Neuro-physiology research has shown that the lower portion of a brain region called the "medial prefrontal cortex" (MPFC) is active when people are focusing on themselves or when they are liked by others. The upper portion of the MPFC indicates judgments about different people, especially when they do not "look alike." Because the MPFC plays a role when we think about ourselves, research suggests that we empathize more easily with what is going through the mind of those of the same political orientation, and see them as we see ourselves, rather than build up a judgment on a range of objective knowledge about a person (Highfield, 2008). Indeed, CEO turnover is more sensitive to performance when board members are independent, i.e., "different" (Barsh, Nudelman, & Yee, 2013).

Behavioral scientists observed that longstanding implicit gender biases have made it quite difficult to judge facts about men and women objectively. As noted by Belasen (2012), even women, when polled, would prefer to have a male boss. The powerful impact of unconscious biases against women was also affirmed among both male and female senior scientists who noted that the bias was so deeply entrenched that they were unable to maintain complete objectivity when a study proved that each of them was more inclined to hire, mentor, and propose higher pay when the same candidate for a vacancy was identified as John rather than Jennifer (Watts, 2014). This finding supports the agreement among researchers that gender biases are not a result of in-group favoritism. Rather, gender bias is often an outcome of an implicit cognitive process in which pervasive gender stereotypes shape our judgments, regardless of our intentions. Moss-Racusin stressed that the participants in her study were likely unaware they were discriminating against Jennifer (Moss-Racusin, Dovidio, Brescoll, Graham, & Handelsman, 2012).

Social relationships are heavily influenced and constrained by homogeneity and prototypical attributes, which notably include gender. The paucity of women in the upper echelons of management thus creates a significant barrier to advancement by women, reducing their opportunity to acquire the experience that is important for their own advancement. Many studies cited throughout this book cite roadblocks to women's career advancement including: lack of general management or line experience; exclusion from informal networks; stereotypes about women's roles and abilities; failure of senior executives to sponsor high-potential women or assume accountability for women's advancement; and inflexible workplaces that restrict women's commitment to personal/family responsibilities.

Having women on company boards and TMTs may give companies unique and fresh ideas and make connections between consumers and employees (Arfken et al., 2004). With a lack of gender parity on company boards, innovation and creativity might be stifled or suppressed in favor of dominating males' views. Diversity is a necessity for businesses today. Not only does it reduce tokenism, it also enhances innovation (Torchia, Calabrò, & Huse, 2011) and creates a better understanding of customer preferences (Brenner, 2015). Studies have shown that greater diversity in executive leadership can be linked to long-term success for the company as well a competitive advantage. Today, about 60% of Fortune 500 companies have a chief diversity officer or similar executive position. They guide companies in how to integrate multi-generational work styles, building loyalty from the baby boomers who face retirement to the millennials whose technical savvy comes with demands for flexibility (Kampf, 2016).

Because women have a strong influence on what people buy, companies would be able to access the full range of resources available to a company. To that end, Catalyst reported in 2004 that Fortune 500 companies with the highest percentage of women corporate officers achieved, on average, a whopping 35% higher return on equity and 34% higher stakeholder satisfaction than did competitors with less diversity in the corporate suites (Catalyst, 2004).

Since 2004, however, the ratio of women on boards remained fundamentally unchanged. How can we explain the discrepancy between mounting evidence of women leadership effectiveness on one hand and the shortfall of women in boardrooms and executive suites on the other? If women are as good as men on most competency evaluation criteria and leadership traits (see Chapter 1), and if men excel primarily on traits associated with less formidable transactional, command, and control attributes, how can we resolve the contradiction between desired leadership qualities and the shunning of talented women? If coaching, mentoring, and sponsoring work better to inspire people than authority and control as sources of motivation, why aren't women more prevalent in upper executive positions? Is it possible that women's relational communication and communal leadership style put them at a disadvantage when it comes to overseeing financial performance, navigating strategic business operations in a cutthroat marketplace, and how well the organization stacks up against the competition?

2020 Women on Boards Gender Diversity Index

2020 Women on Boards conducts research studies about the gender composition of the boards of directors of US companies. The goal is to influence and increase the percentage of board seats held by women to 20% or greater by 2020. The cornerstone is the 2020 Gender Diversity Index (GDI), which has tracked the number of women on boards since 2011 using the Fortune 1000 list from 2010 as a baseline of comparison. Companies are ranked on a "W" (Winning) to "Z" (Zero) scale. Winning "W" companies have 20% or greater women on their boards; Very Close "V" companies have 11–19% women on their boards; Token "T" companies have one woman; and Zero "Z" companies are those without women on their boards. As Figure 5.1 shows, as of December 2015, the GDI included 810 active companies with approximately 50% in the "W" category;

18% were "V" companies; 25% were categorized as "T" companies; and 8% as "Z" (2020 Women on Boards, 2016).

Key findings of the 2016 GDI report included:

- In the 810 active GDI companies, women hold 19.7% of board seats, an increase from 18.8% in 2015, and from 14.6% in 2011, the first year of reporting.
- Women gained 75 board seats in 2015; an increase from 52 board seats gained in 2014.
- The number of "W" companies (greater than 20%) has increased in 2016 to 50%; from 45% in 2015 and 40% in 2014.
- The number of "Z" companies (no women) continued to decline from 11% in 2014 to 9% in 2015 and 8% in 2016.
- The percentage of women on boards has increased in all sectors, but six sectors have increased in 2016 to over 20% compared to five sectors last year: consumer cyclical; defensive; financial services; healthcare; real estate; and utilities.

The overall GDI showed a slightly brighter picture when compared with companies on the 2016 Fortune 1000 list. Women held 18.8% in 2016, a slight increase from 17.9% of the board seats in the 2015 Fortune 1000 companies, compared with 16.9% of the board seats in 2014. The minor change was due to the fact that smaller and new companies entering Fortune 1000 are historically less diverse than older, more established companies.

Getting Board Composition Right

Although women and men have reached numerical parity in lower management, fewer women than men lead from the top. By 2012 women occupied 53% of entry-level jobs, 35% at the director level, 24% of senior vice-presidents, and 19% of the C-suite positions of Fortune 500 companies (Barsh & Yee, 2012). Similar statistics showed that 19.2% of the board seats of S&P 500 companies in 2014 were held by women, unchanged from 2013 (Figure 5.2).

The US does not fare well against other countries, especially European countries. In the UK, the ratio of women on boards in 2014 stood at 22.8%, a marked increase from the 12.5% board seats in 2012; and in France, women held 29.7% of board seats. Scandinavian countries fared even better: Norway (35.5%), Finland (29.9%), and Sweden (28.8%) have led the Eurozone in women's share of board seats in 2014 (Figure 5.3). There are signs that Australian companies are making progress, too, at least at the board level. Women represent 26% of board appointments in ASX 200 companies in 2011 and 13% of total director positions—up from 8% in early 2010 (Sanders, Hrdlicka, Hellicar, Cottrell, & Knox, 2011). In fact, a 2015 report from the International Labour Organization indicates that

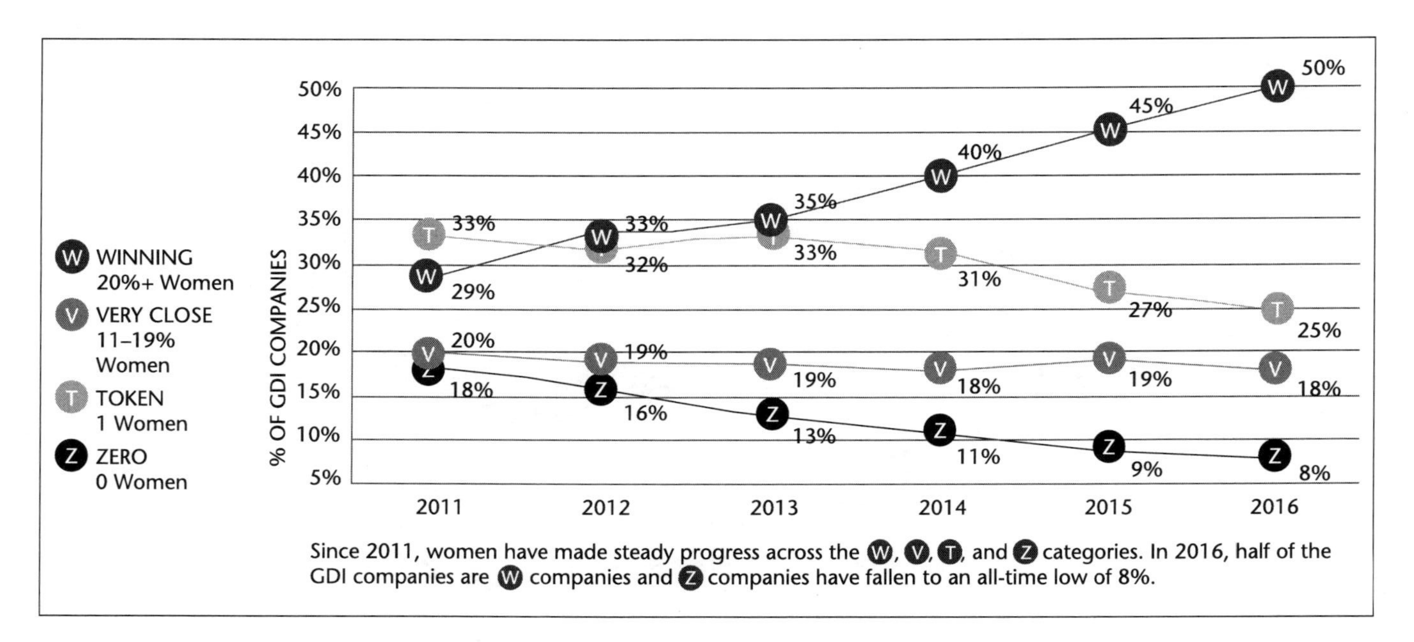

FIGURE 5.1 2011–2016 Trends in the GDI

Source: 2020 Women on Boards (2015). Reprinted with permission.

Note: Percentages may not add to 100% due to rounding.

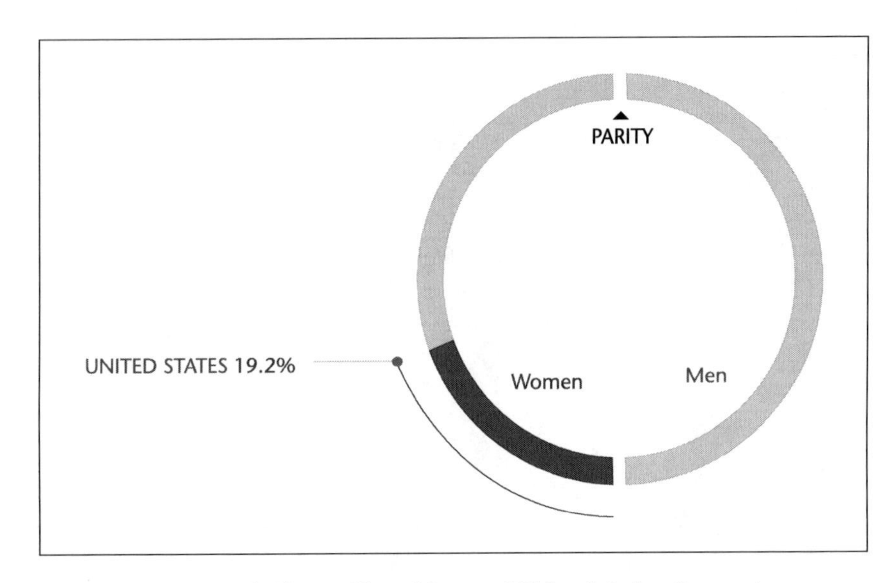

FIGURE 5.2 Women's Share of Board Seats at US Stock Index Companies

Source: Catalyst (2015a).

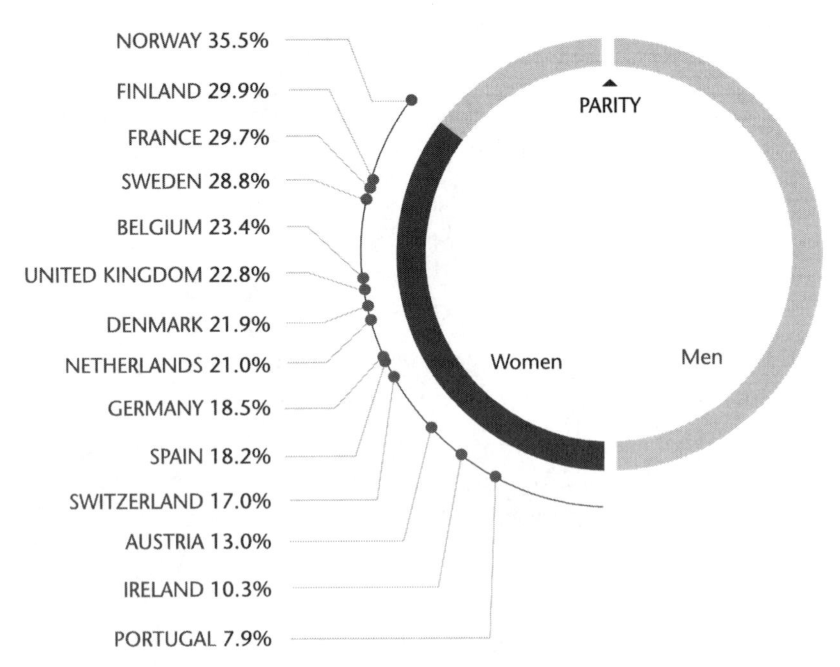

FIGURE 5.3 Women's Share of Board Seats at European Stock Index Companies

Source: Catalyst (2015a).

post-Soviet countries such as Russia, Belarus, Latvia, and Moldova have the highest percentage of women in TMTs.

Having the right attributes on the board is critical for understanding the financial, industrial, and operational aspects of the business. Companies with more women on their boards and with diverse TMTs are not just opening doors to gender equality but are also reaping greater financial rewards and improving the bottom line (Adler, 2001). Women on boards may also facilitate and pressure their companies to hire more women to management positions as well as trigger a trickle-down effect of stopping the leaking pipeline and influencing the promotion of women from within. Furthermore, if boards have a role in the selection of C-suite executives, female board members might be active sponsors of female candidates for these positions, or might be able to leverage their influence to promote female candidates for these positions. This should also stimulate strong social ties, increase the likelihood for active mentoring relationships, and upturn the social capital of women in organizations.

CEO Gender Turnover

While the CEO suite continues to be dominated by men, there was a significant increase in the number of outgoing male CEOs being replaced by women in 2014 (Challenger, Gray, & Christmas, Inc., 2015). Of the 1,036 replacements Challenger has tracked in 2014, 881 or 85%, were men, compared to 2013, when 89% of replacements were men. The number of women replacing men increased by nearly 70% from 61 in 2013 to 103 last year. The number of women replacing women also increased. Meanwhile, the number of instances where departing female CEOs were replaced by men declined by 25%. Through December 2014, 198 women have left the CEO position. Of those, 22 reportedly became CEOs elsewhere. In 2013, 158 women left the CEO position, 11 of whom reportedly went on to become CEO of another organization. The year 2015 failed to see much change in the way of female leaders. Of the 1,025 replacements Challenger has tracked in 2015, 868 or 85% were men, which was equal to the percentage in 2014. The number of women replacing men increased slightly by 5% from 103 in 2014 to 108 in 2015. This number fell to 95 in 2016. The number of women replacing women stayed virtually constant in 2013–2016, as did the number of instances where departing female CEOs were replaced by men. In 2015, 179 women, or 14.6% of all CEOs, left the CEO position. Of those, 21 reportedly became CEOs elsewhere. In 2014, 198 women left the CEO position, 14.7% of the 1,341 2014 CEO changes, 22 of whom reportedly went on to become CEO of another organization (Table 5.1).

Economic Value

Corporate governance theory[1] turned the debate of having a pluralistic board composition and greater diversity in the C-suite into an economic argument by

TABLE 5.1 CEO Replacements by Gender

	Jan-Sept 2016 (interim)	*2015 (interim)*	*2014 (interim)*	*2013 (interim)*
Women Replacing Men	95 (14)	108 (8)	103 (9)	61 (12)
Women Replacing Women	50 (6)	49 (1)	52 (0)	45 (2)
Men Replacing Women	78 (11)	88 (6)	87 (9)	116 (18)
Men Replacing Men	556 (55)	780 (65)	796 (55)	755 (54)
TOTAL REPLACEMENTS	**779**	**1025**	**948**	**977**
TOTAL CEO CHANGES	**944**	**1,222**	**1,314**	**1,246**

Source: Challenger, Gray, & Christmas, Inc. (2015).

Note: Source updated on October 27, 2016 thanks to Colleen Madden, Challenger, Gray, & Christmas, Inc.

linking a greater number of women at the top with sources of competitive advantage. Diversity is beneficial for business and development of effective succession planning is translated into good business. It has been shown that having female directors in a company leads to increased profitability. In fact, 87% of US CEOs whose organizations have a diversity and inclusiveness strategy say it helped enhance performance (PwC, 2015). Burgess and Tharenou (2002) pointed out that of the 50 most profitable US companies in the Fortune 500 listing, 82% had at least one female director, and all top-10 companies had female directors on their boards leading Margaret Heffernan of Fast Company to proclaim, "the future of business depends on women" (Burgess & Tharenou, 2002, p. 9). Evidence has shown that companies with at least one female board member had a ROE of 14.1% over the past nine years, greater than the 11.2% for those without any women (Women in Technology, 2015), and companies that have focused on increasing gender diversity also experienced better results than those that let women's representation slip or fall.

Studies have shown that female leaders are better able to manage the increasingly diverse workplace, focusing on interpersonal relations, supportive communication, and listening skills. Indeed, employees often rate female leaders as providing more idealized influence, inspirational motivation, individual consideration, and intellectual stimulation—all transformational qualities of leadership, which are important for sustaining adaptive organizations—than their male peers. In addition, companies with a significant percentage of female senior managers and board members have greater chances to perform above the average on several key performance indicators (Catalyst, 2007) including:

- ROE: On average, companies with the highest percentages of women board directors outperformed those with the least by 53%.
- ROS: On average, companies with the highest percentages of women board directors outperformed those with the least by 42%.
- ROIC: On average, companies with the highest percentages of women board directors outperformed those with the least by 66%.

In a later study Catalyst (2011) looked at Fortune 500 companies and found that companies with boards having 19%–44% women had a 16% ROS (i.e., ROS or net income as a percentage of revenue) higher than companies with no women on their boards. According to Broderick and Keefe, unprecedented economic value will occur if women are afforded the same educational and economic opportunities as men. For example, reports have shown that as a result of women entering the workforce over the past four decades, GDP in the US is about 25% higher than it would have been. Goldman Sachs economist Kevin Day has calculated that eliminating the remaining gap between male and female employment would boost GDP in the US by 9%, by 13% in the Eurozone, and by 13% in Japan (Broderick & Keefe, 2015). According to Ellingrud et al. (2016), "[e]very state and city in the United States has the opportunity to further gender parity, which could add $4.3 trillion to the country's economy in 2025."

The correlation between gender diversity on boards and corporate performance can also be found across industries—from consumer discretionary to information technology. In all, based on results from companies with strong female leadership presence, the increase of female leaders in workplaces will likely become a competitive advantage for companies who embrace women's leadership and their contributions to the organization.

LEVERAGING DIVERSITY TO MAXIMUM ADVANTAGE: THE BUSINESS CASE FOR APPOINTING MORE WOMEN TO BOARDS

[T]he Conference Board of Canada tracked the progress of Canadian corporations with two or more women on the board from 1995 to 2001. The Conference Board found that these companies "were far more likely to be industry leaders in revenues and profits six years later." Interestingly, this 2002 Conference Board report also refutes some of the most common myths about the impact of women on corporate boards. These myths include widely held misconceptions such as: women only care about the "soft" issues; women don't have the financial or strategic acumen needed at the board level; and women will hamper board unity. To the contrary, the Conference Board concludes that: "Far from focusing on traditionally 'soft' areas, boards with more women surpass all-male boards in their attention to audit and risk oversight and control." Specifically, its research shows that:

- "74% of boards with three or more women explicitly identify criteria for measuring strategy; only 45% of all-male boards do;" and
- "94% of boards with three or more women explicitly monitor the implementation of corporate strategy; 66% of all-male boards do."

The Conference Board further concludes that the diversity that women bring enriches "the leadership palette with different perspectives" and that this "diversity enables constructive dissent that leads to board unity." The Conference Board's research points to other critical benefits. For instance, gender diversity on the board and senior management team helps organizations to attract and retain valuable female talent. Also, "CEOs report that having women on boards contributes to positive attitudes among female employees." In addition, the advantages that women bring in terms of ethical conduct are clearly significant:

- "94% of boards with three or more women ensure conflict of interest guidelines, compared with 68% of all-male boards;" and
- "86% of boards with three or more women ensure a code of conduct for the organization, compared with 66% of all-male boards."

Women apparently broaden the focus of a board as well. When more women are on the board, the Conference Board found a major increase in the use of non-financial performance measures – such as innovation and social and community responsibility. As the Conference Board believes, "the factors that appear to be influenced by more women on boards are precisely those that have the most impact on corporate results." Another important consideration is the fact that women have a deep and intimate knowledge of consumer markets and customers. Women, for example, control 80% of household spending, and using their own resources, make up 47% of investors. They buy more than three-quarters of all products and services in North America.

The influence of women in business-to-business markets is also growing, especially here in Canada. There are more women entrepreneurs per capita in Canada than in any industrialized country. According to the Prime Minister's Task Force on Women Entrepreneurs, more than 821,000 Canadian women entrepreneurs annually contribute in excess of $18 billion to Canada's economy. Their numbers have increased more than 200 percent over the past 20 years and they represent the fastest growing demographic in our economy today.

(Stephenson, 2004)

SOX and Board Seats

Although the Sarbanes-Oxley Act (SOX) did not expressly address board composition, increasing the independence of public company boards was a primary objective of the legislation. Prior to SOX, boards in United States, as well as in most other countries, were dominated by insiders who were members of the TMT. The Act, which was proposed in 2002, approved in 2003, and became effective in 2004, requires a majority of independent directors for firms listed on the New York Stock Exchange and NASDAQ. The intent was to make boards more independent from management and thus induce them to more effectively monitor strategic decisions and guide company executives toward greater shareowner accountability. For publicly held companies without a majority of independent directors, SOX imposes a ceiling on the percentage of dependent or internally appointed directors. In 2002, CEOs were the only non-independent directors on 31% of S&P 500 boards compared with 59% of boards in 2012. The percentage of independent directors on S&P 500 boards has increased from 79% in 2002 to 84% in 2012 (PR Newswire, 2012). US public company boards today are more independent from management, more financially savvy, and more diverse.

WHY MORE WOMEN AREN'T LANDING BOARD SEATS AND WHAT IT WILL TAKE TO CHANGE THINGS

Companies need to have the right talent in place in order to stay relevant and get ahead—from entry-level positions to the C-suite and the boardroom. One option to help promote more women in the workplace is through succession planning, especially on boards. But only 44% of directors "very much" agree that they're spending sufficient time on director succession, according to PwC's 2015 Annual Corporate Directors Survey.

Boards need (and can) do more to increase this number. Effective succession planning requires routine assessment of board members' collective attributes, experience, expertise and, most importantly, diversity. And by diversity, I mean gender and ethnic diversity, as well as diversity of skills, backgrounds, personalities, and opinions. Boards should consider the company's strategy when thinking about director succession and upcoming board member retirements. What aspect of diversity will the board need to help the company deliver on its strategy and stay one step ahead of the competition?

Once the board lays out its succession plans and considers the diversity it needs, the board should proactively get ahead of the search for new directors. Currently, women account for only 20% of all S&P 500 directors despite making up 47% of the U.S. workforce and controlling or influencing nearly three-quarters of household spending and more than 50% of personal wealth in the U.S. With the average S&P 500 board having eleven members, that's about two women per board.

Typically, boards look for a candidate that has been a CEO or held another executive role, as boards often want current or former CEOs as directors. But a mere 4% of S&P 500 CEOs are female and only 14% of the top five leadership positions at the companies in the S&P 500 are held by women. That doesn't make for a big pool of potential candidates. The pipeline for that pool isn't an encouraging picture, either: young women aged 25 to 34 are more likely than young men of the same age to be college graduates or have a graduate degree, and account for almost half of the students in JD, MBA, and MD programs, but the number of ethnically diverse and female executives fell from 2013 to 2014.

Adding to the problem is that boards typically seek recommendations from sitting directors when looking for new board members. This can create a similarly small pool of potential candidates. So how can more women become part of these pools to begin with? I believe good networks are key. Women need to start building their networks early in their career. They need to meet senior executives and ask them for introductions to other senior executives, as well as CEOs and board members. They need to make it known that they want to have leadership roles at their companies and, ultimately, board roles. They need to continue to foster and improve those relationships so that when the time is right they leverage them.

Twenty-seven percent of directors say they don't believe there are enough qualified diverse candidates available. Perhaps they're not looking hard enough. I believe that there are many untapped highly qualified and diverse candidates just a few steps down from the C-suite. In fact, most of the women in these roles are functioning like CEOs and running large segments of the business. They're driving strategies and dealing with risks. These people have the skills to be board members, they just need to know how to get there. And having the right networks is the best way to do so.

(Loop, 2016)

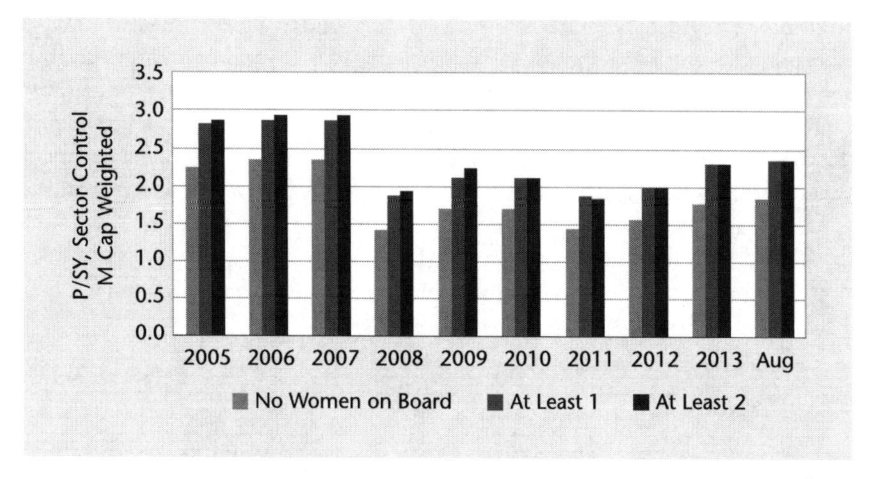

FIGURE 5.4 Representation of Women on Boards

Source: Credit Suisse Research Institute (2014).

US public company boards today are becoming more independent from management, more financially savvy, and slightly more diverse.

As highlighted by the Credit Suisse Research Institute (2014), at an aggregate level, the overall representation of women in senior management positions is in fact quite comparable with that of the board data—12.9% versus 12.7% or 15.3% and 14.1% excluding Japan and South Korea (see also Figure 5.4).

Gender-balanced Boards Through Quotas

In December 2003 Norway passed a law requiring 40% representation of women on boards of public limited companies (PLCs). The primary objective of this reform was to increase the representation of women in top positions in the corporate sector and decrease gender disparity in earnings within that sector. The law became compulsory in 2006 and firms that did not comply by January 2008 would have to be dissolved. As a result, the median percentage of female board members among PLCs has reached 40% by 2008. Following Norway's lead, Spain, Iceland, Italy, Finland, France, and the Netherlands have all passed similar reforms.

Subsequent to political and media discussions, the subject of female participation on boards has been introduced into governmental regulations in Europe, too. The Commission of the European Union (EU), for example, has been supporting the promotion of women into senior executive positions and accepted a proposal for an EU-wide gender equality quota on supervisory boards. Accordingly, 40% of all board seats must have women directors by 2020. The proposal also includes a "flexi quota" or an obligation for publicly listed companies to set themselves specific self-regulatory targets regarding the gender representation among executive directors to be met by 2020 (European Commission, 2012). With this law, the EU will follow in the footsteps of several European countries' initiatives requiring gender quotas, such as Norway (40.5%), Sweden (27%), and Finland (26.8%). This intervention will help improve gender diversity in upper corporate echelons through regulation, EEO, legislation, organizational diversity leadership programs, and pressure from external stakeholders. Indeed, Gregoric, Oxelheim, Randoy, and Thomsen (2015) found that gender quota, when supplemented by policies to ensure the transparency of board, helps prevent the crowding out of other diversity dimensions.

Mixed Results

Quotas can be effective mechanisms for improving gender equality as well as the efficiency of allocating, fitting, and managing talent. Because qualified women might be affected by an absence of supporting networks to guide them through the corporate ladder, quotas can provide the initial boost that women need to break the glass ceiling. If discrimination is the key factor for the underrepresentation of women, quotas might help overcome institutional barriers and prejudice by forcing more exposure to talented women in positions of power (Beaman, Raghabendra, Esther, Rohini, & Petia, 2009). However, if high-quality women cannot be found, the quotas may backfire and reinforce negative stereotypes. Credit Suisse Research Institute (2014), for example, pointed out in its report that while Norway has a 40% quota for female representation on boards with at least 10 directors, the number of women in senior management roles is less than 22% (Figure 5.5). Similarly, a study by Bertrand, Black, Jensen, and Lleras-Muney (2014) showed that the implementation of quotas in Norway failed to improve female participation in TMTs more broadly and have done nothing to address the pipeline issues. Key findings from the Bertrand et al. (2014) study included:

- The newly (post-reform) appointed female board members were observably more qualified than their female predecessors.
- The gender gap in earnings within boards fell substantially.
- While the reform may have improved the representation of female employees at the very top of the earnings distribution (top five highest earners) within firms that were mandated to increase female participation on their board, there is no evidence that these gains at the very top trickled down.
- There is little evidence that the reform was accompanied by any change in female enrollment in business education programs, or a convergence in earnings trajectories between recent male and female graduates. While young women preparing for a career in business report being aware of the reform and expect their earnings and promotion chances to benefit from it, the reform did not affect their family plans.

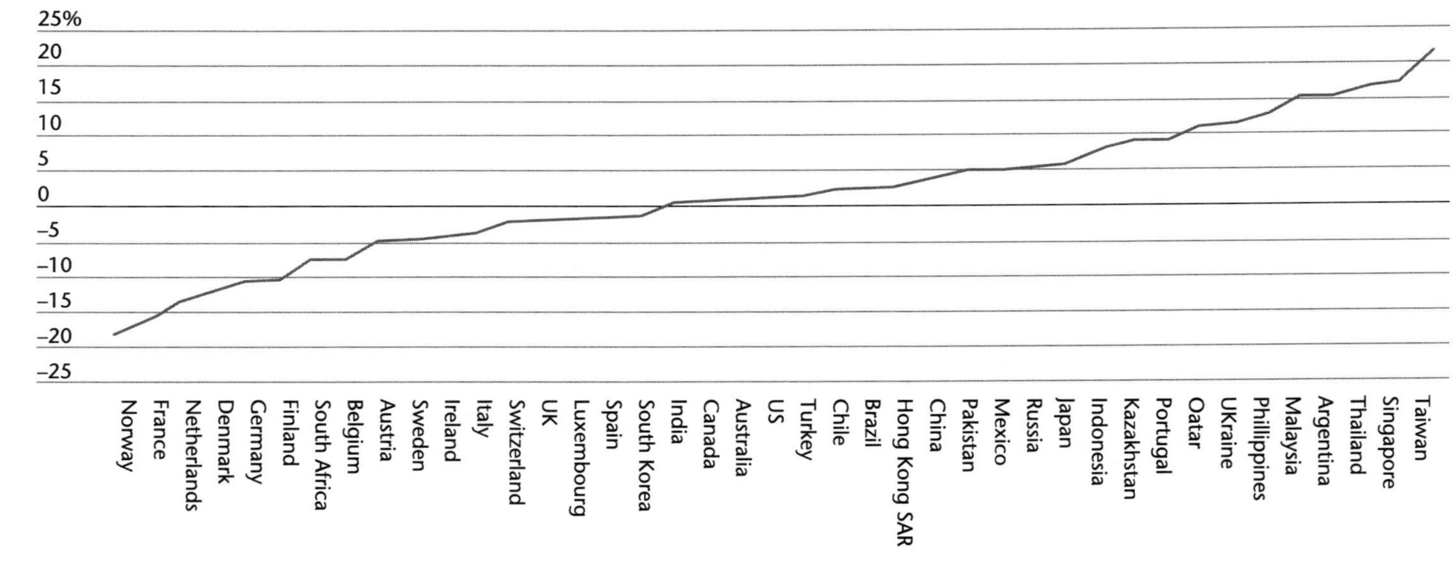

FIGURE 5.5 2013 Female Management Gap by Country (Board versus Top Management)

Source: Credit Suisse Research Institute (2014).

- Overall, in the short run, the reform had very little discernable impact on women in business beyond its direct effect on the newly appointed female board members.

However, these authors concluded that the "lack of positive spillovers beyond the very top [is due to the fact that] it may be too early to tell whether or not a larger number of female employees will benefit from the gender quota in the boardroom" (Bertrand et al. 2014, p. 20).

Possible Effects of Gender Quotas on Boards

The introduction of quotas has generated a healthy debate and led companies and policy makers to consider other measures to improve the gender gap and stop the leaking pipeline. Arguably quotas have led to a possible "tokenism" in some areas rather than an opportunity to create a better management structure. However, gendered-balanced boards reduce the pressures associated with token status, increase women leaders' access to professional networks and support, and increase the likelihood of performance success and satisfaction. Not only does diversity increase women's odds of being promoted to CEO, but it also increases women leaders' tenure duration (Cook & Glass, 2015). More than 80% of board directors at least somewhat believe diversity enhances board effectiveness and company performance, but only 22% say they very much believe there are enough qualified diverse candidates available (PwC, 2015). Paradoxically, women accounted for 53% of entry-level jobs but their presence at the director level (37%), as senior vice-presidents (28%), and in the C-suite (14%) shrinks significantly (Women in the Economy, 2011) underscoring the problem with the leaking pipeline. The corporate pipeline disproportionally loses women at every level.

Potential effects of gender quotas are:

They Might Help in Reducing the Gender Gap

- Lots of qualified women that were not being vocal enough/not competing enough for these high profiles jobs now being eased into them.
- Higher representation of women in top corporate echelons fosters thinking about organizational change to increase family amenities of work ("Women watching out for other women").
- Accelerate changes in social norms by increasing society's exposure to high-ability women in leadership positions.
- Incentivize more "at risk" women to stay on the fast track as likelihood of "board membership" increases; incentivize more "at risk" women to stay on the fast track as female-heavier boards expect to consider more women for other top corporate jobs.

- Increase demand for organizational structures that can accommodate these women; more exposure to high-ability women in leadership position (board and non-board).

They Might Do Nothing, or Even Backfire

- Total number of board positions is fairly limited.
- 40% is lower than the 51% of women in the US.
- Power of the board may be limited (non-executive positions).
- Women *may not* be more "tolerant" or "accommodating" of other women.
- Incentive effects, role-model effects strongly dependent on the assumption that high-quality women will be appointed to these boards.
- Possible issues: limited supply of qualified women; appointment of token women with limited voice by "gaming" the system e.g., stuffing boards with sub-par women.
- Board membership takes away from other more productive activities?

(Bertrand, 2013)

Gender-balanced boards could help shape organizational policies toward pay equity and flexible work schedule that accommodate working mothers and improve work–family integration. Building gender diversity in management could become a goal for results-based leadership (Ulrich, Zenger, & Smallwood, 1999)—delivering positive outcomes for employees, the organization, customers, and investors—while also promoting the advancement of women in the workplace.

Women on Boards and Corporate Performance

The evidence in favor of leveraging diversity in senior management generally supports the claim for appointing more women to boards of directors although a recent meta-analysis (see box "Diversity among Norwegian Boards of Directors") has shown that the overall mean weighted correlation between the percentage of females on corporate boards and firm performance was small and rather non-significant (Pletzer, Nikolova, Kedzior, & Voelpel, 2015).

Thomsen, Gregoric, Randøy, and Oxelheim (2009) examined the relationship between board diversity and economic performance among listed companies in Scandinavia (Denmark, Norway, Sweden, and Finland) over the period 2001–2007 and found that board homogeneity has had an expected negative effect on firm value and growth and that diverse boards outperformed homogeneous boards on all performance measures, i.e., firm value, return on assets, and growth. Board diversity was measured by gender, nationality, and age dispersion. It was found that companies with diverse boards generally perform better than companies with homogeneous boards. These authors were also able to find some statistical support for a causal effect. However, their findings were highly sensitive to model specification including choice of control variables, econometric techniques, and measurement. Other studies, however, found that firms generated on average 1% (or over $40 million) more economic value with at least one woman on their TMT and also enjoyed superior accounting performance (Dezsö & Ross, 2012).

DIVERSITY AMONG NORWEGIAN BOARDS OF DIRECTORS: DOES A QUOTA FOR WOMEN IMPROVE FIRM PERFORMANCE?

At the end of 2002 women comprised only 10% of the boards of directors of public limited companies (PLCs) in Norway. By April 2008, roughly 40% of directors of such firms were women. This leap in representation was the result of Norwegian laws that set a 40% quota for women on boards of PLCs. Quota reform of this magnitude provides a massive shock to boards' structures, thereby providing new empirical evidence on how board diversity and use of quotas affects firm performance. The Norwegian reform is important as an example of government intervention to improve gender equality in both corporate management and in general. It is also the forerunner of similar reforms in Spain, Iceland, France, the Netherlands, Belgium, Italy, and Malaysia.

The authors treat the reform as a natural experiment (that is, determined by events or forces beyond the control of researchers – in this case, the Norwegian legislation). For the 2003–07 period they identify changes in returns on assets (ROA) – a measure of how profitable a company is in relation to its total assets – for firms affected by the reform and compare the change in ROA with the change in ROA for Norwegian ordinary limited firms, which were not subject to the quota reform and could therefore serve as a control group. PLCs, a subgroup of limited firms, face stricter rules with regard to capital stock and board composition and size, their board members are not personally liable for debt, and only PLCs can be listed on Oslo Stock Exchange. As a major owner of PLCs, the state could not endorse the gender imbalance on PLC boards, thus legitimizing the quota reform. Initial impact is small. The main results show that the impact of the reform on firm performance is negligible. Neither ROA nor operating revenues changed, and operating costs can be attributed to the increase in women's representation. These findings imply either that the short-run influence of boards is small, or that the newly recruited women did not contribute markedly different resources and perspectives than the men they replaced, at least in this initial period.

However, the authors infer that the reform may be important from a gender-equality perspective. It has increased women's representation on Norwegian boards. This success may have positive long-term effects on women's opportunities and willingness to seek other high-ranked positions in the labor market, which is an important and more wide ranging "second round" effect on gender equality. The reform also appears to have inspired similar reforms in several other countries, improving gender equality in the corporate world. Thus, at this stage, given the negligible economic performance effects but clearly improved gender equality, the overall impression is that the reform has been a success.

(Dale-Olsen, Schøne, & Verner, 2013)

The correlation between gender diversity on boards and corporate performance can also be found in most industries—from consumer discretionary to information technology. In all, based on results from companies with strong female leadership presence, the increase of female leaders in the workplace over the next decade will likely be a great asset to companies that embrace women's leadership and contributions to the organization. In a 2011 study, others argued that if a firm elects board members to maximize value, the quota may trigger reactions by affected firms with adverse effects on shareholder value.[2] Ahern and Dittmar (2012), for example, provided evidence that the quota had a significantly negative impact on shareowners' value due to suboptimal alignment between members' characteristics and shareholders' expectations.

FEMALE REPRESENTATION ON CORPORATE BOARDS AND FIRM FINANCIAL PERFORMANCE—A META-ANALYSIS

In recent years, there has been an ongoing, worldwide debate about the representation of females in companies. Our study aimed to meta-analytically investigate the controversial relationship between female representation on corporate boards and firm financial performance. Following a systematic literature search, data from 20 studies on 3097 companies published in peer-reviewed academic journals were included in the meta-analysis. On average, the boards consisted of eight members and female participation was low (mean 14%) in all studies. Half of the 20 studies were based on data from developing countries and 62% from higher income countries. According to the random-effects model, the overall mean weighted correlation between percentage of females on corporate boards and firm performance was small and non-significant (r = .01, 95% confidence interval: –.04, .07). Similar small effect sizes were observed when comparing studies based on developing vs. developed countries and higher vs. lower income countries. The mean board size was not related to the effect sizes in studies. These results indicate that the mere representation of females on corporate boards is not related to firm financial performance if other factors are not considered.

(Pletzer et al., 2015)

Signaling Value and Finding Talent

Kanter (1993) suggested that the appointment of women to executive and director positions has also symbolic value that may influence firm performance through indirect channels. The business case for diversity postulates two possible internal symbolic effects. First, with the shortage of skilled workers, the acquisition and retention of qualified employees is a competitive advantage, and minorities embody a talent pool that should not remain untapped. Having the right individuals on boards of directors is important as companies increasingly are recognizing the need for a robust talent pipeline to remain relevant as a strategic differentiator. According to the 2015 PwC study, most CEOs are using multiple channels to find talent, including platforms and social media, and 93% of board directors are at least somewhat in agreement that their companies' hiring, retention, and incentive programs support the need to build a strong talent pipeline (PwC, 2015). Thus, diversity at the top contributes to the amelioration and expansion of the talent pool. Second, women on corporate boards and TMTs may have a spillover effect and positively contribute to an increase of the number of women in mid-level positions due to mentoring and role modeling effects (Konrad, Kramer, & Erkut, 2008; Kurtulus & Tomaskovic-Devey, 2012).

Variation in demographic characteristics, including gender, provides greater benefits to companies such as multiple perspectives in problem-solving communications through an increase of the group's collective "intelligence," creativity, and less conformity or groupthink, removal of prejudice, and greater independence. According to principal agency theory, boards are mechanisms for ensuring the separation of ownership and management, increasing transparency and mitigating self-serving utility maximization by company managers. Diverse boards may be more effective in monitoring managers on behalf of shareholders. This is important as more and more boards are navigating an aggressive activist environment. According to the PwC study, 49% of directors say they are extensively involved in discussions of activism and 55% of directors say their board reviewed strategic vulnerabilities that can be targeted by activists (PwC, 2015). Diversity may also have signaling value. For example, female board members may send an important signal to employees and customers that women's rights are respected, thus improving a company's image.

Companies with both women and men leaders in the boardroom and at the executive table are poised to achieve sustainable big wins for the company and society. Data from Catalyst and researchers from Harvard Business School suggest that gender-inclusive leadership and corporate social responsibility, examined through the lens of corporate philanthropy, are linked. Findings in *Gender and corporate social responsibility: It's a matter of sustainability* (Soares, Marquis, & Lee, 2011) include:

- Compared to companies without women executive leaders, companies with gender-inclusive leadership teams contributed, on average, more charitable funds.
- Even after controlling for key factors that might influence total donations, the presence of women leaders in Fortune 500 companies still has a significant, positive effect: more women leaders are correlated with higher levels of philanthropy.
- By keeping gender issues prominent, gender-inclusive leadership likely also affects the quality of corporate social responsibility initiatives.

When it comes to corporate sustainability, the presence of gender-inclusive leadership both on the board and in executive leadership teams should become a new benchmark for stakeholders for judging the long-term health of a company.

DOES FEMALE REPRESENTATION IN TOP MANAGEMENT IMPROVE FIRM PERFORMANCE?

In essence, our econometric specification compares each firm with itself, that is, when the firm has female representation in top management with when it does not. We find that, ceteris paribus, a given firm generates on average 1% (or over $40 million) more economic value with at least one woman on its top management team than without any women on its top management team and also enjoys superior accounting performance. Moreover, while the benefits of female representation in top management are increasing in the innovation intensity of a firm's strategy, even firms without any significant emphasis on innovation do not experience impaired performance as a result of female representation in top management. Thus, our results suggest that even CEOs who believe their firms have gender-neutral recruitment and promotion processes should ensure that their firms maintain at least some level of gender diversity in top management. We believe that these results make a powerful business case for gender diversity and suggest that a CEO who goes the extra mile to help women overcome barriers to their managerial advancement will often be rewarded with improvements in firm performance.

There may be a similar explanation for why we find that a firm's strategy must be at least somewhat focused on innovation for female representation in top management to benefit firm performance. By including a separate fixed effect for each firm in our data, our empirical testing strategy creates a high hurdle for finding a statistically significant effect of female representation in top management. Firms where one is more likely to observe a woman on the top management team are also those that are more likely to have women at senior levels just below the top management team in years when there is no woman on the top management team. Female representation just below top management may provide these firms some of the benefits that we hypothesize arise from female representation in top management, reducing the power of our statistical tests. If so, then, the performance benefits from female representation in top management would be even larger than our analysis implies and could accrue even to firms for which innovation is not important to strategy.

(Dezsö & Ross, 2012)

The Credit Suisse Gender 3000

The Credit Suisse study by the end of 2013 was extended to board structure and corporate performance by drawing on the Credit Swiss Gender 3000. This brought together data for over 26,000 company directors worldwide including 3,400 women directors at YE2013, a global average of 12.7%. Key findings included: board diversity has increased in almost every country and every sector, progressing from 9.6% in 2010 to 12.7% at the end of 2013; and female participation in top management (CEO and directors reporting to the CEO) stood at 12.9% at the end of 2013, but varied considerably from sector to sector and country to country (Credit Suisse Research Institute, 2014) (Table 5.2).

On a widely used risk metric—the debt to equity ratio—no difference was found between companies without women on the board and those with at least one woman on the board in terms of their appetite for debt. In fact, companies with more than 15% of women in the top management show significantly higher debt to equity ratios, compared to those with less than 10%. This may confound some who have suggested that women exercise an inherently risk-averse approach in decision making. However, little evidence was found to support this where debt was concerned.

Three main obstacles to achieving greater gender diversity were deeply interwoven, making them even harder to untangle: cultural biases; workplace-related biases; and structural/policy issues. Each one of these obstacles was analyzed in detail and dispelled some of the most commonly accepted justifications for a "natural" gender gap. Cultural and education issues were the most challenging to

TABLE 5.2 Market Capitalization and Women on the Board

	Number of women on the board				*Average*
	0	*1*	*2*	*>=3*	*M Cap*
Telecommunication Services	19,729	26,013	21,301	44,254	25,943
Energy	16,968	20,773	44,227	31,257	25,616
Consumer Staples	11,266	10,845	21,888	45,650	22,156
Consumer Discretionary	11,259	14,743	21,202	23,824	16,491
Technology	9,111	25,718	38,767	65,494	23,384
Financials	8,500	12,259	18,563	35,296	17,737
Utilities	8,308	7,802	11,190	20,019	11,692
Health Care	8,112	14,417	39,907	52,921	26,587
Materials	7,759	8,971	18,784	16,742	11,422
Industrials	7,692	11,104	16,777	27,224	12,952
Total	**9,891**	**14,569**	**23,295**	**34,268**	**18,161**

Source: Credit Suisse Research Institute (2014).

overcome in the short term, and policy—not quotas—can help improve the current situation significantly. The Scandinavian model in areas such as paternal leave of absence, for example, has produced positive changes in terms of increased representation of women in the work force at all levels.

The good news from the 2014 Credit Suisse Gender study is that organizations are making steady strides toward achieving greater balance of women representation on boards. Companies displaying greater board gender diversity also show better stock-market returns adjusted for sector bias. Companies with more than one woman on the board have returned a compound 3.7% a year over those that have none since 2005. Companies with higher female representation at the board level or in top management exhibited higher returns on equity, higher valuations, and also higher payout ratios (Figure 5.6).

Hardwiring Diversity

High-achieving women who sponsor the promotion of other women in the organization send strong signals both internally and externally that their organizations are adaptive and open to equality and that they seek broad input on how to overcome the systemic barriers that prevent women from reaching the top (Figure 5.7). The other good news is that women remain ambitious and aspire to leadership positions. In fact, women and men share similar aspirations. For example, McKinsey's study (Women in the Economy, 2011) found that 74% of all men and 69% of all women in their sample aspire to advance.

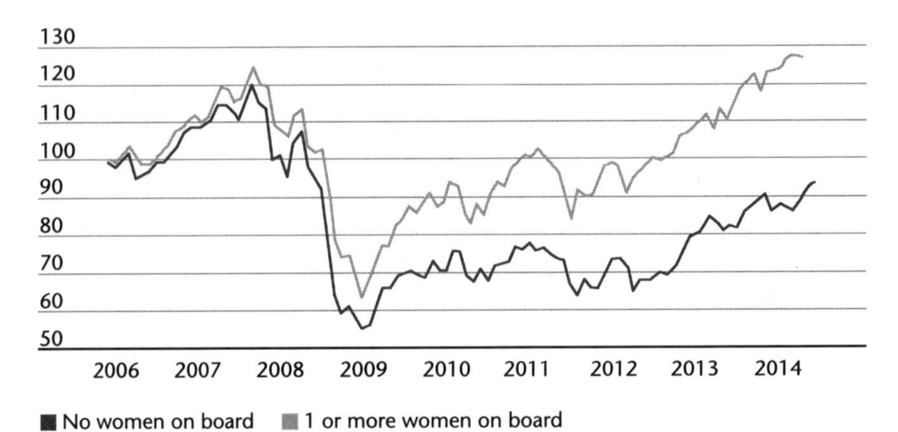

FIGURE 5.6 Global Performance: Companies Market Cap > USD 10 Billion

Source: Credit Suisse Research Institute (2014).

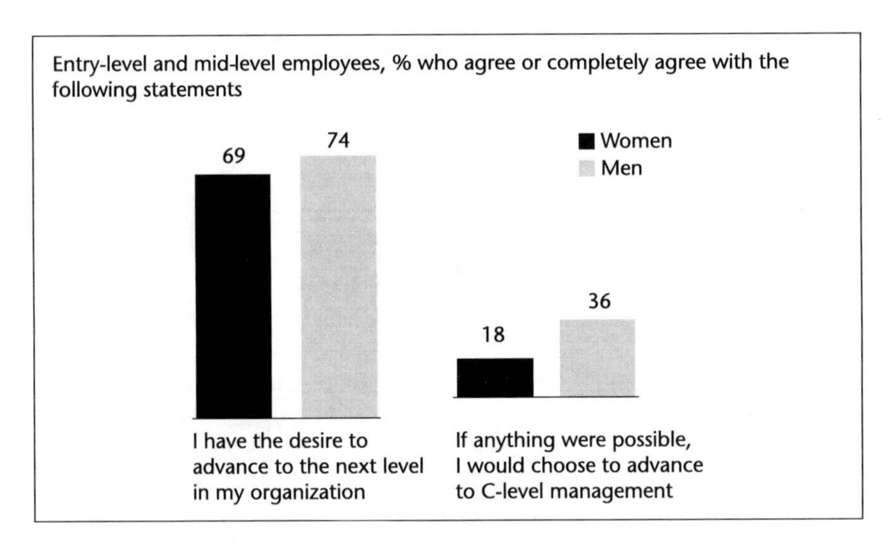

FIGURE 5.7 Women and Men Both Desire to Advance but Few Women Aspire to the C-suite

Source: Barsh & Yee (2012, p. 5).

However, according to the research of Australian companies conducted by Bain & Company there is still a wide gap between intention and outcome (see Figure 5.8). There has been no improvement in the perceptions of a level playing field for women. In fact, there has been a decline, as only 15% of women in 2011 believed that they had equal opportunity (compared with 20% in 2010) for promotion to senior management positions. The widening gap between intention and outcome has also been observed in North America (see Figure 5.9). With all the focus on gender parity, the slow pace of change is confounding.

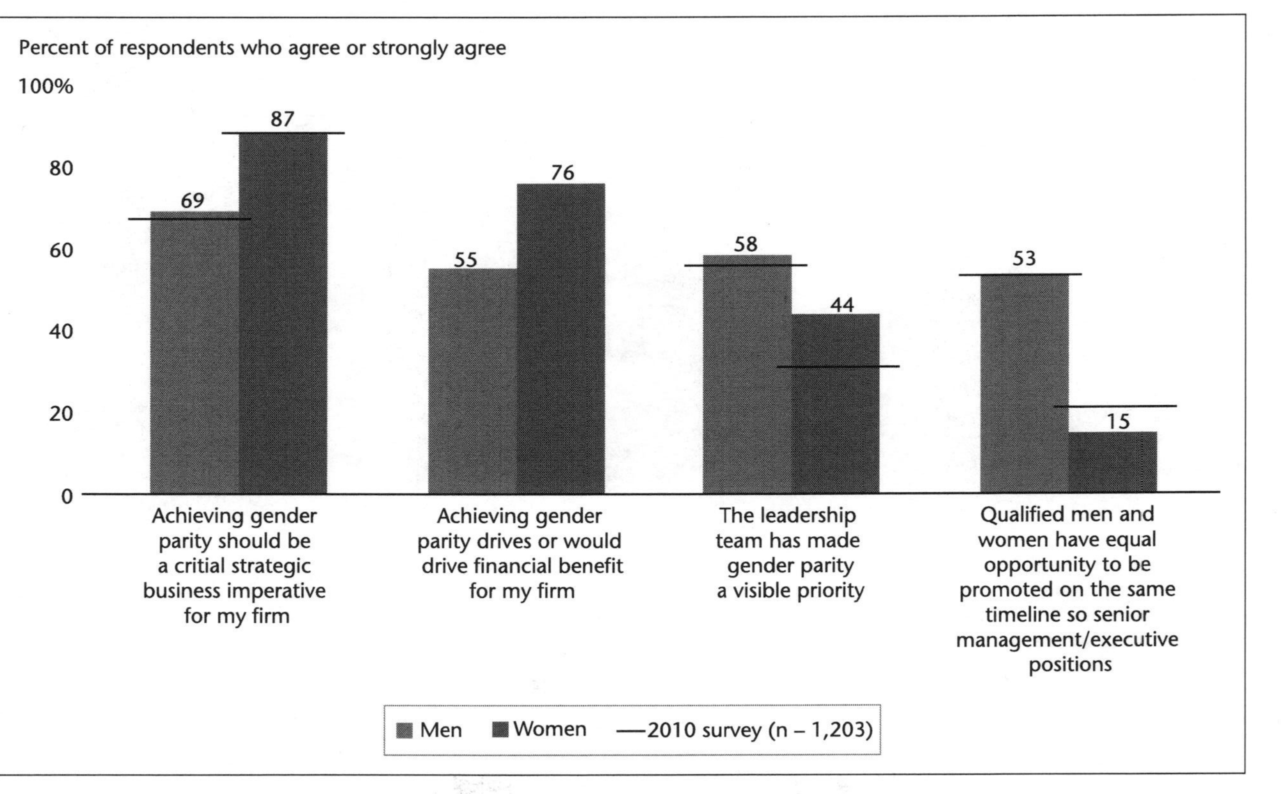

FIGURE 5.8 Gap Between Intention and Outcome Is Still Wide

Source: Sanders et al. (2011).

Why do want to join the C-suite?

- "I enjoy creating a workplace –making decisions that affect people's lives for the better."
- "I think I have a strategic mind and good business acumen and I understand people: I could have a big impact putting that together. It would be rewarding to have the business be successful and to create an engaging work enviroment for our employees."
- "I love being on the inside circle and making decisions. I love seeing how it all goes on. It's daunting, but I'm an information junkie. I want a seat at the table."

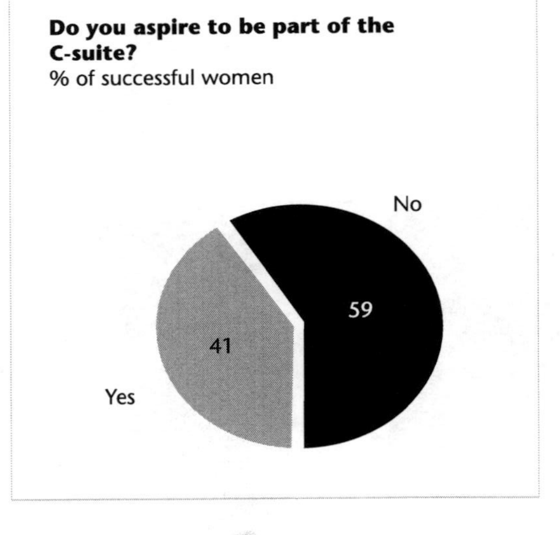

Why are you *not* interested in the C-suite?

- "I'm happy doing what I'm doing. I have 600 employees I manage, and I love interacting with them and giving them purpose. I want to leave a legacy of a sustainable, profitable business."
- "When you see it up close ... it's not clean at the top. Motives are not always enterprise-related. It's more about personal agendas."
- "My ego aspires to make it happen, but my authentic self is not sure if it is worth it. It would require me to do more and more politics, and I don't want to. I don't enjoy that."

FIGURE 5.9 Even Successful Women Executives Offer Mixed Responses

Source: Barsh & Yee (2012).

As business leaders seek to achieve higher levels of financial performance by attracting, developing, promoting, and retaining talent, they need to realize that women, 50% of the talent pool, have exceptional leadership skills. Evidence throughout this chapter and the book shows that these leadership skills are strongly correlated with key success indicators such as retaining talent, organizational commitment, employee engagement, customer satisfaction, and profitability. Women have certain attributes such as high emotional intelligence, attention to details, and adaptability with which they excel (Belasen & Frank, 2013). These attributes have become increasingly more important in an economy more oriented to human service than to the production of material objects.

THE HARD TRUTH ABOUT ECONOMIC INEQUALITY THAT BOTH THE LEFT AND RIGHT IGNORE

Inequality is an inevitable product of capitalist activity, and expanding equality of opportunity only increases it—because some individuals, families, and communities are simply better able than others to exploit the opportunities for development and advancement that today's capitalism affords. Some of the very successes of western capitalist societies in expanding access and opportunity, combined with recent changes in technology and economics, have contributed to increasing inequality. And at the nexus of economics and society is the family, the changing shape and role of which is an often overlooked factor in the rise of inequality.

Though capitalism has opened up ever more opportunities for the development of human potential, not everyone has been able to take full advantage of those opportunities or to progress very far once they have done so.

Formal or informal barriers to equality of opportunity, for example, have historically blocked various sectors of the population—such as women, minorities, and poor people—from benefiting fully from all capitalism offers. But over time, in the advanced capitalist world, those barriers have gradually been lowered or removed, so that now opportunity is more equally available than ever before.

The inequality that exists today arguably derives less from the unequal *availability* of opportunity than it does from the unequal *ability to exploit* opportunity. And that unequal ability, in turn, stems from differences in the inherent human potential that individuals begin with and in the ways that families and communities enable and encourage that human potential to flourish.

The Rising Status of Women

One crucial impact of the rise of the post-industrial economy has been on the status and roles of men and women. Men's relative advantage in the pre-industrial and industrial economies rested in large part on their greater physical strength—something now ever less in demand. Women, in contrast, whether by biological disposition or socialization, have had a relative advantage in human skills and emotional intelligence, which have become increasingly more important in an economy more oriented to human services than to the production of material objects. The portion of the economy in which women could participate has expanded, and their labor has become more valuable—meaning that time spent at home now comes at the expense of more lucrative possibilities in the paid work force.

This has led to the growing replacement of male-breadwinner/female-homemaker households by dual-income households. Both advocates and critics of the move of women into the paid economy have tended to overemphasize the role played in this shift by the ideological struggles of feminism, while underrating the role played by changes in the nature of capitalist production. The redeployment of female labor from the household has been made possible in part by the existence of new commodities that cut down on necessary household labor time (such as washing machines, dryers, dishwashers, etc.).

The trend for women to receive more education and greater professional attainments has been accompanied by changing social norms in the choice of marriage partners. In the age of the breadwinner/homemaker marriage, which predominated from the nineteenth century and the first two-thirds of the twentieth, women tended to place a premium on earning capacity in their choice of partners. Men, in turn, valued the homemaking capacities of potential spouses more than their vocational attainments. It was not unusual for men and women to marry partners of roughly the same intelligence, but women tended to marry men of higher levels of education and economic achievement. As the economy has passed from an industrial economy to a post-industrial service and information economy, women have joined men in attaining recognition through paid work, and the industrious couple today is more likely to be made of peers, with more equal levels of education and more comparable levels of economic achievement.

(Muller, 2013)

The imperative is clear—both morally and commercially. And the commercial case for change is as compelling as the moral one. Women represent an underutilized talent pool in an increasingly talent-constrained

> environment. In addition, decision-making effectiveness in organizations is improved by a diversity of perspectives. That is especially true in a global economy, where women increasingly drive the majority of consumer activity.
>
> *(Sanders et al., 2011, p. 1).*

Women drive an estimated 70–80% of consumer spending with their purchasing power and influence (Figure 5.10); roughly 75% of women identified themselves as the primary shoppers for their households; women now own 40% of America's privately owned businesses and hold half its wealth—estimated to be $11 trillion of a total $22 trillion by 2020 (Femalefactor.com, n.d.).

Ibarra, Ely, and Kolb (2013) suggested three key factors to support women's access to leadership positions:

- Educate women and men about the effects of the second-generation gender bias which is embedded in stereotypes and organizational practices that can be hard to detect, but when people are made aware of it, they see possibilities for change.
- Create leadership development programs for learning, experimentation, and community that help support transitions of high-potential women to bigger roles; provide "identity workspaces" where women are apt to try out unfamiliar behaviors or roles with the active support of sponsors.

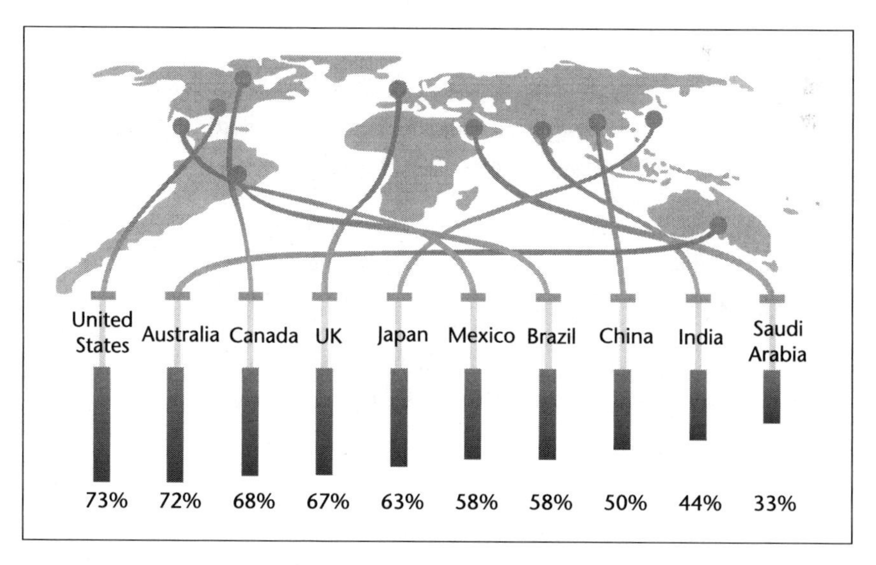

FIGURE 5.10 Percentage of Household Consumption Controlled or Influenced by Women

Source: Catalyst (2015b).

- Manage the competence–likability trade-off by anchoring women's development efforts in a sense of leadership purpose rather than in how women are perceived. Anchoring in purpose enables women to redirect their attention toward shared goals.

In 'Why the future of our organizations depends on having more women in management,' Morgan (2015) noted that more mentoring opportunities, gender diversity programs, and increase in sponsorship for leaders who act as advocates for women are needed to ensure that greater number of women occupied leadership positions.

> The difference between committed CEOs and others is subtle: the former make the goal clear and specific, and they tell everyone about it, while the latter fold "women" into "diversity" and "diversity" into "talent," diffusing focus. In addition, hands-on CEOs reach out to get other senior male leaders involved in the effort, making them catalysts for change. These leaders recognize that gender diversity starts with personal consciousness; once they are committed to the issue, they encourage others to shift mindsets and behaviors in support of the cultural transformation.
>
> *(Barsh & Yee, 2012, p. 10)*

A task force of business, government, and academic leaders sponsored by the *Wall Street Journal* (Women in the Economy, 2011) was set out to confront obstacles that keep women from participating fully in the economy. The group identified ideas and shared best practices from investing personal capital and actively role modeling the desired mindsets and behaviors to building a more open and adaptive culture that could made a real difference and help to drive change and expand gender diversity goals. High-potential women have a proactive role here too as they are expected to initiate queries, network, and bond with key players, male and female, who can sponsor them. Aspiring women own their accomplishments, tone down failures, and volunteer for high-risk assignments. They build momentum through trusting relationships, confidently engage in networking, anticipate responses, negotiate for what they want, use language as a tool for influence, and learn to interrupt effectively. Other recommendations for executives and sponsors include:

- Start at the top by engaging the C-suite in sponsoring emerging mid-level leaders, including 50% women, and provide opportunities to collaborate and make presentations.
- Hold senior managers accountable by tying promotion and compensation to meeting diversity goals and requiring regular reports to the board; use performance dialogues.

- Examine assumptions about how women leaders are "supposed to behave" and help managers understand the view from women's perspectives; make explicit the hidden mindsets that emerge in talent-management discussions.
- Have senior vice-presidents and top executives, rather than direct managers, nominate diverse talent for leadership development and visible roles. Set clear career paths.
- Create a high-performance culture by embedding performance-based indicators and processes at key decision making points; hold executives accountable for using metrics to measure progress; make talent a true source of competitive advantage.
- Provide high-potential women training in "executive presence" starting at midcareer, helping them to be seen as "leadership material."
- True work–life flexibility should be an inclusive part of company strategy and culture, for every employee. Create a culture that celebrates work–life integration.
- Create a climate where senior women reach out to younger women to share encouragement and a sense of purpose and hope.
- Expect all leaders, male and female, to sponsor three diverse successors; link incentives to increasing gender diversity.
- Challenge women to take on risky, high-stakes assignments.
- Enforce term limits on boards and rotate committee memberships; include women directors on the nominating committee; encourage women to submit their names.
- The board should do succession planning on a rolling five-year-plan basis; make gender diversity non-negotiable.
- Find at least one female candidate for every technical job.
- Reward the C-suite for retaining and promoting talented women.

As top executives and board directors conduct fact-based discussions and hold managers accountable to achieving concrete gender diversity results, they will also begin to spread practices that drive success and that help remove impediments to women advancement. The key is making execution more consistent across the organization by developing an inventory of promotion and succession-planning practices and policies and by sharing success stories on gender diversity and high-potential women throughout the organization. The challenge for senior executives and boards of directors is to hardwire the new mindsets and behaviors to sustain this cultural transformation through top-down role modeling and investments in relevant leadership development programs. Over time, what once seemed like a significant milestone will become part of organizational DNA.

Notes

1 Corporate governance theory involves the culmination of principal-*agent* theory, stewardship theory, *stakeholder theory*, *resource dependency theory*, *transaction cost theory*, political theory, legitimacy theory, and social contract theory as well as ethical theories. Corporate governance theory explains the cause and consequence of variables such as the formation of board structures, audit committees, independent non-executive directors, and the duties of upper management and their organizational and social responsibilities (see Wan Fauziah Wan & Alhaji, 2012).

2 For strong theoretical arguments against quotas see Adams, Hermalin, & Weisbach (2010).

References

Adams, R. B., Hermalin, B. E., & Weisbach, M. S. (2010). The role of boards of directors in corporate governance: A conceptual framework and survey. Journal of Economic Literature, *48*(1), 58–107.

Adler, R. D. (2001). Women in the executive suite correlate to high profits. *Harvard Business Review*, *79*(3), 30–32. Retrieved from www.researchgate.net/publication/267822127_Women_in_the_Executive_Suite_Correlate_to_High_Profits.

Ahern, K., & Dittmar, A. (2012). The changing of the boards: The impact on firm valuation of mandated female board representation. *The Quarterly Journal of Economics*, *127*(1), 137–197. DOI:10.1093/qje/qjr049

Arfken, D. E., Bellar, S. L., & Helms, M. M. (2004). The ultimate glass ceiling revisited: The presence of women on corporate boards. *Journal of Business Ethics*, *50*(2), 177–186.

Barsh, J., & Yee, L. (2012). Unlocking the full potential of women at work. *McKinsey Company*. Retrieved from www.mckinsey.com/business-functions/organization/our-insights/unlocking-the-full-potential-of-women-at-work.

Barsh, J., Nudelman, S., & Yee, L. (2013). Lessons from the leading edge of gender diversity. *McKinsey Quarterly*, *4*. Retrieved from www.mckinsey.com/business-functions/organization/our-insights/lessons-from-the-leading-edge-of-gender-diversity.

Beaman, L., Raghabendra, C., Esther, D., Rohini, P., & Petia T. (2009). Powerful women: Does exposure reduce bias? *The Quarterly Journal of Economics*, *124*, 1497–1540.

Belasen, A. T. (2012). *Developing women leaders in corporate America: Balancing competing demands, transcending traditional boundaries*. Santa Barbara, CA: Praeger.

Belasen, A. T., & Frank, N. M. (2013). Using the Competing Values Framework to evaluate the interactive effects of gender and personality traits on leadership roles. *The International Journal of Leadership Studies*, 7(2), 192–215.

Bertrand, M. (2013, July 1). The remaining gender gap(s): Causes and policy responses. *Chicago Booth School of Business*. Retrieved from https://bfi.uchicago.edu/sites/default/files/file_uploads/bertrand_gendergaps_070113.pdf.

Bertrand, M., Black, S. E., Jensen, S., & Lleras-Muney, A. (2014). Breaking the glass ceiling? The effect of board quotas on female labor market outcomes in Norway. Discussion paper series, *IZA DP* No. 8266.

Brenner, L. (2015, March 11). Women in the boardroom: Necessary for business success. *Digitalist*. Retrieved from www.digitalistmag.com/future-of-work/women-in-the-boardroom-necessary-for-business-success-02417818.

Broderick, E., & Keefe, J. (2015, May 25). Male business leaders need to support women's empowerment. *The Huffington Post*. Retrieved from www.huffingtonpost.com/elizabeth-broderick/male-business-leaders-nee_b_6939208.html.

Burgess, Z., & Tharenou, P. (2002). Women board directors: Characteristics of the few. *Journal of Business*, *27*(1), 39–49.

Catalyst. (2004, January 15). The bottom line: Connecting corporate performance and gender diversity. *Catalyst*. Retrieved from www.catalyst.org/knowledge/bottom-line-connecting-corporate-performance-and-gender-diversity.

Catalyst. (2007). Companies with more women board directors experience higher financial performance, according to latest catalyst bottom line report. *Catalyst*. Retrieved from www.catalyst.org/media/companies-more-women-board-directors-experience-higher-financial-performance-according-latest.

Catalyst. (2011). The bottom line: Corporate performance and women's representation on boards (2004–2008). *Catalyst*. Retrieved from www.catalyst.org/knowledge/bottom-line-corporate-performance-and-womens-representation-boards-20042008.

Catalyst. (2015a, January 13). Catalyst census: Women board directors. *Catalyst*. Retrieved from www.catalyst.org/knowledge/2014-catalyst-census-women-board-directors.

Catalyst. (2015b, May 20). Buying power: Global women, what is buying power? *Catalyst*. Retrieved from www.catalyst.org/system/files/buying_power_global_0.pdf.

Catalyst. (2016, July 1). Women CEOs of the S&P 500. *Catalyst*. Retrieved from www.catalyst.org/knowledge/women-ceos-sp-500.

Challenger, Gray, & Christmas, Inc. (2015, December 12). 2015 December CEO Report: 114 CEOs out in December bring yearly total to 1,221. [Press release]. Retrieved from www.challengergray.com/press/press-releases/2015-december-ceo-report-114-ceos-out-december-bring-yearly-total-1221.

Cook, A., & Glass, C. (2015). Diversity begets diversity? The effects of board composition on the appointment and success of women CEOs. *Social Science Research*, *53*, 137–147.

Credit Suisse Research Institute. (2014). The CS gender 3000: Women in senior management. Retrieved from www.calpers.ca.gov/docs/diversity-forum-credit-suisse-report-2015.pdf.

Dale-Olsen, H., Schøne, P., & Verner, M. (2013). Diversity among Norwegian boards of directors: Does a quota for women improve firm performance? *Feminist Economics Research Notes*, *19*(4). Retrieved from www.feministeconomics.org/media/cms_page_media/257/OlsenSchoneVerner.pdf.

Dent, G. (2015, March 6). There are more men called Peter leading ASX 200 companies than women. *Women's Agenda*. Retrieved from www.womensagenda.com.au/talking-about/item/5406-there-are-more-men-called-peter-leading-asx-200-companies-than-women.

Dezsö, C. L., & Ross, D. G. (2012). Does female representation in top management improve firm performance? A panel data investigation. *Strategic Management Journal*, *33*(9): 1072–1089.

Ellingrud, K., Madgavkar, A., Manyika, J., Woetzel, J., Riefberg, V., Krishnan, M., & Seoni, M. (2016, April). *The power of parity: Advancing women's equality in the United States*. Report of the McKinsey Global Institute. Retrieved from www.mckinsey.com/global-themes/employment-and-growth/the-power-of-parity-advancing-womens-equality-in-the-united-states.

Ernst & Young, LLC. (2015, January 12). EY Center for Board Matters Highlights Top Priorities for Corporate Boards in 2015. *PR Newswire US*. Retrieved from www.ey.com/Publication/vwLUAssets/EY_-_Women_on_US_boards:_what_are_we_seeing/%24FILE/EY-women-on-us-boards-what-are-we-seeing.pdf.

European Commission. (2012). *Women on boards: Commission proposes 40% objective* [Press release]. Retrieved from http://europa.eu/rapid/press-release_IP-12-1205_en.htm.

Fairchild, C. (2014, July 8). Women CEOs in the Fortune 1000: By the numbers. *Fortune.Com*, 1. Retrieved from http://fortune.com/2014/07/08/women-ceos-fortune-500-1000/.

Femalefactor.com. (n.d.). *Women by the numbers: Statistics about women*. Retrieved from www.thefemalefactor.com/statistics/statistics_about_women.html.

Gregoric, A., Oxelheim, L., Randøy, T., & Thomsen, S. (2015). Resistance to change in the corporate elite: Female directors' appointments onto Nordic boards. *Journal of Business Ethics*. DOI:10.1007/s10551-015-2703-4

Highfield, R. (2008, March 17). We prefer people we think are similar to ourselves. *The Telegraph, UK*. Retrieved from www.telegraph.co.uk/news/science/science-news/3336375/We-prefer-people-we-think-are-similar-to-ourselves.html.

Ibarra, H., Ely, R. J., & Kolb, D. M. (2013). Women rising: The unseen barriers. *Harvard Business Review*, https://hbr.org/2013/09/women-rising-the-unseen-barriers.

International Labour Organization. (2015). *Women in business and management: Gaining momentum* (abridged version of the global report). Retrieved from www.ilo.org/global/publications/books/WCMS_334882/lang—en/index.htm.

Kanter, R. (1993). *Men and women of the corporation*. New York, NY: Basics Press.

Kampf, J. (2016). The next-generation diversity officer. *Diversity Journal (Spring)*. Retrieved from www.diversityjournal.com/9357-the-next-generation-diversity-officer/.

Konrad, A. M., Kramer, V., & Erkut, S. (2008). The impact of three or more women on corporate boards. *Organizational Dynamics*, *37*(2), 145–167.

Kurtulus, F. A., & Tomaskovic-Devey, D. (2012). Do female top managers help women to advance? A panel study using EEO-1 records. *Annals of American Academy of Political and Social Science*, *639*(1), 173–197.

Loop, P. (2016). This explains why more women aren't landing board seats. *Fortune.Com*, *253*. Retrieved from http://fortune.com/2016/02/15/women-board-seats/.

Morgan, J. (2015, February 15). Why the future of our organizations depends on having more women in management. *Forbes*. Retrieved from www.forbes.com/sites/jacobmorgan/2015/02/18/why-the-future-of-our-organizations-depends-on-having-more-women-in-management/#7a2ae52666a8.

Moss-Racusin, C., Dovidio, J., Brescoll, V., Graham, M., & Handelsman, J. (2012). Science faculty's subtle gender biases favor male students. *Proceedings of the National Academy of Sciences, USA*, *109*, 16474–16479. DOI:10.1073/pnas.1211286109

Muller, J. (2013, April 11). The hard truth about economic inequality that both the left and right ignore. *PBS News Hour*. Retrieved from www.pbs.org/newshour/rundown/the-hard-nut-of-economic-inequality-what-the-left-and-right-both-ignore/.

Pletzer, J., Nikolova, R., Kedzior, K., & Voelpel, S. (2015). *Does gender matter? Female representation on corporate boards and firm financial performance: A meta-analysis*. PLoS One, *10*(6). Retrieved from http://journals.plos.org/plosone/article?id=10.1371/journal.pone.0130005. DOI:10.1371/journal.pone.0130005

PR Newswire. (2012, July 30). 10 years later: Sarbanes-Oxley Act continues to shape board governance. *PR Newswire US*. Retrieved from hwww.prnewswire.com/

news-releases/10-years-later-sarbanes-oxley-act-continues-to-shape-board-governance-164296516.html.

PwC. (2015). *PwC's annual corporate directors survey: Governing for the long term: how boards are adapting to change and reorienting their governance approach*. Retrieved from www.pwc.com/us/en/corporate-governance/annual-corporate-directors-survey.html.

Sanders, M., Hrdlicka, J., Hellicar, M., Cottrell, D., & Knox, J. (2011). What stops women from reaching the top? Confronting the tough issues. *Bain & Company, Inc.* Retrieved from www.bain.com/Images/BAIN_BRIEF_What_stops_women_from_reaching_the_top.pdf.

Soares, R., Marquis, C., & Lee, M. (2011). Gender and corporate social responsibility: It's a matter of sustainability. *Catalyst*. Retrieved from www.catalyst.org/system/files/gender_and_corporate_social_responsibility.pdf.

Stephenson, C. (2004). Leveraging diversity to maximum advantage: The business case for appointing more women to boards. *Ivey Business Journal, 69*(1), 1–5. Retrieved from http://iveybusinessjournal.com/publication/leveraging-diversity-to-maximum-advantage-the-business-case-for-appointing-more-women-to-boards/.

Thomsen, S., Gregoric, A., Randøy T., & Oxelheim, L. (2009). *Nordic board diversity and company economic performance*. Retrieved from www.academia.edu/24557595/Nordic_Board_Diversity_and_Company_Economic_Performance.

Torchia, M., Calabrò, A., & Huse, M. (2011). Women directors on corporate boards: From tokenism to critical mass. *Journal of Business Ethics, 102*(2), 299–317.

2020 Women on Boards. (2016). *Gender Diversity Index 2011–2016: Progress of women corporate directors by company size, state and sector*. Retrieved from www.2020wob.com/companies/2020-gender-diversity-index.

Ulrich, D., Zenger, J., & Smallwood, N. (1999). *Results based leadership: How leaders build the business and improve the bottom line*. Boston: Harvard Business School Press.

Wan Fauziah Wan, Y., & Alhaji, I. (2012). Insight of corporate governance theories. *Journal of Business & Management, 1*(1), 52–63.

Watts, A. W. (2014, June 2). Why does John get the STEM job rather than Jennifer? Corinne Moss-Racusin works to understand and uproot the biases of scientists. *Gender News*. Stanford University. Retrieved from http://gender.stanford.edu/news/2014/why-does-john-get-stem-job-rather-jennifer.

Women in Technology. (2015). *Advancing women to the corporate boardroom*. Retrieved from: www.womenintechnology.org/assets/docs/wit_research_report2015_v7_print_web.pdf.

Women in the Economy, The Journal Report. (2011, April 11). A blueprint for change. *The Wall Street Journal* [Special report]. Retrieved from www.womeninecon.wsj.com/special-report.pdf.

6

RETHINKING WOMEN AND LEADERSHIP

The US Department of Labor, Bureau of Labor Statistics (2015) *Occupational outlook handbook* indicates that top executives held about 2.5 million jobs in 2014. General and operations managers held about 2.1 million of these jobs while chief executives held about 343,400 jobs. Top executives work in nearly every industry. They work for both large and small businesses, ranging from companies in which they are the sole employee to firms with thousands of employees. Top executives in large organizations typically have outsized offices and numerous support staff. However, the work of top executives is often stressful because they are under intense pressure to succeed. They frequently travel to attend meetings and conferences or to visit their company's local, regional, national, and international offices. Executives work many hours, including evenings and weekends. In 2014, about half of the executives worked more than 40 hours per week. Those in charge of poorly performing organizations or departments may find their jobs in jeopardy.

The path to senior management for women in corporate America has not been easy. Despite the recent overall increase in participation of women in the workforce and the attainment of high levels of education, the number of women in executive positions is still disproportionately low compared to men. Consider the following (Warner, 2014):

- Women are 50.8% of the US population.
- They earn almost 60% of undergraduate degrees, and 60% of all Master's degrees.
- They earn 47% of all law degrees, and 48% of all medical degrees.
- They earn more than 44% of Master's degrees in business and management, including 37% of MBAs.

- They are 47% of the US labor force, and 59% of the college-educated, entry-level workforce.

And yet …

- Although they hold almost 52% of all professional-level jobs, American women lag substantially behind men when it comes to their representation in leadership positions.
- They are only 14.6% of executive officers, 8.1% of top earners, and 4.6% of Fortune 500 CEOs.
- They hold just 16.9% of Fortune 500 board seats.
- In the financial services industry, they make up 54.2% of the labor force, but are only 12.4% of executive officers, and 18.3% of board directors. None are CEOs.
- They account for 78.4% of the labor force in health care and social assistance but only 14.6% of executive officers and 12.4% of board directors. None, again, are CEOs.[1]
- In the legal field, they are 45.4% of associates but only 25% of non-equity partners and 15% of equity partners.
- In medicine, they comprise 34.3% of all physicians and surgeons but only 15.9% of medical school deans.
- In information technology, they hold only 9% of management positions and account for only 14% of senior management positions at Silicon Valley startups.

In a 2011 survey that included nearly 3,000 respondents among the UK Institute of Leadership and Management (ILM) members, equally divided between men (49%) and women (51%), women reported lower self-belief and confidence than men. Almost three-quarters of women (73%) believe the glass ceiling exists and say there are still barriers for women looking to be appointed to senior management and board-level positions in the UK (ILM, 2011a). Consistent with Chapter 2 core assumptions about the key drivers behind women's entrepreneurial aspirations, the research also revealed that:

- at every stage the career ambitions of women were found to lag behind those of their male counterparts;
- fewer women than men have ambitions to reach middle management, department head, general management, or director level;
- women are more likely than men to aspire to run their own businesses, and younger women are the most entrepreneurially ambitious, with one-quarter of women under 30 planning to start their own business within 10 years.

AMBITION AT WORK

Before they start work women are less certain than men about the type of role that they want. Throughout their career, women tend to have lower expectations and ambitions in terms of career progression. Women are less confident than men about their own abilities, and more cautious about applying for new roles. They are also more likely to pursue non-linear career paths. The overall picture from female managers is one of a relative lack of career ambition or expectation, coupled with lower levels of confidence and self-esteem. Women managers are well aware of the career challenge they face. Three quarters (73%) of female managers feel that there are barriers to women's management progression – the notorious glass ceiling. The longer a woman's career, the more visible the glass ceiling becomes: 63% of under 30s, 71% of 31–44s and 77% of over 45s acknowledge the barrier. By contrast, only 38% of men believe the glass ceiling exists, though again we saw increased awareness among more experienced male managers, who are likely to be closer to the level at which the glass ceiling comes into effect.

Managers were asked what kind of role they hoped to have at different stages of their careers – after the first ten years, by the time they finished their career, and ten years from the point when they were surveyed. In each scenario, the career ambitions of women managers lagged significantly behind their male counterparts.

Women expected to remain in the same management role for their first ten years in work, or make limited progress. Fewer women than men had ambitions to reach middle management, department head, general management or director level.

Women's end-of-career ambitions when starting their careers were also more limited. More women set the limit of their ambitions at middle management or department head, while more men expected to reach the role of general manager or director.

(ILM, 2011b)

Rethinking Women and Leadership

Significant changes in the US demographics since 1970 have also shaped the profile of stay-at-home mothers. As women's education levels have risen, 25% of 2012's stay-at-home mothers were college graduates, compared with 7% in 1970; and 19% in 2012 had less than a high school diploma, compared with 35% in 1970 (Cohn, Livingston, & Wang, 2014). Whether high-potential women leave because they wish to dedicate more time to their children or because their career prevents them from spending adequate time with their families, the women who opt out of the workforce choose to devote their energy to being caregivers. As Brigid Schulte wrote in her article, "It's the jobs, stupid. Why women really opt out," many women choose to leave work due to the rigid, inflexible corporate culture that is not conducive to parenthood, expecting managers to work evenings and weekends, leaving little time for family obligations (Schulte, 2013). The possibility of a new mother taking a break to raise her child and returning back on the same career ladder is also slim as many leadership positions require not only the right person for the job but also the right timing. Consequently, instead of fighting their way up the ladder, many high-potential women opt out to less demanding fields where the work hours are more flexible.

The problem with the term "opting out" is that it clouds the conscious decision that privileged, educated, and high-achieving women make to care for their family at home with the fact that corporate cultures are not conducive to parenthood, especially when women are faced with binary choices of working or not working. In her book: *Opting out? Why women really quit careers and head home*, Pamela Stone (2007) argues that women are not opting out of the workplace but rather they are being pushed out. When current corporate cultures perpetuate the stereotype that most women will eventually drop out of the workforce for motherhood, it is not helping employers to value their true contributions, or fast-track them to management positions. Stone (2007) contends quite persuasively that well-educated women are forced to leave their high-paying jobs because the requirements for success are simply not compatible with the needs of family. The central question is how do we, as a society, treat women who are trying to reconcile post-feminist workplace goals with the still unchanging stereotypes of women as primarily wives and mothers.

Organizations need to consider tailoring their corporate leadership lifestyles to allow mothers to continue a healthy work–life balance while they are raising children. This is important due to the effects of "brain-drain," especially as many studies have shown that women in corporate leadership positions add value to their companies. McKinsey & Company's recent study found out, for example, that corporations with the highest proportion of women in management had up to a 41% greater ROE over corporations that had no women in management (Borisova & Sterkhova, 2012). At the same time, structural, cultural, and organizational barriers have combined to create a *glass ceiling* that precluded women from achieving senior leadership and executive positions, and even when the overt objections have somewhat diminished, the lingering effects of gender stereotypes have produced repeated cycles of resistance, prejudice, and hostility to women mobility—the *concrete wall*. Over time, pioneering women—some would say superwomen (Cassidy, 2014)—have succeeded in breaking through the glass ceiling, but their success has not been widely replicated.

Many women are expected to balance their professional success with personal fulfillment as their supervisors look for traits manifest in an "ideal employee" and use the a-priori assumption that family responsibilities interfere with work performance, a phenomenon known as the work–family conflict bias (Hoobler, Lemmon, & Wayne, 2011). Both male and female managers tend to harbor work–family conflict bias toward female employees, impeding women's careers and rationalizing the existence of the invisible glass ceiling. Women may also be disincentivized to self-promote by making conscious decisions based on preconceived assumptions. For example, a woman may decline a promotion that requires relocating to a position with greater responsibilities and career advancement potential based on the belief that she eventually plans on getting married and having children. This thinking tends to perpetuate stereotypes about gender roles and to reinforce gender leadership in organizations (Belasen, 2012).

Often women decide not to pursue senior management positions by underestimating their abilities or by choosing alternative paths. The current literature is saturated with a plethora of reasons: women are less likely to self-promote or take risks involving uncertain positions (Bowles, Babcock, & McGinn, 2005; Eagly & Carli, 2007); they have career interruptions due to family responsibilities; and they may lack understanding of internal politics, may experience feelings of isolation, or lack of support and eventually may lose self-confidence.

Unfortunately, female managers have become accustomed to being brushed off until some have surrendered and completely abandoned any desires they had at rising to the top. Women feel that they have to outperform men to get the same reward or win a promotion over their male counterparts (Post, DiTomaso, Lowe, Farris & Cordero, 2009). Contributing factors include: exclusion from informal male oriented networks; limited female role models and mentoring opportunities; work–life challenges and perceived lack of flexibility; gender stereotyping; lack of transparency in role appointments; lack of opportunities (known/communicated); unclear career path; and perceived lack of skills/experience.

VIABLE OPTIONS: RETHINKING WOMEN AND LEADERSHIP

From *Time* to the *New York Times Magazine*, from talk shows to the water cooler, the buzz is all about women dropping out of full-time work, even at the highest professional levels, to stay home with their children. It's this "opt-out revolution," Lisa Belkin argues in the *New York Times Magazine*, and not persistent inequities and stereotypes that accounts for women's under-representation in the leadership ranks of American business and government.

As the term "opt out" implies, Belkin is at odds with Betty Friedan. While Friedan and other leaders of the women's movement stressed women's desire for something more than husbands, children, and well-appointed homes, Belkin claims that many women are reasonably content, for years at a stretch, with exactly that. Friedan described a society that limited women's choices; Belkin sees a society in which women are exercising choices to reject the workplace.

Jamie Gorelick, a former high-ranking official in the Clinton-era Justice Department and a member of the independent 9/11 investigative commission, might be the poster child for Belkin's revolution. In 2003, she left her position as vice chair of Fannie Mae and declined to be considered for its COO post, explaining to *Fortune* magazine that she had two children and didn't want that "pace in my life." The "dirty little secret," she added, "is that women demand a lot more satisfaction in their lives than men do."

Who is correct, Friedan or Belkin? Is the relative shortage of women leaders in government and private enterprise the result of discrimination, or have women chosen not to lead? The two answers, we suggest, are not mutually exclusive. Our findings do not lead us to suspend the struggle to expand women's opportunities for power, authority, and influence. Rather, we argue for reframing the problem of leadership to account for both gender *biases*, which can be addressed through greater equity in the workplace and in society more generally, as well as gender *differences*, which must be addressed through greater diversity in the workplace and society.

(Kellerman & Rhode, 2004)

Opt-out or Pushed-out?

> I hate to say this: It isn't all men's fault. I think some of it is our own attitude and approach. Some of it is very healthy, that women want to make choices about their lives and how they want to spend their time, and what they value.
>
> *(Madeleine Albright cited in Blumenstein, 2012)*

Better-educated women are more likely to be in the labor force than less-educated women and women's decisions to opt out do not represent a return to "traditional" values. Instead, many women's decisions to replace paid jobs with caregiving is due to mismatches between workplace policies and inflexibility that pushes women out, leading to companies' brain-drain or deskilling. This is also a reflection of a vicious cycle in which fathers who are working longer hours than they would like and mothers who are working fewer hours than they would like or who are pushed out of the workplace altogether (Williams, Manvell, & Bornstein, 2006). If the environment of the office is specifically designed to dissuade women seeking management level positions, then why not change that environment? Might it be possible that some women are simply refusing to play a game when the cards are stacked against them? Let's be clear: women leave their jobs because of their workplaces, not their families. They cite long hours with rigid, inflexible schedules and expectations where a common buzzword was that jobs were "all or nothing" (Stone, 2007).

Likewise, as more men continue to play a bigger part in what were traditionally the women's roles at home, it will not only enable women to engage in their own careers but also allow men to get a better understanding of how difficult it is to balance the competing demands of family and work. More than half of American households in 1975 consisted of a male breadwinner and a female homemaker. By 2011, only one in five families matched this description. The majority of families now are dual-income families. This shows that things have changed throughout the years and our society hasn't adapted to these changes. The answer is not to send mothers (or fathers) back to the home front but instead to recognize that the demands of our work life have changed and that workplace policies must change along with them (Glynn, 2012).

Mainiero and Sullivan (2005) argued that women tend to integrate rather than segregate work and non-work needs, the traditional linear career path favored by men. Women's non-work needs go beyond childcare concerns and encompass a quest for spiritual fulfillment, balance, elder care, volunteerism, and the need to be true to oneself. Their research suggests that women's careers are *relational*. Each action taken by a woman in her career is usually viewed as having profound and long-lasting effects on others around her. By contrast men tend to examine career decisions from the perspective of goals and independent actions—targeting the benefits derived from their careers. Men tended to keep their work and non-work lives separate—and often could do this because the women in their lives manage the delicate interplay between work and non-work issues. The focus should be on *integrating work–family* responsibilities. Important considerations include the following:

- Women are the predominant caregivers within the household, as well as other forms of non-market work routines.
- Higher paying jobs for the most part have long hours and inflexible schedules, which disrupt family obligations, making it difficult to integrate work and family life.
- Many of the financially rewarding careers require ongoing and uninterrupted commitment to building the experience curve necessary for promotion to positions of power. Maternity leaves, extended school breaks (snow days, summer camps), and taking care of ill children appear as interruptions (or disincentives for employers).
- Extended leave of absence increases costs for employers of hiring women of child-bearing age, or leading employers to not assign women to important clients or high visibility jobs; it may also keep women out of the workforce for "too long," rendering a re-entry on the fast-track for promotion very unlikely.

According to Ely, Stone, and Ammerman (2014), high-achieving women are not meeting the career goals they set for themselves in their twenties, not because they decide to opt out of the workforce when they have kids, but because they are allowing their partners' careers to take precedence over their own. It's not the children who hold women back in their careers, often it is their husbands (Grose, 2014) who command better work conditions in well-paying professional jobs and especially when women are paid 78% of what men get for equivalent jobs. This wage gap also contributes to the decision of high-educated women to opt out, particularly when those women are only working in part-time jobs to have more time for their children. In these cases, it could turn out to be financially better to stay at home especially if these families have more than one child, making the care costs for them go up to a point where it is just not worth going to work. The list of issues and challenges in trying to juggle work and personal relationships are complex and can be physically and emotionally debilitating.

The choices and frustrations that face many women who want a "full" life that includes executive status usually amount to a burden that often exceeds any normal stress level. Whether it is quality of work life, equal pay, or a decision to stay at home, the stress level is quite enormous. As previously noted, empirical evidence confirms that women in leadership positions significantly improve the companies' performance, yet the support systems to aid the process may not be as readily available for women as they are for men.

"DO-IT-ALL" AND WORK-RELATED STRESS

The pressure to juggle careers, children, and, often, caring for elderly parents is driving soaring levels of workplace stress among middle aged professional women, a leading psychiatrist has warned.

Dr Judith Mohring said official figures showing a spike in cases of workplace stress among women in their 30s and 40s underlined the pressures on the so-called "do-it-all" generation of women. It follows official figures showing middle aged women in Britain are almost 70% more likely to suffer work-related stress. The problem is becoming particularly acute among those in their late 30s and early 40s in which cases have risen by almost a fifth in four years.

Dr Mohring, based at the Priory's Wellbeing Clinic in central London, said the pressure to maintain "traditional women's roles" despite a revolution in the workplace was taking its toll. Recent figures published by the Health and Safety Executive (HSE) show that women aged between 35 and 44 in mainland Britain are 67% more likely to suffer work-related stress than men of the same age.

Cases of work-related stress among women in the age-group stands at 2,090 cases per 100,000 working women, compared with a rate of only 1,250 for men of the same age. The work stress rate among women has jumped 18% in the last four years for those in their late 30s and early 40s. Among women between 45 and 55 the rate is even higher, at 2,180 cases per 100,000 working women but has fallen slightly over the last four years, from 2,200 per 100,000.

(Bingham, 2015)

The Confidence Gap

In a recent interview with *Forbes* magazine, Michelle Shepard, the founder of the Women in Real Life leadership summit, which is an online professional development program for aspiring women seeking career success and a balanced life, stated: "To the men in the room, this was unfathomable. In my experience, it's very common. As women, we often wait until we're competent before we feel confident, whereas men often feel confident before they've achieved full competence" (Kasanoff, 2015). Men, on the one hand, usually overestimate their performance and what the qualifications are. Women, on the other hand, usually underestimate themselves and their performance. Because of this many women usually end up remaining in the same positions they have had for a long time.

In their book, *The confidence code: The science and art of self-assurance—what women should know*, Katty Kay and Claire Shipman (2014) suggest: "Women feel confident only when they are perfect. Or practically perfect." Women tend to underestimate their abilities compared to men who overestimate theirs while all too often the outcomes are the same. This is because women who think that they are less competent than they really are, are also less confident than they should be. Less confidence means less willingness to take risks and to compete. It's a vicious circle. Women will opt out of promotions and positions where they (subjectively) feel that they do not possess the requisite skills. This is the essence of the "confidence gap" cited by the authors. Women's reticence to ask for a promotion and instead reliance on meritocracy and formal channels, is a barrier on their career ladder. Indeed, new research by McKinsey & Company shows that although women and men say they want to be promoted in about equal numbers (75% and 78% respectively), women are significantly less likely to make it to the next tier in their organization. Across all organizational levels, women are 15% less likely than men to get promoted (McKinsey & Company, 2015).

RECOUNT BY KATHERINE GIBAS GIBBONS, PROFESSOR BELASEN'S MBA STUDENT, SUNY EMPIRE STATE COLLEGE, FALL 2015

As far as career goals, mobility for a female reporter is limited. Most often, producers are promoted to management positions. It is rare that an on-air personality would be promoted to management. That is why I am pursuing an MBA, to arm myself with the credentials to affect decision-making in the industry that I am so passionate about. I know how news-gathering in the field works. In many small television markets, producers work almost exclusively within the newsroom, managing the needs there. I know my experience both in-house and in the field would make me a great candidate to lead a newsroom to a great product.

There are other hurdles to climbing the ranks in the news industry, which is male-dominated. According to the Radio Television News Directors Association survey of 2011, only 28% of news directors were women; only 15.8% are general managers of television stations. Of concern is that these data show a decrease in female television and radio executives from previous surveys. These surprising statistics not only demonstrate fewer women in leadership positions but also indicate there are fewer career advancement opportunities for females in my industry.

In many organizations, particularly large corporations, there are a limited number of women in senior management and leadership positions—in some, women hold less than a quarter of those jobs. Fewer women in leadership roles is not only an issue for career development, but it also negatively affects the potential for robust and creative management, which results from a diverse leadership team. It is a critical success factor for any organization to have a healthy balanced workforce and leadership team working collaboratively toward the goals of the organization in a constant learning environment. Several studies indicate women are more vested in motivating others, working collaboratively, and building a team.

The attainment of an MBA levels the playing field and helps minimize the gender gap that exists in many businesses. In addition to the valuable education that speaks for itself, the degree stands for a high commitment to education, desire to hone skills and abilities, and clearly validates the candidate credentials for a leadership position.

In *Empowering yourself: The organizational game revealed*, Harvey Coleman identified PIE (Performance, Image, and Exposure) key factors that influence the advancement of organizational members. In fact, performance only contributes 10% toward promotion decisions, image accounts for 30%, and exposure a whopping 60% (Figure 6.1). These figures stand in stark contrast to professionals'

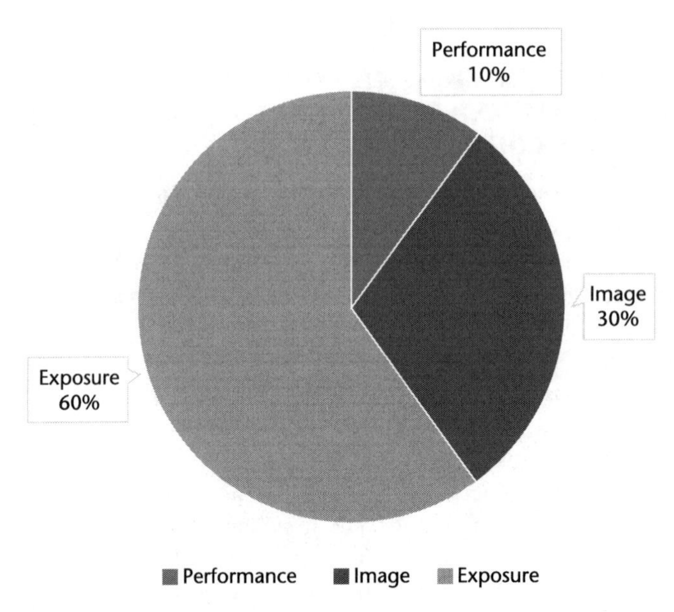

FIGURE 6.1 How Do People Get Promoted?

Source: Adapted from Coleman (2010).

beliefs that superior performance is the way to differentiate themselves. Instead, Coleman (2010) suggests putting much more effort toward achieving high visibility or exposure. Your image is the way you present yourself to the team and to upper management. Coleman (2010) defines exposure as the favorable contact you have with senior managers and decision makers. Unlike women, men are promoted at rates twice as rapidly as women, giving them far broader experience (and access to networks) within an organization and helping them "brand" their image.

Women are not fully understood, their authenticity is not acknowledged or valued and the so-called "female qualities" of relationship and organizational skills are seen as more important at lower levels of the managerial hierarchy (Belasen & Frank, 2012). Women are viewed by their male peers as having weak visionary skills (Ibarra & Obodaru, 2008) and strong relationship skills, which are viewed as being less important top-level leadership skills (Prime, Carter, & Welbourne, 2009).

COMPETENT LEADERSHIP

In my view, the main reason for the uneven management sex ratio is our inability to discern between confidence and competence. That is, because we (people in general) commonly misinterpret displays of confidence as a sign of competence, we are fooled into believing that men are better leaders than women.

This is consistent with the finding that leaderless groups have a natural tendency to elect self-centered, overconfident and narcissistic individuals as leaders, and that these personality characteristics are not equally common in men and women.

For example, women outperform men on emotional intelligence, which is a strong driver of modest behaviors. Furthermore, a quantitative review of gender differences in personality involving more than 23,000 participants in 26 cultures indicated that women are more sensitive, considerate, and humble than men, which is arguably one of the least counter-intuitive findings in the social sciences.

An even clearer picture emerges when one examines the dark side of personality: for instance, our normative data, which includes thousands of managers from across all industry sectors and 40 countries, shows that men are consistently more arrogant, manipulative and risk-prone than women.

The paradoxical implication is that the same psychological characteristics that enable male managers to rise to the top of the corporate or political ladder are actually responsible for their downfall. In other words, what it takes to *get* the job is not just different from, but also the reverse of, what it takes to *do the job well.* As a result, too many incompetent people are promoted to management jobs, and promoted over more competent people.

So it struck me as a little odd that so much of the recent debate over getting women to "lean in" has focused on getting them to adopt more of these dysfunctional leadership traits. Yes, these are the people we often choose as our leaders—but should they be?

Most of the character traits that are truly advantageous for effective leadership are predominantly found in those who fail to impress others about their talent for management. This is especially true for women. There is now compelling scientific evidence for the notion that women are more likely to adopt more effective leadership strategies than do men. Most notably, in a comprehensive review of studies, Alice Eagly and colleagues showed that female managers are more likely to elicit respect and pride from their followers, communicate their vision effectively, empower and mentor subordinates, and approach problem-solving in a more flexible and creative way, all characteristics of transformational leadership, as well as fairly reward direct reports.

(Chamorro-Premuzic, 2013)

Vanessa Hall (2011) described the challenge of building self-confidence as an important part of recognizing and trusting one's own self-efficacy. The greatest challenge and the greatest opportunity for women in leadership is to build and restore trust in the business world, in their homes and families and in the broader community they serve. To achieve that, they also need to build trust in themselves and use it to their advantage.

Commitment to the Value of Diversity

Two observations are clear: First, the glass ceiling continues to persist with the constant preclusion of women from senior executive positions and boards in North America; and second, evidence shows that women have the complete range of the qualities modern leaders need, including social intelligence and authenticity. Formal leadership development programs and succession planning that are inclusive must exist along with willingness by senior executives to recognize the unique value of high-potential women and focus on helping them to gain line experience early on in their career. Effective sponsors need to allow new and different styles of leadership to move in—and up. Sponsorship and advocacy should help high-potential women accelerate their growth and build the prerequisites for high-level positions should the opportunity arise. Royal Bank of Canada, for example, introduced its *Women in Leadership* program in 2013 to increase the representation and visibility of women at executive levels (Seymour, 2015).

The majority of executives believe that leadership development is a key success factor for their organizations (Barrington, 2002). However, a survey of CEOs and human resources executives representing 240 major multinational companies found that while 77% have formal leadership development programs, only 32% believe that they are effective (CEO Survey, 2002). This mismatch needs to change by recognizing the significance of talent management and by promoting women champions meaningfully. The shift must be hardwired as a source of competitive advantage by establishing recruiting, promotion, and succession practices that are women-friendly.

According to Ibarra, Ely, and Kolb (2013), while becoming an effective leader involves a fundamental identity shift, organizations inadvertently undermine this process when they advise women to proactively seek leadership roles without also addressing policies and practices that communicate a mismatch between how women are seen and the qualities and experiences people traditionally tend to associate with leaders. Therefore, mentoring and leadership development programs, while relevant, are insufficient to promote women. These authors suggest that organizations should pursue the following methods proactively: (1) educate women and men about second-generation gender bias; (2) create safe "identity workspaces" to support transitions to bigger roles; and, (3) anchor women's development efforts in a sense of leadership purpose rather than in how women are perceived.

These observations point to a critical area where succession planning practices can and should be improved—the CEO and the board need to hold diversity reviews with senior executives and link the diversity strategy to the overall business strategy. The CEO and board directors need to initiate the selection of internal candidates and ensure their preparation to lead and manage. Senior executives should set out realistic expectations that lead to positive outcomes (Alvarez, 2007). Fulmer and Bleak's (2008) guidelines about successful implementation of leadership development programs in organizations are particularly useful: Start at the top; connect leadership development goals to the organization itself; establish an integrated leadership strategy; be consistent in the execution of leadership programs; and hold leaders across organizational lines accountable.

Communicating Strengths

Barsh and Yee (2012, p. 12) articulated it best:

> [I]f corporate leaders commit to changes that inspire more top women to stay the course through years of family responsibilities and competing interests, then all women and men benefit. It's not easy, but the successful companies and inspiring women reinforce the belief that it is possible. And when a critical mass of high-performing men and women middle managers strive to grow and continue at higher levels, the company builds an advantage that's among the hardest for competitors to copy. Now that's a goal well worth leadership time and attention.

These researchers concluded that if companies opt to increase the number of middle-management women who make it to the next level by 25%, it would significantly alter the profile of the leadership talent pipeline.

More women mean better networks for women, more mentors for less experienced women, and less uncertainty about challenging women's competency or confidence, leading to self-reinforcing cycles that improve women's representation. At the same time, senior executives and board directors must initiate strategies for building a diverse leadership pipeline including systems and practices for making executives trustworthy and holding them accountable, as well as identifying opportunities for changing organizational cultures (Belasen, 2016). Specific strategies for women to promote their careers include (Hampton, 2015):

- Do not limit yourself with self-doubting talks. Don't be too hard on yourselves. In the game of business—confidence is key; visualize yourself succeeding and you will achieve great things.
- Give yourself permission to be successful and influential. Don't wait for opportunity—take it!
- Think BIG; do not confine yourself to conventional choices. Women are born leaders; able to blend imagination, innovation, and skill. So think "outside of the box"!

- Follow other successful women on LinkedIn and discover how they worked to smash the "ceiling."
- Pay NO attention to the folks that say you cannot make it.
- Do not strive for perfection—it is a no-win proposition. However, be the best you can be—at the top of your professional game!

To push through the invisible concrete wall, women are encouraged to act in ways that are genuine and honest to their own values. When necessary, women can use a balance of agentic and communal behaviors through feedback, seek out natural sponsors, and target line roles. It is also important for high-achieving women to communicate their *indispensability* to senior executives (Zenger, Folkman, & Edinger, 2011). Women are encouraged to self-promote within and outside the organization. Women's networks, mentoring, and coaching provides opportunities for men and women to exchange information about each other's professional views and insights as well as benefit from shared experiences (Valerio, 2009). In her TED talk in December 2010, Hanna Rosin suggested re-envisioning the "glass ceiling" as a "high bridge," that is still difficult to reach, but once there, women simply need have the confidence to know that they deserve to be there and have all the skills and experience needed to take the first step (Rosin, 2010).

BALANCE IS NOT THE GOAL, INTEGRATION IS

In fact, some people don't really want balance. Their identity is rooted in work, and that's where they want to be. Outside of work, in the complex dance of family and community responsibilities, they lose their autonomy. Their professional expertise doesn't mean much. They no longer have control. We need better ways to manage work–life boundaries:

- **Shore up the home front:** A lot of stress in our lives, the kind that throws us way off balance, starts with relationship problems at home. Work on them. Get counseling, talk to your spouse and kids. If returning to your family after a day of work fills you with angst, that's a situation only you can repair. Take ownership of the problem, and you'll feel better for it.
- **Quit complaining:** If you feel overworked to the point that you complain about it constantly, how do you think everyone around you feels about it? It's trendy in many companies to run around with multiple, flashing digital devices strapped to our belts or spread out on the table, just so everyone can see how unbelievably busy and important we are. Reinvest that energy in reframing your career possibilities.

- **Say "no" strategically:** The best time to take control of a job is before you accept it. Once you accept it, your negotiating power plummets. So set some ground rules. Be clear on how your performance will be measured. Test the waters. Does everyone in this organization work constantly? If so, don't be surprised when that happens to you a few months later. If your boss loads you up with one more task, try to get an old one off your plate.

(Chappelow, 2012)

Trickle-down Effects

Given that members of TMTs are promoted from within, we can also expect a positive influence of female representation in TMTs on the motivation of lower-level women managers to be stronger than the effect of female board representation. It follows that female representation in top management should help improve the task performance of the TMT itself and also increase the motivation and commitment of women at lower managerial levels. Lower-level managers may regard the presence of a woman on the firm's TMT as a signal that the managerial behaviors associated with the feminine traits are valued by the organization, encouraging them to reach their full potential, and rewarding them for good performance (Eagly, Johannesen-Schmidt, & van Engen, 2003). Not only will female representation effectively legitimize the adoption of these behaviors by women and men, it should also contribute to organizational performance (Dezso & Ross, 2012).

Senior managers who make diversity an explicit focus of talent management processes also hire more women to management positions as well as sponsor and promote women from within. They have the sensitivity skills and urgency of building cultural awareness of subconscious gender stereotypes and responding positively to situations when management took a "risk" by appointing females to leadership roles (PwC, 2008). This creates a winning system in which the social capital of women in the workplace rises, their motivation to integrate work and life increases, and the financial performance of the organization improves through smarter decisions and allocation of resources. Building gender diversity in management delivers positive results for employees and the organization, customers and investors—while also promoting the advancement of women in the workplace.

Inherent Tensions and Competing Values

Paradoxes regarding the work–life landscape exist on an individual employee level as well as on at the managerial and organizational levels. For example, a manager who promotes the use of flexible work arrangements in his/her department can experience greater employee productivity and retention. However, if the manager displays too much flexibility s/he might incur negative consequences from upper management and subordinates. Upper management may see the supervisor as too flexible (e.g., not outcome-focused) and not able to "make difficult decisions." Employees may also see the supervisor as weak and less credible.

On an organizational level, when an organization offers flexible work arrangements (e.g., telecommuting, flextime) to attract diverse, talented employees, it must first consider how individual managers will be able to ensure that their work units can function effectively and efficiently without standardized work hours throughout the organization. It must also consider whether all work–life program options will be available to all employees or whether access will be at a manager's discretion as part of the exchange relationship between a supervisor and his/her most trusted and valued subordinates. And, ultimately, the organization needs to consider the consequences of having firm policies versus policies that allow for greater flexibility. These examples illustrate a few of the paradoxical choices within the work–life landscape.

To more fully examine these paradoxes and provide tools for navigating the work–life landscape, we use the CVF because inherent in the CVF is the notion that organizational and managerial performance are ultimately defined (and judged) by a set of competing criteria and that managerial leaders must consistently confront paradoxical choices that emerge from beliefs that are deeply embedded in organizational and life values (Arsenault & Faerman, 2014; Cameron, Quinn, DeGraff, & Thakor, 2006). For example, managers are expected to ensure stability within the organization yet also face a need to encourage change and innovation in response to external market forces; managers need to look for ways to structure work to enhance employee satisfaction yet must also strive to maximize profitability and meet the demands of external stakeholders.

EMBRACING FAMILY, WORK, AND EDUCATION

Recount by Tina Higgins, Professor Belasen's MBA student, spring 2016

Anne-Marie Slaughter put out an interesting article that sparked controversy in the feminist realm that women cannot have it all. She believes that a generation of feminists did a disservice to a younger generation by leading them to believe that staying home or creating a more flexible work–life balance is wrong. Do I believe you can't have it all as a woman? Absolutely not. I believe that you can, but it's all about timing paired with a shift in perspective. We as women need to let go of the propagated imagery of what it means "to have it all". I had a 4 and 1-year-old when I "opted out", however, I did not leave because I wanted to be a stay at home. It was the working conditions I faced as a young woman trying to navigate her way in a male-dominated environment. An environment that was inflexible carried a double standard and did anything but embrace a family work-life balance.

My career took precedence over my role as both a mother and wife, but ultimately it was because I felt I had no choice. That guilt finally gave way. I will never forget the day when I finally secured a middle management role and had my first at bat, holding a large-scale recruiting event. After being berated by my boss for a non-related issue, I sat in my car and cried, because while I finally "made it", that very moment my daughter was on her very first kindergarten field trip and I chose not to go. I often wonder if I did not have my children would I have still accepted the environment which I was in. I hope not as I also realize that I was not the best version of myself. There was an untapped potential that could not properly be developed in an environment that was merely the perfect backdrop to breed my hyper-effectiveness as a manager. What ultimately came of my "opting out" was an incredible opportunity to develop that potential by being introduced to the CVF. To learn how to communicate, manage and lead effectively while balancing competing tensions in the workplace, I firmly believe will change the trajectory of my career. In closing, I fell in love with being a stay at home mom soaking in every moment without guilt and I also took that same opportunity to go back to school and finish my education. When I finish my MBA, my youngest will be 8 and that timing works for me. So yes, yes I do feel that a woman can have it all and to place a now or never element to this achievement or aspiration to me is redundant. I am growing in confidence as a woman and learned that I do not have to work in an environment like I did ever again. The value of my education in Belasen's course alone has taught me that there are methods to creating a balanced culture using the CVF and I can be a part of that change.

While the CVF has been used primarily to study organizational and leadership performance, the framework generally allows individuals to view of work and life responsibilities holistically from a "both/and," rather than an "either/or" perspective. In doing so, it provides a lens for both researchers and managers within organizations to identify processes, practices, and behaviors that allow for the support of integration of work and life responsibilities. There are many benefits to encouraging managers to take an approach that encourages the coexistence of work and life responsibilities including employee wellness, attraction and retention, career planning, and organizational productivity.

RECOUNT BY KIMBERLY "KIM" GILLESPIE, FORT BRAGG, NC, PROFESSOR BELASEN'S LEADERSHIP DEVELOPMENT PROGRAM, FEBRUARY 2016

I believe some women could remain competitive in the corporate world if they learn how to control their feelings and emotions, like the majority of their male counterparts. There. I said it. In my experience, I have worked in both private and public sectors, from mom-and-pop shops to multi-billion dollar corporations, and about 75% of my female managers and female indirect-supervisors have had a tendency to overtly wear their emotions on their sleeves, hold grudges longer for inconsequential reasons, and justify their thoughts, behaviors, and actions on more social qualifiers than business rationales. Personally, I prefer a male manager to a woman manager for these very reasons. I have always admired how men can disagree in situations, especially with complex subject matter, and quickly and easily rebound to press forward through the project without drama and cattiness, unlike some women managers.

I get that women have a tendency to be emotional thinkers; however, emotions without proper self-control and/or restraint are less than desirable in the corporate world. Advice I give my friends and myself in senior leadership positions in the government and corporate America: Be succinct and decisive when speaking to become relevant and valuable; act with purpose-driven principles not emotions; check your feelings at the door because nobody really cares and it slows progress; and never let them see you sweat. After being one of the women managers that I mentioned earlier, I have taken my own advice and have been more successful in all my leadership positions since. My self-analysis (before/after) demonstrates my personal growth [Figure 6.2].

The *integrative* nature of the CVF allows us to chart internal and external environments, map out roles and competencies, and help women choose the right set of behaviors that are aligned with their goals and priorities. As a *diagnostic* tool, the CVF helps women to see the competing tensions that exist in complex organizational environments and expand the repertoire of their behavioral responses accordingly. As a *development* tool, the CVF helps women identify personal traits, strengths and weaknesses, and align their self-improvement goals with career choices and outcomes. In other words, the CVF helps women increase their *self-efficacy* and at the same time link their personal and family goals with organizational needs and goals. As such, the CVF creates value at both—the personal competency level and the organizational capability level.

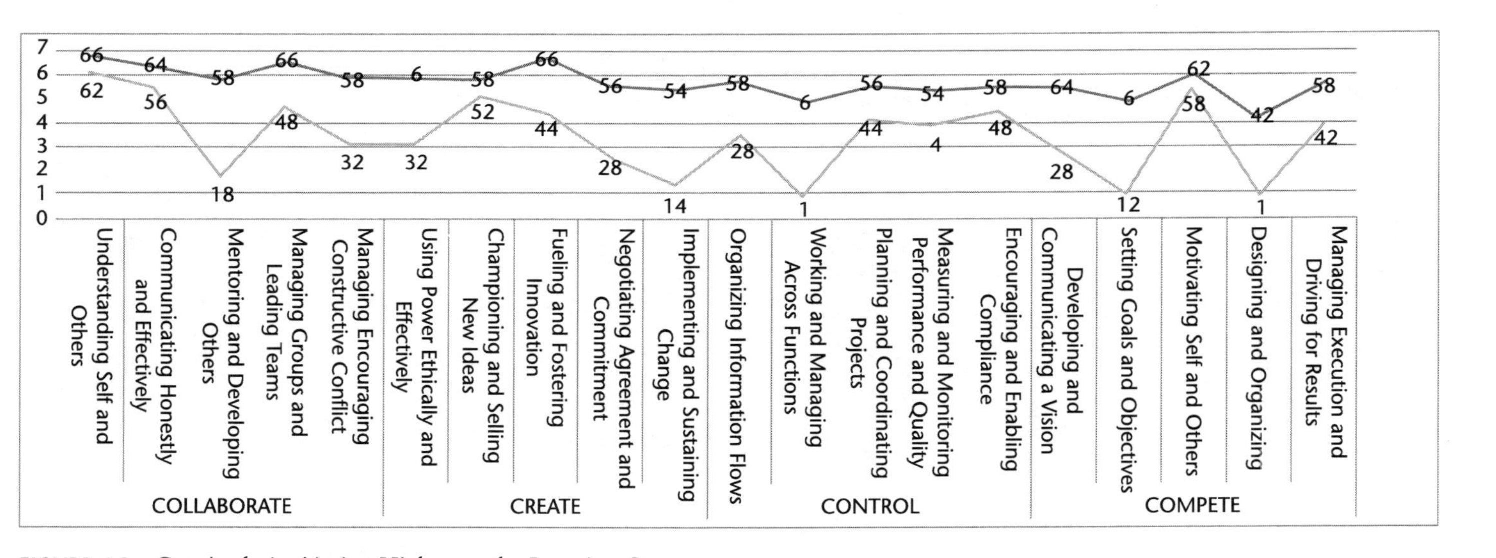

FIGURE 6.2 Gap Analysis: Aiming Higher on the Learning Curve

Source: Student self-analysis, Kimberly "Kim" Gillespie.

Self-improvement

ANN MARIE—LEADERSHIP DEVELOPMENT CASE STUDY[2]

Cameron et al. (2006) describe value creation as a primary motivation that drives both people and businesses. At a personal level, having a positive impact and making a contribution in an area of personal importance is one of the most basic of human needs. Creating value is the way people achieve self-fulfillment, realize their unique potential, and reach self-actualization. The most successful organizations and leaders are those that create superior levels of value. They transform themselves by considering stability and flexibility along with internal and external perspectives. Individuals with a greater capacity to differentiate and integrate concepts in a specific activity can add greater value to that activity than less experienced individuals. Two key dimensions of leadership style are person-centered leadership and task-centered leadership. Effective leaders are able to integrate these two dimensions in their behaviors. Nonetheless, I can identify a multitude of occasions where I have demonstrated both person-centered styles and a multitude of occasions where I have demonstrated task-centered styles. However, I cannot recall nearly as many times where I have demonstrated the two styles simultaneously.

The Competing Values Framework (CVF) has brought to light that achieving valued outcomes in each of the quadrants is crucial for my personal and professional growth, as well as the level of value I add to my organization. As a leader one should consider multiple outcomes in each of the quadrants as they pursue value creation strategies. The CVF has provided me the awareness and ultimately the ability to move from either/or thinking to a both/and thinking.

In conducting my second assessment, I saw point gains in all of the roles with the exception of facilitator and mentor. The second assessment has further strengthened my belief and commitment to developing an improvement plan where these areas are the focus. I am also able to conclude that my conflict resolution skills are particular areas of interest. In order to successfully move from low/middle-level management positions to high-level management positions, I need to master this particular skill set. This desire has also prompted me to become intrigued with the concept of motivation and performance. I am looking forward to including Human Resource Management coursework in my M.B.A. program.

In my current position of Job Developer/Grant Coordinator, I supervise a small staff. This role has been an excellent introductory role to what I hope will become more advanced management roles in the future. I am confident that through gap analysis and the development of a well-rounded outcomes portfolio guided by the CVF I will have a plan for ensuring growth and long-term success [see Tables 6.1 and 6.2].

Belasen (2012)

TABLE 6.1 Self-assessment

Roles	*Post-assessment Score*	*Quadrant*	*Competencies*
Mentor	6.2	Collaborate	The Mentor is helpful and approachable, engaging in the development of people through a caring, empathetic orientation
Innovator	5.7	Vision	The Innovator displays creativity and facilitates adaptation and change
Producer	5.4	Competition	The Producer is task-oriented and work-focused, and motivates members to increase production and to accomplish stated goals (A)
Monitor	5.2	Compliance	The Monitor checks on performance and handles paperwork (C)
Coordinator	5.0	Compliance	The Coordinator maintains structure, schedules, organizes and coordinates staff efforts, and attends to logistical and housekeeping issues (B)
Director	4.8	Compliance	The Director engages in planning and goal setting, sets objectives, and establishes clear expectations (A)
Broker	4.5	Vision	The Broker is politically astute, persuasive, influential, and powerful and is particularly concerned with maintaining the organizations external legitimacy (A)
Facilitator	4.4	Collaborate	The Facilitator encourages teamwork and cohesiveness and manages interpersonal conflict (A).

Source: Belasen (2012).

Note: Items marked with "A" are targeted for immediate improvement; items marked with "B" are targeted for subsequent improvement efforts; items marked with "C" indicate long term improvement plans.

Role Models

In her second year as head of the nation's largest auto-maker, GM, Mary Barra led the $156-billion-in-sales company out from under the shadow of its 2014 ignition-switch recall. She spent $2.9 billion on recalls, which dropped 2014 profits 26%. Yet in recent months she has beaten back headwinds from weak international markets, as sales of expensive trucks and sports utility vehicles have soared (Fortune, 2015). Fortune quotes investment guru Warren Buffett on Barra: "Mary is as strong as they come. She is the person to have there. She is as good

TABLE 6.2 Development Plan

Roles	*Job-specific Tasks*	*Competencies that Support Current Job*	*Competencies to Perform at Higher Levels Areas of Improvement*	*Expected Outcomes*
Mentor	Supervise staff of employment coordinators	Implement programs and procedure that recognize and support growth of human capital	Develop programs and procedures that recognize and support growth of human capital	Improve my knowledge, skill and ability to demonstration person-centered management (C)
Innovator	Grant development and implementation	The development of new programs and processes. The development of continuous improvement plans. The ability to adapt to change	The ability to help others adapt to change, particularly in times of crisis	Improve my ability to guide others through periods of change (C)
Producer	Make certain that program performance standards are met	Set priorities and tasks based on goals and objectives. Motivate others to achieve program goals	Develop tools and techniques related to motivation and performance	Increase my knowledge skills and abilities in the areas of motivation and performance in order to improve my ability to motivate others and assist others in identifying and reaching full potential (B)
Monitor	Track project progress and document results. Write performance appraisals. Maintain records and reports	Monitoring and process records and reports	Develop sophisticated tools for monitoring and tracking progress	Improve my ability to provide constructive feedback. Increase my knowledge and understanding of developing performance appraisal methods and systems (C)

Roles	*Job-specific Tasks*	*Competencies that Support Current Job*	*Competencies to Perform at Higher Levels Areas of Improvement*	*Expected Outcomes*
Coordinator	Manage state-funded employment programs throughout three counties	Attend to logistical and housekeeping issues	Develop and maintain optimal organizational structure	Be able to demonstrate not only the ability to organize my own effort, but also coordinate and organize staff efforts
Director	Grant writing, project and strategic planning, grant implementation	Setting objectives and goals and planning accordingly	Establish clear expectations	Be able to demonstrate the ability to clearly outline expectations both programmatically and personally. This will reduce the amount of time spent on corrective action (A)
Broker	Marketing new projects to consumers, community organizations, state and local governments. Seeking support for community projects	Maintain the organization's external legitimacy	Being politically astute, persuasive, and powerful	An increased level of confidence in my ability influence others (A). An increased awareness of external factors and influences (A)
Facilitator	Hiring, training, and supervision of staff	Encourage teamwork and cohesiveness	Ability to efficiently manage differences between co-workers	Be able to demonstrate mastery of conflict resolution skills (A)

Source: Belasen (2012).

as I've seen" (Gallagher, 2014). Another example is Marissa Mayer, CEO of Yahoo, who gave birth to twin girls and only took two weeks off for maternity leave, which caused some women to cheer her commitment and others to lament the precedent that she was setting. Either way, she became Yahoo's CEO when she was only 38 years old (Walters, 2015).

LAUREN REILLY, CHIEF LEARNING OFFICER, PRACTICE MAKES PERFECT AND FORMER NEW YORK CITY EDUCATOR AND TEACH FOR AMERICA ALUMNA

I began my career teaching in the Bronx and Harlem, as an educator with Teach for America. I focused on fighting for students who were crippled by a lack of safety, shelter, and food. Education was an after-thought among their daily challenges.

But after my first few years teaching—and caring deeply for my students—I realized my profession was crippling me as well. I felt I was equipped to do nothing *but* teach. I wanted to do more to address the growing achievement gap in our society.

In reviewing my options, I found few traditional jobs that served this growing and high-need population. I took a leap of faith in sitting down with the 22-year-old founder of a start-up organization, Practice Makes Perfect [PMP]. PMP is a full-service summer school education organization that drives student outcomes using an innovative near-peer mentorship model. With $100,000 in working capital and two employees, the organization was looking for a volunteer to help with program development and fundraising.

Against all advice from my friends, I decided to work without pay for goals I believed in. Although I knew little about start-ups and fundraising, the founder saw in me a scrappy fast learner who was passionate for the success of his non-profit organization.

Fast forward three years of long nights, continuous professional development, and mentorship meetings. PMP is now a Benefit Corporation with 15 full-time employees and a summer staff of 106. The founder named me Chief Learning Officer [CLO] with a salary to match my thick portfolio of responsibilities. As CLO, I now oversee the nine program staff who serve 1200 inner city students in New York City this year, with the goal of expanding to three additional cities by 2018.

In broadening my professional horizons, I learned that my previous narrow view of my abilities short-changed what I could accomplish in education. Taking a chance on myself to learn new skills has been instrumental in helping PMP bring in over $2 million dollars in earned income to date.

This year, I was recognized by President Obama at a day-long White House seminar and celebration as one of seven Champions of Change for my work in summer learning. I sat on a panel with the US Secretary for Education and spoke about solving the crushing problem of summer learning loss. I stressed the importance of creating a scalable solution to this problem through entrepreneurship dedicated to sustainable change.

Today, at 27 years old, I am the CLO of someone else's start-up. I know this rewarding position is not the end of my professional path. In the future I plan to build my own non-profit educational enterprise. I no longer fear the temporary absence of a particular skillset. I have learned that I *can* learn. I embrace, as an individual and a young woman, the "must-haves" of entrepreneurial success: the drive, the grit, and belief in oneself to achieve goals that once appeared beyond reach.

The reality for *most women and men* is that they must find ways *to integrate multiple responsibilities*—and they may do so in ways that could bring multiple benefits (e.g., less depression, empowerment, financial security). Why not pursue that goal as a win–win solution? Of course, the notion of perfection with its value-maximizing principle of "have it all" is unattainable by most women. This includes the very premise of what "all" means. Does it have to be the very top position in the organization? Everything at one time versus over time? So why not look at experiences of women and men who have managed to combine multiple responsibilities in ways that are right for them but do not conform to a notion of perfection (e.g., they are not the CEO but have fulfilling and challenging jobs and personal lives)?

> There has been a steady and pronounced message in the media that gender roles are changing in American families. Witness, for example, the following: "Behind every great woman: As more women earn high-level corporate roles, more husbands are staying home, raising the kids, and changing the rules."[3]

Sharon Hadary and Laura Henderson in their book *How women lead: 8 essential strategies successful women know* (2013) offer strategies and tools, based on real-life insights from highly successful women, that other women, at any point in their professional career, can use to get on the leadership career path and accelerate their growth potential.[4]

1. *Empower the woman leader within.* Giving women the confidence to lead in a style that is authentic and intuitive to them. Women lead differently than men; qualities such as being holistic, collaborative, inclusive, and consultative are strengths that will help you succeed in a global economy.

2. *Own your destiny.* Assuming control of your life; knowing your values, knowing your goals, and putting in place an action plan that will move you forward.
3. *Be the architect of your career.* Join and leverage social and professional networks.
4. *Advocate unabashedly for yourself.* Promote yourself. Get a mentor. Mentors give you connections, steer you in new or better directions, and save you from making costly mistakes.
5. *Translate the stories that numbers tell to drive strategic results.* To run a successful company, you must understand how your company makes money and how you contribute to it.
6. *Create exceptional teams.* Women are naturals at building teams and managing relationships. Take advantage of your emotional intelligence skills.
7. *Nurture your greatest asset—you.* Understand your strengths and weaknesses. Investing in yourself leads to peak performance. Be a change agent for yourself
8. *Turn possibilities into realities.* Be open to all that life brings your way.

WOMEN IN THE BOARDROOM

To better understand the challenges and opportunities for women in today's workplace, we talked to three women executives at my company, SAP. Below they share their thoughts on how women can move their careers forward today.

Maggie Chan Jones, Chief Marketing Officer (CMO)

Maggie Chan Jones is the chief marketing officer (CMO) of SAP, where she is responsible for the development and execution of marketing strategy across the globe. She champions SAP's mission to help its customers, partners, and employees Run Simple. As a business leader in the marketing industry, she is passionate about women, tech, and early talent. Maggie previously served as a board member of the Women's Bean Project, a nonprofit social enterprise.

Helen Arnold, SAP Global Managing Board and Chief Information Officer (CIO)

Helen Arnold is a member of the SAP Global Managing Board and is the Chief Information Officer (CIO) for the SAP Group and head of Cloud Delivery. As CIO, she leads cloud operations and the SAP HANA Enterprise Cloud, and drives SAP's continuous innovation journey in streamlining and rethinking internal systems at SAP. She focuses on cloud service delivery to private, public, and managed cloud customers and is responsible for the adoption of SAP's solution portfolio internally.

Anka Wittenberg, Chief Diversity and Inclusion Officer (CDIO)

Anka Wittenberg is Chief Diversity and Inclusion Officer at SAP, responsible for the development and implementation of SAP's Diversity and Inclusion strategy globally. Prior to SAP, Anka gained extensive international HR experience, most recently heading Corporate HR globally at Benteler International AG. She is a member of the supervisory board of Westfalen AG, Germany and board member of the Childhood Foundation Germany.

How did you get to where you're at today?

Maggie: I am a firm believer in knowing yourself, understanding what you want, and going after that goal. Be very clear about your talents and skills and how you can use them in a professional role. Make sure you have the right support network – including friends and family. And if possible, find a mentor – someone you respect and can learn from. Don't be afraid to take risks in your career. It's okay if things don't go well at first. Those experiences will always give you confidence. Build positive relationships with people by expressing interest in learning from others and helping others to be successful.

Approximately 60% of Fortune 500 companies now employ a Chief Diversity Officer. Why is it a critical role? And what impact can it have on a company looking to attract more women leaders?

Anka: Given rapidly changing marketplace dynamics and an increasingly diverse world, diversity and inclusion are critical components to competitiveness. Companies with more diverse management teams are linked to stronger financial performance and better reflect the market overall. Diversity enables companies to have a better understanding of their customers, which improves customer satisfaction and expands market share. It strengthens an organization's ability to innovate; improves employee engagement, productivity, and satisfaction; and helps companies outperform the market. Diversity is not just a "nice-to-have" cultural topic – it's a business imperative. That is why companies invest in diversity and inclusion as strategic differentiators. More specific to female leaders, Chief Diversity Officers help build awareness for gender intelligence, facilitate programs that encourage women to pursue leadership opportunities, and help ensure that the corporate culture is attractive to women.

Fewer than 17% of CIOs are women. For women who work in technology, what paths can they take to become a CIO?

Helen: With increasing digitalization and tighter innovation cycles, the role of the CIO has changed. It's no longer about being a technology agent for the business. Instead, it's much more about being an innovation partner. My advice to women who see this as a career path is to carve out roles for themselves in their company's innovation journey – understand what and how your company needs to achieve on a strategic level and make sure you play a key part of that journey. The new technology is about connectivity (such as the Internet of Things and the networked enterprise). These kinds of collaborative, open processes suit women who tend to have strong intuition and the ability to see the big picture. The new world of digitalization requires the ability to think outside the box, and women can take advantage of this.

What is your advice for young women who want to be leaders?

Helen: I always say that women should follow their passions and be authentic. However, it's also essential to take up opportunities to grow their leadership skills. For example, at SAP, we have a Business Women's Network, which provides its 8,000 female members with development experiences such as fellowships, job rotations, and mentorship.

Anka: I encourage young women to find role models and mentors in fields that interest them to get firsthand knowledge of what it takes to be successful. Getting real-world experience through fellowships and job rotations can also allow aspiring female business leaders to "test" an opportunity to ensure it's a good fit. It's always a smart idea to take advantage of the numerous opportunities available to network with other strong, authentic women leaders by working and volunteering for diversity-focused organizations and associations with inclusive cultures.

Maggie: I strongly believe in supporting women in tech – whether they are young and starting out, looking to make a change, or experienced with ambitious career goals. At SAP, we are exploring ways of getting emerging talent on the fast track by offering meaningful opportunities early in their careers, including exposure to executives and exciting projects.

Whenever I talk to the women we are developing, I offer this advice:

Be curious. This is the best time to learn more about yourself, what excites you, and what you are passionate about. Explore as many areas as you can through opportunities such as job rotation.

Be a catalyst. Find an opportunity to lead early in your career. Determine an area or topic you can be great at, in many cases something new and different. Then, paint your vision on how you'll lead. In a highly collaborative environment, your first leadership experience could be a cross-group project, which is a great way to develop your leadership and influencer skills.

Find multiple mentors. Look for mentors from different areas and with competencies you want to emulate. Get a balanced perspective by searching out both male and female mentors who can help open different paths for you.

(Brenner, 2015)

Notes

1 Women currently hold 20 (4.0%) of CEO positions at S&P 500 companies. www.catalyst.org/knowledge/women-ceos-sp-500. Women hold 16.5% of the four positions just below CEO in the S&P 500, http://money.cnn.com/2015/03/24/investing/female-ceo-pipeline-leadership/.

2 For similar assessments see Belasen (2012).

3 "Young women are more career driven than young men," *New York Times*, April, 2012, based on a study done by Pew Research Center; "Men choosing fatherhood over careers," *Forbes*, May, 2012; *The New Yorker*, May 2012, cover art depicts a woman with a stroller entering a playground and every other parent in the playground is a man; "Are dads the new moms?," *Wall Street Journal*, May 2012. www.bc.edu/content/dam/files/centers/cwf/pdf/The%20New%20Dad%20Right%20at%20Home%20BCCWF%202012.pdf.

4 For excellent success stories, see also Geri Stengel, February 20, 2013, "8 strategies successful women entrepreneurs share with their corporate counterparts," *Forbes*, www.forbes.com/sites/geristengel/2013/02/20/8-strategies-successful-women-entrepreneurs-share-with-their-corporate-counterparts/#32913f1639c8.

References

Alvarez, R. (2007). Putting the Pygmalion Effect to work in modernizing healthcare. *Healthcare Information Management & Communications Canada*, 2nd quarter, April, 6–7. Retrieved from http://castleknockcommunications.com/PDF/CHI_Alvarez_2007.pdf.

Arsenault, P., & Faerman, S. (2014). Embracing paradox in management: The value of the competing values framework. *Organization Management Journal, 11*(3), 147–158.

Barrington, L. (2002). Despite hard times companies view leadership development as a priority. Executive action no. 34, *The Conference Board*, New York, NY.

Barsh, J., & Yee, L. (2012). Unlocking the full potential of women at work, *McKinsey Company*. Retrieved from www.mckinsey.com/business-functions/organization/our-insights/unlocking-the-full-potential-of-women-at-work.

Belasen, A. T. (2012). *Developing women leaders in corporate America: Balancing competing demands, transcending traditional boundaries*. Santa Barbara, CA: Praeger.

Belasen, A. T. (2016). Deception and failure: Mitigating leader-centric behaviors. In A. Belasen, & R. Toma. (Eds.), *Confronting corruption in business: Trusted leadership, civic engagement* (pp. 183–216). New York, NY: Routledge.

Belasen, A. T., & Frank, N. M. (2012). Using the competing values framework to evaluate the interactive effects of gender and personality traits on leadership roles. *The International Journal of Leadership Studies*, 7(2), 192–215.

Bingham, J. (2015, November 10). "Do-it-all" generation of women suffering work stress epidemic. *The Telegraph*. Retrieved from www.telegraph.co.uk/women/womens-life/11983974/Do-it-all-generation-of-women-suffering-work-stress-epidemic.html.

Blumenstein, R. (2012, May 7). Madeleine Albright on barriers broken and barriers that remain. *Wall Street Journal*. Retrieved from www.wsj.com/articles/SB1000142405270230474660457738372197423428 2.

Borisova, D., & Sterkhova, O. (2012). Women as a valuable asset. *McKinsey and Company*, April. Retrieved from www.citizencapital.fr/wp-content/uploads/2015/05/Women_as_a_Valuable-Asset_eng.pdf.

Bowles, H. R., Babcock, L., & McGinn, K. L. (2005). Constraints and triggers: Situational mechanics of gender in negotiation. *Journal of Personality and Social Psychology, 89*, 951–965.

Brenner, L. (2015, March 11). Women in the boardroom – Necessary for business success. *D!gitalist Magazine by SAP, Women in Leadership*. Retrieved from www.digitalistmag.com/future-of-work/2015/03/11/women-in-the-boardroom-necessary-for-business-success-02417818.

Cameron, K. S., Quinn, R. E., DeGraff, J., & Thakor, A. V. (2006). *Competing values leadership: Creating value in organizations*. Cheltenham, UK: Edward Elgar.

Cassidy, J. (2014, October 2). The hole in the glass ceiling is getting bigger. *The New Yorker*. Retrieved from www.newyorker.com/news/john-cassidy/hole-glass-ceiling-getting-bigger.

CEO Survey. (2002). Leading indicators: The development of executive leadership. *Chief Executive Magazine*. p. S1.

Chamorro-Premuzic, T. (2013). Why do so many incompetent men become leaders? *Harvard Business Review*. Retrieved from https://hbr.org/2013/08/why-do-so-many-incompetent-men.

Chappelow, C. (2012). Strive for work-life integration, not balance. Retrieved from www.fastcompany.com/1825042/strive-work-life-integration-not-balance.

Cohn, D., Livingston, G., & Wang, W. (2014). After decades of decline, a rise in stay-at-home mothers. *Pew Research Center*. Retrieved from www.pewsocialtrends.org/2014/04/08/after-decades-of-decline-a-rise-in-stay-at-home-mothers/.

Coleman, H. J. (2010). *Empowering yourself: The organizational game revealed*. Bloomington, IN: AuthorHouse.

Dezso, C., & Ross, D. (2012). Does female representation in top management improve firm performance? A panel data investigation. *Strategic Management Journal, 33*(9), 1072–1089.

Eagly, A. H., & Carli, L. (2007). *Through the labyrinth: The truth about how women become leaders*. Boston: Harvard Business School Press.

Eagly, A. H., Johannesen-Schmidt, M. C., & van Engen, M. L. (2003). Transformational, transactional, and laissez-faire leadership styles: A meta-analysis comparing women and men. *Psychological Bulletin, 129*(4), 569–591.

Ely, R., Stone, P., & Ammerman, C. (2014). Rethink what you "know" about high-achieving women, R1412G. *Harvard Business Review, 92*(12), 101–109.

Fortune (2015). Most powerful women list. *Fortune*. Retrieved from http://fortune.com/most-powerful-women/mary-barra-1/.

Fulmer, R. M., & Bleak, J. (2008). What have we learned about strategic leadership development? In C. Wankel & R. DeFillippi (Eds.), *University and corporate innovations in lifetime learning* (pp. 161–179). Charlotte, NC: Information Age.

Gallagher, J. (2014, September 18). Fortune magazine: Barra #2 most powerful woman boss. *Detroit Free Press*. Retrieved from www.freep.com/story/money/cars/general-motors/2014/09/18/gm-mary-barra/15832713/.

Glynn, S. J. (2012). Working parents' lack of access to paid leave and workplace flexibility. *American Progress*. Retrieved from www.americanprogress.org/issues/labor/report/2012/11/20/45466/working-parents-lack-of-access-to-paid-leave-and-workplace-flexibility/.

Grose, J. (2014, November 18). It's not your kids holding your career back, it's your husbands. *Slate*. Retrieved from www.slate.com/blogs/xx_factor/2014/11/18/harvard_business_school_study_it_s_not_kids_but_husbands_that_hold_women.html.

Hadary, S., & Henderson, L. (2013). *How women lead: 8 Essential strategies successful women know*. New York, NY: McGraw-Hill.

Hall, V. (2011). Why women are more trusted than men, and how to use trust to our advantage. Retrieved from http://theglasshammer.com/2011/03/11/why-women-are-more-trusted-than-men-and-how-to-use-trust-to-our-advantage/.

Hampton, S. (2015, May 4). It's 2015: So why aren't there more women CEOs? *Women in Leadership*. Retrieved from www.borderless.net/its-2015-so-why-arent-there-more-women-ceos/.

Hoobler, J. M., Lemmon, G., & Wayne, S. J. (2011). Women's underrepresentation in upper management: New insights on a persistent problem. *Organizational Dynamics, 40*, 151–156.

Ibarra, H., & Obodaru, O. (2008). Women and the vision thing. *Harvard Business Review, 85*(1), 40–47.

Ibarra, H., Ely, R., & Kolb, D. (2013). Women rising: The unseen barriers. *Harvard Business Review, 91*(9), 60–67. Retrieved from https://hbr.org/2013/09/women-rising-the-unseen-barriers.

ILM. (2011a, February 21). *Majority of women say glass ceiling is still a barrier to top jobs* [Press release] Retrieved from www.i-l-m.com/~/media/ILM%20Website/Documents/Information%20for%20media/11.%20Ambition%20and%20gender%20at%20Work_FINAL%20pdf.ashx.

ILM. (2011b). *Ambition and Gender at Work*. Retrieved from www.i-l-m.com/About-ILM/Research-programme/Research-reports/Ambition-and-gender.

Kasanoff, B. (2015). Women: If you're competent, it's time to be confident. *Forbes Leadership*. Retrieved from www.forbes.com/sites/brucekasanoff/2015/03/23/women-if-youre-competent-its-time-to-be-confident/.

Kay, K., & Shipman, C. (2014). *The confidence code: The science and art of self-assurance—what women should know*. New York, NY: HarperBusiness/HarperCollins.

Kellerman, B., & Rhode, D. L. (2004). Viable options: Rethinking women and leadership. *Compass: A Journal of Leadership*, Fall, 14–17, 37.

McKinsey & Company (2015). *Women in the workplace, 2015 corporate America is not on a path to gender equality*. Retrieved from http://womenintheworkplace.com/.

Mainiero, L. A., & Sullivan, S. E. (2005). Kaleidoscope careers: An alternate explanation for the "opt-out" revolution. *The Academy of Management Executive*, *19*(1), 106–120.

Post, C., DiTomaso, N., Lowe, S., Farris, G., & Cordero, R. (2009). A few good women: Gender differences in evaluations of promotability in industrial research and development. *Journal of Managerial Psychology*, *24*(4), 348–371.

Prime, J. L., Carter, N. M., & Welbourne, T. M. (2009). Women "take care," men "take charge": Managers' stereotypic perceptions of women and men leaders. *The Psychologist-Manager Journal*, *12*, 25–49.

PwC. (2008). The leaking pipelines: Where are our female leaders? 79 women share their stories. *Global Human Capital, Gender Advisory Council*. Retrieved from www.pwc.com/gx/en/about/diversity/women-at-pwc/the-leaking-pipeline.html.

Rosin, H. (2010, December). New data on the rise of women [Video file]. Retrieved from www.ted.com/talks/hanna_rosin_new_data_on_the_rise_of_women/transcript?language=en.

Schulte, B. (2013, August 8). It's the jobs, stupid. Why women really opt out. *Washington Post*. Retrieved from www.washingtonpost.com/blogs/she-the-people/wp/2013/08/08/its-the-jobs-stupid-why-women-really-opt-out/.

Seymour, R. (2015, March 5). Tapping into high potentials: Programs guiding female talent to the top. *Women of Influence*. Retrieved from www.womenofinfluence.ca/2015/03/05/tapping-into-high-potentials/#.V7IY1J3D8dU.

Stone, P. (2007). *Opting out? Why women really quit careers and head home*. Berkeley, CA: University of California Press.

US Department of Labor, Bureau of Labor Statistics. (2015, December 17). *Occupational outlook handbook, 2016–17 edition, top executives*. Retrieved from www.bls.gov/ooh/management/top-executives.htm.

Valerio, A. M. (2009). *Developing women leaders: A guide for men and women in organizations*. Oxford, UK: Wiley-Blackwell.

Walters, J. (2015, September 2). Yahoo CEO Marissa Mayer's minimal maternity leave plan prompts dismay. *The Guardian*. Retrieved from www.theguardian.com/technology/2015/sep/02/yahoo-ceo-marissa-mayer-minimal-maternity-leave-plan-prompts-dismay.

Warner, J. (2014). Fact sheet: The women's leadership gap. *Center for American Progress*, 7. Retrieved from www.americanprogress.org/issues/women/report/2014/03/07/85457/fact-sheet-the-womens-leadership-gap/.

Williams, J. C., Manvell, J., & Bornstein, S. (2006). Opt out or pushed out? How the press covers work/family conflict: The untold story of why women leave the workforce. *The Center for WorkLife Law*. Retrieved from www.worklifelaw.org/pubs/OptOutPushedOut.pdf.

Zenger, J. H., Folkman, J. R., & Edinger, S. K. (2011). Making yourself indispensable. *Harvard Business Review*, *89*(10), 84–92. Retrieved from https://hbr.org/2011/10/making-yourself-indispensable/ar/1.

PART IV

Breaking Societal Barriers

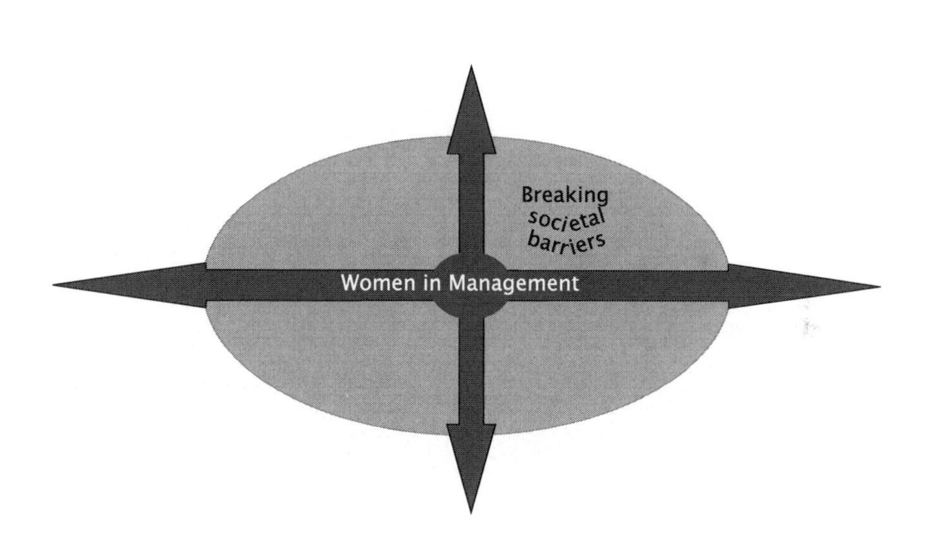

7

CHANGING THE CORPORATE MINDSET

Despite being the majority in the population, obtaining 60% of undergraduate and Master's-level degrees, and holding almost 52% of all professional-level jobs, American women lag substantially behind men when it comes to their representation in leadership positions (Warner, 2014). A common view is that gender leadership styles reflect the power differentials seen in society as a whole (Fine, 2007) and that masculine qualities such as task focus, assertiveness, authoritativeness, and lack of emotionality, more so than communal qualities, appear synonymous with leadership in US and European cultures (Izraeli & Adler, 1994; Schein, 2001; Fine & Buzzanell, 2000).

This view will need to change as women have proven to be exceptional leaders in business, government, and nonprofit organizations, as well as political settings. Women have taken on both transformational and transactional roles that have changed the course of major corporations and political institutions. Look at Elizabeth Warren who has challenged the global financial establishment to provide a fair playing field for middle-class individuals. This has led to oversight capabilities that have brought transparency to areas which did not exist before.

Arlie Russell Hochschild's *The second shift: Working parents and the revolution at home* (1989) describes the double burden women in the late twentieth century had to deal with as employed mothers, juggling the primary responsibilities of domestic affairs and working as diligent professionals. The "second shift" is a metaphor for women who are still responsible for the lion's share of domestic responsibility. This is what fundamentally and unjustly pushes women out of the exclusive echelons of higher leadership. As reported by Ely, Stone and Ammerman (2014), almost two-thirds of the women had returned to work but to different types of work that offered greater flexibility—and lower pay. It is important that women are offered the flexibility to develop their careers and family so that a broader base of thought leaders is developed.

This chapter examines societal and legal norms and practices and provides frameworks for cultural transformations and change leadership.

Slow but Steady Progress

During the 1960s and 1970s women's participation in the workforce had reached 40% with women primarily occupying professions such as teaching, nursing, and social work. The majority of women were still in non-management positions due to the prevailing assumption that managerial responsibilities require managers to be assertive, with an analytic mindset and with commitment that transcends regular work time. Hence, women filled support staff positions such as assistants and secretaries. With the passage of the 1964 Civil Rights Act that made discrimination in employment unlawful on the basis of gender, race, and social status, women began to chisel away at the concrete wall that buffered them from reaching managerial positions that traditionally have been the exclusive territory of men. The concrete wall began to crack in the 1970s and 1980s when women were advancing to lower middle-management positions. Nevertheless, they were still facing tough barriers in the pursuit of top executive jobs.

In the 1990s, as organizations began to shift away from vertical structures rooted in male conceptions of power toward horizontal structures based on commitment, empowerment, and diversity, it also signaled a shift to a new management paradigm. This new paradigm involved a transition toward transformational forms of leadership: from command structures designed exclusively around reporting and compliance to commitment structures emphasizing relational power and open communication lines. Upper-management was expected to shift from "taking charge" to "taking care" and evaluated on abilities to "transform" people and organizations, not only "transact" around core business competencies.

Today's flatter, team-based organizations are no longer looking for top-down authority figures but for more collaborative and inclusive approaches to leadership based on facilitative power and consultation. Leadership is becoming more interactive, and women's style of leadership seems to be more appropriate than that of men's in diversified and globalized work environments. Moreover, the past 40 years marked a significant transformation in women's participation in the labor force. By the end of 2008, women's proportion in the civilian labor force increased steadily from 43.3% in 1970 to 59.5%. Women have also increasingly attained college degrees. Among women aged 25 to 64 who were in the labor force, the proportion with a college degree roughly tripled from 1970 to 2008. Women's earnings as a proportion of men's earning also have grown over time. In 1979, women working full time earned 62% of what men did; in 2008, women's earnings were 80% of men's (Belasen, 2012).

At the same time, the question of why more women, whose feminine gender role suggests teamwork, empowerment, sharing information, and caring for employees, have not yet shattered the notorious glass ceiling. Why are women grossly underrepresented in boardrooms and executive suites?

In 2007, McKinsey & Company conducted a study to offer valuable insights regarding the importance of female representation in top management positions. The report, *Women matter: Gender diversity, a corporate performance driver*, documented the reasons that hinder diversity in senior management positions. The study predominately focused on European companies, providing evidence that gender gaps are palpable globally. Interestingly, the study also pointed out that "companies where women are most strongly represented at board or top-management levels are also the companies that perform best" (Desvaux, Devillard-Hoellinger, & Baumgarten, 2007, p. 3). Credit Suisse reports that from 2005 to 2013, companies with women in senior management had higher price/book value ratios than companies without women in TMTs, and companies with at least two women managers tended to outperform those with only one (Credit Suisse Research Institute, 2014). According to the International Monetary Fund (Elborgh-Woytek et al., 2013), there is ample evidence that when women are able to develop their full labor-market potential, there can be significant macroeconomic gains.

If companies truly do perform best when women hold top positions, one might wonder why gender gaps persist and what can be done to bridge these gaps.

Well Educated, Highly Competent

Women's self-reports of assertiveness, dominance, and masculinity during the 1990s that experienced a major transformation in organizational cultures (Twenge, 1997, 2001), and the value that women place on job attributes such as freedom, challenges, leadership, prestige, and influence, have all become more similar to those of men (Konrad, Ritchie, Lieb, & Corrigall, 2000; Belasen & Frank, 2012). They also work harder and wiser to choose the leadership style that they feel comfortable with, and that does not contradict with their feminine image. They can be go-getters in management and, at the same time, inspire others as transformational leaders. Moreover, women are not submissively waiting for opportunities, but rather they seek them proactively and diligently. They reach for those opportunities by themselves. Nevertheless, in order to prove that they are able to achieve the same level of managerial leadership as men, women need to "prove" that they have strong upper management skills in many areas.

Women now outnumber men at almost every level of higher education, with three women attending college and graduate school for every two men. They get more Master's degrees and more PhDs. Most law school students are women, as are almost half of the medical students. In Canada, women earned 35.3% of all MBAs in 2007, up from 33.4% in 2006. In the US, in 2013/2014, they earned more than 44% of Master's degrees in business and management, including 37% of the MBAs (Warner, 2014).

According to the US Bureau of Labor Statistics (2015), the occupational distributions of female and male full-time workers differ considerably. Compared with men, relatively few women work in construction, production, or transportation occupations; women are far more concentrated in office and administrative support jobs (see Figure 7.1).

At lower managerial levels, women are slated to earn more money than men. The number of women with $100,000+ income is rising at a much faster pace than it is for men. Nationwide, about 1 in 18 women working full time earned $100,000 or more in 2009, a jump of 14% over two years; In contrast, 1 in 7 men made that much, up just 4% (Morello & Keating, 2010). Furthermore, the February 2010 US Bureau of Labor Statistics report provided evidence confirming that women outnumbered men on the nation's payroll for the first time in history. Interestingly, surveys indicate that women, and especially highly-educated women, are more likely to be motivated by a job's intrinsic values than by extrinsic rewards.

Gender Pay Gap

In November 2015, the US Bureau of Labor Statistics released its newest report, which provides an overall review of women's earnings in the United States (US Bureau of Labor Statistics, 2015). In 2014, women who were full-time wage and salary workers had median usual weekly earnings of $719. Women's median earnings were 83% of those of male full-time wage and salary workers ($871). In 1979, the first year for which comparable earnings data are available, women's earnings were 62% of men's. Since 2004, the women's-to-men's earnings ratio has ranged from 80% to 83% (see Figure 7.2). This report drew on earnings data from the Current Population Survey, a national monthly survey of about 60,000 households conducted by the US Census Bureau for the US Bureau of Labor Statistics.

The Bureau of Labor Statistics report breaks down the gender pay gap by age, race, occupation, and hours worked. Findings included:

- In 2014, among workers age 35 and older, women earned between 76% and 81% of what their male counterparts earned in 2014. For those under age 35, the earnings differences between women and men were smaller, with women earning 90% to 92% of what men earned.
- Among women, whites ($734) earned 87% as much as Asian women ($841), blacks ($611) earned 73%, and Hispanics ($548) earned 65%. In comparison, white men ($897) earned 83% as much as Asian men ($1,080); black men ($680) earned 63% as much; and Hispanic men ($616), 57%.
- Education is a key determinant of pay for both women and men. Median weekly earnings vary significantly by educational attainment. Among all

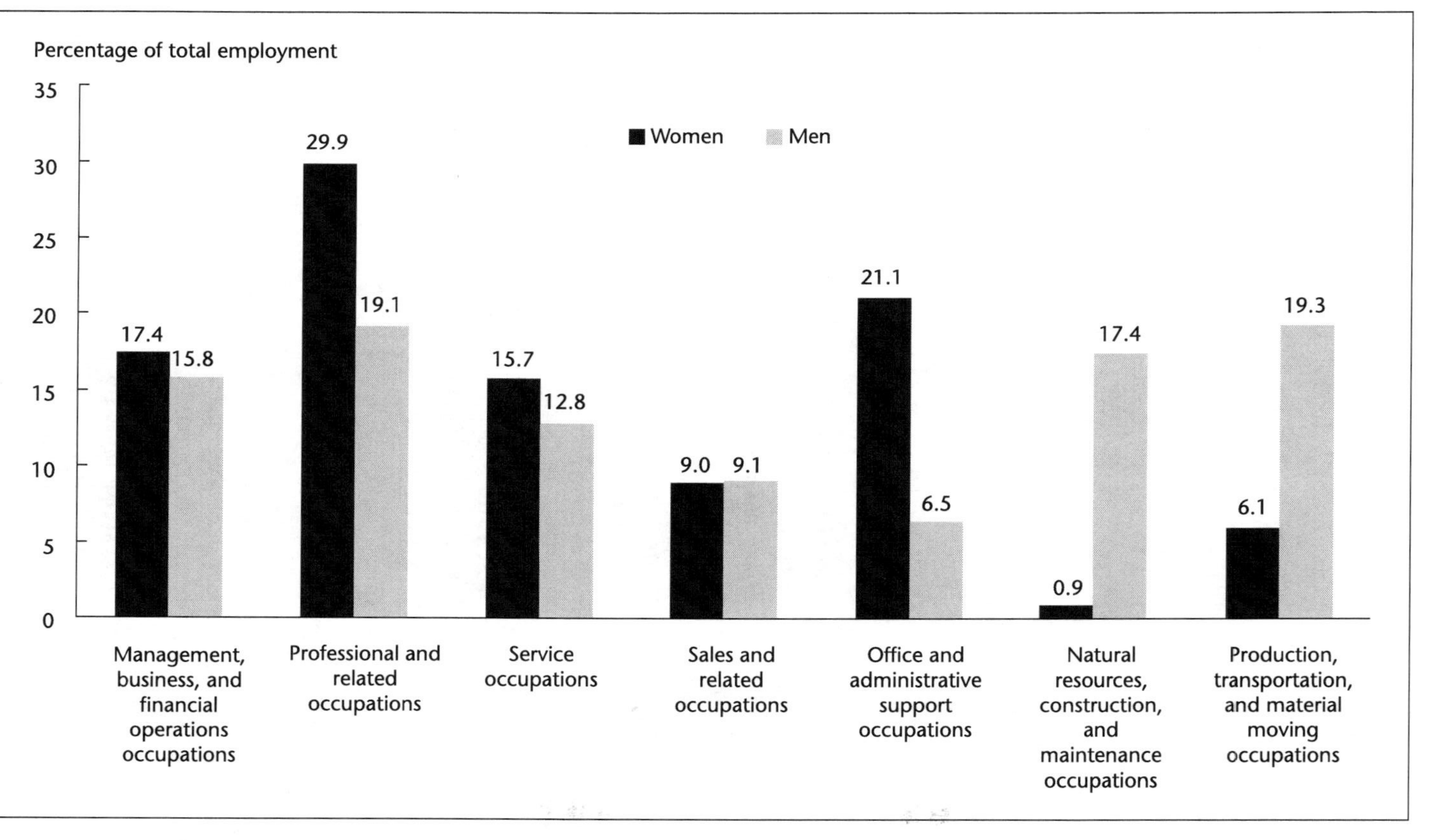

FIGURE 7.1 Distribution of Full-time Salary Employment for Women and Men by Occupation, 2014 Annual Averages

Source: US Bureau of Labor Statistics (2015).

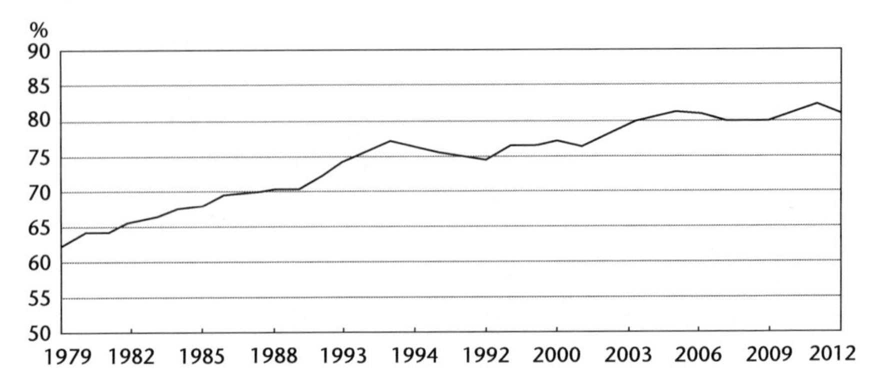

FIGURE 7.2 Women's Earnings as a Percentage of Men's, 1979–2012

Source: US Bureau of Labor Statistics (2015).

Note: Data relate to annual averages of median usual weekly earnings for full-time wage and salary workers.

workers age 25 and older, the weekly earnings of those without a high school diploma ($488) were two-fifths of those with a bachelor's degree or higher ($1,193) in 2014. For workers with a high school diploma who had not attended college, median earnings ($668) were a little more than half of the earnings of those with a bachelor's degree or higher. Those with some college or an associate's degree ($761) made just under two-thirds of what workers with a bachelor's degree or more made.

- Women and men working full time in management, business, and financial operations jobs had higher median weekly earnings than workers in any other major occupational category in 2014 ($1,056 for women and $1,416 for men). In management, business, and financial operations occupations, women who were chief executives and computer and information systems managers had the highest median weekly earnings ($1,572 and $1,529, respectively). Among men in this occupational category, chief executives and architectural and engineering managers had the highest earnings ($2,246 and $1,975, respectively). This holds true even at the top of the scale, as female CEOs and directors earned 42% less than their male counterparts (Shin, 2012).
- The occupational distributions of female and male full-time workers differ considerably. Women are more likely than men to work in professional and related occupations.
- In 2014, 30% of women worked in professional and related occupations, compared with 19% of men. Within this occupational category, though, the proportion of women employed in the higher paying job groups is much smaller than the proportion of men employed in them.

- In 2014, 10% of women in professional and related occupations were employed in the relatively high-paying computer and engineering fields, compared with 44% of men.
- Women in professional and related occupations were more likely to work in education and healthcare jobs, which generally pay less than computer and engineering jobs. Indeed, 68% of women in professional occupations worked in education and healthcare jobs in 2014, compared with 30% of men.
- Among full-time workers (that is, those usually working at a job 35 hours or more per week), men are more likely than women to have a longer workweek.
- In 2014, 26% of men who usually work full time worked 41 or more hours per week, compared with 15% of women who worked those hours.
- Women were more likely than men to work 35 to 39 hours per week: 12% of women worked those hours in 2014, while 5% of men did. A large majority of both male and female full-time workers had a 40-hour workweek. Among these workers, women earned 89% as much as men earned.

PAYSCALE'S LATEST REPORT SHOWS THAT THE GENDER PAY GAP IS REAL

A few highlights from the report:

- The gender pay gap is highest between married men with children and married women with children.
- Married men earn the highest salaries, and single moms the lowest. Married men with children make median salaries of $67,900; those who do not have children earn $60,800. Single moms make $38,200 (median, uncontrolled for other factors) and $45,500 (median, controlled for factors like job, experience, etc.).
- Men's salaries increase until ages 50 to 55, where they level off at a median salary of $75,000; women's salaries plateau between the ages of 35 to 40 at a median of $49,000.
- The tech industry has the smallest controlled (1.4%) and uncontrolled (20.7%) pay gaps, until you get to the executive level, where the controlled gender pay gap of 5.6% is slightly higher than other industries. In general, the pay gap gets wider the higher up the ladder you go: male executives earn 32.8% more than female executives (uncontrolled) and 6.1% more (controlled).
- The highest overall controlled pay gap is for Gen X (3.6%).
- The pay gap increases with more education: PhD holders have the highest controlled pay gap (5.1%), followed by MBA holders (4.7%), and MDs (4.6%).

> Perhaps the biggest surprise is that men were more likely to report that they prioritize home and family obligations over work (52%, compared with 46% of women) – pretty much the opposite of what you might expect. On the other hand, the more often women report prioritizing home and family over the work, the larger the controlled pay gap becomes, suggesting that women who are up front about their desire to concentrate more energy on their personal lives are punished at work.
>
> *(Luckwaldt, 2015)*

The Bureau of Labor Statistics report on women earnings in 2014 discussed above demonstrates that the gender pay gap still permeates every segment of society—by age, race, education level, occupation type, and hours worked. Evidently, the gender pay gap has widened further in 2015 with male executives earning many times more than their female counterparts (Reaney, 2015). One stipulation is that women's choice of jobs and positions is largely determined by the type of disciplinary education and training that they pursue prior to entering the workforce (Figure 7.3). A 2014 UCLA survey of college freshmen shows large gender gaps in students' intention to major in subjects such as finance, which tend to be higher-paying, while women are more likely to focus on tourism and hospitality (Eagan et al., 2014). This differential focus of area choice leads to

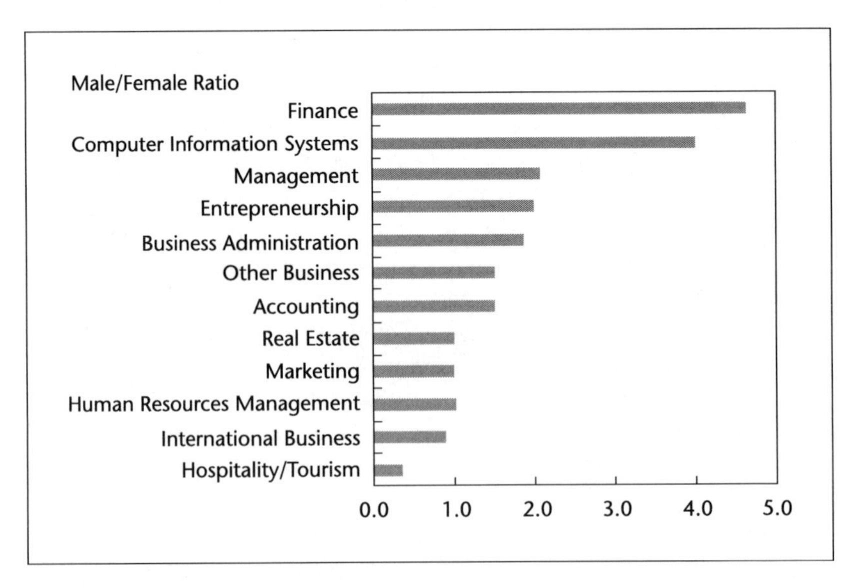

FIGURE 7.3 Women in Graduate Education: Ratio of Males to Females Reporting Intended Business Major by Focus Area

Source: Council of Economic Advisers (2015).

wage gaps for men and women from the start of their careers. For example, the expected early career salary for finance is over 40% higher than the expected early career salary for hospitality and tourism in which women outnumbered men (Council of Economic Advisers, 2015).

Work–Family Conflict

Many organizations associate being a woman as incompatible with being a leader. However, work–life conflict appears to provide another reason for the underrepresentation of women in upper management.

> The work–family conflict bias means that just being a woman signals to a manager that her family will interfere with her work, irrespective of whether or not that woman actually has work–family conflict, is married, has children, or has children of certain age.
>
> *(Hoobler, Lemmon, & Wayne, 2011, p. 152)*

It is noteworthy that Title VII of the Civil Rights Act of 1964 protects women from workplace biases and discrimination based on perceived difference and the FMLA provides job protection for new parents.

In addition to early preparation, the pay gap between men and women could also be associated with expected length of career interruptions as well as differences in number of hours worked. Deviations from the corporate culture and standard of non-interruption and loyalty are harshly imposed in the conversion of long hours and hard work to earnings. This is especially true if a woman chooses to have children or take maternity leave. Studies show that

> much of the growth in the earnings gap in the first decade was due to women being more likely to take time away from work – closely associated with childbirth and child care needs (10 or more years out, there is a 22 percentage point gender gap in having taken time out of work including parental leave) – and the gender gap in hours with women more likely to work shorter hours including part-time employment – also typically related to family and caregiving responsibilities.
>
> *(Council of Economic Advisers, 2015)*

Corporate Mental Blinders

If women have the ability to influence followers to emulate their actions as well as the ability to motivate them to embrace and enact their vision, then they certainly possess qualities of successful managerial leaders. Nevertheless, about 70% of women and 57% of men "believe an invisible barrier – a glass ceiling – prevents women from getting ahead in business, according to a study of 1,200 executives in eight countries, including the U.S., Australia, Austria and the Philippines" (Clark, 2006). Notably, very few women have upper management line experience in the areas of marketing, finance, or operations, which are typically needed to become a company CEO. Moreover, it was recognized a long time ago that only 4% of the companies interviewed in a study attempted to get women the line experience they needed to become a CEO (Oakley, 2000).

Another corporate practice that hinders women's chances of success includes compensation practices. In general, women receive a lower salary as well as less perks and time off. In fact, according to a 2008 survey of CEO pay (Jones, 2009), female CEOs on average made only 85% of what men CEOs made. Furthermore, a study conducted by Kulich, Ryan, and Haslam (2007) suggested that decisions about performance-based pay related directly to male CEOs, while they were mediated by evaluations of leadership characteristics and abilities in the case of female CEOs. These authors indicated that

> while men were both rewarded and punished in line with their company's performance, the amount of bonus received by the female CEO did not significantly differ in contexts of increasing versus declining company performance. Apparently, relative to male executives for whom the standard evaluation of leadership capabilities was applied, company performance did not matter so much when a bonus was allocated to female executives. Hence, for women, leadership performance was evaluated based on perceptual dimensions (i.e., assessments of charisma and leadership ability) rather than demonstrated outcomes . . . [Thus] men's success seemed to be acknowledged without needing to scrutinize their leadership abilities, whereas women's abilities were subject to greater interrogation before conclusions about their leadership were inferred from company performance.
>
> *(Kulich, Ryan, & Haslam, 2007, p. 595)*

As discussed throughout the book and later in this chapter, female CEOs may also receive higher pay when the diversity of the board is much greater. Moreover, helping behaviors among female executives (e.g., active mentoring, sponsorship) may also reduce gender pay gap among CEOs.

Aside from the barriers in company policies and procedures for women, behavioral and cultural prohibitions also exist. For one thing, there is the double-bind situation with implicit corporate mental blinders—a woman cannot succeed no matter what she does. In these cases, women are told to act authoritatively in order to be taken seriously but are then perceived as "bitches" for acting tough, but when women act in ways that are consistent with the feminine stereotype, they are seen as too nice (Valerio, 2009). Ultimately, the double-bind view depicts women in a paradoxical lose–lose situation.

Intrinsically Motivated, Proficiently Fitted

The majority of women have multiple goals in life, and don't just set out to snag the biggest monetary prize when they plan their career (Pinker, 2008). Women seem to prefer intrinsic rewards such as self-development and quality of work–life whereas men value more extrinsic rewards and opportunities to advance up the corporate ladder (Sturges, 1999). In 2008, the Pew Research Center conducted and published the survey *Men or women: Who's the better leader?* The survey was based on telephone interviews with a nationally representative sample of 2,250 adults living in the continental United States. The survey respondents were asked to report if they believed eight traits—honesty, intelligence, hardworking, decisive, ambitious, compassionate, outgoing, and creative—were true for men or women. The findings from this particular survey question were quite revealing: On seven of eight leadership traits measured in this survey, women were rated either better than or equal to men. Of those eight traits men only prevailed over women on decisiveness.

Although women were viewed as more likely to possess most leadership traits, the survey findings unveiled a puzzling paradox: When respondents were asked whether men or women make better political leaders, only 6% stated they believe women make better political leaders than men and 21% stated they felt men make better leaders than women (Pew Research Center, 2008). The predominant view of women's suitability for political leadership positions remained the same in 2015 as indicated in Figure 7.4, although the success of Hillary Clinton in the 2016 Democratic campaign trail has signified a major change in the overall perception of women's efficacy and fitness for the top position in the world.

Who Is the Boss?

In a report titled "Americans prefer male boss to a female boss," Carroll (2006) explains that Gallup first asked this question in 1953, and at that time, two in three Americans said they would prefer a male boss, while just 5% said they would prefer a female boss, with 25% volunteering it would make no difference. Beginning in 1982, sentiments shifted and greater numbers of Americans said they would prefer a female boss or said their boss's gender didn't matter to them. In more recent years, a plurality of respondents indicated that gender makes no difference to them, but the preference for a male boss among those who have a preference has been observed in every poll in which this question has been asked over the years.

More recently, by a 37% to 19% margin, Americans indicated that, if they were taking a new job, they would prefer their boss to be a man rather than a woman. Some 43% of Americans volunteer that it would not make a difference to them. The results on this question have fluctuated substantially over the years, but relatively few Americans—no more than 22%—have said they would prefer a female boss.

About two-thirds of Americans, including majorities of men and women alike, say it is easier for men than women to get elected to high political offices and to get top executive positions in business, but women are more likely to express this view. About three-quarters of women say men have a better shot at these roles, compared with about six-in-ten men, a pattern that is repeated across generations.

For example, Millennial and Boomer women are 13 percentage points more likely than their male counterparts to say it is easier for men to get top executive positions in business; there is a 14-point gender gap among Gen Xers and a 17-point gap among the Silent generation on this question. Similarly, there are double-digit gender gaps across generations on views that it is easier for men to get elected to high political offices.

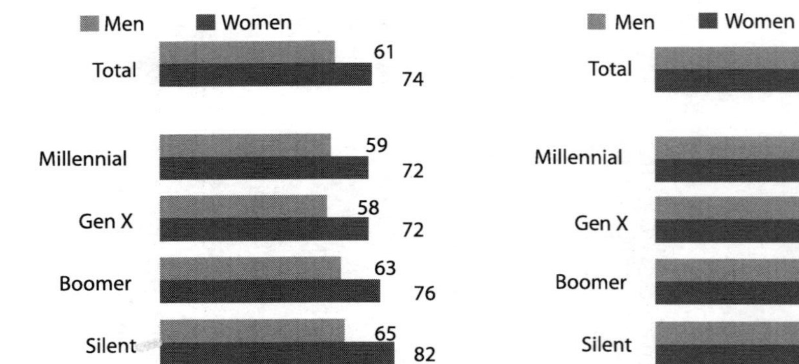

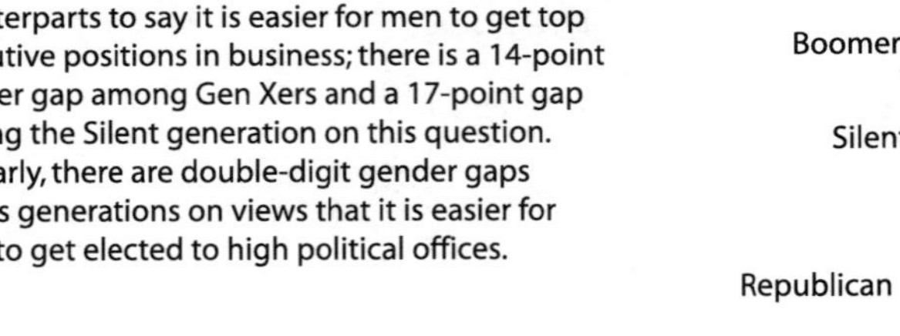

FIGURE 7.4 Most Say it is Easier for Men to Get Top Positions in Business and Politics

Source: Pew Research Center (2015).

Women are somewhat more likely than men to say they would prefer a female boss, but only about one in four women typically do (Carroll, 2006). By 2010–2015 these percentages shifted dramatically as millennials (both men and women) began to rearticulate career paths by re-balancing social, educational, and financial goals. As many as 72% of them would like to be their own boss but if they do have to work for a boss, 79% of them would want that boss to serve more as a coach or mentor. Moreover, 88% prefer a collaborative work culture rather than a competitive one; 74% want flexible work schedules; and 88% want "work–life integration," which isn't the same as work–life balance, since work and life now blend together inextricably (Asghar, 2014).

Underrepresented and Unaccounted for

On September 28, 2010, the US Government Accountability Office released the findings of its 2000–2007 study, using the US Census Bureau's American Community Survey, covering three important questions:

1. What is the representation of women in management positions compared to their representation in non-management positions by industry?
2. What are the key characteristics of women and men in management positions by industry?
3. What is the difference in pay between women and men in full-time management positions by industry?

Overall, the US Government Accountability Office results (2010) showed that female managers' representation and differences between female and male managers' characteristics remained largely similar. However, the differences narrowed substantially in level of education and slightly in pay. In 2007, women comprised an estimated 40% of managers and 49% of non-managers across 13 industry sectors, virtually unchanged from 2000. On average for the 13 industry sectors, an estimated 14% of managers in 2007 were mothers to children under age 18 in the household, compared to 17% of non-managers. The largest proportion of women managers were healthcare and social assistance (70%), educational services (57%), financial activities (50%), and leisure and hospitality (45%). While both male and female managers experienced increases in obtaining undergraduate degrees or higher (up 6%), women's gains surpassed men's, up 3%. Across the industry sectors, on average, female managers earned 81 cents for every dollar earned by male managers in 2007 as compared to 79 cents in 2000.

The narrowing of the gap between 2000 and 2007 for all managers without children in the household was statistically significant at the 95% confidence level. These results bear the question of why, with women advancing in both education and leadership, the number of women in top corporate positions is so small. While women pursue more education and earn more money, they are still hitting the glass ceiling when it comes to corporate upper echelons. Although women are going to great lengths to educate themselves, they continue to be marginally represented in higher-level positions in the corporate world (Perry, 2009).

In 2012, women accounted for 53% of entry-level jobs and made it to "the belly of the pipeline" in large numbers. But then female presence fell off a cliff, to 35% at the director level, 24% among senior vice-presidents, and 19% in the C-suite (Barsh & Yee, 2012). One of the most serious issues regarding the scarcity of women in executive suites and corporate boards is the vicious cycle where negative stereotyping, discrimination, and prejudice traverse from traits (women are friendly, cooperative, relational, inclusive) to consequences (women are dominated and opportunities for upward mobility are blocked) leading many successful women to believe that there is little or no incentive for women to fight through systemic barriers (McEldowney, Bobrowski, & Gramberg, 2009). The paradox that exists reveals the prevailing gap: "In an era when women have made sweeping strides in educational attainment and workforce participation, relatively few have made the journey all the way to the highest levels of political or corporate leadership" (Pew Research Center, 2008, p. 3).

Women are more likely to be siloed into "soft" positions and staff roles such as public relations, human resources, ethics, and diversity although they often play key roles in marketing and customer relations mainly because of their superior people and communication skills (Belasen, 2012). Further, they often find themselves on a cliff with appointments to positions associated with negative energy, suboptimal outcomes, or less attractive assignments where the prospects for failures and subsequent criticisms are inescapable (Haslam & Ryan, 2008). Unlike men who self-promote quite aggressively, many of the contributions women make to the companies they work for do not get noticed.

Contrast the majority of women's staff positions with their male counterparts who occupy line positions with profit and loss responsibilities that are often reserved for men, supporting their upward career movement. Why is this? How can we explain the consistency and integrity between women's leadership effectiveness on one hand and the small number of women serving on corporate boards or fulfilling executive and senior leadership positions on the other? If coaching and mentoring, collaboration, trust, honesty and emotional intelligence are so essential for inspiring employee engagement, enhancing their leadership capability and improving organizational performance, why aren't women more prevalent in corporate leadership roles? If the humanistic rather than the rationalistic models of management are key success factors for achieving high commitment and for motivating employees at all levels (Belasen, 2000), and if women's leadership and social intelligence skills are vital for achieving competitive advantage (Belasen, 2012), why not select women for senior leadership positions? I raised the same mind-boggling question in Chapter 5. Is it possible that women's predominant relational style and communal leadership qualities create gender biases in recruiting women for top positions or for selecting them to manage bottom-line operations or lead high-risk business environments?

The short answer is the unseen "artificial barriers" that block women from advancing to top executive jobs. Furthermore, the "glass ceiling" is no longer a single barrier, but a combination of multiple factors that push against women in management. Anna Marie Valerio (2009) concluded that even with the progress that has been made so far in corporate America, women seeking upper executive positions face persistent barriers to their success. The "glass ceiling" is not just one wall that women strive to shatter, but "many varied pervasive forms of gender bias that occur frequently in both overt and covert ways" (Oakley, 2000, p. 321). In 2016, regardless of the progress that has been made, this statement still holds true. Even today, in male-led companies, the voices of women are often stifled and the current approaches that exist to help women move up in the hierarchy usually are geared toward getting women to blend in rather than speak their minds.

Ultimately, women who seek top management positions must weed through culturally formed stereotypes and at the same time avoid crossing culturally generated barriers. Eagly and Carli (2007) describe this barrier as "labyrinth leadership." In Chapter 3, I refer to this as a centripetal force, invariably unicursal, that sends women to the center followed by a centrifugal force that then keep them from reaching their goals. This centrifugal force is associated with inertia that moves in a circular path—a catch 22 (Belasen, 2012). Women are judged against male norms, often eliciting negative evaluations about their behaviors and performance. When gendered organizations value the disembodied employee, the expectations are for women to fit this male-normed mold regardless of the perceived incongruity between the predominantly agentic qualities and the predominantly communal qualities characterizing women. The perceived incongruity could lead to two forms of prejudice: a less favorable evaluation of women's fitness for leadership roles; and a less favorable evaluation of the actual leadership behavior displayed by women because agentic behavior is perceived as less desirable in women than men (Eagly & Karau, 2002). When women perform leadership roles they are often perceived as having violated their stereotypically prescribed feminine roles.

Gendered Leadership

Eddy and Cox (2008, p. 72) pointed out that even women presidents in community colleges are judged against male norm. One of the women presidents told the story of being forceful on her side of an argument and being called a "bitch." She reflected, "I walked out of his office and said, 'I can't work for this man, and what's more, I probably can't work for anyone. I've got to be my own boss."' Indeed, she was penalized for acting tough outside her gender. Another president, petite in stature, noted that a female board member advised her to wear glasses "to appear more serious. The women needed to act tougher to meet the expected work roles but could not appear too tough" (p. 74).

Men in leadership roles, however, are seen as acting in congruence with their prescribed masculine roles. Therefore, successful female leaders generally work hard and seek leadership styles that do not elicit resistance to their authority by challenging norms dictating that women be egalitarian and supportive of others (Eagly, Johannesen-Schmidt, & Van Engen, 2003). Hence, gender role congruence theory, consistent with social identity theory and similarity attraction models of interactions, typecasts males as high in masculine traits who are more task-focused or agentic, whereas females are high in feminine traits in tune with interpersonal and communal orientations.

Existing structures of pay and reward systems tend to reinforce this incongruity—women are judged less favorably than men despite exhibiting similar behaviors and accomplishments. Male contributions are measured in terms of bottom line results and numeric values such as ROI and ROE. Dominance, aggression, and competitiveness are overvalued and overemphasized. Traditional women's strengths such as maintaining relationships, resolving conflicts, sharing power, caring for employees, and reaching a consensus tend to be undervalued.

Good communication skills, collaboration, mentoring, and developing others are important but less significant than quantitative measures of success—bottom-line factors used to reward male managers. Women are particularly vulnerable to these evaluative biases when they work in male-dominated settings, paradoxically suffering harsh consequences for displaying excellent leadership, communication, and sensitivity skills (Heilman, Wallen, Fuchs, & Tamkins, 2004). Female managers reportedly need to work harder to persuade senior managers to see their side, while male managers are able to negotiate, bargain, and obtain concessions. Feminine traits such as concern for others (relatedness), consensual approach to decision making, and consideration of feelings of others prior to initiating action may limit the extent of upward influence since women may act on different kinds of opportunities.

Organizations, particularly those which are male-dominated, are not gender-neutral—they reflect settings in which women's behavior and accomplishments are scrutinized, measured, and evaluated differently from men's (Hopkins, O'Neil, Passarelli, & Bilimoria, 2008). Success becomes increasingly challenging in organizations with bosses that see loyalty and "fit" with their norms and values. Managers whose styles match those of their executives and senior managers may benefit from "fit effects" in performance evaluation and promotion decisions.

The perceived incongruity and subsequent prejudice reinforces a vicious cycle from two directions: Because leaders are expected to have more agentic than communal qualities, women, on the one hand, conforming to their gender role are "failing" to meet the requirements of their leadership role; while conforming to their leader role can produce a failure to meet the requirements of their gender role (Eagly & Johannesen-Schmidt, 2001). Men, on the other hand, produce expectations that are consistent with current views of agentic leadership roles and behaviors (e.g., confidence and assertion), their natural tendencies. However, because agentic behaviors are perceived as incompatible with communal behaviors, women are particularly vulnerable to becoming targets of prejudice, placing them at a disadvantage (e.g., rewarded differently).

Corporate Long-term Success

Sometimes people view women as lacking the stereotypical directive and assertive qualities of good leaders—that is, as not being tough enough or not taking charge. The anomaly of a woman executive in a male-dominated executive suite may itself affect the ratings of her leadership skills and abilities. A second major reason for female disadvantage is due to prevailing assumptions that male executives are preferred by their male colleagues as male executives typically land positions of COO or CEO. This is often referred to as a *contagious effect*. Predominantly male boards are much more likely to appoint male CEOs and only a few firms have equal gender representation in compensation committees (Shin, 2012). Because CEOs are usually men and board members are usually chosen from the pool of CEOs, many CEOs will select mirror-like board members who possess the qualities that they have, surrounding themselves with figureheads who match their own attributes. Having women on company boards can give the company unique and fresh ideas and make connections between consumers and employees (Arfken, Bellar, & Helms, 2004). Studies have shown that having women in positions of executive leadership can be linked to long term success for the company as well a competitive advantage (Women in Technology, 2015).

Because women have a strong influence on what people buy, companies would be able to access the full range of resources available to a company. Notably, the Fortune 500 companies with the highest percentage of women corporate officers achieved, on average, a whopping 35% higher return on equity and 34% higher stakeholder satisfaction than did competitors with less diversity in the corporate suites (Catalyst, 2004). Similar results were found in 2011 (Catalyst, 2011).

Women help boost companies' public image and reputation through support of social responsibility and philanthropic programs. They add value to the company with unique adaptability skills and are masters in creating positive work climates based on inclusion and diversity. They typically have a stronger moral orientation and possess more social sensitivity than men, a necessary attribute to have on a socially accountable company's board. It is not that women and men compete in a zero-sum game—it is that they bring something new or complementary to the table for an organization. As Eagly (2007) pointed out: Business journalists often echoed some of these themes by highlighting the important role that women have in dealing with employees and stakeholders while delivering consistent results – CEO qualities that are pursued by many boards of directors (Belasen, 2012).

Beyond Tokenistic: The Black Box of the Boardroom

While male CEOs and senior vice-presidents are praised for forceful and assertive behavior and given low marks for being cooperative and empathic, the exact opposite is "reserved" for women. Notably, the gender stereotypes that are preventing women from reaching the top still exist especially when standards of success are measured in male terms where hierarchy and power are preferred over egalitarianism and persuasion. One is prejudice, which is when someone holds a negative view of another based on their cultural identity. The other is discrimination, which is when prejudice becomes observable. Research shows that both of these components exist in the workplace where agentic or instrumental behaviors are valued rather than empowerment, influence, and care for employees. Assessments of leadership inherently reflect gender stereotypes and prejudices.

There is also a widely held stereotypical belief that women will allow their emotions to get in the way of their work and managing others, especially men (Huffman & Cohen, 2004). A woman who loses composure may be seen as weak and lose credibility. Conversely, a man who loses composure may be seen as sensitive. Women also experience cross pressures for their time and the constant need to balance competing priorities across life and career goals that are different for men (Mainiero & Sullivan, 2006; O'Neil & Bilimoria, 2005). Consequently, women choose to work part-time or not at all so they can attend to their families at home. Others telecommute by working from home, most commonly on a part-time basis. Indeed, Ruderman and Ohlott (2004) reported a higher turnover rate for women than for their male counterparts in executive positions with at least 10 years of experience.

Stereotyping can be particularly risky due to the fact that the descriptions of certain groups are often mutually exclusive. Moreover, the fact that women in upper-management positions are almost always "tokens" instead of "dominants" hurts their chances of making it to the top (Oakley, 2000). Because "dominants" have a tendency to act in ways that affirm the group's solidarity, the "tokens" are often made to feel excluded as well as face more pressure at work. Kanter's (1977) theory of tokenism suggests that underrepresented individuals at the senior ranks require unique strategies and talents since they must respond to different expectations and are evaluated with different lenses than mainstream peers. In fact, the likelihood of women who work with groups of 85% or more men to experience negative consequences associated with tokenism is relatively high (Yoder, 1991). The 2020 GDI, which tracks the number of women on boards, indicates that as of December 2015 there were 619 "Token Companies" in the GDI that included 1,823 companies (2020 Women on Boards, 2015).

Women directors tend to be viewed as "out-group" and less trustworthy members and their appointment often comes with a negative social bias. Many women shared their concerns about board development, gaining credibility, and fitting into the board environment as board leadership is a critical component in board participation and consultation (Kakabadse et al., 2015). This is unfortunate since gender diversity on corporate boards influences corporate governance outcomes that in turn impact performance (Terjesen, Sealy, & Singh, 2009). Attaining critical mass—going from one or two women (a few tokens) to at least three women (consistent minority)—also makes it possible to enhance the level of firm innovation (Torchia, Calabrò, & Huse, 2011). Paying attention to how directors are appointed to governance committees (e.g., audit, compensation, nomination), the black box of the boardroom (Minow, 2009), and the roles that women assume can enhance our understanding of how diversity impacts firm performance. Participation in board leadership helps reduce groupthink and provides important challenges to existing practices, norms of behavior, and boardroom dynamics (Huse & Solberg, 2006). Board leadership is a critical component in board participation and discussion, and women should not be invited through symbolic appointment but rather through substitution of male directors.

A real shift in the corporate mindset involves a critical increase in the number of women directors through laws and regulations. In Norway, it was not until quota laws were put into place that women began to gain access to boards in a meaningful way. Pressure could also come from further academic, fact-tank groups, and nonprofit organizations to find out more about dynamics within the "black box" of corporate boardrooms, current perceptions of women participation, and their contributions to boards. One example is Elstad and Ladegard's (2012) study of 458 women on Norwegian corporate boards where the ratio of women directors among board members ranged from 11% to 100%. They found that women perceived that they had a high level of information sharing, a low level of self-censorship, and a high level of influence across the different ratios of board membership held by women directors. These results support the notion of women directors as significant influencers.

A related question is whether quota laws can provide strong incentives for women to shift the current work–family conflict in favor of their professional careers. The answer to this question is also affected by the national norms and culture. For example, the success of quota laws in motivating women to invest in their careers could be smaller in cultures characterized by stronger family integration and much greater in countries in which family functions are outsourced to the market. Likewise, countries with greater emphasis on social equity, economic freedom, or gender-friendly political institutions could affect women's willingness to re-allocate time from family to career.

Strong external pressure to appoint women to boards could play a significant role in the adoption and diffusion of corporate practices. One possible alternative, which more closely fits the American business culture, is to create a system of incentives based on a company's success in gender equity as the federal government already uses tax incentives to encourage certain business practices. Unlike the Norwegian model of liquidating a company for not meeting a quota, tax incentives in the US are less threatening (Lee, 2014).

Career Interruptions, Parenthood, and Work–Family Conflict

It seems that while women feel they would relocate for the right opportunity, most women do not actually make the move when the opportunity presents itself. There is also the question of whether women have appropriate financial incentives to relocate. Women may hold the same position as men but their salaries are significantly lower. It is not a secret that women have been outpaced by men in salary throughout their careers. It is clear that in order for these numbers to continue to shift, there needs to be a fundamental change in how leading companies proactively and diligently break the systemic barriers that prevent women from reaching the top and achieving equality in pay.

Considering the choice of relocation or not joining the workforce from a financial perspective, a stay-at-home parent has been estimated to have a monetary value of anywhere from around $60,000 to $115,000. Salary.com estimates $112,962 per year and a stay-at-home mom's workweek to average 94.7 hours a week in 2012 (Salary.com, 2012). Salary.com increased the estimation to $113,586 in 2013 (Salary.com, 2013). An intelligent husband estimated that the value of his wife's work in 2014 was worth $73,960 in 2014 (Fuller, 2015). According to Business Insider, Insure.com was far less generous with its salary estimate, estimating the 2013 market value of a mom's work at $59,862 (Woodruff, 2013).

The convention of women having to stay at home to care for the children has completely changed as well. Many of these beliefs stem from antiquated notions of the past. As more fathers are staying home with the kids and taking on more housework and childcare duties, the roles that men and women used to portray are now converging. Additionally, as fewer fathers are the family's sole breadwinner, the work–family balance is becoming more of a challenge overall with dads juggling the competing demands of family and work. Meanwhile, women have increased their share of earned income and while significant pay gaps still remain, there is clearly a more equal distribution of labor, at home and outside, between mothers and fathers (see Figure 7.5). In fact, men are now opting out in favor of taking care of children as women, in some occupations (e.g., technology, sales or marketing) are making more money than men (Sahadi, 2016).

> Among working fathers, 50% say that it is difficult for them to balance the responsibilities of their job and their family. This is roughly equal to the share of working mothers who told us they have difficulty balancing work and family.
>
> *(Parker, 2015)*

While staying home may not be the best available option, many men will need to increase their caregiving roles at home to help meet their partnering expectations (Harrington, Van Deusen, & Humberd, 2011).

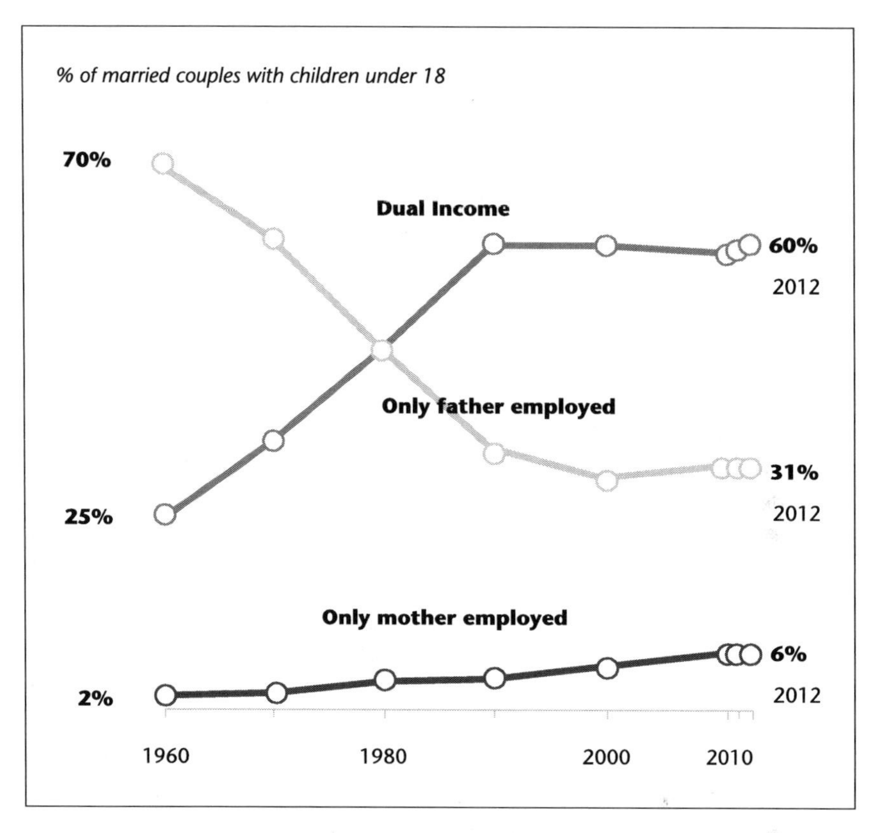

FIGURE 7.5 The Rise in Dual-income Households

Source: Parker (2015).

The major factors parents need to take into consideration when making the decision of one or both going to work are the cost of the labor that a stay-a-home parent provides and the approximate wages the parent would receive from working. Looking at the data described in the previous section, we can infer that whichever number is higher makes the most financial success for the individual and their needs. The salary estimations broke down the tasks of a stay-at-home parent into different job occupations and the hours spent in each role. The different positions (for the stay-at-home parent) considered are childcare, CEO, psychologist, cook, housekeeper, laundromat, computer operator, facilities manager, janitor, and driver (Salary.com, 2013). Some positions may have been left out or overestimated depending on the individual household roles. There can be stay-at-home mothers who largely take care of the finances and taxes on top of their normal roles previously listed, as well as event planner and secretary. As indicated above, according to Business Insider, Insure.com estimated an average salary for a stay at home mom in 2013 to be $59,862 (Woodruff, 2013).

Therefore, at a bare minimum, a salary of $60,000 is needed to justify a second parent going to work.

This trend of one spouse choosing to remain home and care for the children is not causing men to opt out but more so causing women to opt out even though women are on average receiving higher levels of education. A big factor contributing to the less-educated spouse being the one to work is most likely due to the increased hours required when working in corporate leadership and the wage inequality that is still seen in this day and age. Women, on average, make 78% of the wages that are experienced by men for the exact same positions (Kessler, 2015). Females need to be much higher up the corporate ladder when compared to their male counterparts to make more than the $60,000 baseline and overcome the wage gap.

The turn-around began in the mid-1990s though, which would lead to the conclusion that there have been increasingly more educated women than men entering the workforce for roughly two decades. Other factors, such as the social stigma associated with women in the workforce, may still be suppressing the representation or there has not been enough time or enough men in power deciding to retire.

The only area of education where men in OECD (Organization for Economic Cooperation and Development) countries out-represented women was at the doctorate level in 2005. All countries in the OECD Index are projected by 2025 to have more than 50% women graduating except for Switzerland and Turkey. As for whether women will begin to establish themselves in more male-dominated industries, there has not been a large shift in the educational degrees women are receiving. Overwhelmingly, they still have a larger presence in education and a smaller presence in engineering (Vincent-Lancrin, 2008).

The decreased presence of educated women in the workforce can harm organizations in the long run. One area in particular that might experience a large decline from a decreased presence of women is marketing. Women notoriously spend more time shopping and therefore purchase a greater amount of goods, whereas men tend to be more focused on what needs to be purchased (Lewis, 2013). Marketers need to focus on both genders but place more emphasis on women as

> women make more than 85% of the consumer purchases in the United States, and reputedly influence over 95% of total goods and services purchased. Women as a whole are considered more sophisticated shoppers than men, taking longer to make a buying decision.
>
> *(Lewis, 2013)*

Another factor that must be considered if the female is going to work as opposed to the male is the potential lost future earnings. A couple needs to account for the lower wages of the present value but it is also important to consider the decreased chance of being promoted in the workplace. People like those who are similar to themselves; the opposites attract theory when it comes to relationships has been disproven (Lilienfeld, Lynn, Ruscio, & Beyerstein, 2011). We tend to lean toward the old adage of "birds of a feather flock together." The majority of the higher-up workforce is comprised of men, and men are likely to select other men to follow them. Male leadership is different from female leadership; the selection process is (hopefully) not based on gender but probably a similar work style and leadership style. This could be a leading factor of why men who are in leadership positions promote those who are like-minded (Pew Research Center, 2015; Highfield, 2008).

The article "Trust and gender: An examination of behavior, biases, and beliefs in the investment game" was aimed at understanding the main question of whether gender influences a person's chance of being trusted and their trustworthiness (Buchan, Croson, & Solnick, 2008). As previously pointed out, women are consistently found to be more trustworthy than men but men trust easier than women. Women feel more obligated and men are more strategic.

The Buchan et al. article stated, "Women tended to see the interpersonal aspect of the partnership and therefore did not take advantage of the opportunity for increased profit (even when both parties could potentially gain)." These authors argued that the stereotypes stay strong with women being relationship-oriented and men being more task oriented. The scenario with the highest level of trust is a male sender (negotiator) who would be more trusting presenting to a female who would be more trustworthy (Buchan et al., 2008). This causes an increased emphasis on the fact that women tend to be below men in the workforce and the increased comfort level of each gender with these roles.

RECOUNT BY JENNETTE M. TARIO, MBA, CLARKSON UNIVERSITY SCHOOL OF BUSINESS, SUMMER 2016

The Birchbox CEO, Katia Beauchamp, talks on CNN about the difficulties women investors face (CNN Money, 2016) and highlights many of the issues I have heard about; it echoes warnings I received prior to choosing to enter the world of finance. Each place I interviewed brought up the fact that I was a woman. Some places pointed out that I would be better at building client relationships and that there was a lack of women in the financial industry, while others insisted that people would be less likely to work with me as I am not the quintessential financial advisor.

I have a mentor at AXA and she is a female. She is also one of the top producers of our office and highly intelligent. She always says the old way of thinking is out as more women become involved in the household's financial picture as she always reminds me "women want to work with women and men want to work with men." Essentially, the more women continue to control the financials of the house then more women advisors will be sought after.

A recent edition of *The Motley Fool* describes a portion of the book *Warren Buffet Invests like a Girl: And Why You Should, Too*: "he's patient and does thorough research. He doesn't buy into the latest popular technology company that he doesn't understand. He doesn't take excessive risks or jump in and out of stocks." It also cites that in 2014 women outperformed men by 12% as well as the fact that men were 25% more likely to lose money in the market. This is partly a tangent but also draws attention to the fact that women and men think differently, their temperaments are also different, leading to different outcomes. Another reason why a man is more likely to promote or respect a man, they are similar with regard to their thought process and temperament.

Pushing Through the Invisible Wall

A fundamental change in the fabric of top leadership positions is called for. Organizations must reassess their mission statements and remove corporate barriers that limit or inhibit women's access to upper positions. Even a small increase in the percentage of female managers is expected to contribute to the implementation of successful practices, such as inclusive leadership or participative decision making. Past research shows that there is positive correlation between participation in decision making and superior organizational performance (Fernie & Metcalf, 1995; Capelli & Neumark, 2001), especially when decisions are made by teams (Foote, Matson, Weiss, & Wenger, 2002). Participative decision making generates more complete information and knowledge, brings more breadth and depth into the process, and leads to increased acceptance and support. As long as organizations include women in their management teams, they should expect superior performance (Melero, 2011).

Prejudices against female managers are expected to be less intense and their peers and superiors are less likely to perceive them as tokens when women's proportions in decision making authority centers are higher. Tokenism is a phenomenon that leads to the informal isolation of minority members who, in turn, respond by keeping low profiles (Kanter, 1977). If women have preferences for specific leadership styles (i.e., democratic), the likelihood that such styles and practices (i.e., involvement, interpersonal orientation) will become widespread will increase. Melero (2011) found that workplaces with a higher percentage of female managers tend to allocate more time to group decision making processes and to giving and receiving feedback. Managers are also more open to improving the collective performance and discussing career development opportunities with employees.

To push through the invisible wall, women must act in ways that are genuine and honest to their own values. Arguably, if women have to hide their own values and succumb to organizational pressure to mold into current norms and practices, their motivation to remain with an organization for a long period of time is lessened (Ruderman & Ohlott, 2004). At the same time, women need to find the right balance of agentic and communal behaviors through feedback, mentoring, and developmental plans. Balanced behaviors will allow women to communicate competence and self-confidence.

Women are encouraged to self-promote and make connections laterally and vertically. This expectation may seem quite rudimentary, however, studies show that men also do a better job at networking with male peers and supervisors who have access to points of influence. Moreover, research has shown that women have limited access to or are excluded from informal networks in the workplace. These networks are vital during socialization processes, decision making communications, and conflict resolutions. Limited access can also make it more difficult for women to create alliances and be close to point of information leading to limited mobility (Miller, 2006). This is especially true in highly male-dominated or masculine settings where women are challenged to act tough and exercise competitive styles to gain acceptance into influential networks (Timberlake, 2005). Women's networks, mentoring, and coaching provide opportunities for men and women to exchange information about each other's professional experience (Valerio, 2009, p. 83).

Often, human resources organizations may emphasize the positive skills that women possess, but may not actually follow through on hiring women for top leadership positions. Because of this frustrating situation, women tend to just give up instead of fight the injustice or engage in self-promoting behaviors. As a result, women are also less likely to use self-promoting behavior, are less "networked", and less likely to negotiate their "cards" aggressively.

Women do not tend to promote themselves as well as men do and they also have less mobility within and between organizations and are more dependent on formal advancement procedures than are men (Lyness & Thompson, 2000). Existing training and development programs tend to focus on current competencies and short-term performance expectations rather than long-term strategic planning goals putting women at obvious disadvantage. Women also often take jobs where there is no opportunity for promotion to the top, such as human resources/public relations. Moreover, many of the contributions of women to the companies they work for do not get noticed as much as men's contributions.

Willingness to relocate provides flexibility that can make women both competitive and attractive for employers. According to a 2004 CareerWomen.com survey (Hazard, 2004), over 60% of the women sampled stated they would relocate for the right position or promotion. However, when asked how willing they would be to make the move, only 4% responded "very willing." By contrast, 77% of job seekers with MBAs claimed that they would move and of that, 46%

replied "very willing." Moreover, 73% of women stated that they have moved for their spouses or partners, while only 9% responded that their spouse or partner moved for them. It appears that while women feel they would relocate for the right opportunity, most women do not actually make the move when the opportunity presents itself.

In a 2010 World Economic Forum report on corporate practices for gender diversity in 20 countries, of the companies participating in the survey, 100% of those in the United Kingdom and the United States appeared to offer support to employees in their effort to balance work and personal responsibilities through flexible working patterns, remote/distance working, and part-time work possibilities. Companies in Turkey and Mexico appeared to offer the fewest options in this regard. Change in the right direction, however, does occur as 82% of all respondent companies offered flexible working arrangements, while 55% offered remote/distance working, and 74% provided part-time working methods (see Figure 7.6).

Positive Change

Following Benjamin, Heffetz, Kimball, and Rees-Jones' (2012) proposition that women may strive to "have it all" because it will lead to a sense of purpose, sense of control, prestige or social status, not necessarily personal happiness, Bertrand (2013) found no evidence of greater life satisfaction or greater emotional well-being among educated women who have achieved the double goal of combining a successful career with a family life. The proposition of this book, however, is that organizations must change proactively to meet the professional needs of career women by reducing the stress associated with meeting incongruent expectations and performance standards and by adjusting work schedules, reward systems, succession planning, and leadership development programs.

Women make up the vast majority of the professional and service-related workforce but have not attained a proportional level of top executive positions. This imbalance is driven by multiple factors including long-held stereotypical and cultural biases about women in leadership and a lack of emphasis on corporate strategies to support the advancement of women to the top. Some of the strategies recommended to address this issue include development of a corporate priority for gender diversity in executive leadership with CEO and board accountability; effective succession planning; implementation of leadership development programs that focus on gender diversity; adoption of objective performance evaluation process; and creation of corporate initiatives such as flexible work schedules, mentor programs, networking events, and corporate women networks (McDonagh, Bobrowski, Hoss, Paris, & Schulte, 2014). Fulmer and Bleak's (2008) guidelines about successful implementation of leadership development programs in organizations are particularly relevant: Start at the top; connect leadership development goals to the organization itself; establish an

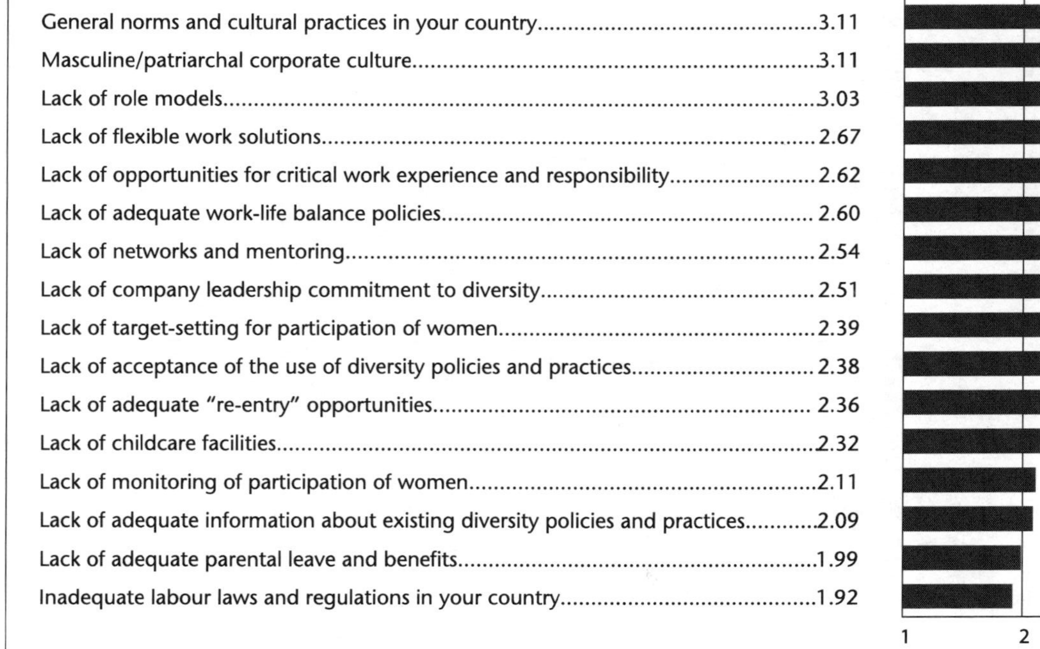

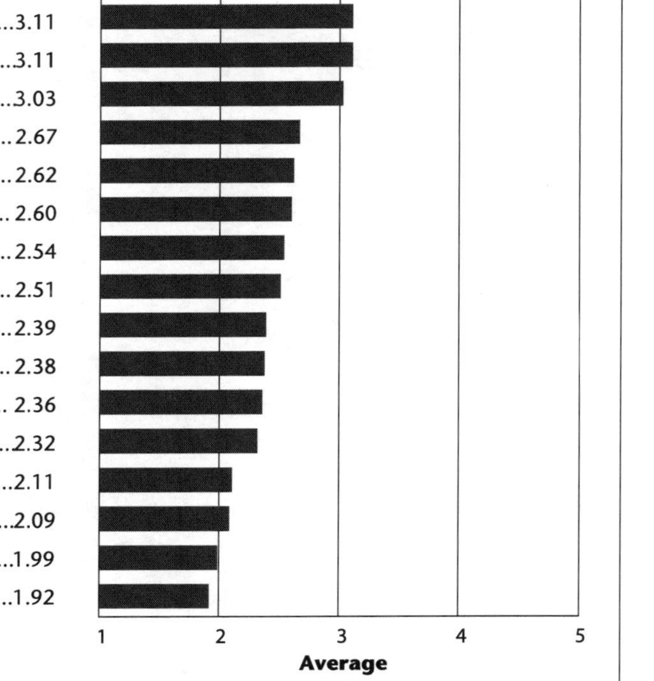

FIGURE 7.6 Barriers to Women's Rise to Positions of Leadership

Source: Zahidi & Ibarra (2010).

integrated leadership strategy; be consistent in the execution of leadership programs; and hold senior leaders accountable.

EXPANDING OPPORTUNITIES FOR WOMEN IN BUSINESS

Business educators have a critical role to play in shaping the leaders of tomorrow and facilitating diverse leadership. Given the demographic changes both underway and on the horizon, business schools must adapt in order to ensure that their students are trained looking forward to the business environment in which they will lead. To be competitive, future leaders will increasingly need to be involved in recruiting and retaining talent and therefore will need to be aware of the work/family issues they, their colleagues, and their employees may face.

By taking further steps to encourage more female students to pursue business careers, to ensure greater inclusivity in the classroom and on campus, and to better consider the lifetime career paths of their students, business schools can help our nation's workplace policies catch up with the needs of our modern-day workers and employers.

In particular, business schools can help ensure access to business school and business careers for women by taking concrete steps to pursue outreach and engagement to build the pipeline of women interested in business careers, to partner with companies to help women get back on the fast track, and to ensure that business school is a viable investment for a range of students, especially those with a lower earnings profile.

In addition, business schools have the opportunity to combat gender disparities by altering the business school experience to better address obstacles faced by women, including life-cycle challenges, facilitating mentorship and sponsorship opportunities, making curricula and faculty more representative, and ensuring that a diverse group of perspectives are brought into the classroom that business schools are providing.

To improve the outcomes and success of women in the workplace, it will be critical to improve career support and services, build tools for entrepreneurs, and expand workplace flexibility. By being model employers, business schools can lead by example, creating opportunities for all workers to succeed, including recognizing the need for balance between work and family responsibilities, ensuring diversity in leadership positions, and recognizing the importance of value, tone, and a culture of inclusiveness.

(Council of Economic Advisers, 2015)

References

Arfken, D. E., Bellar, S. L., & Helms, M. M. (2004). The ultimate glass ceiling revisited: The presence of women on corporate boards. *Journal of Business Ethics, 50*(2), 177–186.

Asghar, R. (2014, January 13). What millennials want in the workplace (and why you should start giving it to them). *Forbes*. Retrieved from www.forbes.com/sites/robasghar/2014/01/13/what-millennials-want-in-the-workplace-and-why-you-should-start-giving-it-to-them/#c008fb92fdfb.

Barsh, J., & Yee, L. (2012). Unlocking the full potential of women at work. *McKinsey & Company*. Retrieved from www.mckinsey.com/business-functions/organization/our-insights/unlocking-the-full-potential-of-women-at-work.

Belasen, A. T. (2000). *Leading the learning organization: Communication and competencies for managing change*. Albany, NY: SUNY Press.

Belasen, A. T. (2012). *Developing women leaders in corporate America: Balancing competing demands, transcending traditional boundaries*. Santa Barbara, CA: Praeger.

Belasen, A. T., & Frank, N. M. (2012). Using the Competing Values Framework to evaluate the interactive effects of gender and personality traits on leadership roles. *The International Journal of Leadership Studies*, 7(2), 192–215.

Benjamin, D. J., Heffetz, O., Kimball, M. L., & Rees-Jones. A. (2012). What do you think would make you happier? What do you think you would choose? *American Economic Review, 102*(5): 2083–2110.

Bertrand, M. (2013). Career, family, and the well-being of college-educated women. *American Economic Review, 103*(3), 244–250. DOI:10.1257/aer.103.3.244

Buchan, N. R., Croson, R. T., & Solnick, S. (2008). Trust and gender: An examination of behavior and beliefs in the investment game. *Journal of Economic Behavior & Organization, 68*(3/4), 466–476. DOI:10.1016/j.jebo.2007.10.006

Capelli, P., & Neumark, D. (2001). Do "high performance" work practices improve establishment level outcomes? *Industrial Labor Relations Review, 54*, 737–775.

Carroll, J. (2006). Americans prefer male boss to a female boss. *Gallup News Service*. Retrieved from www.gallup.com/poll/24346/americans-prefer-male-boss-female-boss.aspx.

Catalyst. (2004). The bottom line: Connecting corporate performance and gender diversity. Retrieved from www.catalyst.org/knowledge/bottom-line-connecting-corporate-performance-and-gender-diversity.

Catalyst. (2011). The bottom line: Corporate performance and women's representation on boards (2004–2008). Retrieved from www.catalyst.org/knowledge/bottom-line-corporate-performance-and-womens-representation-boards-20042008.

Clark, H. (2006, March 8). Are women happy under the glass ceiling? *Forbes*. Retrieved from www.forbes.com/2006/03/07/glass-ceiling-opportunities—cx_hc_0308glass.html.

CNN Money. (2016, April 8). Birchbox CEO: "Easier for men to get funding." *CNN Money*. [Video file]. Retrieved from http://money.cnn.com/video/news/2016/04/08/birchbox-ceo-beauty-products-investors.cnnmoney/.

Council of Economic Advisers. (2015, August). Expanding opportunities for women in business. Issue brief. Retrieved from www.whitehouse.gov/sites/default/files/docs/women_in_business_issue_brief_final_nonembargoed.pdf.

Credit Suisse Research Institute. (2014). The CS gender 3000: Women in senior management. Retrieved from www.calpers.ca.gov/docs/diversity-forum-credit-suisse-report-2015.pdf.

Desvaux, G., Devillard-Hoellinger, S., & Baumgarten, P. (2007). *Women matter: Gender diversity, a corporate performance driver.* McKinsey & Company. Retrieved from www.raeng.org.uk/publications/other/women-matter-oct-2007.

Eagan, K., Stolzenberg, E. B., Ramirez, J. J., Aragon, M. C., Suchard, M. R., & Hurtado, S. (2014). The American freshman: National norms fall 2014. *Los Angeles: Higher Education Research Institute, UCLA*. Retrieved from www.heri.ucla.edu/monographs/TheAmericanFreshman2014-Expanded.pdf.

Eagly, A. H. (2007). Female leadership advantage and disadvantage: Resolving the contradictions. *Psychology of Women Quarterly, 31*, 1–12.

Eagly, A. H., & Carli L. (2007). *Through the labyrinth: The truth about how women become leaders.* Boston: Harvard Business School Press.

Eagly, A. H., & Johannesen-Schmidt, M. C. (2001). The leadership styles of women and men. *Journal of Social Issues, 57*, 781–797.

Eagly, A. H., & Karau, S. J. (2002). Role congruity theory of prejudice toward female leaders. *Psychological Review*, 109, 573–598.

Eagly, A .H., Johannesen-Schmidt, M. C., & Van Engen, M. L. (2003). Transformational, transactional, and laissez-faire leadership styles: A meta-analysis comparing women and men. *Psychological Bulletin, 129*(4), 569–591.

Eddy, P. L., & Cox, E. M. (2008). Gendered leadership: An organizational perspective. *New Directions for Community Colleges, 142*, 69–79. DOI:10.1002/cc.326

Elborgh-Woytek, M. K., Newiak, M. M., Kochhar, M. K., Fabrizio, M. S., & Kpodar, K. et al. (2013). *Women, work, and the economy: Macroeconomic gains from gender equity.* International Monetary Fund. Retrieved from www.imf.org/external/pubs/ft/sdn/2013/sdn1310.pdf.

Elstad, B., & Ladegard, G. (2012). Women on corporate boards: Key influencers or tokens? *Journal of Management and Governance, 16*(4), 595–615.

Ely, R., Stone, P., & Ammerman, C. (2014). Rethink what you "know" about high-achieving women, R1412G. *Harvard Business Review 92*(12), 101–109.

Fernie, S., & Metcalf, D. (1995). Participation, contingent pay, representation and workplace performance: evidence from Great Britain. *British Journal of Industrial Relations, 33*(3), 379–415.

Fine, M. G. (2007). Women, collaboration, and social change: An ethics-based model of leadership. In J. L. Chin, B. L. Lott, J. K. Rice, & J. Sanchez-Hucles (Eds.), *Women and leadership: Visions and diverse voices* (pp. 177–191). Boston: Blackwell.

Fine, M. G., & Buzzanell, P. M. (2000). Walking the high wire: Leadership theorizing, daily acts, and tensions. In P. M. Buzzanell (Ed.), *Rethinking organizational and managerial communication from feminist perspectives* (pp. 128–156). Thousand Oaks, CA: Sage.

Foote, N., Matson, E., Weiss, L., & Wenger, E. (2002). Leveraging group knowledge for high-performance decision-making. *Organizational Dynamics, 31*(3), 280.

Fuller, G. (2015, April 6). Man's letter to wife calculates how much stay-at-home moms should earn. *Elite Daily*. Retrieved from http://elitedaily.com/news/world/mans-letter-calculates-stay-at-home-moms-earn/990159/.

Fulmer, R. M., & Bleak, J. (2008). What have we learned about strategic leadership development? In C. Wankel & R. DeFillippi (Eds.), *University and corporate innovations in lifetime learning* (pp. 161–179). Charlotte, NC: Information Age.

Harrington, B., Van Deusen, F., &. Humberd, B. (2011). *The new dad: Caring, committed and conflicted.* Chestnut Hill, MA: Boston College Center for Work & Family.

Haslam, S. A., & Ryan, M. K. (2008). The road to the glass cliff: Differences in the perceived suitability of men and women for leadership positions in succeeding and failing organizations. *The Leadership Quarterly, 19*(5), 530–546.

Hazard, E. (2004, August 11). Women hesitant to relocate: Most women would move if the right job came along, but few would be completely willing. *PLANSPONSOR*. Retrieved from www.plansponsor.com/Women-Hesitant-to-Relocate/.

Heilman, M. E., Wallen, A. S., Fuchs, D., & Tamkins, M. M. (2004). Penalties for success: Reactions to women who succeed at male gender-typed tasks. *Journal of Applied Psychology, 89*(3), 416. Retrieved from http://dx.doi.org/10.1037/0021-9010.89.3.416.

Highfield, R. (2008, March 17). We prefer people we think are similar to ourselves. *The Telegraph*. Retrieved from www.telegraph.co.uk/news/science/science-news/3336375/We-prefer-people-we-think-are-similar-to-ourselves.html.

Hochschild, A. R. (1989). *The second shift: Working women and the revolution at home*. New York, NY: Viking.

Hoobler, J. M., Lemmon, G., & Wayne, S. J. (2011). Women's underrepresentation in upper management: New insights on a persistent problem. *Organization Dynamics, 40*, 151–156.

Hopkins, M. M., O'Neil, D. A., Passarelli, A., & Bilimoria, D. (2008). Women's leadership development: Strategic practices for women and organizations. *Consulting Psychology Journal: Practice and Research, 68*(4), 348–365.

Huffman, M. L., & Cohen, P. N. (2004). Occupational segregation and the gender gap in workplace authority: National versus local labor markets. *Sociological Forum, 19*(1), 121–147.

Huse, M., & Solberg, A. G. (2006). Gender-related boardroom dynamics: How Scandinavian women make and can make contributions on corporate boards. *Women in Management Review, 21*(2), 113–130.

Izraeli, D. N., & Adler, N. (1994). Competitive frontiers: Women managers in a global economy. In N. Adler & D. N. Izraeli (Eds.), *Competitive frontiers: Women managers in a global economy* (pp. 3–21). Cambridge, MA: Blackwell.

Jones, D. (2009, January 1). Women slowly gain on Corporate America. *USA Today*. Retrieved from http://usatoday30.usatoday.com/money/companies/management/2009-01-01-women-ceos-increase_N.htm.

Kakabadse, N. K., Figueira, C., Nicolopoulou, K., Hong Yang, J., Kakabadse, A. P., & Ozbilgin, M. F. (2015). Gender diversity and board performance: Women's experiences and perspectives. *Human Resource Management, 54*(2), 265–281.

Kanter, R. M. (1977). Some effects of proportions on group life: Skewed sex ratios and responses to token women. *American Journal of Sociology, 82*, 965–990.

Kessler, G. (2015, April 2). The "Equal Pay Day" factoid that women make 78 cents for every dollar earned by men. *The Washington Post*. Retrieved from www.washingtonpost.com/news/fact-checker/wp/2015/04/02/the-equal-pay-day-factoid-that-women-make-78-cents-for-every-dollar-earned-by-men/.

Konrad, A. M., Ritchie Jr., J. E., Lieb, P., & Corrigall, E. (2000). Sex differences and similarities in job attribute preferences: A meta-analysis. *Psychological Bulletin, 126*, 593–641.

Kulich, C., Ryan, M. K., & Haslam, A. S. (2007). Where is the romance for women leaders? The effects of gender on leadership attributions and performance-based pay. *Applied Psychology: An International Review, 56*(4), 582–601.

Lee, A. (2014, September 5). Gender quotas worked in Norway. Why not here? *New Republic*. Retrieved from https://newrepublic.com/article/119343/impact-quotas-corporate-gender-equality.

Lewis, M. (2013). Men vs. women: Differences in shopping habits and buying decisions. *Money Crashers*. Retrieved from www.moneycrashers.com/men-vs-women-shopping-habits-buying-decisions/.

Lilienfeld, S. O., Lynn, S. J., Ruscio, J., & Beyerstein, B. L. (2011). *50 great myths of popular psychology*. Malden, MA: Wiley-Blackwell.

Luckwaldt, J. H. (2015, November 5). PayScale's latest report shows that the gender pay gap is real. Career news. *PayScale*. Retrieved from www.payscale.com/career-news/2015/11/the-gender-pay-gap-is-real.

Lyness, K. S., & Thompson, D. E. (2000). Climbing the corporate ladder: Do female and male executives follow the same route? *Journal of Applied Psychology, 85*, 86–101.

McDonagh, K., Bobrowski, P., Hoss, M., Paris, N., & Schulte, M. (2014). The leadership gap: Ensuring effective healthcare leadership requires inclusion of women at the top. *Open Journal of Leadership, 3*, 20–29. DOI:10.4236/ojl.2014.32003

McEldowney, R. P., Bobrowski, P., & Gramberg, A. (2009). Factors affecting the next generation of women leaders: Mapping the challenges, antecedents, and consequences of effective leadership. *Journal of Leadership Studies, 5*(2), 24–30.

Mainiero, L. A., & Sullivan, S. E. (2006). *The opt-out revolt: Why people are leaving companies to create kaleidoscope careers*. Mountain View, CA: Davies-Black Publishing.

Melero, E. (2011). Are workplaces with many women in management run differently? *Journal of Business Research, 64*, 385–393.

Miller, K. (2006). *Organizational communications: Approaches and practices*. Boston: Wadsworth.

Minow, N. (2009). *Women on corporate boards of directors: international research and practice*. In S. Vinnicombe, V. Singh, R. Burke, D. Bilimoria, & M. Huse (Eds.), *Corporate governance: An international review*, 17(5), 661. DOI:10.1111/j.1467-8683.2009.00765.x

Morello, C., & Keating, D. (2010, October 7). More U.S. women pull down big bucks. *The Washington Post*. Retrieved from www.washingtonpost.com/wp-dyn/content/article/2010/10/06/AR2010100607229.html.

O'Neil, D. A., & Bilimoria, D. (2005). Women's career development phases: Idealism, endurance, and reinvention. *Career Development International, 10*, 168–189.

Oakley, J. G. (2000). Gender-based barriers to senior management positions: Understanding the scarcity of female CEOs. *Journal of Business Ethics*, 27(4), 321–334.

Parker, K. (2015, June 18). 5 facts about today's fathers. *Pew Research Center*. Retrieved from www.pewresearch.org/fact-tank/2014/06/12/5-facts-about-todays-fathers/.

Perry, A. (2009, March 6). Women climbing corporate ranks: Study. *Toronto Star*. Business section, B3.

Pew Research Center. (2008, August 25). A paradox in public attitudes—men or women: Who's the better leader? Retrieved from http://pewsocialtrends.org/2008/08/25/men-or-women-whos-the-better-leader/.

Pew Research Center. (2015). Women and leadership: Public says women are equally qualified, but barriers persist. Chapter 3: Obstacles to Female Leadership. Washington, DC: Pew Research Center. Retrieved from www.pewsocialtrends.org/2015/01/14/chapter-3-obstacles-to-female-leadership/.

Pinker, S. (2008, March 24). Why women earn less, men are fragile and more. *USA Today*. Retrieved from www.today.com/id/23558979/ns/today-today_books/t/why-women-earn-less-men-are-fragile-more/#.V2JKOfkrLIU.

Reaney, P. (2015, November 5). Women in the US are paid less than men at every level in all industries, according to a new study. *Business Insider*. Retrieved from www.businessinsider.com/us-women-paid-less-than-men-at-every-level-in-all-industries-2015-11.

Ruderman, M. N., & Ohlott, P. J. (2004). What women leaders want. *Leader to Leader, 31*, 41–47.

Sahadi, J. (2016, April 12). Young women are asking for (and getting) more pay than men. *CNNMoney*. Retrieved from http://money.cnn.com/2016/04/12/pf/gender-pay-gap/index.html?section=money_pf.

Salary.com. (2012). What is a stay-at-home mom worth? Infographic. *Salary.com*. Retrieved from www.salary.com/stay-at-home-mom-infographic/.

Salary.com. (2013). What's a mom worth? Salary.com releases 13th annual mom salary. *Salary.com*. Retrieved from www.salary.com/whats-mom-worth-pr/.

Schein, V. E. (2001). A global look at psychological barriers to women's progress in management. *Journal of Social Issues, 57*(4), 675–688.

Shin, T. (2012). The gender gap in executive compensation: The role of female directors and chief executive officers. *The ANNALS of the American Academy of Political and Social Science, 639*(1), 258–278.

Sturges, J. (1999). What it means to succeed: Personal conceptions of career success held by male and female managers at different ages. *British Journal of Management, 10*, 239–252.

Terjesen, S., Sealy, R., & Singh, V. (2009). Women directors on corporate boards: A review and research agenda. *Corporate Governance: An International Review, 17*(3), 320–337.

Timberlake, S. (2005). Social capital and gender in the workplace. *Journal of Management Development*, 24, 34–44.

Torchia, M., Calabrò, A., & Huse, M. (2011). Women directors on corporate boards: From tokenism to critical mass. *Journal of Business Ethics, 102*(2), 299–317.

Twenge, J. M. (1997). Changes in masculine and feminine traits over time: A meta-analysis. *Sex Roles*, 36, 305–325.

Twenge, J. M. (2001). Changes in women's assertiveness in response to status and roles: A cross-temporal metaanalysis, 1931–1993. *Journal of Personality and Social Psychology*, 81, 133–145.

2020 Women on Boards. (2015). Gender diversity index, 2011–2015: Progress of women corporate directors by company size, state and sector. Retrieved from www.2020wob.com/sites/default/files/2020GDI-2015Report.pdf.

US Bureau of Labor Statistics. (2015, November). Highlights of women's earnings in 2014. BLS Reports. REPORT 1058. Retrieved from www.bls.gov/opub/reports/womens-earnings/archive/highlights-of-womens-earnings-in-2014.pdf.

US Government Accountability Office. (2010). Women in management: Female managers' representation, characteristics, and pay. *GAO Reports*, 1–7. GAO-10-1064T. Washington, DC: United States Government Accountability Office. Retrieved from www.gao.gov/new.items/d101064t.pdf.

Valerio, A. M. (2009). *Developing women leaders: A guide for men and women in organizations*. Oxford, UK: Wiley-Blackwell.

Vincent-Lancrin, S. (2008). The reversal of gender inequalities in higher education: An on-going trend. *Higher education to 2030*, 265–298. Retrieved from www.oecd.org/edu/ceri/41939699.pdf.

Warner, J. (2014, March 7). The women's leadership gap: Women's leadership by the numbers. *Washington, DC: Center of American Progress*. Retrieved from www.americanprogress.org/issues/women/report/2014/03/07/85457/fact-sheet-thewomens-leadership-gap/.

Women in Technology. (2015). *Advancing women to the corporate boardroom*. Retrieved from www.womenintechnology.org/assets/docs/wit_research_report2015_v7_print_web.pdf.

Woodruff, M. (2013, May 8). Here's how much it would cost to replace your mom. *Business Insider*. Retrieved from www.businessinsider.com/value-of-stay-at-home-moms-2013-5.

Yoder, J. D. (1991). Rethinking tokenism: Looking beyond numbers. *Gender & Society*, *5*, 178–192.

Zahidi, S., & Ibarra, H. (2010). The corporate gender gap report 2010. In *World Economic Forum. Geneva, Switzerland*. Retrieved from www3.weforum.org/docs/WEF_GenderGap_CorporateReport_2010.pdf.

8

SUSTAINING DIVERSITY AND INCLUSION

Women and men in organizations must act in ways that are genuine and honest to their own values and also find the right balance of agentic and communal behaviors through feedback, mentoring, and developmental plans. Caprino (2013) observed the following:

- the differences between men and women are not fully understood or valued;
- whole-self authenticity is a must-have for many women, yet impossible still in many corporate environments;
- life, family, and work priorities clash fiercely;
- extreme work demands can drum women out;
- marginalizing of women is more common than we want to admit;
- personal accountability needs to be expanded.

Integration of work–life dynamics will allow women to communicate competence and self-confidence. Belasen (2012) also notes that companies need to systemically break down the cultural barriers and stereotypical biases that prevent women from reaching the top.

In most cases women are the primary caregivers and caretakers in the household in addition to being the physical carriers of children, all of which can slow down upward movement at work. Many times in business, opportunities arise unexpectedly and the woman employee at home taking care of a sick child misses out on an opportunity to advance. It may not be intentional, just a simple "out of sight, out of mind" situation, but often it is deliberate as men perceive women to be incapable of balancing work and home without neglecting either one. This is where the proverbial "glass ceiling" situation appears—as long as standards in business are made and enforced by men, women will continue to be absent from top positions.

As organizations reinforce masculine qualities through rewards and incentives (Chin, 2004), images such as "the glass ceiling" and "the glass cliff," or the high levels of stress and burnout at the top, continue to reflect reality (Weyer, 2007; Haslam & Ryan, 2008). The "glass cliff" describes situations where women executives can be set up to work under conditions that lead to job dissatisfaction, feelings of disempowerment, and higher employee turnover. Eagly and Carli (2007) go so far as to argue that since there are actually several barriers that women must overcome to reach senior positions, we should move beyond the glass-ceiling metaphor, and that a more accurate metaphor would be the "labyrinth" associated with inertia that moves in a circular path—a catch 22. Gender discrimination, stereotypical biases, unequal expectations, and the "pipeline" circular argument postulating that insufficient numbers of qualified women exist in the pool of managers to equalize positions in senior management are causing career women to re-consider mobility options. Bridging the gap may be acceptable for most women who are willing to adapt and retrofit themselves into a culture dominated by males, but oftentimes, women considered for leadership roles are opting out for this very reason. The conversation is archaic and the fabric of leadership needs to evolve in order to retain highly talented female leaders.

Work–Family Conflict

A critical issue involves the work–family conflict bias. Employers concede that family considerations interfere with work obligations, irrespective of whether or not women actually have work–family conflict, are married, or have children of a certain age. This is a prevalent bias that managers (both male and female) hold against women that is associated with lower performance reviews, and ultimately fewer promotions for women (Hoobler, Lemmon, & Wayne, 2011). This bias propels a self-fulfilling prophecy with women at lower levels laying low or staying away from seeking out promotion to higher managerial levels, which are perceived as unattainable. According to Schwanke (2013), research indicates that the average American woman works 13.2 hours per week on housework, compared to her spouse who works approximately 6.6 hours. This constant barrage of work "after work" can at times force females to maintain the middle-management position versus attempting to climb the ladder, which would require more commitment of hours at their professional work.

Another issue is the sunk cost factor or the cost associated with investments in current areas of specialization, training, and development. Transitions into senior management roles or even laterally to a comparable but different functional area involve shedding previously effective professional identities and acquiring new skills suitable for performing the new roles (Ibarra, Ely & Kolb, 2013). Yet people often feel ambivalent about leaving the comfort of previous roles in which they excelled, because doing so means moving toward an unknown terrain.

> Organizations inadvertently undermine this process when they advise women to proactively seek leadership roles without also addressing policies and practices that communicate a mismatch between how women are seen and the qualities and experiences people tend to associate with leaders.
>
> *(Ibarra et al., 2013)*

"Opting Out" and Brain-drain

A study by Deloitte & Touche, which was conducted two decades ago, is still relevant now. It found 70% of women who left their companies were still working full-time a year later, just for a different employer, and less than 10% had left the workforce to take care of their families (Kanter & Roessner, 1999). When examining the total population of mothers who stay at home with their children, *opt-out moms*[1] make up a very small fraction (4%) of the total number of stay-at-home moms (Figure 8.1). The majority of these women left reluctantly, finding they had been passed over for high-visibility assignments, offered dead-end positions, or given projects with less satisfying tasks. Most women (77%) still believe that the reason why they are not advancing in their careers is because they chose family over work (Livingston, 2014). However, according to a recent

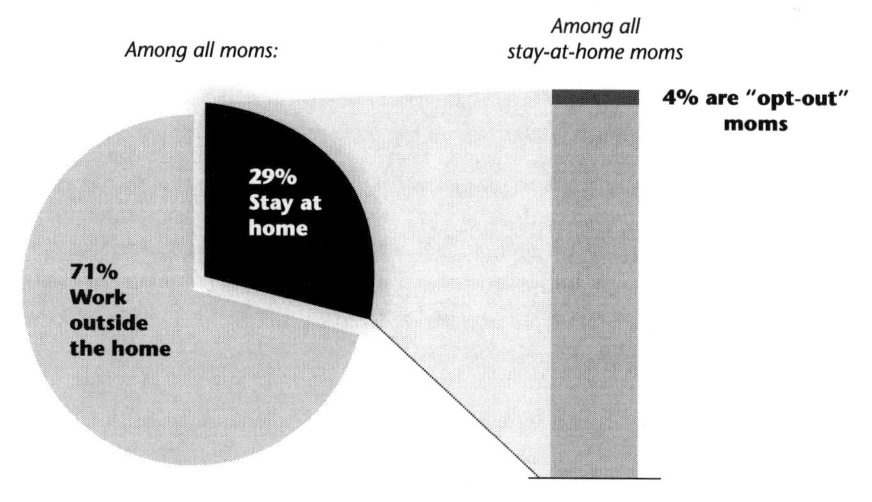

FIGURE 8.1 Highly Educated "Opt-out" Moms Are a Small Group

Source: Pew Research Center (2013).

Pew Research Center report, much of the recent growth in stay-at-home moms has been driven by those with less education (Cohn, Livingston, & Wang, 2014).

The vast majority of women in the study by Ely, Stone, and Ammerman (2014) believed their careers would rank equally in importance with those of their partners, while more than 50% of male respondents expected their careers to take priority over their partners' careers. Nearly 75% of Generation X and baby-boomer men reported their careers had taken precedence over their partners', and 40% of women reported their careers had taken a back seat to their partners'. When it comes to childcare, the study found that about 50% of the women expected to take on the majority of child-caring responsibilities while 75% of the men believed their partners would take on that role. Women who believed their careers would be equal in importance to their partners', as well as believed a more equal division of labor for child-care responsibilities, had their expectations dashed on both fronts (Lavine, 2014).

THE RHETORIC AND REALITY OF OPTING OUT

The imagery surrounding "opting out" and policies such as off-ramping reinforce the idea that women are marginal, uncommitted workers and provide an enduring rationale for statistical discrimination (women will "only leave anyway," the refrain that formerly shut them out of the professions) and more overt forms of discrimination such as the now well-documented motherhood penalty. By positioning women as taking "time out" during the prime years of career advancement, women's workforce exists and career interruptions clear the field for men to advance, the "leaky pipeline" of women's own choices further perpetuating the male breadwinner-dominated professional workplace unresponsive to caregiving and family.

(Stone & Hernandez, 2012, p. 52)

Women may be opting to stay home to raise their children because the options available to them once they return from maternity leave are limited, leading them to opt for a support role in which their jobs are secondary. For a growing number of women, staying home is not a choice. More mothers say they're staying home because they can't find work that pays for the rising cost of childcare. Many simply can't find a job at all. For those women that are able to return to work, not only do they sacrifice status or stature for leaving in the first place, but also most of their paycheck ends up going to daycare (Berman, 2014). If a mother were to put her child in daycare versus overseeing care herself there could be a significant cost difference. Child Care Aware of America (2015) found average daycare center costs for New York State to be $14,144. This cost alone could contribute significantly to the estimated salary of an opt-out mother.

There is yet another factor that should be considered: Many new parents rely on the grandparents to care for the children, but with the retirement age going up and lack of retirement savings to fall back on, more and more elders are choosing not to retire and no longer present a viable alternative to daycare. Without grandparents to provide free care, or a high-paying job that can pay all the bills, the trend to stop working after a newborn until the child reaches the age where they can attend school seems to be on the rise.

Opting out can be understood as a response to the challenge of integrating work and family but primarily as a workplace's failure to transform its culture, not a choice among worthwhile options.

> Opting out rhetoric ignores the real problems even educated, privileged working mothers continue to encounter in the workplace and that undermine their career attachment. The true culprits are: the ideal worker concept of job commitment; a dearth of positive role models; inadequate policies to accommodate employees with dependent children; mommy-tracking; a persistent gender wage gap; and the ongoing gendered division of labor in the home that defines caregiving as women's work. All these problems are made to disappear in stories about opting out.
>
> *(Stone & Hernandez, 2012, p. 51)*

Opting out should not be viewed as a choice, let alone solution, but rather a symptomatic problem to the work–family dilemma.

Work and family are not dichotomized and should not be viewed as mutually exclusive categories (either/or) but are contextualized as "both/and," with workplace flexibility and sharing responsibilities at home. Rather than employing on and off ramping (when women can take time off for caregiving and re-enter the workforce later), organizations need to adopt policies that integrate work and family, with enhanced flexibility and greater part-time opportunities. Women want more meaningful work and more opportunities for career growth and companies need to provide adequate entry points to full-time work for women who have, for instance, recently been on a part-time schedule or taken a career break.

Women opt out for a variety of reasons, including unequal pay, lack of role models, the extra burden of being the primary caregiver as well as the wage earner, and limited opportunities (Cabrera, 2007). Successful women abandoning their careers are less concerned about salary and status and more about lack of intellectual fulfilment and development opportunities. Women such as Oprah Winfrey and Eileen Fisher have found success by rejecting the system and by striking out on their own as entrepreneurs. To retain or attract high-achieving women and reduce the risk of brain-drain, leaders should articulate a vision of inclusion and equity and champion a cultural transformation that value women's talents. Talent thrives when it has new and meaningful challenges and opportunities to pursue. Smart leaders recognize the importance of integrating work and family, offer flex time, value part time, offer back up childcare, and create a culture that support diversity and inclusion.

> **QUOTE FROM A DISCUSSION BOARD OF ONE OF PROFESSOR BELASEN'S MBA STUDENTS, SPRING 2016**
>
> When I gave my notice at my all-consuming, never-thankful, poor-paying job today, I had gone in with very strong convictions . . . but when push came to shove, I found myself saying that "perhaps I was not cut out for the role" . . . nothing could have been further from the truth but I do believe that a male-driven workplace with an air of a male superiority complex meant that no matter how much I gave, it could never be enough.
>
> Workplace and pay inequality . . . these are very real struggles that are happening in the workplace every day. I have devoted the better part of two decades working to better myself and advance my knowledge and career, never opting to be the stay-at-home mom (primarily due to financial restrictions), and yet time and again have found myself up against a wall working far too hard for far less pay/benefits than my male counterparts.

Second-generation Bias

Dubbed by Ely, Ibarra, and Kolb (2011) as "second-generation bias" the discourse has moved from investigations of intended or unintended exclusion of women from positions of power to root causes of women's persistent underrepresentation in leadership roles putting them at a disadvantage. Second-generation bias is embedded in stereotypes and organizational practices that exist below the surface and that can be hard to detect, but when people are made aware of it, they see possibilities for change. Primary factors include:

1. Fewer female leaders at the top and the limited opportunity for viewing senior women as credible sources of advice and support.
2. Gendered career paths and fewer chances for fitting in line positions or joining formal rotations in sales or operations that have traditionally been a key step on the path to senior leadership. The researchers pointed out that organizations tend to give less priority to supporting roles or activities (e.g., building a team, avoiding a crisis, intelligence, and analysis), which women are more likely to do, while rewarding heroic efforts or outcomes, which are most often done by men. The cumulative effect of these practices disadvantages women, as men continue to seek and attain high-visibility positions, thus reinforcing the vicious circle that men are simply better leaders.

3. Women's networks are limited or less influential in terms of proximity to decision authority centers. Men's networks provide more opportunities for connectivity and informal support with sponsors and active mentors than women's do. Meanwhile, men in positions of power tend to direct developmental opportunities to junior men, whom they view as more likely than women to succeed.
4. Most definitions link leadership with masculinity and action oriented mindsets and behaviors where being decisive, assertive, and independent are desirable. In contrast, women are expected to be nice, caretaking, and unselfish. This mismatch puts female leaders in a double bind: If they excel in traditionally male domains they are viewed as competent but less likable than their male counterparts but if they are assertive they often appear arrogant or abrasive. Meanwhile, women in positions of authority who enact a conventionally feminine style may be liked but less respected. They are deemed too emotional to make tough decisions and too soft to be strong leaders.

ARE WOMEN MORE EMOTIONALLY INTELLIGENT THAN MEN?

Women tend to be better at emotional empathy than men, in general. This kind of empathy fosters rapport and chemistry. People who excel in emotional empathy make good counselors, teachers, and group leaders because of this ability to sense in the moment how others are reacting.

Neuroscientists tell us that one key to empathy is a brain region called the insula, which senses signals from our whole body. When we're empathizing with someone, our brain mimics what that person feels, and the insula reads that pattern and tells us what that feeling is.

Here's where women differ from men. If the other person is upset, or the emotions are disturbing, women's brains tend to stay with those feelings. But men's brains do something else: they sense the feelings for a moment, then tune out of the emotions and switch to other brain areas that try to solve the problem that's creating the disturbance.

Thus women's complaint that men are tuned out emotionally, and men's that women are too emotional—it's a brain difference.

(Goleman, 2011)

Stopping the Leaking Pipeline

The pipeline of female middle managers during the 1990s has not resulted in the expected flood of female executives (Ragins, Towsend, & Mattis, 1998).

Disappointingly, the pipeline even in the last few years has only yielded a trickle of female senior executives, those such as Indra Nooyi and Marjorie Kaplan who have struggled through the "labyrinth" and the excessive scrutiny, double standards, and the challenges of balancing work and family.

Two factors that may explain the little progress in achieving parity in TMTs involve lack of awareness of the need to change and misperceptions of women's ability to lead. For example, although 76% of the men in the study of Australian companies by Bain & Company (Sanders, Hrdlicka, Hellicar, Cottrell, & Knox, 2011) believed that gender parity *could* result in financial benefits for their organizations, only 55% of them agreed in reality that it would, implying that gender diversity is still not well understood or accepted. Until that happens, achieving gender parity remains quite an elusive goal as it requires a shift in underlying values and beliefs. These beliefs appear to be linked to differences in style. Challenging these beliefs will require a cultural transformation over the long term.

Lagging behind men in achieving positions of power has been exacerbated by the absence of gender diversity climates in organizations due to the innate male-dominated culture, leaky pipeline, and limited opportunities for building social capital or obtaining high-visibility assignments. Absence of active mentoring, descriptions of higher level positions in masculine terms not congruent with women's authentic or prototypical behaviors, use of different performance standards for evaluation, and limited access to networks lessen women's involvement as leaders.

For the most part women find themselves stuck in lower levels and compared to male counterparts fewer continue to middle management and farther. Women enter the white-collar workforce in greater numbers than men: 53 for every 47 males. Yet as they move from entry-level to middle management, and from mid- to senior-level positions, men advance disproportionately, outnumbering women nearly two to one. At the very top of the career ladder, men outnumber women nearly four to one (Hewlett, Peraino, Sherbin, & Sumberg, 2010).

A shortage of women in senior positions may send misguided signals to aspiring career women that upper-level jobs are out of reach. Moreover, highly qualified and experienced women may not find higher level positions too appealing. As a result, organizations may lose the opportunity to capitalize on the skills and talents of a well-qualified part of their workforce. Further, when employees take notice about the absence of women in senior management positions, they may form ideas about the implicit values and perceived culture of the organization, such as it being an "old-boys club," or discriminatory in its hiring and retention practices. Many women internalize these stereotypes, which creates a self-fulfilling prophecy. Moreover, underrepresentation of women in upper management reduces the opportunity to have female mentors with experience in upper management (Figure 8.2).

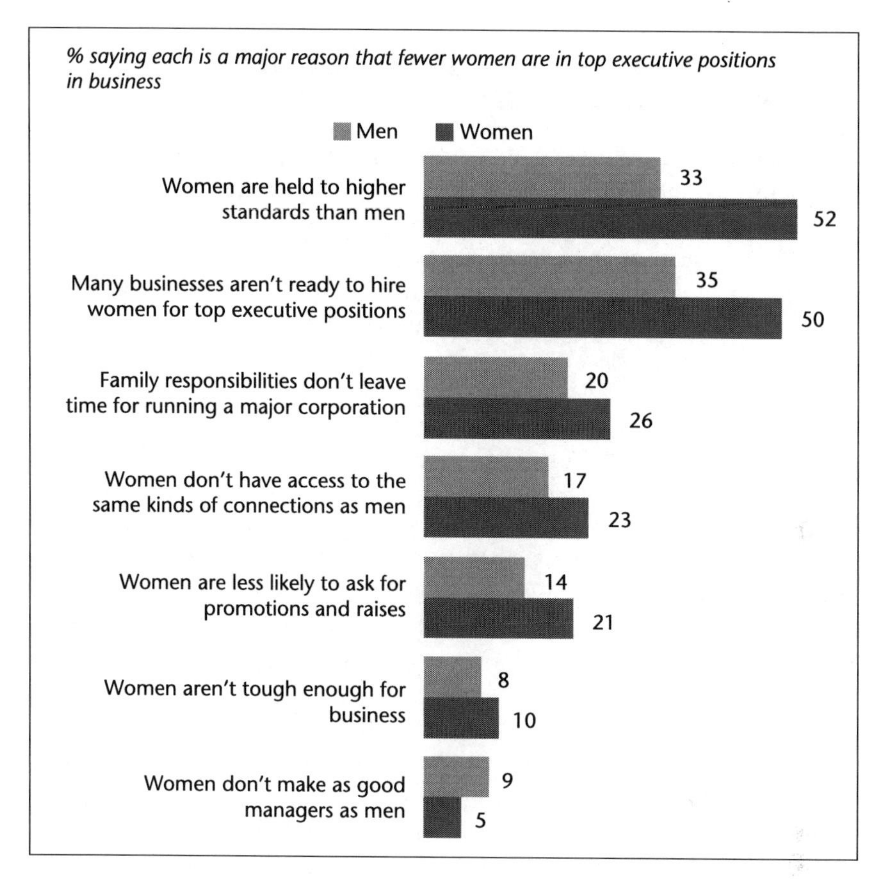

FIGURE 8.2 Why Aren't More Women in Top Business Positions?

Source: Pew Research Center (2015).

Women can continue their path toward leadership positions more optimally when they benefit from active mentoring, networking, or by having a high-level advocate or sponsor (Roebuck & Smith, 2011). Without seasoned female mentors to guide women through what can be a politically driven succession-planning process, women may feel unprepared for upper-management positions and thus avoid self-promoting themselves. The invisible glass ceiling is problematic because it stymies the opportunity for a substantial section of the US workforce, that is, women, to contribute their full potential to the society at large and to organizations in particular. Sponsoring women earlier in their career and building and sustaining inclusive work environments can create more success.

A RECOUNT BY A STUDENT IN PROFESSOR BELASEN'S LEADERSHIP DEVELOPMENT PROGRAM, APRIL 2016

I have also experienced this type of behavior in predominately male-based departments in business organizations. Not only are there golf-outings, there are also the after work happy hour, cigars and "weekend at Bernie's" events. I believe that so many corporations are stuck on operating in this manner that leaders tend to overlook the fact that there may be discriminating behaviors against members who that may not fall into the "good old boys" club.

In many "predominantly male" organizations, women tend to be just a number for meeting the "diversity quota." In many instances, the women involved in such an environment tend to lose their sense of self, as they are trying to fit in or not become too overly sensitive to comments and behaviors by male colleagues. But what if the comments are excessive or borderline harassment? Many are left with the choices and questions including 1) Complaining to management/HR, but some may contemplate just where would this get them? This may lead to dropping the complaint altogether; 2) Wondering whether their workload will increase as a retaliatory act; 3) Will she be ostracized from the group entirely? 4) Wondering if she should leave the company, and find a more diverse organization where they stress that harassment, & discrimination of any kind are not tolerated (which could lead to termination) and are strongly enforced by the company.

It's understandable that there are times when outings and discussions are not deemed fit for everyone, whether male or female, but when is the line drawn? Does leadership ask the question, if I do or say this, would someone be offended? If the answer is probably yes, then most likely it may be offensive to others. It's a long road ahead, and we have seen progress where companies are emphasizing the fact that they are an equal opportunity work environment, but in my opinion, many corporations are not fully there as yet.

Sponsors create opportunities for the talented women they help, open the door to growth opportunities, counsel them and advocate for their advancement. Of course, these relationships are hard to institutionalize and often occur informally. CEO champions who hold their managers accountable can invite high-potential women to shadow members of TMTs as well as expose them to the company's strategy and business operations. TMTs and sponsors can accelerate women's growth so that once women begin to form families, they will already have learned the ropes for advancement. It is particularly important to find a sufficient number of high-achieving female middle managers who can help companies reach the tipping point. As Figure 8.3 demonstrates, over time, hardwiring diversity as an

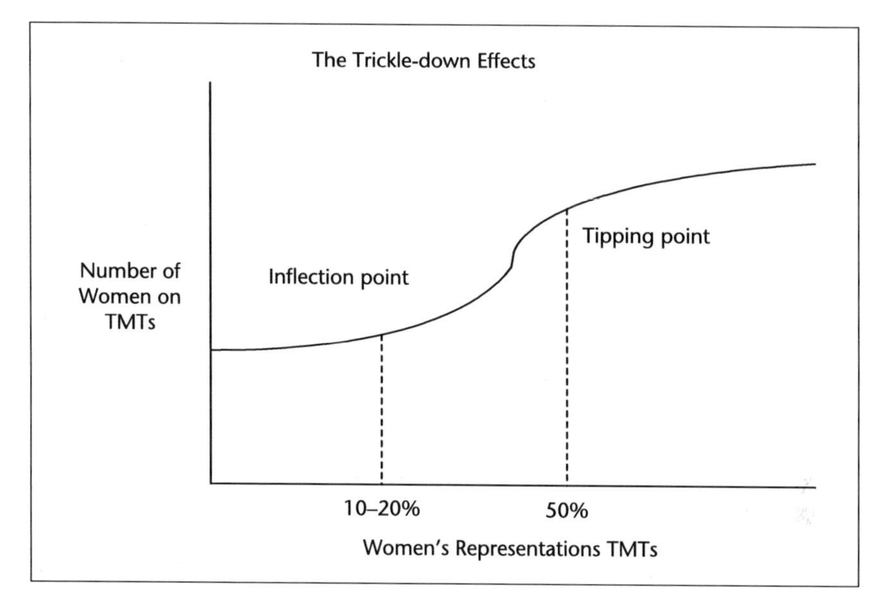

FIGURE 8.3 The Trickle-down Effects

integral part of the fabric of the organization can help change the underlying values and behaviors of organizational members and create a culture of openness and acceptance.

Importance of Diversity and Women's Competencies

In her article, "It's time for a new discussion on women in leadership," Avivah Wittenberg-Cox (2014) calls "to shift the discussion away from a lingering women's problem or an issue of equality and instead focus on this as a massive business opportunity." Evidence from the field and the literature on leadership effectiveness (Cameron, Quinn, DeGraff, & Thakor, 2006) suggests that creating value in organizations, which is an enormous strategic goal, requires balanced leadership skills and smart leaders who know that gender balance delivers better and more sustainable performance.

Effective leaders understand more deeply and act more effectively to integrate women in executive decision processes to obtain better results. On the one hand, all-male boards or predominantly male boards are much more likely than diverse boards to appoint male CEOs. On the other hand, gender integration on boards reduces the perception of women leaders as outsiders, thus allowing women greater access to top leadership positions. There is also a significant positive relationship between the proportion of women on the board of directors and women CEOs' length of tenure. Diverse boards increase the duration of women leaders' tenure, allowing them a greater opportunity to demonstrate their leadership capacity. Thus, diversity among decision makers plays a strong role in women's ability to overcome institutional barriers (Cook & Glass, 2015).

Kellie McElhaney and Sanaz Mobasseri of the Haas School of Business at the University of California, Berkley found that companies that explicitly place value on gender diversity perform better in general, and perform better than their competitors on multiple dimensions of corporate sustainability (McElhaney & Mobasseri, 2012). This finding also mirrors the results of a longer-term study led by Roy Adler, of Pepperdine University in Malibu, California and executive director of the Glass Ceiling Research Center. His study tracked the number of women in high-ranking positions at 215 Fortune 500 companies between 1980 and 1998. The 25 companies with the best record for promoting women to senior positions, including the board, posted returns 18% higher and returns on investment 69% higher than the Fortune 500 median in their respective industries (Adler, 2001). With critical mass of female board members, the board is expected to provide a more balanced and equitable review of women's concerns and career paths. The best leaders prefer leading the charge to following it. So it would now make sense to focus on the leadership competencies that enable certain leaders to build gender-balanced organizations (Wittenberg-Cox, 2014). Women will be more likely to speak out in board meetings, pose challenging questions, and encourage board members and TMTs to become more sensitive and collaborative and less hierarchical.

Take Warren Buffet as an example. In the book *Warren Buffett invests like a girl: And why you should too*, Lofton (2011) drew on behavioral economic studies that have analyzed the investment styles of men and women—and articulated eight essential principles about women's investment tendencies, ranging from trading less than men, and being less overconfident and overoptimistic than their male counterparts. At the same time female investors are more susceptible to peer pressure, learn from failure, are more risk-averse, and more willing to spend time and effort researching their investments before they make a move. These traits, according to Lofton, characterized Warren Buffet's successful career. He is patient and does thorough research. Warren appreciates relationships, is fair, and acts ethically at all times. He doesn't buy into the latest popular technology company that he doesn't understand. He doesn't take excessive risks or jump in and out of stocks. This comment is part tangent but also draws attention to the fact that while women and men may think differently or have different temperaments, they may need to apply similar competencies for attaining organizational outcomes. Here, too, the female advantage is greater.

Consider the study by Zenger and Folkman[2] (2012a) who found that women scored higher in 12 of the 16 competencies that measure outstanding leadership. Two of the competencies in which women outscored men—taking initiative and driving for results—traditionally have been thought of as particularly male strengths. Their findings suggest that organizations should promote from within rather than go outside to help increase the effectiveness of the top leadership team.

ARE WOMEN BETTER LEADERS THAN MEN?

Our latest survey of 7,280 leaders, which our organization evaluated in 2011, confirms some seemingly eternal truths about men and women leaders in the workplace but also holds some surprises. Our dataset was generated from leaders in some of the most successful and progressive organizations in the world both public and private, government and commercial, domestic and international.

In the confirmation category is our first finding: The majority of leaders (64%) are still men. And the higher the level, the more men there are: In this group, 78% of top managers were men, 67% at the next level down (that is, senior executives reporting directly to the top managers), 60% at the manager level below that.

Similarly, most stereotypes would have us believe that female leaders excel at "nurturing" competencies such as developing others and building relationships, and many might put exhibiting integrity and engaging in self-development in that category as well. And in all four cases our data concurred—women did score higher than men.

But the women's advantages were not at all confined to traditionally women's strengths. In fact, at every level, more women were rated by their peers, their bosses, their direct reports, and their other associates as better overall leaders than their male counterparts—and the higher the level, the wider that gap grows [see Table 8.1].

TABLE 8.1 Overall Leadership Effectiveness by Gender by Position (Percentile Scores)

	Male	*Female*
Top Management, Executive, Senior Team Members	57.7	67.7
Reports to Top Management, Supervises Middle Managers	48.9	56.2
Middle Manager	49.9	52.7
Supervisor, Front Line Manager, Foreman	52.5	52.6
Individual Contributor	52.7	53.9
Other	50.7	52.0
Total	51.3	55.1

Specifically, at all levels, women are rated higher in fully 12 of the 16 competencies that go into outstanding leadership. And two of the traits where women outscored men to the highest degree—taking initiative and driving for results—have long been thought of as particularly male strengths. As it happened, men outscored women significantly on only one management competence in this survey—the ability to develop a strategic perspective [Table 8.2]. Top leaders always score significantly higher in this competency; since more top leaders are men, men still score higher here in the aggregate. But when we measure only men and women in top management on strategic perspective, their relative scores are the same.

Why are we not engaging and fully employing these exemplary women leaders? Yes, blatant discrimination is a potential explanation. If not actual then certainly perceptual. We shared our findings with a group of women outside this particular survey and asked them to suggest why they thought

TABLE 8.2 Top 16 Competencies Top Leaders Exemplify the Most

	Male Mean Percentile	*Female Mean Percentile*	*T value*
Takes Initiative	48	56	–11.58
Practices Self-development	48	55	–9.45
Displays High Integrity and Honesty	48	55	–9.28
Drives for Results	48	54	–8.84
Develops Others	48	54	–7.94
Inspires and Motivates Others	49	54	–7.53
Builds Relationships	49	54	–7.15
Collaboration and Teamwork	49	53	–6.14
Establishes Stretch Goals	49	53	–5.41
Champions Change	49	53	–4.48
Solves Problems and Analyzes Issues	50	52	–2.53
Communicates Powerfully and Prolifically	50	52	–2.47
Connects the Group to the Outside World	50	51	–0.78
Innovates	50	51	–0.76
Technical or Professional Expertise	50	51	–0.11
Develops Strategic Perspective	51	49	2.79

their colleagues had been rated so highly on taking initiative and self-development. Their answers pointed to the still-tenuous position they feel themselves to be in the workplace: "We need to work harder than men to prove ourselves"; "We feel the constant pressure to never make a mistake, and to continually prove our value to the organization."

That is, anecdotally, at least, the women we queried don't feel their appointments are safe. They're afraid to rest on their laurels. Feeling the need (often keenly) to take initiative, they are more highly motivated to take feedback to heart. The irony is that these are fundamental behaviors that drive the success of *every* leader, whether woman or man. What should leaders and managers do with these findings?

(Zenger & Folkman, 2012a, 2012b)

Building Social Capital

The caveat is that women tend not to promote themselves as well as men do, have less networking opportunities, and typically are dependent on formal advancement procedures more so than are men (Lyness & Thompson, 2000). However, inflexibility of the workplace and seemingly unfair expectations of a woman versus a man may lend themselves to an abbreviated career for an educated woman. Furthermore, existing training and development programs tend to focus on current competencies and short-term performance expectations rather than long-term strategic-planning goals putting women at obvious disadvantage. Women also often take jobs where there is no opportunity for promotion to the top, such as human resources and public relations, and where many of the contributions of women to the companies go unnoticed, unlike men's contributions.

THE SPONSOR EFFECT

Women's aversion to this kind of naked quid pro quo translates into a wealth of supportive peers but a dearth of relationship capital. Furthermore, it tends to manifest as a lack of leadership skill—a more serious oversight, according to Adam Quinton, a former managing director at Bank of America Merrill Lynch, who led the firm's 175-person Global Macro Research team. "As you advance in an organization, you start off doing what is typically a specific task, something with a relatively narrow impact, and you interact with a narrow group of people," he says. "As time goes by, however, your success is defined less by specific tasks and more by getting others to come together

> to execute those tasks. There's a crucial point in the business where you must go from that narrow, task-based role to becoming more of a broader contributor." And this transition, he adds, "is where I see women stumble." To their detriment, women perceive cultivating relationships and mobilizing them on their own behalf as, at best, an occasional necessity rather than the very exercise of leadership. They fail to see that the practice of seeking out powerful people, cultivating their favor, and cashing in those chips is itself a demonstration of leadership potential.
>
> *(Hewlett et al., 2010, p. 6)*

Effective methods for developing equitable talent and building social capital could very well be supported by active mentoring and proactive sponsorship. In a 2010 World Economic Forum report on corporate practices for gender diversity in 20 countries, 59% of the companies surveyed say they offer internally led mentoring and networking programs, 43% provide employees with the opportunity to participate in externally run programs, and 28% of companies offer women-specific mentorship and networking programs (Zahidi & Ibarra, 2010). Possessing a large amount of social capital in the form of rich developmental networks is fundamental for women's advancement (Hunt et al., 2009; Ibarra, Kilduff, & Tsai, 2005). Are these efforts and mechanisms translating into actual promotions and appointments of women to high-visibility positions?

Value in the Middle

Implementing innovation requires effective balance of strategic awareness with operating experience and an optimal mix of leadership and management roles. This is important as crowdsourcing often creates different identities for the organization that also require effective communication strategies (Belasen & Rufer, 2013). A broader identity gives employees the permission to engage in various strategies—to exploit existing products and services while simultaneously explore new offerings and business models. Female managers, especially in middle-management positions, more so than senior managers or operating-level managers, have the communication competencies to handle the complexity of information and high number of interactions (Belasen & Luber, 2017). Since women were found to excel in both transformational and transactional elements of initiating and managing change (Belasen, 2012), their advantage in leading organizations and operations adds strategic value to organizations and industries.

Leadership effectiveness is positively associated with all of the dimensions of transformational leadership and the contingent reward dimensions of transactional leadership. Since women were rated much higher than men in behaviors that contribute to effective leadership, then female leadership advantage should be considered seriously and responsibly in promoting women from within the ranks of management. Providing women with high-visibility positions can only support the strategic objectives of the corporation, add credibility, and create value rooted in ethics and high performance. As Figure 8.4 indicates, investments in women middle-management development might help avoid the exit of high-potential women from their current jobs.

Furthermore, women are also seen as more effective and in tune with the needs and values of a multicultural environment. Women naturally bring human relations skills into the workplace, which help create a productive work environment and build strong relationships based on trust and transparency. A shift in culture will encourage more women to seek higher level positions because the environment will be more conducive to accepting them. The process of cultural acceptance and the increased desire to pursue senior management will create a trickle effect of greater parity in corporate leadership.

Gender Fatigue

According to a survey by Hewlett et al. (2010), 56% of men compared with only 39% of women think that women have made considerable progress at their companies since 2000. One the one hand, the majority of men (58%) say that the reason for the progress is that their company has been trying harder to promote women. On the other hand, the majority of women (57%) say it is because women have made great strides in terms of performance and educational credentials. Coined "gender fatigue" by Kelan (2009), men are far less likely to recognize that gender bias is still prevalent in the workplace. While 49% of women think gender bias is alive and well today, only 28% of men agree. Conditioned by decades of initiatives dedicated to correcting gender inequities, male CEOs simply do not see the absence of women around them as caused by gender discrimination.

Gender fatigue marginalizes productive discussion regarding inequalities between men and women, making gender bias difficult to address. Research in the UK found that while 60% of male CEOs "recognize the problem of an inhospitable culture, they do not actually understand how this manifests itself in their organizations" (Catalyst, 2000, pp. 33–34). The study, *Breaking the barriers: Women in senior management*, reveals that 77% of female UK CEOs cite stereotyping as a barrier to women's advancement to senior levels but only 57% of the male senior managers think alike (see Table 8.3).

Ethical Mindfulness

Executives must believe that openness, candor, and respect—all women qualities—are the fundamental tenets of trusted leadership that should be imbedded in the social fabric of the organization. In the end, we need top executives with true

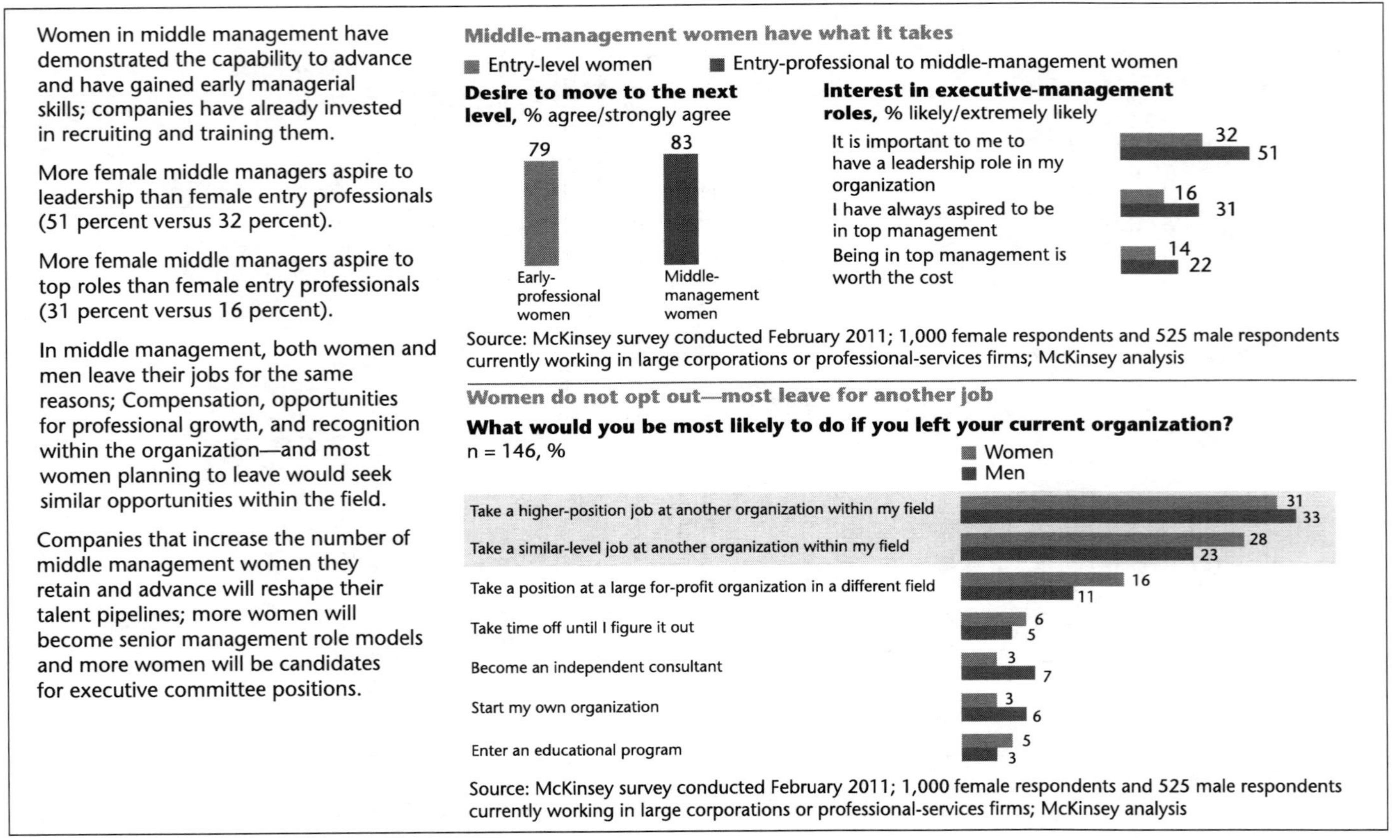

Women in middle management have demonstrated the capability to advance and have gained early managerial skills; companies have already invested in recruiting and training them.

More female middle managers aspire to leadership than female entry professionals (51 percent versus 32 percent).

More female middle managers aspire to top roles than female entry professionals (31 percent versus 16 percent).

In middle management, both women and men leave their jobs for the same reasons; Compensation, opportunities for professional growth, and recognition within the organization—and most women planning to leave would seek similar opportunities within the field.

Companies that increase the number of middle management women they retain and advance will reshape their talent pipelines; more women will become senior management role models and more women will be candidates for executive committee positions.

Middle-management women have what it takes

■ Entry-level women ■ Entry-professional to middle-management women

Desire to move to the next level, % agree/strongly agree

Early-professional women: 79
Middle-management women: 83

Interest in executive-management roles, % likely/extremely likely

	Entry-level women	Entry-professional to middle-management women
It is important to me to have a leadership role in my organization	32	51
I have always aspired to be in top management	16	31
Being in top management is worth the cost	14	22

Source: McKinsey survey conducted February 2011; 1,000 female respondents and 525 male respondents currently working in large corporations or professional-services firms; McKinsey analysis

Women do not opt out—most leave for another job

What would you be most likely to do if you left your current organization?
n = 146, %

	Women	Men
Take a higher-position job at another organization within my field	31	33
Take a similar-level job at another organization within my field	28	23
Take a position at a large for-profit organization in a different field	16	11
Take time off until I figure it out	6	5
Become an independent consultant	3	7
Start my own organization	3	6
Enter an educational program	5	3

Source: McKinsey survey conducted February 2011; 1,000 female respondents and 525 male respondents currently working in large corporations or professional-services firms; McKinsey analysis

FIGURE 8.4 A Focus on Developing and Advancing Middle-management Women Can Have the Biggest Impact

Source: Arora et al. (2011)

TABLE 8.3 Male and Female CEOs' Views

Male and female CEOs have distinctly different perceptions about the extent to which several factors listed in the question are barriers, differences that mirror those between senior women and CEOs as a group. The largest areas of lack of agreement are:

	Male %	*Female %*
Stereotyping	57	77
Organisational politics	19	58
Exclusion	34	63
Style	11	49
Harassment/discrimination	16	42
Mentoring	49	72
Lack of development opportunities	35	54

Source: Catalyst. (2000).

humility—enlightened leaders who draw heavily on self-regulation and ethics mindfulness. Mindfulness as a state of active awareness is characterized by the continual creation and refinement of categories, an openness to new information, and a willingness to view contexts and respond to situations using multiple lenses of inquiry (Langer, 1989; Levinthal & Rerup, 2006).

When organizational members are exposed to trusted leaders who display self-regulatory behaviors, they also learn and subsequently follow such behaviors. Trusted leaders help trigger ethical mindfulness in others. Trusted leadership begins and ends as an important leadership responsibility. Ethical mindfulness becomes a form of self-regulation that causes one to behave with an ethical consciousness from one decision or behavioral event to another (Aquino & Reed, 2002; Thomas, Schermerhorn, & Dienhart, 2004). Self-regulation is associated with persistence toward accomplishing goals and resistance against attempts that inhibit or hinder the achievement of goals (Carver & Scheier, 1998; Mischel, Cantor, & Feldman, 1996; Wegner & Bargh, 1998).

Trusted leaders pursue transparency and accountability, credibility and honesty, attributes that are manifested in women's inner capabilities and antecedents. Organizational leaders that pursue ethical mindfulness move from a "leader-centric" to a "leadership-centric" approach focusing on excellence, ethics, and endurance (Belasen, 2012; Vanourek & Vanourek, 2012). Mindful leaders do not think in terms of "either/or" dichotomies or by attaching mutually exclusive categories to people and values or by developing stereotypical biases toward women in organizations. These biases are translated into mindsets, values, and patterned behaviors that often inhibit women's advancement to TMTs. Trapped by their dysfunctional styles and unable to explore or employ other modes of positive behaviors, senior executives may succumb to continuing their behaviors as usual, avoiding any signals of wrongdoing. They need to unlearn the old habits and completely shift their mindset in words and deeds, by aligning their espoused values with decisions and actions.

The position of this chapter is that top executives must be attentive to their blind spots, or the behavioral and perceptual areas known to others but unknown to them, to maintain a good balance and avoid poorly made judgments or dysfunctional forms of behavior. Acknowledging women's contributions to the workplace requires two-way leadership in which care and sensitivity, transparency and accountability, are the principles that drive mutual respect and confidence. Ultimately, leadership is about character and doing the right things, moral maturity, self-control, and appreciation of others. Trust-based reciprocal relationship enables leaders to serve the people who rely on them, listen to their needs, give praise and recognition, show kindness, display true honesty, and be authentic. Trusted leadership is characterized by the absence of arrogance, pride, and deception. It is acting unselfishly.

> Providing ethical leadership means making ethical values visible—communicating about not just the bottom line goals (the ends) but also the acceptable and unacceptable means of getting there (the means). Being an ethical leader also means asking very publicly how important decisions will affect multiple stakeholders—shareowners, employees, customers, society—and making transparent the struggles about how to balance competing interests.
>
> *(Trevino & Brown, 2004)*

Notes

1 "These so-called 'opt-out moms' (roughly 10% of all highly-educated mothers) make up just 1% of the nation's 35 million mothers ages 18 to 69 who are living with their children younger than 18. For our purposes, 'opt-out moms' are mothers who have at least a Master's degree, an annual family income of $75,000 or more; a working husband; and who state that they are out of the workforce in order to care for their family." See www.pewresearch.org/fact-tank/2014/05/07/opting-out-about-10-of-highly-educated-moms-are-staying-at-home/.

2 John H. "Jack" Zenger, DBA, is the co-founder and CEO of Zenger Folkman. Jack's vast experience ranges from serving on the faculty of Stanford to serving as CEO of three highly successful training firms. He is a world expert in the field of leadership development, a best-selling author, and a highly respected and sought-after speaker, consultant, and executive coach.

Joe Folkman, PhD, is co-founder and president of Zenger Folkman. He is globally recognized as a top leader in the field of psychometrics, leadership, and change. He is a respected authority and consultant to some of the world's most successful organizations, a best-selling author, and a frequent keynote speaker and conference presenter.

References

Adler, R. D. (2001). *Women in the executive suite correlate to high profits*. Retrieved from www.csripraktiken.se/files/adler_web.pdf.

Arora, S., Ayanova, A., Barsh, J., Lund, S., Malhora, V., Manyika, J., Sumner, H., & Yee L. (2011). *Women in the economy: Selected exhibits*. McKinsey & Company. Retrieved from www.mckinsey.com/client_service/organization/latest_thinking/~/media/mckinsey/dotcom/client_service/organization/pdfs/womeneconomy_exhibits_v3_10282011.ashx.

Aquino, K., & Reed, A., II. (2002). The self-importance of moral identity. *Journal of Personality and Social Psychology*, *83*(6),1423–1440.

Belasen, A. T. (2012). *Developing women leaders in corporate America: Balancing competing demands, transcending traditional boundaries*. Santa Barbara, CA: Praeger.

Belasen, A. T., & Luber, E. (2017). Innovation implementation: Leading from the middle out. In N. Pfeffermann & J. Gould (Eds.), *Strategy and communication for innovation: Integrative perspectives on innovation in the digital economy* (3rd ed.) (pp. 229–243). Berlin, Germany: Springer.

Belasen, A. T., & Rufer, R. (2013). Innovation communication for effective interprofessional collaboration: A stakeholder perspective. In N. Pfeffermann, T. Minshall, & L. Mortara (Eds.), *Strategy and communication for innovation* (2nd ed.) (pp. 227–240). Heidelberg, Germany: Springer.

Berman, J. (2014, June 30). When being a stay-at-home mom isn't a choice? *Huffington Post*. Retrieved from www.huffingtonpost.com/2014/06/30/stay-at-home-moms_n_5537503.html.

Cabrera, E. (2007). Opting out and opting in: Understanding the complexities of women's career transitions, *Career Development International*, *12*(3), 218–237.

Cameron, K. S., Quinn, R. E., DeGraff, J., & Thakor, A. V. (2006). *Competing values leadership: Creating value in organizations*. Cheltenham, UK: Edward Elgar.

Caprino, K. (2013, February 12). The top 6 reasons women are not leading in corporate America as we need them to. *Forbes*. Retrieved from www.forbes.com/sites/kathycaprino/2013/02/12/the-top-6-reasons-women-are-not-leading-in-corporate-america-as-we-need-them-to/#71c924c86d6d.

Carver, C. S., & Scheier, M. F. (1998). *On the self-regulation of behavior*. New York, NY: Cambridge University Press.

Catalyst. (2000). Breaking the barriers: Women in senior management in the UK. *Catalyst*. Retrieved from www.catalyst.org/system/files/Breaking_the_Barriers_Women_in_Senior_Management_in_the_U.K..pdf.

Child Care Aware of America. (2015). Parents and the high cost of child care: 2015. *Child Care Aware of America*. Retrieved from www.usa.childcareaware.org/advocacy-public-policy/resources/reports-and-research/costofcare/.

Chin, J. L. (2004). Feminist leadership: Feminist visions and diverse voices. *Psychology of Women Quarterly*, 28, 1–8.

Cohn, D., Livingston, G., & Wang, W. (2014). After decades of decline, a rise in stay-at-home mothers. *Pew Research Center*. Retrieved from www.pewsocialtrends.org/2014/04/08/after-decades-of-decline-a-rise-in-stay-at-home-mothers/.

Cook, A., & Glass, C. (2015). Diversity begets diversity? The effects of board composition on the appointment and success of women CEOs. *Social Science Research*, *53*, 137–147.

Eagly, A. H., & Carli L. (2007). *Through the labyrinth: The truth about how women become leaders*. Boston: Harvard Business School Press.

Ely, R.J., Ibarra, H., & Kolb, D.M. (2011). Taking gender into account: Theory and design for women's leadership development programs. *Academy of Management Learning & Education, 10*(3), 474–493.

Ely, R., Stone, P., & Ammerman, C. (2014). Rethink what you "know" about high-achieving women, R1412G. *Harvard Business Review, 92*(12), 101–109.

Goleman, D. (2011, May 6). Are women more emotionally intelligent than men? Retrieved from www.danielgoleman.info/are-women-more-emotionally-intelligent-than-men/.

Haslam, S. A., & Ryan, M. K. (2008). The road to the glass cliff: Differences in the perceived suitability of men and women for leadership positions in succeeding and failing organizations. *The Leadership Quarterly, 19*(5), 530–546.

Hewlett, S., Peraino, K., Sherbin, L., & Sumberg, K. (2010). The sponsor effect: Breaking through the last glass ceiling. *Center for Work-Life Policy Survey*. Research sponsored by American Express, Deloitte, Intel, and Morgan Stanley. Retrieved from http://wliut.com/wp-content/uploads/2015/09/The-Sponsor-Effect.pdf.

Hoobler, J. M., Lemmon, G., & Wayne, S. J. (2011). Women's underrepresentation in upper management: New insights on a persistent problem. *Organization Dynamics*, 40, 151–156.

Hunt, L., Laroche, G., Blake-Beard, S., Chin, E., Arroyave, M., & Scully, M. (2009). Cross-cultural connections: Leveraging social networks for women's advancement. In M. Barreto, M. K. Ryan, & M. T. Schmitt (Eds.), *The glass ceiling in the 21st century: Understanding barriers to gender equality* (pp. 49–71). Washington, DC: American Psychological Association.

Ibarra, H., Ely, R., & Kolb, D. (2013). Women rising: The unseen barriers. [Cover story]. *Harvard Business Review, 91*(9), 60–67.

Ibarra, H., Kilduff, M., & Tsai, W. (2005). Zooming in and out: Connecting individuals and collectivities at the frontiers of organizational network research. *Organization Science, 16*, 359–371.

Kanter, R. M., & Roessner, J. (1999). Deloitte & Touche (A): A hole in the pipeline. Harvard Business School Case 300-012, September 1999. [Revised May 2003.]

Kelan, E. (2009). Gender fatigue: The ideological dilemma of gender neutrality and discrimination in organizations. *Canadian Journal of Administrative Sciences, 26*(3), 197–210.

Langer, E. J. (1989). *Mindfulness*. New York, NY: Perseus.

Lavine, L. (2014, November 24). The real reasons why women's careers stall after parenthood: A new study from Harvard Business School sheds light on what happens after graduation, and the answer isn't what you'd expect. *Fast Company & Inc.* Retrieved from www.fastcompany.com/3038938/strong-female-lead/the-real-reasons-why-womens-careers-stall-after-parenthood.

Levinthal, D., & Rerup, C. (2006). Crossing an apparent chasm: Bridging mindful and less-mindful perspectives on organizational learning. *Organization Science, 17*, 502–513.

Livingston, G. (2014). Opting out? About 10% of highly educated moms are staying at home. *Pew Research Center*. Retrieved from www.pewresearch.org/fact-tank/2014/05/07/opting-out-about-10-of-highly-educated-moms-are-staying-at-home/.

Lofton, L. (2011). *Warren Buffett invests like a girl: And why you should too*. Harper Collins.

Lyness, K. S., & Thompson, D. E. (2000). Climbing the corporate ladder: Do female and male executives follow the same route? *Journal of Applied Psychology, 85*(1), 86–101.

McElhaney, K., & Mobasseri, S. (2012). *Women create a sustainable future.* UC Berkeley Haas School of Business. Research sponsored by KPMG with Women Corporate Directors. Retrieved from www.haas.berkeley.edu/groups/online_marketing/facultyCV/papers/Women_Create_Sustainable_Value_FINAL_10_2012.

Mischel, W., Cantor, N., & Feldman, S. (1996). Principles of self-regulation: The nature of willpower and self-control. In E. T. Higgins & A. W. Kruglanski (Eds.), *Social psychology: Handbook of basic principles* (pp. 329–360). New York, NY: Guilford Press.

Pew Research Center. (2013). Analysis of March current population surveys integrated public use microdata series (IPUMS-CPS), 2013. Retrieved from www.pewresearch.org/fact-tank/2014/05/07/opting-out-about-10-of-highly-educated-moms-are-staying-at-home/.

Pew Research Center. (2015). Women and leadership: Public says women are equally qualified, but barriers persist. Chapter 3: Obstacles to female leadership. Washington, DC: Pew Research Center. Retrieved from www.pewsocialtrends.org/2015/01/14/chapter-3-obstacles-to-female-leadership/.

Ragins, B. R., Towsend, B., & Mattis, M. (1998). Gender gap in the executive suite: CEOs and female executives report on breaking the glass ceiling. *The Academy of Management Executive, 12*(1), 28–42.

Roebuck, D. B., & Smith, D. N. (2011). Wisdom from executive female leaders: What can organizations, executive education programs, and graduate students learn? *Journal of Executive Education, 10*(1), 43–73.

Sanders, M., Hrdlicka, J., Hellicar, M., Cottrell, D., & Knox, J. (2011). What stops women from reaching the top? Confronting the tough issues. *Bain & Company, Inc.* Retrieved from www.bain.com/Images/BAIN_BRIEF_What_stops_women_from_reaching_the_top.pdf.

Schwanke, D. (2013). Barriers for women to positions of power: How societal and corporate structures, perceptions of leadership and discrimination restrict women's advancement to authority. *Earth Common Journal, 3*(2). Retrieved from www.studentpulse.com/a?id=864.

Stone, P., & Hernandez, L. A. (2012). The rhetoric and reality of "opting out": Toward a better understanding of professional women's decisions to head home. In B. D. Jones (Ed.), *Women who opt out: The debate over working mothers and work-family balance* (pp. 33–56). New York, NY: NYU Press. Retrieved from www.jstor.org/stable/j.ctt9qg9pg.5.

Thomas, T., Schermerhorn, J. R., & Dienhart, J. W. (2004). Strategic leadership of ethical behavior in business. *Academy of Management Executive, 18*(2), 56–66.

Trevino, L. K., & Brown, M. E. (2004). Managing to be ethical: Debunking five business ethics myths. *Academy of Management Executive, 18*(2), 69–81.

Vanourek, B., & Vanourek, G. (2012). *Triple crown leadership: Building excellent, ethical, and enduring organizations.* New York, NY: McGraw.

Wegner, D. M., & Bargh, J. A. (1998). Control and automaticity in social life. In D. Gilbert, S. T. Fiske, & G. Lindzey (Eds.), *Handbook of social psychology* (4th ed., Vol. 1) (pp. 446–496). New York, NY: McGraw-Hill.

Weyer, B. (2007). Twenty years later: explaining the persistence of the glass ceiling for women leaders. *Women in Management Review, 22*(6), 482–496.

Wittenberg-Cox, A. (2014). It's time for a new discussion on "Women in leadership." *Harvard Business Review.* Retrieved from https://hbr.org/2014/03/its-time-for-a-new-discussion-on-women-in-leadership/.

Zahidi, S., & Ibarra, H. (2010). The corporate gender gap report 2010. In *World Economic Forum. Geneva, Switzerland.* Retrieved from www3.weforum.org/docs/WEF_GenderGap_CorporateReport_2010.pdf.

Zenger, J., & Folkman, J. (2012a). Are women better leaders than men? *Harvard Business Review, 15*, 80–85. Retrieved from https://hbr.org/2012/03/a-study-in-leadership-women-do.

Zenger, J., & Folkman, J. (2012b). A study in leadership: Women do it better than men. Retrieved from http://zengerfolkman.com/media/articles/ZFCo.WP.WomenBetterThanMen.033012.pdf.

CONCLUSION

Quality of Work–Life

> Balance suggests perfect equilibrium. There's no such thing. That's a false expectation . . . . There are going to be priorities and multiple dimensions of your life, and how you integrate that is how you find happiness.
>
> *(Denise Morrison, President and CEO of Campbell Soup Company)*

Although women, more so than men, go to great lengths to educate themselves and gain important leadership skills, they continue to be represented only marginally in high-level positions in the corporate world. They are also grossly underrepresented in boardrooms and executive suites. As of September 2013, there were only 36 women CEOs listed in the Fortune 1000. By mid-2014, about 5% of the Fortune 1000 companies had women CEOs or presidents (Fairchild, 2014) and in February 2015 the number of women occupying board positions on S&P 1500 companies was 2,150 (out of 13,850 seats), a meager 15.5% (Ernst & Young, 2015). As of January 2016, women held 20 (4.0%) of CEO positions at S&P 500 companies (Catalyst, 2016). One of the most serious issues regarding the paucity of women in TMTs and corporate boards is the perseverance of gendered leadership that mitigates or deters women from pursuing senior management positions (Carnes & Radojevich-Kelley, 2011), leading many to believe that this problem is associated with a "pipeline condition," the untested explanation that women leaders with the appropriate skills and abilities are very scarce. High-potential women advance more slowly in both pay and career progression than men even though they are on par in skills and talents.

The facts remain the same—regardless of their educational accomplishments over the years (see Figure C.1) and adding value to companies' success, women are underrepresented in TMT positions and still have a long way to go before achieving parity with their male counterparts in the workplace. In what is

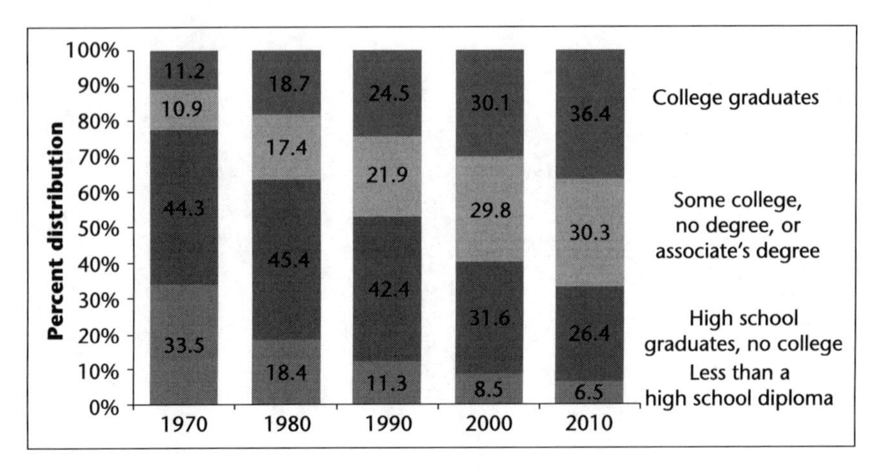

FIGURE C.1 Women in the Civilian Labor Force, Aged 25 to 64 Years, by Educational Attainment, 1970–2010

Source: US Department of Labor, Bureau of Labor Statistics (2011).

described as the notorious "glass cliff," often women executives are given problematic assignments or positioned in high-risk situations leading to job dissatisfaction, feelings of deprived power and authority, and higher employee turnover (Ryan, Haslam, & Postmes, 2007). Women are granted fewer opportunities to prove their leadership capabilities compared to men, and the positions that they do get are statistically higher in risk of failure. On average, women in these types of positions will have shorter tenures and will be more likely to be replaced by men, should their organization experience negative growth under their leadership. When a management job ad lists nine requirements for a position, women, on the one hand, wait until they've fulfilled 10 to apply. Men, on the other hand, throw their hats in the ring if they meet six of the nine requirements (Williams & Dempsey, 2014). At work, unlike their male counterparts, many women need to repeatedly perform tasks at a high level for comparable recognition.

Other evidence indicates how women are only considered for leadership positions in companies that are facing financial difficulty and more studies show how business leaders were more unlikely to pick females to head their companies (Long, 2014). A study by Keziah (2012), for example, showed that male recruiters favored male candidates for low-risk positions. Furthermore, the methodical exclusion from informal networks (aka men's clubs), lack of opportunities to assume line roles, and limited access to visible and/or challenging assignments block women from reaching the top.

The prevailing gap between women's education and workforce participation has persisted, too: "In an era when women have made sweeping strides in educational attainment and workforce participation, relatively few have made the journey all the way to the highest levels of political or corporate leadership"

(Pew Research Center, 2008, p. 3). Alice Eagly and Linda Carli (2007) describe the problem of gendered leadership and accessibility as *labyrinth leadership*. Ultimately, women who seek top management positions must clear through culturally saturated biases and stereotypes and at the same time avoid crossing culturally generated barriers such as misrepresentation of the commitment to personal and family responsibilities as an inability to meet tough schedules. High-potential women are less likely to promote themselves as well as men do, have less mobility within the organization, and are more dependent on formal advancement procedures than are men. This is especially true in highly male-dominated settings where women are challenged to act tough and exercise competitive styles not congruent with their authentic styles to gain acceptance into influential networks (Timberlake, 2005).

Leveraging Differences, the Power of Synergistic Effects

Mainiero and Sullivan (2005) argued that women tend to integrate rather than segregate work and non-work needs, the traditional linear career path favored by men. Women's non-work needs go beyond childcare concerns and encompass a quest for spiritual fulfillment, balance, elder care, volunteerism, and the need to be true to oneself. Their research suggests that women's careers are relational. Each action taken by a woman in her career is usually viewed as having profound and long-lasting effects on others around her. By contrast men tend to examine career decisions from the perspective of goals and independent actions—targeting the benefits derived from their careers. The box below describes further research on the neural connections within the human brain as markers for sex-based differences (see also Figure C.2).

THE HUMAN BRAIN: GENDER-BASED DIFFERENCES

New research on the neural connections within the human brain suggests sex-based differences that many have suspected for centuries: women seem to be wired more for socialization and memory while men appear geared toward perception and coordinated action. The female brain appears to have increased connection between neurons in the right and left hemispheres of the brain, and males seem to have increased neural communication within hemispheres from frontal to rear portions of the organ. University of Pennsylvania researchers announced the results, generated by scanning the brains of about 1,000 people using a technique called diffusion tensor imaging, on Monday (December 2) in the *PNAS*.

UPenn Perelman School of Medicine radiologist Ragini Verma and colleagues scanned the brains of more than 400 males and more than 500 females from 8 to 22 years old and found distinct differences in the brains of male versus female subjects older than age 13. The cortices in female brains were more connected between right and left hemispheres, an arrangement that facilitates emotional processing and the ability to infer others' intentions in social interactions. In male brains, however, the cortex was more connected to rear brain regions, such as the cerebellum, which suggests greater synergy between perception and action.

"There is biology to some of the behavior we see among men and women," Verma told the *Los Angeles Times*:

> In the population, men have stronger front-back connectivity, and women have inter-hemispheric or left-right connectivity more than the men. It's not that one or the other gender lacks the connectivity altogether, it's just that one is stronger than the other.

These physiological differences, which didn't appear in stark contrast in those under 14, could possibly give rise to behavioral differences between the sexes. "So, if there was a task that involved logical and intuitive thinking, the study says that women are predisposed, or have stronger connectivity as a population, so they should be better at it," Verma told the *LA Times*:

> For men, it says they are very heavily connected in the cerebellum, which is an area that controls the motor skills. And they are connected front to back. The back side of the brain is the area by which you perceive things, and the front part of the brain interprets it and makes you perform an action. So if you had a task like skiing or learning a new sport, if you had stronger front-back connectivity and a very strong cerebellum connectivity, you would be better at it.
>
> *(Grant, 2013)*

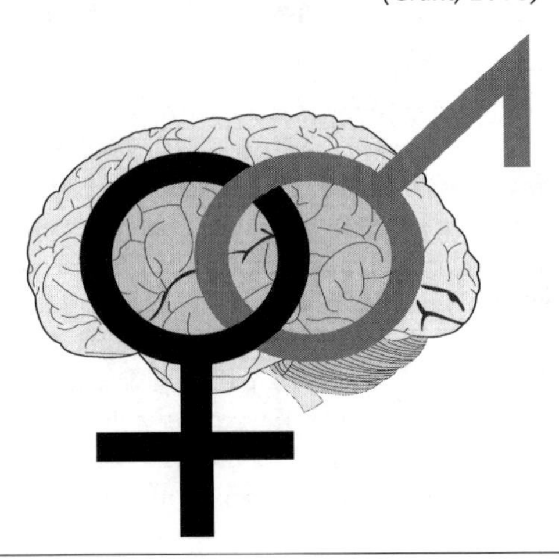

FIGURE C.2 Physiological Differences as Indicators for Behaviors

Source: Grant (2013).

In a study of senior managers' stereotypical perceptions of leadership behaviors, Prime, Carter, and Welbourne (2009) reported that female respondents perceived that women were more effective than men on "supporting," "rewarding," "mentoring," "consulting," "team-building," and "inspiring." Male respondents attributed female effectiveness to "supporting others" and "rewarding subordinates" behaviors. In terms of "problem solving," "upward influence," and "delegation," male respondents rated male managers as more effective than women on all three variables while women rated male managers higher on all three except for "problem solving." These findings suggest that gender is a reliable indicator of perceived differences in women's and men's leadership performance. At the same time, one could argue that these differences also imply different skills and preferences and therefore are complementary. In other words, men and women are expected to behave differently and complementarily creating opportunities for co-leadership and synergistic effects. Companies have come to recognize and embrace diversity by establishing co-ed teams reaping benefits for consumers and investors as well as team development. Borisova and Sterkhova (2012), for example, found out that corporations with the highest proportion of women in management had up to a 41% greater return on equity over corporations that had no women in management.

Shift in Paradigm

Organizations, particularly those that are male-dominated, are not gender-neutral, reflecting settings, performance criteria, and leadership styles in which women's behaviors and accomplishments are judged against male norms. Men in leadership roles, however, are seen as acting in congruence with expected masculine roles. The gender stereotypes that inhibit women from reaching the top still exist, especially when standards of success are measured in male terms, where hierarchy and power are preferred over social equality and persuasion.

The passage of the 1964 Civil Rights Act initiated a prospect for women to define the workplace by not just participating but revolutionizing the leadership found in organizations. However, even by the 1980s, the stereotypes that had existed for decades continued and women did not find themselves as contenders for top executive jobs. It wasn't until the 1990s that characteristics such as commitment and empowerment, and new values such as diversity, participation, integrity, honesty, and inclusion began to alter the idea of what management structure should look like.

The 1990s began the shift away from vertical structures rooted in male conceptions of power that emphasize command and control approaches designed exclusively around reporting and compliance. This structure has been perpetuated with the mindset that woman's role is providing care within the family and society. The demand for having to care for others often restricts what many women can achieve in their careers, in effect, penalizing them for motherhood.

For this reason, women in leadership are too often burdened with difficult choices: to have children and sacrifice or delay their careers, or to sacrifice or delay having children to pursue their careers. These choices are unreasonable for obvious reasons, choices that men do not have to make. Most importantly, childcare responsibilities can force career breaks on women in their prime working age years. It is a vicious cycle that is fading as more and more women are breaking through the barriers: barriers that were instituted by men. Bias is deep seated, and it nourishes on the tyranny of experience. Those with experience (particularly men) are those who are already doing well and who have not gone "off ramp" (e.g., to care for children).

FOR YAHOO CEO, TWO NEW ROLES

Marissa Mayer, Who Was Named to Top Post Monday, Is Expecting Her First Child in October

Just hours after Yahoo Inc. named Marissa Mayer as its new chief, the real conversation kicked in: how she will juggle pregnancy and being the CEO charged with saving a foundering Internet giant.

(Lublin & Kwoh, 2012)

Over the last four years, the decline of business at Yahoo! has frequently made headlines and with the negativity, so has Marissa Mayer's name (see box "For Yahoo CEO, Two New Roles"). While many thought the under-40-year-old CEO would be a game changer for women in business, the failing company and her deliberate efforts to shy away from stereotypical gender roles (e.g., maternity leave, work–life–family balance) have done little to help the barriers to corporate success women face. More recently, in 2016, Yahoo! was acquired by Verizon. With the purchase, it is unclear at the time of writing whether Marissa Mayer will have a job. She may be the best example of a high-profile corporate women to fall from the glass cliff.

Positive signs of change, however, begin to emerge everywhere as many companies are embracing the value of sustained diversity by providing mechanisms such as parental leaves, part-time policies, and travel-reducing technologies to help women stay the course. The new paradigm that is emerging begins to spell out new values such as diversity, participation, integrity, trust, honesty, and inclusion. The most important leadership attributes for success in the new organizational environments include intellectual stimulation, inspiration, participatory decision making, and setting expectations/rewards (Barsh & Yee, 2012), notably, characteristics more commonly found among women leaders and that are also embedded in the new paradigm. Not only does diversity increase women's odds of being promoted to top executive positions, but it also increases women leaders' tenure duration (Cook & Glass, 2015). The female CEOs in Fortune 500 companies all seem to harbor a similar pattern: they combine the powerful ability to impact the bottom line with a passion for motivating employees and caring for consumer needs, giving them a dynamic edge in business today (Belasen, 2012). Women also make better decisions when it comes to ethical dilemmas (Women in the Workplace, 2013). Organizations that neglect this critical talent-management issue risk lagging their competitors in attracting, developing, and retaining the best candidates to serve as the next generation of leaders.

Hopeless Romantic

In her now infamous article "Why Women Still Can't Have It All," Anne-Marie Slaughter, Princeton University Professor and former director of policy planning at the State Department, states the following:

> [T]he minute I found myself in a job that is typical for the vast majority of working women—working long hours on someone else's schedule, I could no longer be both the parent and professional I wanted to be.

Indeed, work–life integration, or lack thereof, is the real driving force behind the lack of female leadership. Research has shown that women are more likely than men to leave a job due to domestic or social responsibilities, which could explain the higher voluntary departure rate (Klampe, 2010). Highly talented women are more likely to start their own businesses than climb the corporate ladder. Between 1997 and 2014, when the number of businesses in the United States increased by 47%, the number of women-owned firms increased by 68%—a rate 145% greater than the national average. Indeed, the growth in the number (up 68%), employment (up 11%), and revenues (up 72%) of women-owned firms from 1997 to 2014 exceeded the growth rates of all but the largest publicly traded firms (Womenable, 2014). In 2014, the US ranked number one among 17 countries on having the conditions that foster high-potential female entrepreneurship (Stengel, 2014).

Successful integration of work–life is the preeminent issue facing working mothers today with many becoming social entrepreneurs capitalizing on their skills and creating the much needed flexibility to integrate career choices with family responsibilities. Indeed, Thébaud (2015) found out that organizations with paid leave, subsidized childcare, and part-time employment opportunities lower the motivation to become a business owner as fewer women are attracted to entrepreneurship out of a need to resolve work–family conflicts.

Many women choose to leave work due to the rigid, inflexible corporate culture that is not conducive to parenthood, expecting managers to work nights and weekends, leaving little time for family obligations. Likewise, the strongest motivation for women starting their own businesses involve setting their own work schedule and the opportunity to integrate family and work. Flexibility is needed to handle childcare obligations, participate in community affairs, respond to personal health concerns, provide caregiving for aging parents, and perform other family obligations. Flexibility does not necessarily mean working fewer hours, but having more control over when to work. This gives women at work the ability to manage their family responsibilities and at the same time have successful careers.

According to Ely, Stone, and Ammerman (2014), high-achieving women are not meeting the career goals because they are allowing their partners' careers to take precedence. Male partners who command better work conditions in well-paying professional jobs (especially when women are paid 78% of what men get for equivalent jobs) create a wage gap that cannot be easily bridged, particularly when those women are only working in part-time jobs to have more time for their children. For the most part, the culture of corporate America does not support the ideal work scenario of the modern working mothers. These women, typically, are still responsible for the lion's share of domestic responsibilities. Until there is a cultural shift in both the home life and corporate America in which men/fathers participate more fully in the responsibilities of childcare and domestic chores, women will continue to opt out of highly demanding positions of leadership in order to pursue a better quality of work–life. Changes, however, in stay-at-home dads are beginning to take roots (see Figure C.3).

Arlie Russell Hochschild's *The Second shift* (1989), characteristic of women who are still responsible for the most part of the household responsibilities, is what essentially pushes women out of the race for senior leadership positions.

RECOUNT FROM A STUDENT IN PROFESSOR BELASEN'S LEADERSHIP DEVELOPMENT CLASS, FALL 2014

The substance of these kinds of gender roles is antiquated for our day and age. Call me a "Hopeless Romantic," but marriage is an equal partnership, which requires equitable effort by both partners in domestic affairs; the man washes the dishes, the wife dries the dishes after dinner, fair enough.

The idea of trusting a man comes from our patriarchal culture with the belief that a "man" should head the household, family, business, and country. Unfortunately, the patriarchal piece of the puzzle does not seem to fit as well as the matriarchal one would, according to research and statistics. It will be interesting to see how this tension will evolve as the millennials start coming into the workforce and the baby-boomer generation begins to retire at a higher rate.

Soon millennials will make up the majority of the workforce, around 50% by 2020, and if these areas are not addressed companies will lose productivity. The

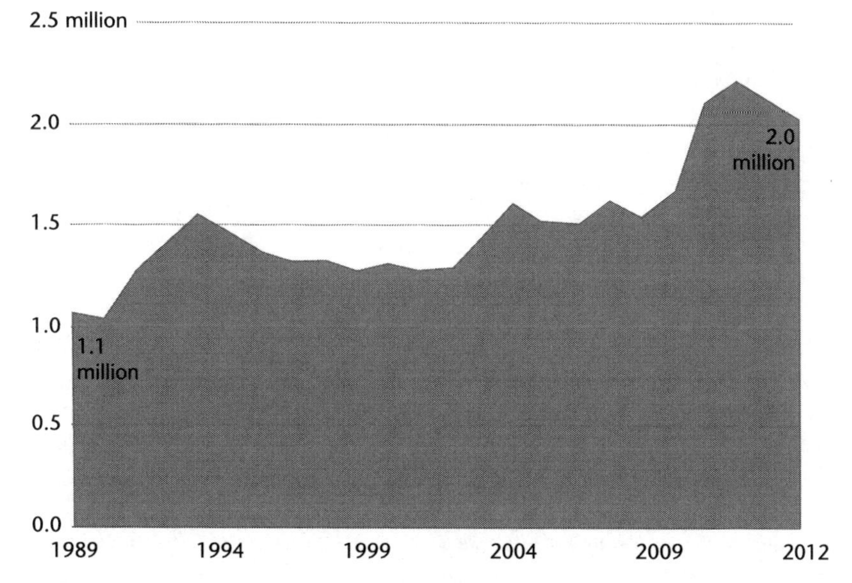

FIGURE C.3 Rising Number of Stay-at-home Dads

Source: Pew Research Center analysis of March Current Population Surveys Integrated Public Use Microdata Series (IPUMS-CPS),1990–2013.

Note: Based on fathers ages 18–69 with own child(ren) younger than 18 in the household. Fathers who live apart from their children are not included. Fathers are categorized based on employment in the year prior to the survey.

concerns and issues of millennials include improving the world, being their own boss or having a mentor relationship with their boss, collaboration instead of competition, flexible hours, engagement, reputation, and work–life balance (Gilbert, 2011).

Millennials seek careers in which they can make a difference and that provide opportunities for better work–life integration. Interrole conflict between future work and family roles are predicated on the assumed incompatibility of these roles (Weer, Greenhaus, Colakoglu, & Foley, 2006). Millennials are not eager to make early sacrifices and may actually limit their career options in anticipation of work–family conflict (Westring & Ryan, 2011). However, while women tend to limit their career aspirations in anticipation of work–family interferences (Friedman & Greenhaus, 2000), men often adopt a more traditional view of gender ideology and roles (Davis & Greenstein, 2009) and tend to develop greater number of career aspirations. The following questions were used by Wittmer and Koepke (2016) in their study of 335 working undergraduate and graduate business students:

1. How would you describe your balance between work and your personal life?
2. What types of pressures, conflicts, or strains do you typically experience balancing work and personal life?
3. What factors (school, work, family) create the most imbalance for you?
4. What type of career are you looking to have when you complete your education?
5. If you had no constraints, would this be the career you would pursue?
6. Do you anticipate your work–life balance will be better or worse once you are in your future career?
7. What types of pressures, conflict, or strains do you anticipate having in the future balancing work and personal life?

Wittmer and Koepke (2016) found that students who experienced reduced levels of work–life conflict in their organizations were also more optimistic about their future work–life balance than students who experienced more work–life conflict in their current roles. Students who were less dependent financially on their jobs were more optimistic about their future work–life balance. Younger students, as expected, were more optimistic about their future work–life balance than older students.

Anne-Marie Slaughter pointed out that women must ask for what they need and believe in themselves (Slaughter, 2013). Women need to take more responsibility for their career paths and be more assertive when pursuing higher positions. They cannot and should not pattern themselves or look to males as role models because there are certain unspoken rules and perks men have dating back over 50 years that are still present today. In corporate America, knowing all that we know about the unique leadership qualities women possess, that should not be too hard, should it?

Gender Pay Gap and Negotiation

In 2012, of the five best-paid executives at each of the S&P 500 Index companies, 198 were women, or about 8% of the total. Those high-achievers on average earned $5.3 million, 18% less than men (Hymowitz & Daurat, 2013). Carnegie Mellon economics professor Linda Babcock, who studies the gender pay gap, says men are four times more likely to negotiate their pay. That keeps women at a disadvantage, though they're not always aware of it (Noguchi, 2015). In negotiations, men are more task oriented and women are more interpersonally oriented (Walters, Stuhlmacher, & Meyer, 1998). Women don't ask for what they want for fear of being perceived negatively. This brings up another good point—how "aggressiveness" is accepted in both men and women. As others have discussed, a man can be called aggressive while a woman is called "bossy" for the same actions. Can the same be said about "aggressiveness" when applied to salary negotiations (Baer, 2014)?

Men, however, perceive the task of "asking" as a useful means to achieve greater gains. The net result is a sustained gender pay gap. In particular, men have

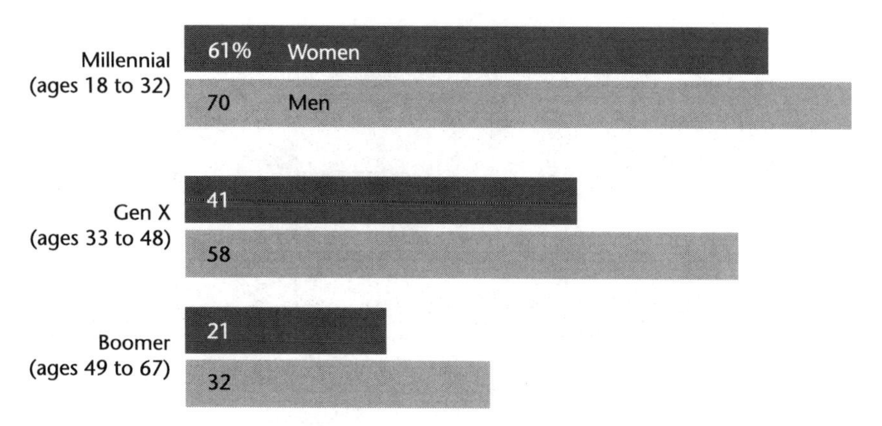

FIGURE C.4 Percentage Saying They Would Like to Be a Boss or Top Manager

Source: Pew Research Center (2013).

Note: Based on those who are not retired and not currently the boss/top manager (n = 1,539).

more of a tendency to define success by the level of their incomes and professional achievements, whereas women generally place more emphasis on the quality of their family and community relationships (Kiesel, 2015). Women of all ages, just like men, want a secure job they enjoy, but they are less likely than men to ask for raises or aspire to top management jobs (see Figure C.4). This is especially true once they reach their thirties and forties, when many men and women face the tradeoffs that go with being a working parent (Pew Research Center, 2013).

Behaviorally and cognitively, women must understand, at a very deep level, the forces that shape their beliefs, attitudes, and impulses. Simply telling women what they should do differently without helping them understand the root causes of their behavior will not help them achieve meaningful change. With a sponsor, for example, 38% of women summon the courage to negotiate (Hewlett, Peraino, Sherbin, & Sumberg, 2010, p. 11). Changes, however, are beginning to take shape as millennials are now asking for (and getting) more pay. Women in technology, sales, or marketing with two years' or less experience actually got salary offers that were 7% higher than those received by equally inexperienced men (Sahadi, 2016).

> At each level of education, women have fared better than men with respect to earnings growth [see Figure C.5]. Although both women and men without a high school diploma have experienced declines in inflation-adjusted earnings since 1979, the drop for women was much smaller than that for men: a 12% decrease for women as opposed to a 34% decline for men. On an inflation-adjusted basis, earnings for women with a bachelor's degree or higher have increased by 32% since 1979, while those of their male counterparts have risen by 18%.
>
> *(US Department of Labor, Bureau of Labor Statistics, 2014)*

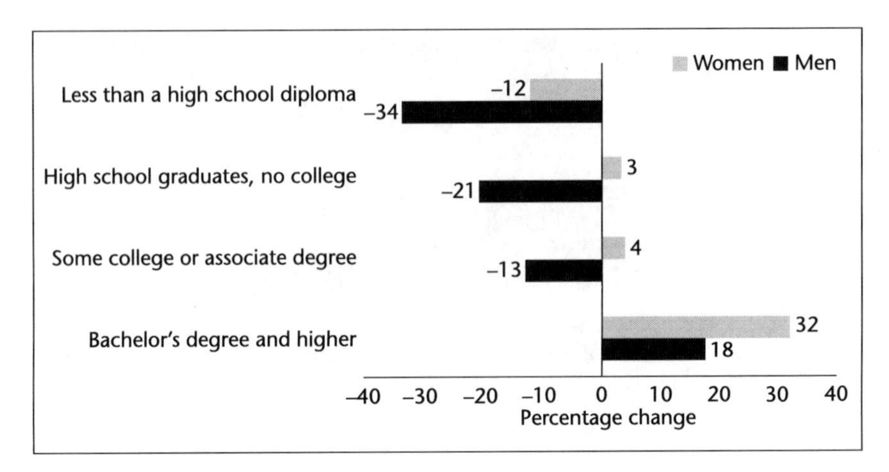

FIGURE C.5 Percentage Change in Inflation-adjusted Median Usual Weekly Earnings of Women and Men, by Educational Attainment, 1979–2013

Source: US Department of Labor, Bureau of Labor Statistics (2014).

Note: Data relate to earnings of full-time wage and salary workers, 25 years and older.

Equality and Inclusion

Two levels of intervention could help reduce gender inequality in organizations: Personal initiatives and change in policies, performance evaluation criteria, and codes of behavior (see Table C.1). These two levels converge at leadership development and succession planning and integrate management education and development goals with organizational interests and needs. In fact, as shown in Figure C.6, women are much more likely than men to say more change is needed to achieve gender equality in the workplace. The gap is especially wide among millennial women and men (Pew Research Center, 2013).

Discovery and Control

The Quality of Work Life (QWL) framework, which appears in Figure C.7, is based on the dimensions of the CVF for women's leadership discussed in Belasen (2012). Note how the framework provides a roadmap for identifying the main issues (personal, organizational, institutional, cultural) that high-achieving women face, while at the same time charts the critical domains of women's work–life aspirations. For example, the patterns identified by Williams and Dempsey (2014) can be categorized using the framework to reinforce the magnitude of the issues that they describe in their book. *Prove-It-Again!*: a descriptive bias that requires women to constantly demonstrate their competence (cultural); "The Tightrope," a prescriptive bias that forces women to find a balance between the competing

TABLE C.1 Personal and Institutional Initiatives for Reducing Gender Inequality in Organizations

Individual Initiative	*Organizational Change*
Go above or around the barrier; initiate a dialogue on gender among peers	Use contingent reward leadership
Be a strong, skillful, and persistent woman leader	The gendered context of organizations must be recognized in any assessment process
Compete head on for those lucrative corporate positions when they become available	Create mentoring opportunities that match women with senior managers' programs including women mentors for men
Seek out significant impact on how resources are allocated	Create a tracking system that monitors the equity by which performance ratings are developed and used
Stay connected	Clarify the demonstrative outcomes of problem solving skills in performance evaluation by emphasizing problem solving competence
Pursue executive coaching and role modeling; get an executive mentor	Develop transformational-based mentoring programs
Get transformational mentor to promote confidence and trust	Balance agentic with communal norms and standards
Seek out other women who have broken that glass barrier	Help women think and act strategically
Reframe your work context to make it more meaningful: integrate your roles to achieve wholeness	Focus career advancement and management development programs on future, strategic-planning goals rather than present, short-term goals
Break down institutional gender stereotypes; redefine the power structure, then use it to initiate change	Design different approaches to leadership development
Actively manage your mentoring relationships; identify a sponsor	Support mentoring systems that sympathize with the need to integrate work and family roles
Seek visibility through networking	Promote policies that encourage diversity and reward collaboration
Be in charge of your destiny; develop agency behaviors (e.g., assertiveness)	Increase group diversity by including more women on work groups
Follow your deeply held values and beliefs rather than organizational norms and expectations; be authentic—live up to your values	Provide employees and managers with leadership training that focuses on upward leadership practices including self-assertion and involvement strategies
Identify alternative routes, including external sources, for self-development and ongoing learning	Monitor and encounter disempowering experiences targeted at women managers

(continued)

TABLE C.1 Personal and Institutional Initiatives for Reducing Gender Inequality in Organizations *(continued)*

Individual Initiative	*Organizational Change*
Develop self-awareness and self-clarity	Abolish practices where women constantly need to validate their qualifications before assuming leadership roles
Continue to display transformational leadership qualities especially individualized consideration and intellectual stimulation	Develop and deliver ethical training programs that focus on commitment and respect for fairness and egalitarianism
Continue to develop leadership competencies; get feedback from others about your strengths and weaknesses; pursue holistic development that considers the balance of family and work–life goals in women's careers	Initiate radar (360-degree) assessments
Seek out relationship with peers to build rapport and credibility	Emphasize different expectations such as challenge, balance, and authenticity in career roles and responsibilities
Be proactive in searching creative ideas to resolve the tension between organizational values and your personal values	Use differential coaching methods following the life cycle approach to development
Seek out high-risk positions such as international assignments that might lead to greater visibility and leadership opportunities	Assign women to high-visibility jobs
Demonstrate your success stories; Communicate competence and self-confidence	Initiate change in organizational and institutional structures, existing performance evaluation criteria and standards
Work with your employers to identify alternative means to accomplish work expectations; Get your sponsor to model the way and support your career throughout.	Create flexible work schedules; promote multiple options for working from remote locations; formalize part-time arrangements; support paid leave

Source: Based on Belasen (2012).

poles of masculinity and femininity (organizational); "The Maternal Wall," which pushes working mothers to be at home rather than in the workplace (institutional); and "The Tug of War," which compels women to defend their own coping strategies and condemn those of others (personal).

This QWL framework encourages organizational members (men and women) to see these paradoxes not as "either/or" pressures but, instead, as "both/and" opportunities. In encouraging a "both/and" perspective, the framework calls for

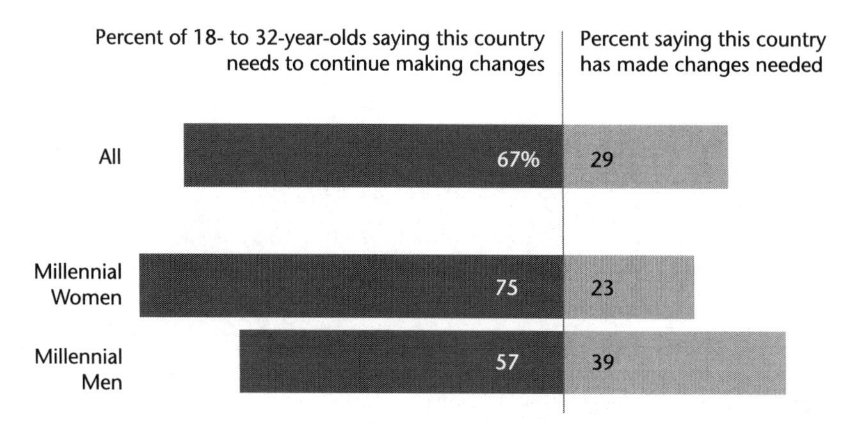

FIGURE C.6 Percentage of Millennial Women and Men Who Indicate That More Change Is Needed to Achieve Gender Equality in the Workplace

Source: Pew Research Center (2013).

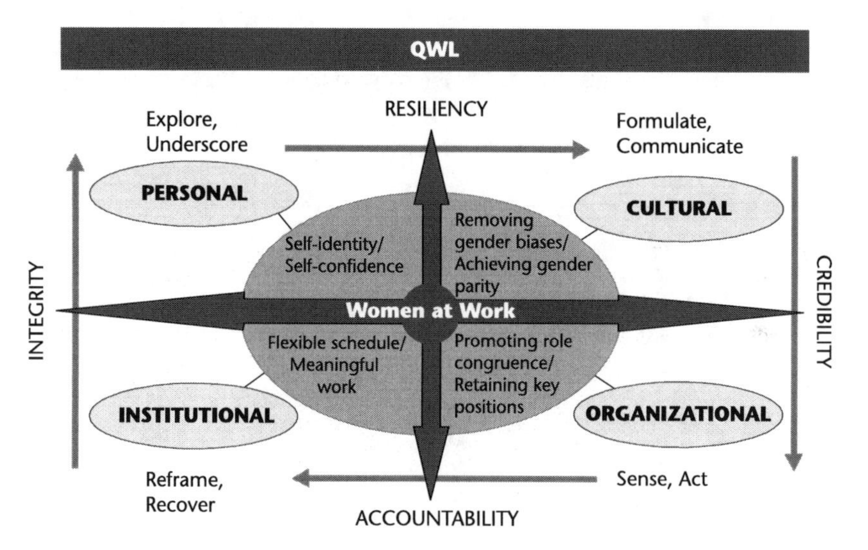

FIGURE C.7 Balancing the Dimensions of the QWL Framework

managers to display a range of behaviors to meet these multiple pressures (Belasen & Frank, 2012). For example, they can work with their employees to develop new and innovative processes and practices that maintain internal stability and also provide appropriate levels of flexibility to women to meet their work–life goals. Most importantly, by using the CVF as a lens (Belasen & Frank, 2010) that allows us to view organizational life through a "both/and" perspective, we can avoid the question that is regularly posed to women, and increasingly to men, regarding whether they can realistically expect to "have it all" in their work and personal life domains. That is, we can avoid the assumption that focusing on one domain necessitates ignoring, or at least minimizing, one's focus on other domains. Arguably, a CVF-based approach offers new perspectives for how women (and men) can reconcile and navigate multiple domains since it encourages us to focus on multiple competing values in order to maximize overall effectiveness (Belasen & Frank, 2012).

Moreover, rather than seeking maximum utility levels on each dimension (all of family, all of work), the CVF allows us to integrate solutions and to raise important questions about what it means to maximize value in different circumstances. Additionally, some applications of the CVF approach caution that the display of behaviors at the outermost extreme level can result in negative consequences (Belasen & Frank, 2008). This cautionary note is relevant as managers seek to implement work–life practices within organizations.

The QWL self-assessment questionnaire provided here is based on the survey scale developed and validated by Swamy, Nanjundeswaraswamy, and Rashmi (2015). These researchers identified nine significant dimensions explaining 82.24% of the total variance based on factor analysis: work environment; organization culture and climate; relation and co-operation; training and development; compensation and rewards; facilities; job satisfaction and job security; autonomy of work; and adequacy of resources. The survey questions were adapted and redistributed across the CVF quadrants by relevance.

QWL QUESTIONNAIRE

Rate each item from 1 to 5 where: 5—Strongly agree; 4—Agree; 3—Uncertain; 2—Disagree; 1—Strongly disagree.

Personal (Self-Identity, Self-Confidence)

1. I feel confident when performing my job
2. I feel quite secure about my relationships with others
3. I feel that my work allows me to succeed
4. People can speak up and voice their opinions frankly without fear of being punished
5. I feel empowered and supported by peers and supervisors
6. I identify my values with the values of the organization
7. I feel affiliated with my organization
8. Overall, I would say my morale on the job is high
9. I plan to stay with this organization for the foreseeable future

Institutional (Flexible Schedule, Meaningful Work)

10. My organization allows a flextime option
11. I can do my job from home
12. I am involved in making decisions that affect work
13. Conditions on my job allow me to be as productive as I could be
14. My work environment is good and highly motivating
15. Taking time off during work to take care of personal or family matters is tolerated
16. I feel empowered in fulfilling my managerial duties
17. I get personal satisfaction from my work
18. The organization offers me opportunities to grow and apply my skills

Cultural (Removing Barriers, Achieving Parity)

19. I have open channels to executives
20. The wage policies adopted by my organization are fair
21. The exchange of communication within the organization is transparent
22. I feel safe around people in my organization
23. I am treated fairly and respectfully
24. The culture and values in my organization are based on honesty and integrity
25. I feel that I am given an adequate and fair compensation for the work I do
26. People have an equal chance to get ahead in this organization regardless of gender
27. I am not discriminated in my job because of my gender

Organizational (Promoting Role Congruence, Retaining Key Positions)

28. My organization does a good job of linking rewards to job performance
29. My supervisor handles performance problems constructively and objectively
30. Promotions in my organization are handled fairly
31. My supervisor shows appreciation for the contribution I make
32. My performance is evaluated objectively and positively
33. I am not judged or discredited when performing my leadership role
34. I have equal opportunity to climb up the hierarchy in my organization
35. Coaching by female mentors is available in my organization
36. My contributions are highly appreciated by men and women in my organization

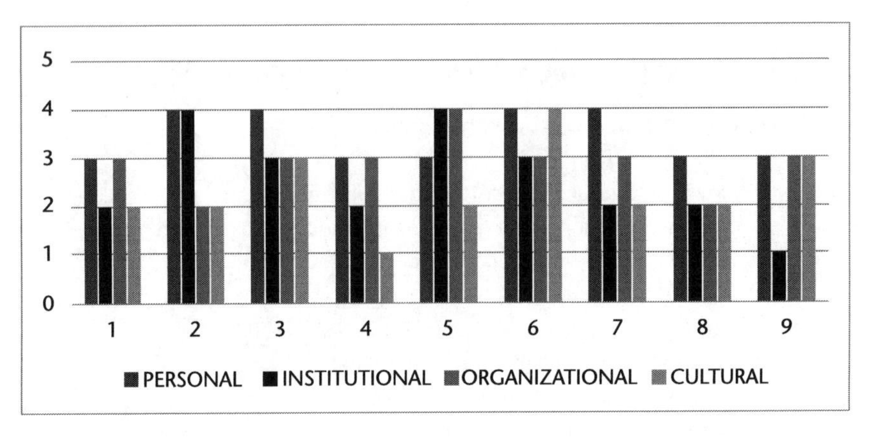

FIGURE C.8 Assessment 1

Reflecting on institutional and organizational constraints and opportunities (policies, structures) and cultural and personal biases and possibilities (communication, autonomy) gives respondents a chance to assess the current predicaments and dynamics through self-understanding, discovering their identities (see Figure C.8 for assessment 1), and taking back control (see Figure C.9 for assessment 2).

Chappelow's (2012) suggestions (see box "Understanding Your Behavior") are particularly relevant in providing guidelines and insights to help high-potential women to go past the existing barriers in their organizations.

UNDERSTANDING YOUR BEHAVIOR

Research shows that a critical aspect of integrating work/life facets is the degree to which you manage family-interrupting work or work-interrupting family. How does that play out in your case? Do you tend to blend personal and work tasks? If so, you might be an *Integrator*. Maybe you are more of a *Separator* and you tend to keep these tasks separated into defined blocks of time. If you are a *Cycler* you might switch back and forth between cycles of either highly integrating family and work followed by periods of intentionally separating them.

Recognizing which of these behavior patterns most naturally fit you and creating a strategy that takes them into account becomes a starting point for integration. Also understand this: None of these types is inherently better, so it's important to recognize which of these are ideal for you—not which you think you *should* be.

Discovering Your Identity

How we view ourselves plays a critical part in integrating work/life roles. Do you mostly identify yourself as *work-focused, family-focused*, some combination of those two—or something else altogether? (Hint: don't answer this one the way you think you should answer it; be honest with yourself).

Work-focused people tend to identify themselves through their work roles—manager, vice president, leader. Family-focused people see themselves primarily as a parent, spouse, or friend. *Dual-focused* individuals identify with and invest in themselves equally in both roles. (Hint 2. Most executives initially claim to be dual-focused. More often than not, their actions say otherwise.) *Other-focused* individuals primarily invest in interests that do not connect directly to work or family.

Taking Back Control

The reality is, there are some jobs that make successful work/life integration very difficult. More important is how they make you feel about the degree of control you have. To what degree do you feel in control of how you manage the boundaries between your work and personal life? Someone with *high boundary control* has a high degree of ability to decide when to focus on work or, by comparison, to focus on family.

So here are a few key takeaways. First, do not try to balance anything. Second, try to integrate instead, which requires some real awareness of your preferred behaviors, self-identity, and sense of control. You need to dedicate some time to figuring out those preferences. Finally, there's no "right" way to create an integrated life. The possibilities of what success looks like are as endless as the potential plot lines in a parking lot booth operator's novel.

(Chappelow, 2012)

The second assessment (Figure C.9) illustrates the progress that has been made both proactively and responsibly to close the "gender gap" and improve QWL in all of the dimensions of the framework. Recently, Forbes conducted an interview with 75 high-level women in marketing and strategy, and collected a list of leadership advices to guide women navigating at the top (Goudreau, 2013). Some of the suggestions were based on experience while others on wisdom and intuition. These include: "stay determined" and never quit, even when you are facing obstacles; be "courageous" and continuously challenge yourself; "think bigger" by having a wider vision; "take calculated risks" to achieve your goals and plans but also use a workable plan to make your goal achievable; "remain disciplined" and execute your plan strictly; "hire smart people" and then listen closely to their perspectives; be reflective by asking

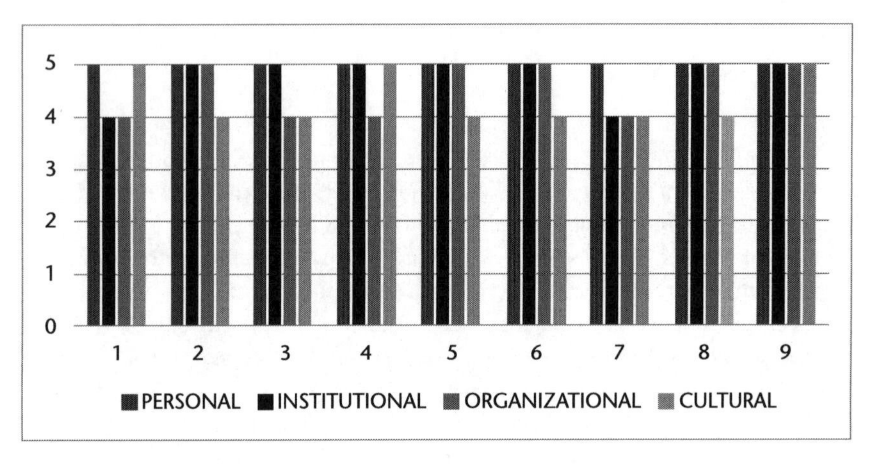

FIGURE C.9 Assessment 2

"where have I been? Where am I now?" "Is what I am doing right now beneficial for reaching my ultimate goal?" These questions keep women with advancement aspirations focused and mindful, and make the goal of retaining senior-level positions achievable.

Respondents can also look at assessment 2 (Figure C.9) as the relatively desired situation (compared to the current situation depicted in assessment 1, Figure C.8) and therefore look at the gap between the two sets of ratings as opportunities for improvement. This gap is illustrated in Figure C.10 (before and after).

To achieve your personal goal and to sustain the "desired" situation, you can continue to review the situation to identify mitigating factors in order to help manage the boundaries between your work and personal life and sustain the integration. Henna Inam's blog provides good suggestions:

- Start by believing in yourself. You are here to make an important difference. You have strengths and gifts that have been given to you to make that difference. You have a very important leadership purpose so pursue it.
- Help a woman leader believe in herself by letting her know what strengths you have observed in her. Encourage her to reach for her goals.
- Sponsor a woman by giving her access to powerful people and assignments in your organization.
- Partner up with a woman leader who you admire and mutually become accountability partners in helping you reach your goals.
- Start or sponsor a women's mentoring circle in your organization or community.

(Inam, 2013)

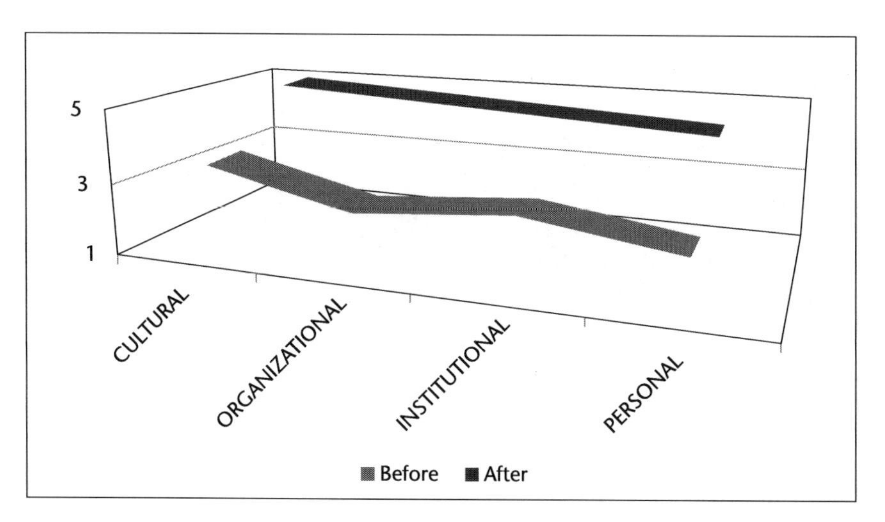

FIGURE C.10 Gap Analysis

Much of the research on work–life integration has focused on the negative effects associated with work–family conflict that triggers burnout, role conflict, stress, and anxiety. Increasingly, however, companies are developing means such as wellness and benefit programs to facilitate work–life issues as they also impact employee morale and organizational performance. In top-performing companies, for example, it is common for colleagues to support each other (Amabile, Fisher, & Pillemer, 2014) benefiting themselves and the organization creating win–win–win outcomes. Typically, helping colleagues has positive spillover effects (Greenhaus & Powel, 2006) on work–life integration as the social support at work is translated into more time for family and greater emotional support at home. The existence of a dual effect is also possible with greater spouse involvement at home reducing work–family conflict at home while also triggering higher job satisfaction. Both employers and employees should collaborate in lowering the rigid boundaries that existing policies and work schedules have around work–life integration. Many employers, for example, go as far as inviting families to parties, employee appreciation events, career achievements, recognition awards, or retreats to celebrate important milestones in the life of the organization or the careers of employees. Indeed, employee loyalty, happiness, and retention are positively affected by the congruence of work–family integration (Ilies, Wilson, & Wagner, 2009). Organizations, business, and nonprofits should take note.

References

Amabile, T. M., Fisher, C. M., & Pillemer, J. (2014). IDEO's culture of helping. *Harvard Business Review*, January/February, 54–61.

Baer, D. (2014, March 24). Here's why banning the word "bossy" is great for women. *Business Insider.* Retrieved from www.businessinsider.com/what-bossy-words-says-about-gender-at-work-2014-3.

Barsh, J., & Yee, L. (2012). Unlocking the full potential of women at work. *McKinsey & Company.* Retrieved from www.mckinsey.com/business-functions/organization/our-insights/unlocking-the-full-potential-of-women-at-work.

Belasen, A. T. (2012). *Developing women leaders in corporate America: Balancing competing demands, transcending traditional boundaries.* Santa Barbra, CA: Praeger.

Belasen, A. T., & Frank, N. (2008). Competing values leadership: Quadrant roles and personality traits. *Leadership & Organization Development Journal, 29*(2), 127–143.

Belasen, A. T., & Frank, N. M. (2010). A peek through the lens of the Competing Values Framework: What managers communicate and how. *The Atlantic Journal of Communication, 18*(3), 5–30.

Belasen, A. T., & Frank, N. M. (2012). Using the Competing Values Framework to evaluate the interactive effects of gender and personality traits on leadership roles. *The International Journal of Leadership Studies*, 7(2), 192–215.

Borisova, D., & Sterkhova, O. (2012). Women as a valuable asset. *McKinsey & Company, April.* Retrieved from www.citizencapital.fr/wp-content/uploads/2015/05/Women_as_a_Valuable-Asset_eng.pdf.

Carnes, W. J., & Radojevich-Kelley, N. (2011). The effects of the glass ceiling on women in the workforce: Where are they and where are they going? *Review of Management Innovation & Creativity, 4*(10), 70–79.

Catalyst. (2016, July 1). *Women CEOs of the S&P 500.* New York, NY: Catalyst. Retrieved from www.catalyst.org/knowledge/women-ceos-sp-500.

Chappelow, C. (2012, March 16). Leadership: Strive for work–life integration, not balance. *Fast Company & Inc.* Retrieved from www.fastcompany.com/1825042/strive-work-life-integration-not-balance.

Cook, A., & Glass, C. (2015). Diversity begets diversity? The effects of board composition on the appointment and success of women CEOs. *Social Science Research, 53*, 137–147.

Davis, S. N., & Greenstein, T. (2009). Gender ideology: Components, predictors, and consequences. *Annual Review of Sociology, 35*, 87–105.

Eagly, A. H., & Carli, L. L. (2007). *Through the labyrinth: The truth about how women become leaders.* Cambridge, MA: Harvard Press.

Ely, R., Stone, P., & Ammerman, C. (2014). Rethink what you "know" about high-achieving women, R1412G. *Harvard Business Review, 92*(12), 101–109.

Ernst & Young, LLC. (2015, January 12). EY Center for board matters highlights top priorities for corporate boards in 2015. *PR Newswire US.* Retrieved from www.ey.com/Publication/vwLUAssets/EY_-_Women_on_US_boards:_what_are_we_seeing/%24FILE/EY-women-on-us-boards-what-are-we-seeing.pdf.

Fairchild, C. (2014, July 8). Women CEOs in the Fortune 1000: By the numbers. *Fortune. Com*, 1. Retrieved from http://fortune.com/2014/07/08/women-ceos-fortune-500-1000/.

Friedman, S. D., & Greenhaus, J. H. (2000). *Work and family—allies or enemies? What happens when business professionals confront life choices.* New York, NY: Oxford University Press.

Gilbert, J. (2011). The millennials: A new generation of employees, a new set of engagement policies. *Ivey Business Journal, 75*(5), 26–28. Retrieved from http://iveybusinessjournal.com/publication/the-millennials-a-new-generation-of-employees-a-new-set-of-engagement-policies/.

Goudreau, J. (2013, March 21). Eight leadership lessons from the world's most powerful women. [Editorial]. *Forbes*. Retrieved from www.forbes.com/sites/jennagoudreau/2013/03/21/eight-leadership-lessons-from-the-worlds-most-powerful-women/.

Grant, B. (2013, December 4). Male and female brains wired differently: The brains of men contain stronger front-to-rear connections while those of women are better connected from left to right. *The Scientist*. Retrieved from www.the-scientist.com/?articles.view/articleNo/38539/title/Male-and-Female-Brains-Wired-Differently/.

Greenhaus, J., & Powell, G. (2006). When work and family are allies: A theory of work–family enrichment. *The Academy of Management Review, 31*(1), 72–92. Retrieved from www.jstor.org/stable/20159186.

Hewlett, S., Peraino, K., Sherbin, L., & Sumberg, K. (2010). The sponsor effect: Breaking through the last glass ceiling. *Center for Work–Life Policy Survey*. Research sponsored by American Express, Deloitte, Intel, and Morgan Stanley. Retrieved from http://wliut.com/wp-content/uploads/2015/09/The-Sponsor-Effect.pdf.

Hochschild, A. (1989). *The second shift*. New York, NY: Avon Books.

Hymowitz, C., & Daurat, C. (2013, August 13). Best-paid women in S&P 500 settle for less remuneration. *Bloomberg, Technology*. Retrieved from www.bloomberg.com/news/articles/2013-08-13/best-paid-women-in-s-p-500-settle-for-less-with-18-gender-gap.

Ilies, R., Wilson, K. S., & Wagner, D. T. (2009). The spillover of daily job satisfaction onto employees' family lives: The facilitating role of work–family integration. *Academy of Management Journal, 52*(1), 87–102.

Inam, H. (2013, April 15). Why aren't there more women CEO's? [Blog post]. Transformational Leadership Inc. Retrieved from www.transformleaders.tv/why-arent-there-more-women-ceos/.

Keziah, H. E. (2012). Falling over a glass cliff: A study of the recruitment of women to leadership roles in troubled enterprises global business and organizational excellence. *Global Business and Organizational Analysis, 31*(5), 44–53.

Kiesel, L. (2015, January 21). Men and women define success differently: Who cares about the money? *Mainstreet.com*. Retrieved from www.mainstreet.com/article/men-and-women-define-success-differently-who-cares-about-the-money.

Klampe, M. (2010, October 4). Women executives twice as likely to leave their jobs as men. *Oregon State University News and Research Communications*. Retrieved from http://oregonstate.edu/ua/ncs/archives/2010/oct/women-executives-twice-likely-leave-their-jobs-men.

Long, C. (2014). Women, leadership and the "glass cliff": Research roundup. *Journalist's Resource*. Retrieved from http://journalistsresource.org/studies/society/gender-society/women-leadership-glass-cliff-research-roundup.

Lublin, J. S., & Kwoh, L. (2012, July 17). For Yahoo CEO, Two new roles. *The Wall Street Journal*. Retrieved from www.wsj.com/news/articles/SB10001424052702303612804577533332960888756.

Mainiero, L. A., & Sullivan, S. E. (2005). Kaleidoscope careers: An alternate explanation for the "opt-out" revolution. *The Academy of Management Executive, 19*(1), 106–120.

Noguchi, Y. (2015, April 23). Some companies fight pay gap by eliminating salary negotiations. *WAMC Northeast Public Radio, Morning Edition*. Retrieved from www.npr.org/2015/04/23/401468571/some-companies-fight-pay-gap-by-eliminating-salary-negotiations.

Pew Research Center. (2008). Men or women: Who's the better leader? A paradox in public attitudes. *Pew Research Center*. Retrieved from http://pewsocialtrends.org/2008/08/25/men-or-women-whos-the-better-leader/.

Pew Research Center. (2013, December 11). 10 findings about women in the workplace. *Pew Research Center*. Retrieved from www.pewsocialtrends.org/2013/12/11/10-findings-about-women-in-the-workplace/.

Prime, J. L., Carter, N. M., & Welbourne, T. M. (2009). Women "Take Care," Men "Take Charge": Managers' stereotypic perceptions of women and men leaders. *The Psychologist-Manager Journal*, *12*, 25–49.

Ryan, M. K., Haslam, S. A., & Postmes, T. (2007). Reactions to the glass cliff: Gender differences in the explanations for the precariousness of women's leadership positions. *Journal of Organizational Change Management*, *20*(2), 182–197.

Sahadi, J. (2016, April 12). Young women are asking for (and getting) more pay than men. *CNNMoney*. Retrieved from http://money.cnn.com/2016/04/12/pf/gender-pay-gap/index.html?section=money_pf.

Slaughter, A. M. (2013, March 7). Yes, you can. Sheryl Sandberg's *Lean In*. *New York Times. Sunday Book Review*.

Stengel, G. (2014, January 8). 11 reasons 2014 will be a breakout year for women entrepreneurs. *Forbes*. Retrieved from www.forbes.com/sites/geristengel/2014/01/08/11-reasons-2014-will-be-a-break-out-year-for-women-entrepreneurs/#7c77cab91ef1.

Swamy, D. R., Nanjundeswaraswamy, T. S., & Rashmi, S. (2015). Quality of work life: Scale development and validation. *International Journal of Caring Sciences*, *8*(2), 281–300.

Thébaud, S. (2015). Business as plan B: Institutional foundations of gender inequality in entrepreneurship across 24 industrialized countries. *Administrative Science Quarterly*, *60*(4), 671. DOI:10.1177/0001839215591627

Timberlake, S. (2005). Social capital and gender in the workplace. *Journal of Management Development*, 24, 34–44.

US Department of Labor, Bureau of Labor Statistics. (2011, December 29). TED: The economics daily: Educational attainment of women in the labor force, 1970–2010. Retrieved from www.bls.gov/opub/ted/2011/ted_20111229.htm.

US Department of Labor, Bureau of Labor Statistics. (2014, December). Highlights of women's earning in 2013. BLS Report. Retrieved from www.bls.gov/opub/reports/womens-earnings/archive/highlights-of-womens-earnings-in-2013.pdf.

Walters, A. E, Stuhlmacher, A. F., & Meyer, L. L. (1998). Gender and negotiator competitiveness: A meta-analysis. *Organizational Behavior & Human Decision Processes*, *76*, 1–29.

Weer, C. H., Greenhaus, J. H., Colakoglu, S. N., & Foley, S. (2006). The role of maternal employment, role-altering strategies, and gender in college students' expectations of work–family conflict. *Sex Roles*, *55*: 535–544.

Westring, A. F., & Ryan, A. M. (2011). Anticipated work–family conflict: A construct investigation. *Journal of Vocational Behavior*, *79*, 596–610.

Williams, J. C., & Dempsey, R. (2014). *What works for women at work: Four patterns working women need to know*. New York, NY: New York University Press.

Wittmer, J. L., & Koepke, C. (2016). Work–life balance: Current conflict and anticipate conflict. Paper presented at the Academy of Management, Anaheim, CA.

Women in the Workplace. (2013). A research roundup. *Harvard Business Review*. September. Retrieved from https://hbr.org/2013/09/women-in-the-workplace-a-research-roundup.

Womenable. (2014, March). *The 2014 State of Women-owned Businesses Report: A Summary of Important Trends, 1997–2014*. Commissioned by American Express OPEN. Los Angeles, CA: LaLa Press. Retrieved from www.womenable.com/content/userfiles/2014_State_of_Women-owned_Businesses_public.pdf.

INDEX